Leadership and Liberation

How do leaders influence the people around them?

Is leadership about having particular personality traits or is it about what leaders actually do and the types of relationships they build?

This book looks at how to be an effective leader. It presents a model of leadership that has many practical implications for those who occupy formal leadership roles or who seek to influence events informally. By looking at leadership in the context of liberation, it provides the reader with an alternative perspective, enabling them to think about their own aims and effectiveness as a leader. It analyses our understanding of oppressed and oppressor groups and how processes of mistreatment develop and become institutionalized. From this standpoint, effective leadership is presented as a means of confronting inequality and initiating positive change. The practical skills required by leaders to assist them in becoming agents of change and influence, and in dealing with the inevitable conflicts that arise in complex interpersonal situations, are considered. The reasons why leaders are targets of attack are also looked into, as well as the situations in which they can act as a positive force for transformation.

Containing an in-depth review of the development of leadership theory, *Leadership and Liberation* also critically evaluates mainstream approaches and analyses the implications for leaders on the ground. The lessons to be learned are applicable to leaders in all types of groups and organizations and will be of interest to those studying psychology, business and management.

Seán Ruth is an Organizational Psychologist who was formerly Senior Lecturer in Psychology and Head of the Department of Organizational and Social Studies at the National College of Industrial Relations, Dublin, Ireland. He now runs his own training and consultancy business specializing in leadership development, conflict resolution, liberation and equality.

Leadership and Liberation

A Psychological Approach

Seán Ruth

LONDON AND NEW YORK

First published 2006
by Routledge
27 Church Road, Hove, East Sussex BN3 2FA

Simultaneously published in the USA and Canada
by Routledge
270 Madison Avenue, New York NY 10016

Reprinted 2007

Routledge is an imprint of the Taylor & Francis Group, an informa business

Copyright © 2006 Seán Ruth

Typeset in Times by RefineCatch Ltd.
Printed and bound in Great Britain by
TJ International Ltd, Padstow, Cornwall
Cover design by Louise Page

British Library Cataloguing in Publication Data
A catalogue record for this book is available from the British Library

Library of Congress Cataloging-in-Publication Data
Ruth, Seán.
    Leadership and liberation : a psychological approach / Seán Ruth.
        p. cm.
    Includes bibliographical references and index.
    ISBN 0-415-36459-0 (hardcover)
    1.   Leadership–Psychological aspects.   2.   Liberty.   I. Title.
    BF637.L4R88 2005
    158′.4–dc22

2005017916

ISBN 978-0-415-36459-1

Contents

Preface   vii

PART I
The content of leadership   1

1 Core functions of leaders   3

2 Other key functions of leaders   18

3 Leadership, authority and collaboration   34

4 Leadership: character or competence?   50

5 Destructive reactions to leaders: The isolation-attack
   dynamic   70

6 Handling attacks on leaders   89

PART II
The leadership context   113

7 Oppression and leadership   115

8 Internalized oppression   136

9 Theories of internalized oppression   155

10 A psychology of the middle class   174

11 Identity and the process of liberation   198

PART III
Strategies and skills   225

12 Change and influence strategies   227

13 Conflict resolution skills   246

14 Problem-solving skills   264

Bibliography   284

Author index   296

Subject index   298

Preface

This book has arisen out of a long-standing personal and professional interest in the process of leadership and a deep commitment, both personal and professional, to the process of liberation. In its essence, it is impossible to separate leadership from the process of liberation. While many of the available works on leadership have shed useful insights into how to be effective in a leadership role, few put this in the context of the day-to-day struggles faced by people because of oppression. Yet true leadership, as I hope to show, is inherently liberating in its effects. It changes people's lives. For this reason, the focus of this book is not just on understanding leadership but also on how to make leadership a resource for liberation. It is about a workable model of leadership that can guide our actions in the context of social change. It is not just about understanding what leadership is about but also about understanding how we can become a liberating resource for the people around us.

For this reason, a significant portion of what will be covered is focused on understanding the dynamics of oppression and liberation. There is a growing awareness in psychology and other disciplines of the importance of these issues. However, until now, the implications of these issues for the process of leadership have not been explored in great depth. If anything, leadership has been viewed suspiciously by many people as an oppressive and authoritarian process and the focus has been on how to minimize the influence or intrusion of leaders. In contrast to that, the approach here is to view leadership as a resource to be cultivated. Leadership, as such, is not inherently oppressive. Properly understood and practised, leadership is a huge resource for transformation and liberation.

In the same way that it has tended to ignore the social context of leadership, much of leadership theory is narrowly focused on, and confused with, the formal roles of managers and Chief Executive Officers (CEOs) in business and industry. True leadership, however, is much wider than this and deals with a very broad range of groups, organizations and situations. It operates at all levels, both formally and informally, in work organizations and also in social, community, non-profit, voluntary, family, cultural and other contexts. The model presented here is applicable to all of these different contexts and I have tried to avoid restricting it to any one type of organization or to any one type of role. Those with formal leadership roles and those who act informally will find this model equally useful.

Much of what is written reduces leadership to a set of practical skills that overlook the much deeper developmental and transforming aspects of the role. Many of these skills are actually management skills and are not unique to leadership. Their goal is also often about compliance rather than leadership. The goals of true leadership are much bigger than simply getting people to do what we want as is implied in much of the existing theory. As we shall see, leadership is much more about the ability to think clearly about people, to build close, solid relationships with them, and to take initiatives to develop them. It is fundamentally about assisting people to claim their full leadership ability. While this book also includes many practical suggestions about how to deal with challenging difficulties, all of these are located in the context of a deep awareness of the broader developmental role of leadership.

The usual approaches to leadership also fail to acknowledge the very personal nature of leadership, the fact that being a leader can bring up many difficult feelings about ourselves, our relationships and our work. I do not know of anyone who does not find leadership a challenge at a personal level. It has a way of bringing us face to face with our deepest fears and doubts. To be effective in a leadership role challenges us to go against and overcome these personal difficulties and it is this that can make leadership one of the quickest forms of personal development. In some ways, existing leadership theory makes it seem too easy. Learning some practical skills, however, does not, on its own, turn someone into an effective leader. For that, we need a much deeper awareness of the role of a leader and of the ultimate, liberating goals of leadership, along with a process of personal growth and liberation that mirrors what we are trying to help other people to achieve. It is not possible to become an effective leader without being transformed personally in the process. Many of the implications of this will be explored in the coming chapters.

The different elements of this leadership model are described over the coming chapters. The book is divided into three sections. Part I (Chapters 1 to 6) explores the *content* of leadership and what it means to be an effective leader. The emphasis here is on the key functions that leaders perform and the leadership qualities that make a difference. Part II (Chapters 7 to 11) focuses on the leadership *context*, namely, oppression and liberation. This gives a particularly powerful way of thinking about the role of the leader and how leaders can play a liberating role in relation to those around them. Part III (Chapters 12 to 14) deals with some of the practical *strategies* and *skills* that are especially important for anyone who wishes to play an effective leadership role. In particular, it examines influence, change and conflict-resolution strategies.

The combination of leadership and liberation in this book makes it of interest to a wide range of people. Students of psychology will find that it offers a much more wide-ranging and sophisticated model of the dynamics of leadership than more traditional and mainstream approaches. Among other aspects, this model avoids the common problem of looking at leadership in a social and political vacuum and integrates much of the awareness provided by recent developments in the psychology of liberation. In addition, those in managerial roles with an interest in understanding the leadership aspects of what they do and how to develop their staff will also find much to assist them. The model here has many practical implications for how to build and maintain solid and effective relationships with people. Similarly, leaders and activists in social change organizations and groups (community, educational, political, social and voluntary) will find an approach that throws considerable light on these dynamics and offers an extremely useful perspective on how non-oppressive models of leadership can operate. Finally, leaders in many other contexts, both formal and informal, will find a model that allows them to appreciate more clearly their role and how best to be a positive and transforming influence.

Writing this book has drawn on many years of experience in teaching psychology to people in a wide range of leadership positions in work organizations, trade unions, educational bodies, health care organizations, community groups, religious institutions, civil and public service bodies and many other types of organization. It has also drawn on many years' experience as a consultant and trainer working with such organizations and assisting them to tackle demanding leadership and organizational issues. Equally importantly, however, it has drawn on my own personal journey to develop my own leadership and to confront my own oppression and liberation. In deciding what to include and what to emphasize, I have been guided by the ways in which I have been able to use in my own life the perspectives and ideas contained in this theory. I have tried to avoid including material that would have no immediate or practical implications for anyone reading it. In this I have been strongly influenced by many years of teaching psychology to mature students and their well-developed sense of what constitutes useful knowledge.

Many people have played hugely important roles in helping me to understand this work and to challenge the blocks to my own leadership. My parents, Angela and Sean, were the first models for me of what it means to develop respectful, supportive relationships with the people around them, characterized by uncompromising integrity. From their example I learned many valuable lessons. Also, it would be hard to overestimate the influence of the people of Letterkenny, the place where I grew up. Much of my understanding of leadership and the context for leadership was formed in the crucible of that small town and I am forever proud and grateful to call it home. Many other people, too numerous to list, have played significant roles in the development of my awareness about leadership and liberation. In particular, however, I owe a huge debt of gratitude to my wife, Margaret, whose unwavering belief in me and unstinting support and encouragement and whose refusal to accept any limitations whatsoever have led, more than anything, to me putting together all that I have learned over many years. Among other things, her down-to-earth, practical and incisive intelligence has taught me the difference between purely academic knowledge and knowledge that is socially useful and makes a difference.

Part I

The content of leadership

1 Core functions of leaders

INTRODUCTION

What is the role of a leader? Whether it be a team leader, a manager, a trade union leader, a CEO, a school principal, a community or religious leader, a social change activist or any other kind of leader, they all must grapple with what exactly their role is as leaders. What are the functions of a leader? As a leader, what am I supposed to do? If I want to be an effective leader, where do I begin? What do I focus on? Where do I put my energy or my attention? How can I tell if my priorities are right? For someone who is new to a leadership role or for someone who has been in a leadership role for some time, these are key questions. Even if the person does not occupy a formal leadership position but is informally trying to make a difference to those around them, the same questions apply.

Many writers on the nature of leadership have focused on identifying the *qualities* of an effective leader. While these are often very helpful, they have not always thrown sufficient light on what it is that leaders are supposed *to do*. They tell us about the leader as a person but not necessarily about leadership as a process (Rost, 1993b, 1997; Rost and Barker, 2000). In this chapter, I want to look at the key functions, the role, or the job of a leader. The qualities of effective leaders, which we shall look at in more detail further on, will tell us more about *how* the leader carries out these functions or about the personal characteristics that contribute to being effective in this role. To begin with, however, we need to have a clear picture of what an effective leader is trying to do. We can get a sense of this by looking at what stands out about people who are influential in other people's lives.

In workshops over many years, in different parts of the world, I have asked participants to describe what was special about individuals who had made a positive impact on their lives. What were the qualities of the people who stood out in their minds? People from a wide cross-section of backgrounds (different occupations, ages, genders, religions, nationalities, cultures) are remarkably consistent in what they highlight. Time and again, for example, they point to someone who cared about them, someone who was understanding, someone who was a good listener, someone who was approachable, or someone who brought out the best in them. (See Table 1.1.) These are characteristics of people who were influential in their lives, people who made a difference to them. In this sense also, they are characteristics of good leadership.

Now if we were to think of these qualities as a description of one single person, we would notice that none of them seems out of character. They are not inconsistent with one another. They sit well together. This is interesting because, in fact, this is not actually one person but a collection of different people. What it does seem to indicate, however, is that there is some harmony or consistency in the things that people respond to. They have some underlying feature in common. In fact, implicit or embedded in these characteristics of influence is an actual model of the leadership process and that is what we want to extract here.

In themselves, these characteristics do not tell us a lot about what the role of a leader is. They simply provide us with examples, expressions or manifestations of good leadership. In practice, no one person is likely to have all of these qualities to the same degree. We each have our strong points and our weak points. However, it is not these specific qualities as much as what lies beneath them that I am most interested in at this point. When we examine these characteristics in more depth, we can get a clear picture of what it is that good leaders do.

To get at this underlying model, we can ask what is going on between the people involved when any or all of these characteristics are being demonstrated. In particular, what is the leader doing in that situation? What function is the leader carrying out? In reply to these questions, many people point out that these qualities highlight the fact that leaders are involved in a relationship, that they listen and communicate well, that they are able to put themselves in the other person's shoes. Each of these is significant but I want to emphasize one in particular. At the heart of these general characteristics is a very simple process of one person empathizing with, or, more simply, *thinking clearly about*, someone else.

Table 1.1 Characteristics of Influential People

Some of the most commonly cited characteristics of individuals who had a positive impact on others are listed below. These have been taken from a wide range of groups, varying in terms of gender, age, religion, occupation, culture and nationality.

Caring	Positive
Approachable	Enthusiastic
Has integrity	Supportive
Accepting of people	Has a vision
Respectful	Good listener
Affirming	Challenging
Brings out the best in people	Inspiring
Understanding	Has a sense of humour

Many of the characteristics highlighted are expressions of one person's ability to empathize with, think clearly about and respond appropriately to the needs of another. In reply to the question of who made a difference to them, people may describe someone, for example, who was able to see clearly a talent or ability they had and who was able to offer the challenge or encouragement they needed to realize their potential. This person was able to think well about them and to respond in some helpful, appropriate way. People are described who had their finger on the pulse of the situation, who were aware, thoughtful, sensitive, intuitive, or in touch with what was going on. Put simply, they were able to think clearly about the other person and what they needed. If we place this at the core of the process, it has profound implications and allows us to see leadership in ways that are radically different from traditional, hierarchical or authoritarian conceptions of leadership.

The essence of this alternative model is that leadership, at its core, is a very simple process of thinking well or *thinking clearly* about people and the situation facing them. (In this sense also, leadership is something people do rather than a position they occupy.) Essentially, the key function of a leader is to think. We could sum this up in terms of two questions that a leader is continually trying to answer. The first of these is "What is going on here?" The second is "What needs to happen in order to tackle this situation?" In practically any leadership situation, the leader is grappling with these two questions. This, as we shall see, does not mean doing the thinking for people, telling them what to do or thinking in isolation from them. Rather, it is the job of the leader to collaborate with people and *facilitate* the process of finding answers to these questions. This puts the emphasis on the leader being a facilitator, a listener, a team builder, an enabler, a developer of other people, and, fundamentally, a thinker. So, what does it mean to say that the leader's job is to think?

THINK ABOUT PEOPLE AND THE SITUATION FACING THEM

In carrying out this role, people have to be thought about on several levels. First, people have to be thought about *individually*. How is each member of the group doing? What is going well for them and where do they need a hand? What potential do they have and where are they stuck? Where do they need support from us? Essentially, thinking about people entails being able to see where they struggle while, at the same time, seeing their strengths and their potential. It means being able to separate that struggle and its effects from what is true of them positively and inherently as humans. We think about Anne, for example, and notice the great potential she has to become a leader but also the places where she lacks confidence in herself. We think about Barry and notice the talent he has for organizing but also his tendency to get overwhelmed because he takes on too much work. We notice Jane and her deep commitment to the work but also the places where she is inclined to become isolated from the group. Without a picture of this struggle and of the person's potential, it will be difficult for a leader to figure out what makes sense in any given situation.

Secondly, people have to be thought about *collectively*. This is quite different from just thinking about each individual. What is the situation facing the *group* or organization as a whole? What is going on in the group or organization? Where is it experiencing difficulties? What issues does it need to address? Is it achieving what it set out to do? Is it on track? What are the challenges and what are the opportunities that it faces? What is the potential of this group? What stops it being more effective or reaching this potential? Thinking about these questions often involves taking account of such issues as relationships, communication, organization, morale, power, roles, goals, conflict and, as we shall see in later chapters, oppression. We are trying to put our finger on the pulse of the group. Just as with the individual, we are trying to understand where the group as a whole is struggling and how we can assist it with that struggle. So, for example, we may notice that the group has become so preoccupied with short-term, day-to-day crisis management that it has lost sight of the long-term goals. Or perhaps trust has broken down and people no longer feel safe to communicate openly with each other. There is a need for people to stop and take stock of what has been happening to them and where they need to do things differently.

Thirdly, the leader must think about what is happening in the *wider situation* that has implications for the individuals, the group or the organization. What do we need to take account of in the world at large outside this group or organization? Where does this group or organization fit into the wider scheme of things? What is going on in the wider environment that has, or will have, some impact on us and that we need to think about? What are key issues in the environment of this group or organization that might affect how we see our task or how we attain our goals? How can events or processes in the wider environment help us to make sense of what is happening within our group? Thus the leader tries to understand the processes operating within the group and between the group and the world at large. Bennis (1998) talks about the leader as someone who helps define reality, interpreting events and making sense of the complexity around people. Tichy (2002) says the role of a leader is to see reality. The ability of a leader to name or describe clearly what is happening is often a powerful resource for any group.

Sometimes the leader offers people a theory, a model or a context that makes sense of what is happening around them. Being able to put a name on what is going on and give an accurate description of the wider context or the bigger picture is a powerful contribution for any leader. It is closely related to the leader's ability to listen and empathize. If the leader has listened and empathized well, and understood the struggles, this theory, model or context will resonate deeply with people and also hold out a challenge to them.

Finally, both the group or organization and the individuals within it need to be thought about *over time*. What has happened in the past for this group? What might happen in the future for the group? Where is it heading? In a similar way, a good leader thinks about individuals in terms of their previous experience, what is happening to them in the present and what is possible in the future. It is not enough to think only in the short term. The leader must think about how things will be over the longer term, having a clear understanding of both the past and the present and how things might evolve in the future.

Having a vision of how things could be different is a key feature of effective leadership. What often distinguishes effective leaders is the clarity of the vision they have evolved about the future of the group or the organization. Leaders are able to hold out a view of the "big picture" that can excite and inspire people. There is a proactive movement towards a future goal rather than merely reactive, short-term responses to immediate crises. This ability to evolve a meaningful, relevant and challenging vision depends on the leader having a clear understanding of both the history and experience of the individuals and of the group and also of their present circumstances. The vision that emerges is deeply rooted in an understanding of the struggles that people face and have faced, both individually and collectively. As we get a clear picture of those struggles, we also get a picture of how things could be different. A good leader has a picture of the possibilities for change and development in the people around them. In this sense, vision is directly related to our ability to listen deeply and empathize. In many cases, the vision that emerges gives expression to a deeply felt need that has never been clearly articulated before. People may not have realized how important it was to them until they heard it described like this.

Thinking on all these different levels is at the heart of leadership. More than any other ability, being able to think well is essential for effective leadership. Saying this, however, does not mean that it is something leaders do in isolation.

GET OTHER PEOPLE'S THINKING

Thinking about people and the situation facing them cannot be done on our own. In order to get clarity about what is going on and what needs to happen, it is absolutely necessary to involve other people in this process. A problem with this central, *thinking* role of leadership is that no one person is smart enough, or has access to enough information, to be able to answer all the important questions on their own. As a leader, there are almost certainly several gaps in my knowledge and understanding of any complex situation. There are also some things that are beyond my experience, situations about which I am not good at thinking clearly and that I find it difficult to appreciate fully. Other people are likely to have a deeper understanding, or more information, about these than I do at this point in time. So, in fulfilling this basic role of leadership, an essential requirement is to get other people's thinking. What has become very clear, as Jackins (1984, 1987, 1997) has pointed out, is that it is not possible for a leader to do the thinking *for* people. It is not the function of leaders to have answers to all the questions that need to be answered nor is it realistic to expect leaders to have all the answers. It is not the leader's job to know everything. What leaders can do is try to get *other people's thinking* and use it to fill in the gaps in their own thinking and, in the process, get greater clarity about problems and their solutions. At its core, the role of a leader is to *facilitate* the process of finding clarity. Essentially, this is a collaborative process that draws on the contributions of everyone involved.

At one level, this simplifies the role of leadership enormously and lifts the burden of always having to know what to do off the leader's shoulders. It shifts the emphasis in the role from that of expert, fixer or commander to that of facilitator. At the same time, fulfilling this facilitator role demands a number of particular skills that are often in short supply, not least being the abilities to listen deeply and to create safety.

Listen deeply

An essential requirement in getting other people's thinking is the ability to listen deeply and pay thoughtful attention to what they are thinking, experiencing and feeling. It is hard to over-emphasize the importance of this ability. Without it, we simply cannot be effective in a leadership role over the longer term. There is no doubt that anyone who takes the time to listen closely to the people around them will learn an enormous amount about the challenges and opportunities facing individuals and the group. What often separates effective leaders from less effective leaders is the extent to which they are able to understand the issues and the struggles facing the people they are leading and this can only be achieved by listening deeply. Beynon (1984) described how the most effective trade union leaders were the ones who stayed close to the membership and had their fingers on the pulse of their group. They spent time on the shop floor listening to the concerns, fears and issues of individual members. Much of this listening takes place one-to-one and informally. Block (1993) describes one good lunch room conversation as being worth a hundred surveys. We stop to greet someone in a corridor or spend time with them over a break in the work. Or, we chat informally while we work together on some task. As we listen, we get a picture of what is going well for them or where they are struggling. Effective leaders will often use these informal interactions as an opportunity to get a sense of how people are doing. Listening in formal meetings, performance reviews, appraisals, or other communication sessions is no substitute for this ongoing, "spontaneous" listening. In many ways, one of the least developed skills is the ability to "hang out" with people, apparently to waste time, in ways that give them a chance to tell us about the issues that matter to them.

One of the concerns that leaders sometimes have about this listening aspect of the role is that it seems, at first glance, to require quite an amount of time. However, true listening is an ongoing, concurrent, non-stop process rather than a separate or additional process to other aspects of the role. Only some of it takes place in formal meetings set up for this process. It is the quality of the informal listening we do minute by minute rather than the quantity of formal listening that often makes the difference. If we get this right, it is not only not a burden but is actually a positive boon to our overall effectiveness.

To listen to people in this way is not necessarily a straightforward process. At its core it embodies respect, caring, appreciation and acceptance of people as they are. Unfortunately, deep listening is more often preached than practised. Much of what passes for listening is, in fact, a type of pseudo-listening where the attention of the "listener" is actually on their own thoughts, experiences or feelings. Sometimes, there is a hidden agenda they are working from and this pseudo-listening is a way to manipulate compliance. Perhaps listening is seen as good for motivating people. They are listened to not with the expectation of learning anything but simply to make them feel better. Without relaxed, deep, respectful listening we cannot hope to be true leaders. Listening deeply, however, operates on a number of levels. We have to listen not just to what people think but also to how they are feeling.

Listen to feelings

When we try to get other people's thinking, we may notice that, often, they will communicate not so much what they are thinking as how they are feeling. However, if we listen carefully and pay enough attention to how people feel, we can learn a lot from this about the current situation and what needs to happen. In fact, some of the most important things we hear will be communicated at the level of feelings. We may hear them in the words people use, or in their tone of voice, or observe them in their body language. These feelings give us an insight into the difficulties, the struggles, the hurts, the history and the hurdles to be overcome.

The key thing is that a full understanding of the current situation requires us to listen with an open, non-defensive mind and to understand how people are feeling as well as thinking. This means that, as leaders, we have to be comfortable listening to the expression of feelings, and in particular, to painful feelings such as anger, frustration, hurt, fear or worry. At times, people will share these feelings spontaneously given any kind of interested listening. In other cases, we will actively have to go after and draw out these feelings. As we listen, we are getting a picture of the issues, the concerns, the difficulties, the challenges and the struggles that will have to be addressed as we move ahead. Often we will also get glimpses of solutions or ways forward.

Sometimes, it can be hard to keep listening to people's feelings. What we are hearing triggers our own feelings. We may feel hurt, moved, upset, scared or troubled by what we are hearing. If we are truly listening, this is not surprising. However, we do not want our own feelings to get in the way of hearing what it is like for others. It will help enormously if, as leaders, we have someone who, periodically, will listen to us and the feelings that come up for us in this role. This is something that many leaders do not have access to and yet it can enable us to listen much more effectively and not get confused by what we are hearing. It makes it easier not to take things personally and to leave the feelings behind at the end of the day.

As we listen to a range of people individually, and to a group collectively, we begin to get a clearer sense of the struggles facing the group as a whole and how we can assist them to deal with these struggles. We listen to people because it is actually a huge source of enlightenment and clarity. In practice, we will not have a sufficiently clear understanding of the issues until we see clearly how people are feeling. One of the things I have come to realize more deeply in recent years is the extent to which, as a leader, I need to accept that, in many situations, I actually know very little and that the real expertise lies with the people I am trying to assist – if only I can learn to listen to them. This is particularly true of situations where my background is that of a dominant, privileged or oppressor group. As a White middle-class man, for example, there are many things I simply do not understand sufficiently, especially in my relationships with people of colour, working-class people and women. If I am to have a non-oppressive, peer relationship with any of these, I will have to give up any assumption that my thinking is clearer than theirs. I will have to learn to listen well and be guided by what I hear. This is something we will return to in later chapters.

Apart from leading to greater clarity, it is also the case that the process of paying attention to people's feelings can itself be hugely important in helping to release individual initiative and developing the people we lead. As people are listened to thoughtfully and respectfully, they are enabled to process and make sense of what has been happening in their situation. Their thinking is enhanced. They can re-evaluate and move on from painful emotions and hurts that may otherwise operate as rigid blocks. Listening, in this sense, is a healing process that can empower people to take initiative. In fact, listening that is truly healing will often lead to the discharge or venting of what we can call painful emotion on the part of the person being listened to. They will release feelings of hurt, anger, fear or grief that are associated with what they are relating to us. This will show up in the form of tears or laughter or storming or shaking, for example. As these feelings are released, the person is able to reconnect with their clear thinking and their power. This process of emotional discharge will be discussed in more detail in Chapter 2. Listening in this way and playing a healing role is a key aspect of effective leadership. It is part of developing the leadership ability of those around us.

Getting access to how people are feeling is not necessarily a straightforward process. It involves two key elements, the creation of safety and the combating of isolation. For people to show us their feelings, they need to feel safe and they need to feel connected to others. As leaders, we have to think about how to create these conditions that will enable people to be open with us and with each other.

Create safety

A common experience in many groups is for a number of people to sit down together to try to discuss a problem and then find that individuals stay quiet, do not speak openly and do not address the real issues facing them. Sometimes, rather than going quiet, they may actively set about attacking, blaming and hurting one another as they defensively try to discuss the issues. Before this meeting begins, people can be seen discussing the issues privately with one another and having much to say about the problems facing them. These discussions may be quite animated at times. They may display a deep concern or interest and throw up many ideas about what steps should be taken. During the subsequent formal meeting, however, none of this animation is evident and suggestions are slow to emerge. Something has happened to stifle the energy and openness of the group. Afterwards, when people return to their trusted confidants and cliques, they once again become animated and energized. We may hear comments such as, "Well, I knew that meeting was going to be a waste of time" or "I could have told you nothing useful would emerge from that meeting". At the risk of being facetious, sometimes, the most revealing parts of a meeting are the things people say just before they go in and the comments they make when they come out. When you look at a group like this from the outside, it is painfully clear that the people do not feel safe enough with one another to be able to listen or have a useful discussion. Argyris (1985, 1986, 1999) talks about the "defensive routines" that people engage in and the difficulties in moving towards non-defensive "double-loop learning". Mitchell and Rossmoore (2001) look at this same model in explaining why leaders are unable to implement advice that they know makes sense. Harvey (1988) describes this type of situation as the Abilene Paradox. (See Table 1.2.) A key challenge for leaders in this situation is to create the conditions for people to be honest with themselves and with each other.

   If we are to get a clear picture of what is happening in a situation and what needs to happen, we have to be able to create enough safety for people to tell us honestly where it hurts, where it gets difficult, what the issues or concerns are, or where they need a hand, without them being pulled into attacking one another or going silent. This is a key leadership function. Our aim is to create the safety for people to listen and think together without being waylaid by painful emotion and destructive interactions. Much of this safety is created in the one-to-one, listening relationships that the leader builds with individual members of the group. The quality of these relationships will tend to set the tone for the relationships between people when they come together in a meeting. These relationships are built slowly over time and not just in the heat of the moment when a crisis arises. Further safety is created by the relaxed,

Table 1.2 Symptoms of Failure to Deal Constructively with Conflict

---

- People feel unhappy, frustrated, powerless when trying to cope with conflict.
- They agree, *in private*, as individuals, about the nature of the problem facing the group or organization and the steps required to cope with the problem.
- They break into subgroups of trusted friends or associates. They meet over coffee or lunch to discuss the problem, to voice complaints, to share rumours or to plan imagined solutions that they would try.
- There is a lot of blaming of others for the situation they are in. People blame the boss, other sections of staff and so forth for the problem. The boss will be described as incompetent, out of touch, ineffective or having other failings.
- In meetings where the problem is discussed, people act cautiously, "soften" their views, use ambiguous language or even say the opposite of what they think. As a result, they fail to communicate accurately their thinking, their desires and their beliefs to others.
- With such invalid and inaccurate information, people make collective decisions that not only fail to solve their problems but sometimes make them worse.
- As a result of such counterproductive actions, people feel more frustration, anger, irritation and dissatisfaction with the group or organization.

Adapted from Dyer (1977) and Harvey (1988)

non-threatening and constructive tone that the leader sets for the meeting. Finally, a lot of safety can be created by structuring the meeting in ways that encourage good listening. On many occasions, I have worked with groups that were experiencing destructive conflict or tensions where individuals told me privately in advance that they expected no one to speak honestly, or they expected people to walk out of the meeting or they expected people to attack one another. Making relaxed connections with people individually, setting a relaxed tone to the meeting, and ensuring that people were listened to respectfully and without interruption during the meeting were often sufficient to ensure a productive outcome. Practical guidelines for achieving this in a group will be discussed in Chapter 14.

Break through isolation

In order to protect themselves, some people cut themselves off from others in the group. A feature of many groups and organizations that are in difficulty, when you examine them, is that there are large blocks of isolation within them. Before, during and after a meeting, people are not well connected with each other or do not have a close or trusting relationship. This, of course, is both a cause and a reflection of the lack of safety people feel. The result is that we do not get to hear what is going on or have access to the full potential of a person because of the isolation. As part of building safety and getting a clear picture of what is going on, leaders also need to be able to spot the ways in which people have become isolated from one another and to break through this isolation and establish a meaningful connection with them. This is often done with people on a one-to-one basis or by setting the situation up so that groups of people get to listen respectfully to one another and hear what it is like for the others. (Note that this is different from breaking through people's solitude or need for time alone. The isolation that is being discussed here is a pulling away from people based on painful emotion or distress. A thoughtful approach implies being respectful of the person's need for solitude while having no respect for their isolation).

The skill of breaking through isolation involves being able to communicate that I am a safe person and not a threat, that I am interested and that I care about them. It also means being able to communicate that I can see the other person separately from the difficulties they are experiencing or creating. They can tell that I respect them, like them or admire them. In spite of the language used to describe this – combating or breaking through the isolation – the process essentially involves a relaxed and sensitive reaching out to people in ways that communicate my desire to be there for them. This is a key role of leadership and it echoes the belief of Greenleaf (1977) that an important part of what he calls servant leadership is the building of a sense of community.

Being able to communicate this often involves giving up my own pull to become isolated or keep my distance. It involves making myself accessible to people. Essentially, in order to lead well, I need to be able to spot and break through someone else's isolation *and* be able to spot and give up my own isolation. In certain situations, particularly where we are faced with people who are acting in intransigent, defensive or attacking ways, there can be a pull for us to "disappear" or cut ourselves off from contact. Sometimes, not only do we disappear from the "difficult" people, but we also unconsciously cut ourselves off from everyone else. The stress or pain of dealing with the difficult person uses up the slack, the tolerance, the patience and the energy we have for people in general. To be effective, we have to resist this pull to disappear. This requirement to give up our own isolation, by the way, is one of the ways in which taking leadership can operate as a very powerful form of personal development. If we are to succeed in a leadership role, we have to come to terms with our own fears and blocks and learn how to operate effectively in spite of these. In a similar way, Bennis and Thomas (2002) have highlighted the close link between effective leadership and becoming an integrated, healthy person.

Listen to thinking

Listening deeply to how people are feeling, from which extracting clarity about the situation follows, is one part of this process. People will also show us their thinking. Often, what they say will be a mix of thinking and feelings. Where people do try to give us their thinking, difficulties can still emerge. Sometimes, the thinking is mixed in with painful emotion and we have to listen very carefully in order to separate one from the other. In practice, we may notice a variety of responses to our requests to hear people's thinking.

Some people will have thought a lot about the problem or issue that concerns us. When we look for it, they will give us very clear thinking that will make a big difference to our understanding of the situation, assuming we do actually listen to it and can remain open minded. A major asset of leadership is being able to surround ourselves with individuals who can think clearly and rationally about particular, complicated and pressing issues or who can be depended on to stay thinking clearly when everyone else is being pulled into getting upset.

Other people, however, when we listen to them, will give us confused thinking. They may have even less of an insight into the issue than we do ourselves. They may share with us their own experiences but be unable to make much sense of them or draw any conclusions from them. Beyond describing their experiences they feel very lost and confused about what is going on or what it might be useful to do. However, if we listen carefully to what they say, we will find very useful bits of information or thinking that are worth all the effort we have to make. For example, because of what we have learned from other people, the confused picture that this particular person is giving us may actually begin to make some sense. Perhaps what we are hearing is beginning to form a pattern that we can discern because we have been listening carefully to a range of people. What this person is saying echoes in some way what we have heard from others. What is confusing to this individual is providing us with another piece of the jigsaw. The key thing is that we have to listen carefully and think about what we are hearing. Mao Zedong once said, referring to educators, that their role was to reflect back to people in a challenging way the issues that they themselves raised in a confused way. Exactly the same thing applies to the role of any leader. A key role for a leader is being able to listen deeply, see the bigger picture and reflect this back to people in ways that challenge, inspire or enlighten them. As we saw earlier, part of the role of a leader is to help define reality. Being able to do this, however, depends on the quality of our listening and our ability to extract the patterns or themes that underpin the confusion.

There are still other people who will take the opportunity of being asked for their thinking to bring up their pet complaint or gripe, even if it seems irrelevant to the issue at hand. "I'm glad you have asked me that. It's like I have been saying for the past twenty years, not that anyone ever listens of course, but nothing is going to change around here until we get rid of so-and-so." The tone of this complaint tends to distinguish it. It has a repetitive, hard-to-listen-to, complaining quality that invites little sympathy. Even here, however, if we listen carefully, we may also find useful bits of information or thinking. It may not add much to our understanding of the problem that concerns us, but we may learn that someone is unhappy or that they feel no one ever listens. Separately from the painful emotion or rigid preoccupation with one part of the overall situation, we are getting information about some of the difficulties people are struggling with and some of the difficulties or conflicts facing the group.

The key point in all of this is that, if we want to find the answers to pressing problems, we have to set things up to listen to other people's thinking, other people's feelings and other people's experience. As we sift through all that we hear, we can put the bits that make most sense together into some coherent picture or plan of action. However complicated or messy this process is inclined to be, there is no useful alternative. We cannot do all this thinking on our own.

BUILD RELATIONSHIPS

So far, we have seen that leadership is essentially a process of listening closely to people and thinking about what is going on. We also saw that this involves particular skills on the part of the leader. Crucially, however, if we are to draw on other people's thinking successfully, we need to build close, trusting, one-to-one relationships with them within which it is safe for them to communicate with us. It is clear that we cannot lead people effectively at a distance or in isolation from them. Unless we build these relationships, we will inevitably misjudge the situation and do things that are either unhelpful or counterproductive. During one workshop, a hospital matron spoke out about what she considered to be the important aspect of her leadership and that was making sure that no one saw her as having any favourites among the staff. The way she ensured this was to keep her distance from everyone! She solved the problem of not being seen to have favourites but probably also created many other problems in the process. A key part of the role of leadership is the process of building close relationships and keeping quality contact with people. At the risk of oversimplifying it, we could even see it as simply making friends with people. Jackins (1990) has said that all effective leadership rests on the building of solid one-to-one relationships with people. Everything else, the setting up of committees, the calling of meetings, the mass communications, and so on are, at best, supplementary and complementary to this. It is through the building of these relationships that the real work of leadership is carried out. In a similar way, Kouzes and Posner (2002) emphasize that the clear message coming from their research is that leadership is a relationship. For them, the successful leader will be the person who values people first and profits second. This same point is echoed by Wheatley (2003) who says that the way to prepare for the unknown is to attend to the quality of relationships.

In a related way, it has also been said that to be effective as leaders we have to in some sense fall in love with the people we are trying to change. This does not mean becoming gushy and romantic. It means getting close enough to people to see the full person, the strengths and talents but also the difficulties and struggles. Without this, we are unlikely to have a clear picture of the people we are trying to influence. I once heard a community leader describe the people he had worked with for many years as "just plain lazy". But this says more about the leader than about the people. If that was all he had learned about them over the years, then he had clearly missed something. He had no sense of their inherent strengths or positive qualities nor any sense of their potential. Importantly, he had no clear sense of their struggles.

We can often get a measure of our effectiveness by looking at the depth and quality of the relationships we have built with the people we are trying to lead. As leaders, we can look strategically at our relationships and assess whether we have the range and quality of relationships that we need in order to be effective in the situation where we find ourselves. Are there people with whom we have little or no connection? Are there people from whom we have become isolated? Are there people we have not had good quality contact with recently? Are there individuals it would be useful for us to spend some time with? Do our relationships reflect the full range of diversity in our group? Are there important subgroups within which we have no, or very few, close relationships? Are there particular individuals or subgroups whose experience we know little about? Seeing the building of relationships as a central part of the leadership process is a powerful way to increase our effectiveness enormously. And, as we shall see later, it is also a central part of developing other people's leadership.

I started this chapter by highlighting the role of thinking about people and the situation facing them. We have seen how this requires a focus on building relationships. In actual practice, we could reverse the order in which these have been described and say that *leadership is a process of building close relationships within which we listen deeply to people's thinking and feelings so as, together, to think clearly about what is happening in the current situation and what needs to happen to address the issues facing us.*

These processes are at the heart of effective leadership. They give us a clear picture of what our role is as leaders and how we need to spend a significant portion of our time. They also give us a benchmark against which to strategize and to evaluate our progress. Our job as leaders is to build relationships of influence.

SUMMARY

The focus in this chapter on thinking on different levels and over the longer time period means seeing this model as a type of *big-picture* or *liberation leadership*. The role of the leader is to step back, understand what is going on, understand the wider context and think about where things are going in the longer term. If we are thinking clearly about people we are also automatically going to think about their potential. We are going to think about where they hold back from exercising their full power or their full initiative. We are going to think about the next steps in their liberation. Seeing leadership as a liberating process has many implications that I want to explore in more detail in later chapters.

With this alternative model of liberation leadership we move from an image of leadership as a hierarchical pyramid with the leader on top deciding everything to something more like an inverted pyramid where the leader is underneath supporting their collaborators to achieve their ends. Even this, however, is only a very rough depiction of what this model represents. Its shape is actually much closer to that of a circle of collaborators than to a hierarchical pyramid. With these processes at the centre of this model, we can now look at other important aspects of it in the next chapter.

REFLECTION

You as a leader

Think about yourself as a someone who plays a leadership role, even if you do not happen to occupy any formal position of leadership.

1   Make a list of your key strengths as a leader.
2   What, in particular, is special or unique about you as a leader or the way you lead?
3   In what ways have you modelled good leadership?
4   Describe a situation where you were able to think particularly clearly about people and the situation facing them.
5   What are your strengths in building close and effective relationships with your collaborators?
6   Describe a situation where you built a good relationship with someone within which you were able to listen deeply and empathize with their struggle.
7   If you were to change anything, what would you do differently in order to build closer, more supportive or more effective relationships?

The situation facing you

8   Describe the situation facing your group or organization. What are the key issues or challenges you face?
9   What is happening in your group or organization that needs to be addressed as a key issue?
10   What is happening in the world or the environment around your group or organization that needs to be addressed as a key issue?
11   What do you think needs to happen in your group or organization to address these key issues?

2 Other key functions of leaders

INTRODUCTION

In Chapter 1, we saw some of the core functions of an effective leader. These are absolutely central to how effective leaders operate. However, leadership does not stop there and these are not the only important functions of a leader. Leaders do not just build relationships, listen to people and think about the situation. They also act on the thinking and clarity that emerges from this process. In this chapter, we shall see how taking initiative, being decisive and actively developing new leaders are among the other key features of effective leadership.

TAKE INITIATIVE

As we listen deeply to the people around us and think about what is going on, we begin to get an insight into the nature and scale of the issues facing us. We also get insights into what might be required or what might need to happen to move things ahead. We are able to draw on the experiences, the feelings and the clear thinking of the people around us to figure out what makes most sense. So far, so good. At this point, however, an important aspect of the leader's role is the taking of initiative. Leadership is an active role and goes beyond empathic listening and thinking. Already we have seen how it involves such initiatives as building safety, combating isolation and building close relationships. There are various other significant ways an effective leader will take initiative. Importantly, the leader, having listened deeply, will put proposals or suggestions to the group as to how they might proceed and try to get agreement on these.

Propose ways forward and get agreement

Leaders listen to the thinking, feelings and experience of the members of the group. As they listen, they are all the time asking themselves what makes sense here. Based on what they hear and observe, they separate the good ideas from the not-so-good ideas and put together a picture of the issues facing the group and possible ways of dealing with these. They come up with a proposal that they think will address the situation facing them and they put this to the group. We use various terms in this context. We talk about coming up with plans, or strategies, or suggestions, or workable solutions or ways forward. Whether it takes the form of an informal suggestion or a formally proposed strategy, the role of the leader is to act on the best thinking available. (Note that, in speaking about this, we are talking not just about leadership as a formal position but leadership as a function that anyone can carry out.)

Having put the best thinking available into some kind of proposal, the leader then tries to get agreement to this from the members of the group. Getting agreement is not necessarily easy, and at times it may be messy and complicated. For example, having listened closely to people and come up with ideas for addressing the issues, leaders may find that people throw these back in their face and tell them their proposals are rubbish. They may then have to listen more and their suggestions may have to be modified until they find a way forward that is acceptable and workable. In most cases, there is no alternative to this. As we saw in the last chapter, to do the thinking *for* the group is not possible.

While getting agreement may not be a straightforward process, it is possible. In particular, where the style of leadership has been characterized by ongoing and consistent attempts to listen to people, there tends to evolve a more relaxed, flexible approach to decision making. At the point of decision, people do not dig their heels in. Although things may not be going the way they would ideally prefer, they know they have been heard and will continue to be heard. They seem to adopt an attitude that says "It's not going my way this time, but next time it might." They do not have any sense of the system being biased against them or of never being listened to. They do not have any sense of being "losers". Under these kinds of circumstances, people tend to stay flexible. Their response to finding themselves in a minority position is to say, "I disagree with most of you. However, you seem sure of what you want so I'm willing to go along with you even though I think you are wrong." Effectively, the group operates on a working consensus and does not get bogged down on disagreements.

The likelihood of reaching a good consensus will be enhanced even further if the process of reaching a decision is focused on ensuring people are listened to rather than argued with. I once facilitated a large group of 65 people to reach agreement on a controversial proposal that been the source of much divisive conflict over a number of years. Their discussions had been plagued by antagonism, disrespect, polarization and very little listening. To avoid destructive splits, the decision had been postponed on a number of occasions. I was asked to assist the group to dispose of the issue once and for all over the course of a day-long meeting. At the beginning of this meeting, I announced to the group that we would spend the day simply listening to every individual's thinking. We would have little time for open discussion and would keep the focus on listening to and understanding what people were saying. The group agreed to this process with some misgivings but was pleasantly surprised to note that everyone was listened to without interruption, without attack and with great respect. The constitution of this group required a secret ballot on the proposal and when this was held at the end of the day, what had started as a 5 per cent minority grew to a 65 per cent majority. More importantly, everyone in the room was happy with the decision. Those who were outvoted were pleased that a firm decision had finally been made even though it was not the one they preferred. This example highlights a central principle of conflict resolution, namely, that it is possible to 'listen people' into agreement much more easily than it is to argue them into agreement. Guidelines for this type of process will be discussed in Chapter 14.

Act decisively

Occasionally, it will not be possible to reach consensus on a future course of action. This may happen for a variety of reasons. For example, in a crisis or emergency there may not be enough time to continue talking until everyone is agreed. Or, the issue may be so contentious or emotive that, at this time, it is not possible to reach consensus. There may be matters of principle that people are unwilling to yield on at this point. Alternatively, the issue may not be particularly important and it does not make sense to waste a lot of time discussing it. In cases like this, and where it is important that something actually be done, a key role of the leader is to make a decision and act decisively. In the face of indecision, the leader announces, "OK, since we can't agree on a course of action and since we do need to do something, here's what I think we'll do." Such leaders take account of everyone's thinking and make the best decision they can under the circumstances. But they do act. In other cases, where there is enough time or where the issue is not pressing, decisions can be postponed until there is greater clarity or agreement. The essential point is that part of thinking well about a group is knowing when it is time to act decisively. It is not good leadership to abandon people to indecision in situations where action is necessary.

The inability to get a decision can be more destructive in certain situations than any possible wrong decision. At times of prolonged indecision, people's worst qualities can come to the surface as they become impatient, frustrated, blaming, powerless, or bad-tempered. In such situations, it may well be better to make a firm decision and risk getting it wrong than to allow the indecision to persist. When a decision is made, the group will soon find out if it is the wrong one and can set about correcting it. If no decision is made, nothing can be learned and, meanwhile, relationships deteriorate and things fall apart all around us.

In general, as we saw above, where the approach to leadership has been characterized by genuine attempts to listen and use people's thinking, and where the leader has consistently worked to develop close, supportive relationships, the members of the group will tend not to see the leader's decision as arbitrary or biassed against them. Rather than resenting this initiative, they will be pleased that action is being taken by someone. The response may be, "Well, you have heard what we all think and it's clear we are divided in what we believe ought to be done. So, make your best decision and we will go along with whatever you decide."

Normally, of course, it is not the role of the leader to impose decisions or solutions unilaterally on a group. In the type of situation being described here, however, where there is no consensus and, at the same time, a definite need for action, it is important that leaders are prepared to take this initiative and get the backing of the group.

The corollary of this is that where we ask someone to take on a leadership role, it makes sense to allow them to take decisive action where it is called for. Sometimes, leadership is effectively neutralized and undermined by the failure of groups to support the leader's initiative. It can happen that, because of people's bad experiences with authoritarian or abusive leadership in the past, they refuse to allow any leader to act unless there is group consensus. Or they insist on routinely checking up on everything the leader does, so that the person never feels free to act independently. We shall see more about this type of dynamic and its effects in Chapters 5 and 6. While these reactions to a leader's decisiveness may be understandable, they are not based on a clear understanding of the leadership role. The decisive role for leadership being described here is still rooted in ongoing, deep listening and respect for the thinking of other people. It is not fundamentally abusive or oppressive even though it may, in a superficial way, resemble the actions of other abusive or oppressive authoritarians.

Organize

Apart from making proposals, getting agreement and acting decisively, there are other significant areas where leaders will take initiative. An important part of the job of leadership is organizing people to do what needs to be done. The leader thinks about how best to organize the group to achieve its objectives, listens to other people's thinking about this, and, on the basis of the best thinking available, takes initiative to see that things work well. Again, this is not an arbitrary imposition of structures or processes but a thoughtful response to what the leader is hearing and observing. It will commonly be done in consultation with people as equals. In times of chaos, confusion, powerlessness, inertia and other blocks to effectiveness, however, prolonged discussion of what steps to take may not make sense. In fact, to dither or fail to act may make things worse. To make progress, it may be necessary to propose a way of organizing people and ask them to support this. This organization cannot be imposed against the will of the group. However, if the leader has demonstrated a consistent commitment and ability to listen, in the absence of any better alternative, they will be allowed by the group to exercise this initiative and their attempts to organize will be supported. If there is trust within the group, people will be willing to follow the leader's direction or will suggest improvements to the organization proposed by the leader. On the other hand, where people's experience of leadership has not been positive, where they have been exposed to more authoritarian, hierarchical styles of leadership, there may be a reluctance to trust any leader to make decisions or to organize. This has led some groups, particularly religious and social change groups, to experiment with alternative forms of "shared leadership". We shall look at these in more detail in the next chapter.

Model the message

One of the characteristics of effective leaders is that they model what they preach. They "walk the talk" and demonstrate an integrity in how they behave. There is a consistency between their values, their vision, their standards and their behaviour. For many groups, effective leaders are especially able to model a sense of hope and encouragement for people. They also model a belief and confidence in the people around them. These particular aspects of modelling are crucial at this time because of their relative scarcity. Many groups are crying out for anyone who will offer some hope or encouragement. Any leader who can consistently model these has the potential to make an enormous difference. One of the things that distinguished the leadership of people like Martin Luther King and Nelson Mandela was precisely this ability to offer hope and to lend people confidence. This modelling is more than just the expression of high-sounding platitudes. It is not about charisma or oratory. The type of relationships and the actions of the leader reflect, and are consistent with, the values and beliefs espoused by the leader. People do not get mixed messages from them. In many cases, the real modelling takes place non-verbally or indirectly and in the context of developing a close relationship.

Inspire

Through the relationships that they build, through the quality of their listening, through their ability to communicate an accurate picture of reality, and through their ability to model hope, encouragement and confidence, leaders are also able to inspire the people around them. A particularly important part of this, however, is the ability to hold out a vision of how things could be better. True leadership is able to grasp and communicate the "big picture". This raises people's sights beyond the immediate and short-term perspective and shows what is possible. A truly inspiring vision articulates a clear and accurate picture of past experience and current reality, paints a picture of an attractive future, and details how people might move from one to the other.

Some leaders manage to inspire people through a charismatic presence and oratory. People are struck by their magnetic personalities. However, while public-speaking skills, for example, are very valuable, they are not the essence of the ability to inspire. More important is the ability to articulate clearly the struggles facing people, to give voice to pressing concerns and, at the same time, to point a direction and hold out a confident and passionate commitment to a vision for the future. Other characteristics of inspiring leaders can include humility (a relaxed acceptance of self and others) and the ability to speak from the heart. The emphasis here on modelling and inspiring is mirrored in the works of Kouzes and Posner (2002) and of Bennis (1998, 2000) who underline just how central these roles are. For Kouzes and Posner, for example, these are two of five key leadership practices.

One of the difficulties for people in leadership roles is that this inspirational role can be neutralized by the constant demands of day-to-day administration and by the ongoing fire-fighting that consumes both the group's and the leader's time and energy. Over time, the initial vision and passion of the leader are whittled away by these wearying distractions. The values that they held dear and that guided them become blurred. People who started out with a clear sense of what they wanted to achieve, and a deep connection to the importance of what they were doing, gradually lose sight of these deeper motivations and disconnect from their sense of the bigger picture. Many groups and organizations that started out with radical or exciting visions for their work gradually succumb to inertia, low morale and ineffectiveness as the connection to their vision is replaced with short-term considerations of survival or fire-fighting. Creating the time and the opportunities to reconnect with a personal vision for the work and the values that underpin this vision is a key issue for leadership. We cannot hope to expect others to adopt a longer-term perspective if we ourselves have lost sight of our own vision. As a leader, therefore, I have to keep noticing what it is that excites me about this work, what attracts me to it, what aspects of what I do are closest to my heart, what it is that I feel passionate about, what are the values I hold dear or what it is that matters to me. For some people, reconnecting with these involves stepping back regularly from the immediate, day-to-day problems and finding some quiet time to reflect on their own. Heifetz and Linsky (2002a, 2002b) refer to this type of space as a sanctuary for the leader. For others, reconnecting with them is achieved by having someone listen interestedly to them while they speak from the heart about what is important to them. However we do it, effective leadership requires staying in touch with this bigger, longer-term picture of the work we do.

Unlike the tendency in many organizations, a compelling and attractive vision cannot be imposed on others. Putting copies of a mission statement or vision on plaques on the wall, having managers lead discussions of the corporate vision with staff or allowing people to work out the implications of the corporate vision for their particular section or department are not sufficient sources of inspiration. They do not allow people to have ownership of the vision. Often, in fact, the vision is at odds with the actual values experienced by people day to day. Highlighting this concern, Collins (1996) complains that leaders spend too much time drafting and redrafting vision and mission statements and not enough time ensuring that their organizations are aligned with the values and the vision they already espouse. A key question to ask is whether the espoused values actually match the practice on the ground and, if not, what steps need to be taken to bring the practice into line with what is espoused.

Similarly, a truly inspiring vision is highly personal and individualistic. Attempts to develop collective or corporate visions often result in statements of vision that are so watered down as to be vacuous and uninspiring. Huge amounts of time are invested in working out collective statements of mission where discussions, sometimes long, are held over which precise wording to use. By the time agreement has been reached on a wording, the statement no longer excites anyone. Rather than wasting time negotiating a collective vision, we could more usefully find ways to encourage the individuals who feel passionate about the work to speak to us from the heart about what it is that moves them and touches them. So long as I am not *required* to agree with someone else, I can be inspired by them. Often, as people share their individual visions, a curious thing begins to happen. The different visions begin to gravitate towards one another as people are inspired by each other. People find ways to support and encourage one another to pursue their visions without needing to compromise any essential aspects of their own vision. One of the challenges we face in leadership is to assist people to reconnect with a personal vision that inspires and excites them and to begin to share this vision with the people around them. Wheatley (1997) makes the point that giving up a tightly controlled type of leadership and allowing people to follow their own vision does not mean that the organization spins out of control. She says that, if organizations are clear about their purposes and values, the individual initiatives taken by people across the organization will result in an overall coherence.

As a leader, I can hold out and model an overarching vision that challenges and inspires. I do not need to require people to accept my vision. In fact, people cannot be *required* to buy into it. However, if I have been listening well to people, if I have seen clearly their strengths, their talents and their struggles, I can articulate a set of values and a vision that goes to the heart of what matters to them. If I get these other aspects of the leadership role right, many people will gladly follow me. If it is an attractive vision and if I am seen to model it well, people will *choose* to commit themselves to it.

Having said this, it should be noted that mission or vision statements do have other uses that perhaps explain their popularity. For example, they may be useful summaries of corporate direction that leaders can refer to as a benchmark for evaluating progress. Where statements of mission or vision have been held up as leading to significant change in organizations, I suspect it is most likely because such statements clarified the thinking of the leaders of those organizations. Mission statements can also serve as useful public relations vehicles for giving outsiders a sense of what the organization aspires to. As a source of inspiration for members of the organization or as aids to effectiveness, however, they are often overrated. In many ways, the issue is not whether the organization can agree on a *collective* vision but whether *individual* initiative and inspiration can be released and harnessed. Releasing such initiative depends on each individual member of the organization having a connection to their own personal vision and a sense of how this connects with the visions of the people around them.

Take principled stands

Occasionally, leaders will be required to adopt principled positions on issues that put them at odds with the majority of the people around them. Part of modelling for people is being prepared to act with integrity and courage. It is not the role of leadership to follow unthinkingly the wishes of the majority or the outcomes of opinion polls in situations where issues of principle or integrity are at stake. Blair (2002) describes how, in the context of a commitment to cherishing diversity, a school principal may have to institute policies that are unpopular with staff or parents, where she will have to be "resolute in the face of opposition" (p. 190). This is not to say that at this point the leader necessarily becomes autocratic. However, with a commitment to clear thinking, the leader will persist in raising the issue, push for further discussion or analysis, and act as a conscience for the group until a more rational or ethical position has been agreed. Occasionally, as Blair suggests, they will insist on correct policies being implemented or adhered to.

To compromise on important matters of principle is to abdicate responsibility as a leader. Martin Luther King once said that if every Black person in the US were to turn to violence as a means of achieving civil rights, he would be the lone voice preaching that non-violence was the only correct way. In saying this he was highlighting this important role of leadership in certain situations. He said he refused to determine what was right by taking "a Gallup Poll of trends of the time" (quoted in Oates, 1982, p. 407). For King, a true leader was not just a searcher for consensus but someone who also moulded consensus. Of course, acting with integrity and taking a principled stand should be a feature of the normal style of leadership. In most cases, where a liberation approach to leadership is the norm, acting in this way will resonate with other people's value systems and will be a further source of inspiration. In exceptional cases, where the leader takes a different position to the majority, the respect for the leader's integrity will encourage most people to be thoughtful and balanced in their response.

To ensure that the taking of principled stands does not become simply an expression of a leader's prejudices or biases, it is very important that leaders have put mechanisms, processes or structures in place that assist them to clarify continually their own thinking and eliminate any elements of painful emotion that might distort their thinking. Staying close, and listening, to the people around them is an important part of this process. A commitment to their own personal growth and development is also important and, within this, having the opportunity to look at where they are not being honest with themselves or where they have not acted with integrity. In doing this, it is very helpful for the leader to have opportunities to be listened to and "counselled" while they think through issues. As this happens they get to look at, and discharge, any feelings they have about those issues, particularly any painful emotions (such as anger, frustration, fear, hopelessness, shame, worry and so on) that might tend to distort their best thinking about them. This broader issue of support structures for leaders will be explored in Chapter 5.

DISCHARGE

I have referred, on a number of occasions, to the process of discharge. This is a natural human process of feeling and releasing emotions that is sometimes called venting, sometimes called catharsis, that has a beneficial effect on the person doing it. In particular, it can have significantly positive effects for leaders both in terms of their own ability to function effectively and in terms of their ability to assist others to function effectively. It has been described in some detail by Jackins (1970, 1978) and by Kauffman and New (2004). Janov (1978, 1990, 2000) also describes this kind of process, particularly in terms of its physiological aspects and effects. We can see the discharge process most clearly with young children before we socialize them not to show feelings. They will automatically and immediately discharge whenever they get hurt. While a person is discharging painful emotion (and this is usually signalled by the release of tears, by shaking, laughter, angry storming and a number of other indicators), their brain is automatically processing the hurtful or distressing events that led to these feelings. Anyone who has ever had a deep cry will have noticed that, while they were crying, their mind was working furiously, remembering, thinking through and processing whatever hurt them. Often, the hurt we feel in the present is actually related to much older hurts from the past that the present situation has brought to mind. During discharge, the person re-evaluates the original hurtful experience and is assisted in thinking more rationally about that and similar situations in the present. To the extent that someone can discharge whatever painful emotion is pulling at their attention, they will generally be able to think more clearly in that situation. After discharge, people will report that things don't seem as bad as they did beforehand, the situation seems clearer or that they can see a way forward that wasn't obvious before. The process of re-evaluation is automatic and the more we discharge the clearer we get. The feelings do not need to be intellectually analysed by us or anyone else in order to get this clarity. Discharge has the effect of un-numbing our brains or kick-starting our thinking in the places where it had shut down. Where painful emotion wells up and is not discharged, it will tend to distort our thinking and pull us into rigid, inflexible and inappropriate responses to situations. Whether we get overwhelmed by it or else go numb so as not to have to feel it, our reactions are based largely on that painful emotion rather than on a rational perspective on what makes sense.

Leadership is one role that brings up painful emotions for people. Sometimes we get scared. Or we get confused. We feel isolated. We feel stressed or worried. We feel hurt. Whatever the feeling, having the opportunity to discharge in safety can make a huge difference to the quality of a person's leadership. They get to offload the painful emotion rather than having it pile up and overburden them. By providing a safe place for leaders to look at the feelings that come up for them in that role and to discharge whatever feelings get in their way, we can assist them to stay fresh, creative and flexible in the way they lead. Regular opportunities for a leader to step back from the work and be listened to genuinely and interestedly while they discharge whatever is in the way of thinking clearly or acting effectively can make a huge difference to the quality of that person's leadership. This type of listening is a very important means of support that we can give leaders to enable them to stay fresh and to continue to grow as they lead.

To the extent that leaders are comfortable with discharge and have the opportunity to use the process for themselves, they can also help to release the people around them from their painful emotions. Discharge is a natural healing process and leaders can play an important healing role by creating the safety for people around them to discharge when appropriate. The leader's ability to listen deeply and empathize and to encourage the release of painful feelings is a very effective tool in empowering people to think more clearly and act more decisively. This healing role of leaders is something we shall return to when we look at the notion of servant leadership in Chapter 4.

It is also true that, without much access to discharge, some leaders have still been able to hold out powerful perspectives and think clearly about what made sense. There is another process, the process of decision, that has enabled leaders to stay effective in difficult times (Jackins, 1995b, 1997). Where a leader has some important piece of clarity to guide them – a vision or a deeply felt set of values, for example – their connection to this piece of clarity can guide them when things get confusing or painful emotion pulls at them. They can make a decision, in spite of any feelings to the contrary, in spite of fears or doubts, to hold a particular point of view or move in a particular direction. Although it can sometimes require a lot of courage or persistence, this process of decision is an important and powerful aspect of leadership. Many people have done great things by the power of decision. On its own, however, it can also be quite stressful and may sometimes lead to a stubborn intransigence that causes the leader to ignore important and relevant factors in the overall situation. Where we can combine discharge and decision, however, we have an even more powerful type of leadership. The process of discharge followed by decision followed by more discharge in an ongoing cycle enables leaders to keep thinking creatively and to act decisively without being sidetracked, worn down or waylaid by painful emotion.

DEVELOP POTENTIAL – CREATE NEW LEADERS

If thinking clearly about people is at the heart of leadership, then leaders are inevitably going to think about how to develop the talents and potential of other people. A major function of leadership consists of turning the people around us into leaders. Realistically, for example, in many situations, there simply are not enough bodies on the ground to do all the work that needs to be done. The only way the work can be progressed effectively is if we see a central role of leadership as being the development of new leaders. We have to see ourselves, at all levels, as in the business of leading leaders, who, in turn, will lead other leaders, and so on. This is probably one of the least understood and certainly least practised aspects of the leadership role. It means we first have to create and develop those leaders we will lead. It has been said that the most important job of any leader is to spot and train their own replacement and to make themselves redundant in that function as quickly as possible.

Somewhat oversimplifying this, it has been said that the ideal leadership situation is having a leader sitting in a room with their feet up and reading a newspaper. Basically, everything has been delegated and the leader is left with little to do other than keep an eye on things and wait for something to go wrong where they can assist people to sort things out. The leader has delegated everything, not so they can have an easy life, but to where it will do most good. For example, responsibility will have been delegated where it would be helpful in stretching someone or providing a useful challenge to them. Or, it will have been delegated to someone who could actually do it better and for whom it would not be an unhelpful burden. In this way, a key role of leaders is to empower the people around them. This image of a leader with their feet up reading a newspaper is, of course, an idealized picture of how leadership might look. It does, however, capture an important aspect of the role. In reality, just as this person was delegating to other people, they themselves would be taking on new challenges and responsibilities and be moving ahead in their own development.

This function of empowering people and creating new leaders is often preached about but much less often practised. The word "empowerment" is actually becoming debased by its widespread use in situations where there is only a pretence at empowerment. In fact, for many people, their normal experience is of people in authority hoarding information, hoarding influence and hoarding power. Particularly where there is an imbalance of power in the relationship, there seem to be real difficulties in some leaders letting go of control and trusting other people to take leadership. Implicit in their actions is a norm that says control will be handed over only when the leader is comfortable and satisfied that the other person will either do things the way the leader likes or else will make no mistakes. There can be a reluctance to allow people to make mistakes and learn from them or to allow people to apply their own style and approach to leadership. It is as though leaders were only comfortable with clones of themselves. The ability to give up control and trust people who have shown they are ready for leadership is a key part of the leadership role. This is something we shall return to again when we look at this issue in the context of liberation.

If, as a leader, I were to focus the bulk of my energy on assisting the people around me to take leadership and initiative, I would become hugely effective. Many other issues and difficulties would fall into place and be handled elegantly along the way. One of the criteria we can apply in evaluating our own effectiveness is the extent to which the people around us can think for themselves, can take initiative and can exercise leadership independently of us. To what extent are we able to listen to and take on board other people's ideas and suggestions (even when we think we know better than they do)? To what extent are we able to follow other people's suggestions or ideas and allow them to learn from their mistakes? Does it always have to be done our way? One of the tests of servant leadership put forward by Greenleaf was whether other people, "*while being served*, become healthier, wiser, freer, more autonomous, more likely themselves to become servants?" (1977, p. 13).

Encouraging everyone to take leadership, of course, is not meant to imply that everyone will go off doing their own thing without any reference to one another. With thinking at the heart of this model, encouraging people to take leadership necessarily includes encouraging them to be thoughtful, listening and responsible in the steps they take. Thinking clearly means that they will take account of other people and adapt their actions to the requirements of the situation.

Bossy bosses

One variation on this problem occurs where people experience leaders as having an apparent personality transformation when they move into formal leadership roles. They are seen to become bossy, authoritarian or dictatorial. People will be heard to remark that someone was a lovely person until they got this extra power or authority. The conventional wisdom in this situation is that power has gone to the person's head. It is assumed that the leader has too much power and that this is the cause of their becoming so bossy. This has been summed up in the well-known saying that "power corrupts". In contrast with this, research seems to show that, in many cases, it is not so much power that corrupts as powerlessness. (In Chapter 3 we shall see some other possible sources of corruption). Kanter (1979a, 1979b, 1993), for example, has given a detailed account of the respective effects of powerlessness and power in organizations. People who become bossy or dictatorial, or who seem to lord it over everyone else, actually feel quite insecure and powerless. People who relaxedly feel powerful rarely become authoritarian. These people actually seem to delegate more. Because they feel secure in their position, they tend to delegate naturally and do not need to fall back on the trappings of authority to get things done. Issues of status or territory are not of great importance to them. Their main concern is that things work well, however that is best done.

From this point of view, *one* of the ways to deal with authoritarian leaders is to increase their sense of power and security. Research on supervisors in the workplace has shown that where people's jobs are restructured in order to give them more support, more resources and more scope for initiative, they automatically delegate more. In contrast to this, supervisors whose jobs were not restructured, but who were sent on training programmes in communication and human relations, did not significantly improve in their ability to delegate (Kanter, 1979b). In later chapters we shall look at other perspectives on, and strategies for dealing with, such people.

Some authoritarianism is, as Kanter suggests, due to insecurity and powerlessness and is an attempt to feel powerful by lording it over others. Powerlessness, of course, is not the only source of bossiness or authoritarianism. A closely related source of this is internalized oppression and the tendency of oppressed people to switch roles into an oppressor role when they get the opportunity. We shall look at this in more detail in Chapter 8. Some authoritarianism is more unaware and is the result of a conditioning to look down on, feel superior to, or more intelligent than others. Many groups that have traditionally occupied positions of power have, over time, internalized an arrogant belief that they know best. Someone from such a group may not feel insecure or powerless at all. In this case, the authoritarianism comes from lack of awareness and feelings of prejudice towards, or distrust or low expectations of, people from a different background. This has implications for how such people lead and will be explored in greater detail in later chapters. Perhaps, after all, it is the extremes of either too much power or too little power that actually do the damage.

How to develop leaders

If turning other people into leaders is a vital part of the leader's job, what can we do to achieve this? Kanter (1979a, 1979b) highlights three particular sources of power that, when present, enable people to act powerfully. The first of these is access to resources, i.e. the money, the materials, the tools, the personnel and so on that are required to get the job done. The second is access to information, i.e. being "in the loop", knowing what's going on, having inside information. The third is access to support, i.e. being allowed to exercise initiative or discretion and getting encouragement and backup from above for this. While there may, at times, be limits on the amount of available resources, there are practically no limits to access to information or support. The more information and support we can provide, the more we can empower people. People who feel in the know and who feel they have support automatically tend to take initiative.

In a similar way, Jackins (1986) has articulated simple steps to turn people into leaders. First, we have to raise with people the possibility of their becoming leaders. This we can do in a variety of ways. We can ask them for help. We can praise their leadership qualities. We can create roles and ask them to fill them. We can talk about the need for leadership. Anything that encourages people to think of themselves as having a leadership role will be helpful.

Secondly, we repeatedly have to express confidence in the person's ability to lead. We have to provide constant reminders that we are pleased with their efforts and that we have faith in them to meet greater challenges. Showing that we believe in them and that we have a relaxed, non-urgent but high expectation of them provides a lot of safety and encouragement for people to take more initiative and move into leadership.

Thirdly, we have to give them information on how to lead. This we can do by coaching them, providing practical information, training or reading material. More than anything we can model how to lead for them. The combination of warm support and active modelling of good leadership creates the conditions for people to experiment and develop their own leadership.

Fourthly, we have to provide opportunities for them to get experience of leading in situations that do not overwhelm them. We give them opportunities to experience success, discover that they are capable, enjoy doing it and realize that it is possible to learn how to do it better. We look for leadership opportunities that will stretch them and challenge them to take another step in their development.

Finally, when they take leadership or show initiative, we have to lavish praise and appreciation on them and encouragement to take further steps. By following these steps, we can create a climate of safety within which people are able to grow into leadership. They are encouraged to take risks, experiment and learn from their experiences. Notice that this process does not include criticizing people for their mistakes or failures. The focus is on what they have achieved and what they are capable of. The assumption here is that if we provide the safety and the support, they themselves will figure out what they need to do differently or how they can do even better in future.

All through this process, we are there to listen to them celebrate their successes or talk about their fears or disappointments. We offer a shoulder to lean on while they talk about how hard it is to lead, how confused they are or how scared they are of taking the next step. By maintaining a relaxed, confident belief in their ability we provide the safety for them to overcome their own self-doubt, confusion or fears.

This approach to developing new leaders is echoed by Pierce (1984) when he asserts that there is only one way to get new leaders and that is to ask them personally, individually and one to one. He also emphasizes the importance of relationships when he stresses that people can only be encouraged into leadership by someone with whom they already have a relationship of trust.

Turning the people around us into leaders is not a difficult task once we understand that it is central to the role of leadership. As leaders, our job is to provide the encouragement, the support and the safety for people to take initiative and grow into leadership. This is something that has to be all the time at the centre of our relationships.

SUMMARY

In this chapter, we have added to the list of functions carried out by effective leaders. In particular, we have emphasized the importance of seeing leadership as an active role based on the listening and thinking that are always at its core. This active role includes, among other functions, taking initiative to move things forward, being decisive, organizing people and developing new leaders. Having a clear picture of the functions of a leader allows us to think about what we are doing and what we are trying to achieve in any situation. It also reminds us that leadership is something we do and not just a position we occupy. This model of leadership has a number of important implications that we shall look at in the next chapter, particularly how it relates to the concept of authority.

REFLECTION

Other aspects of your leadership

1   Describe a situation where you modelled taking initiative or acting decisively in a way that made a positive difference.
2   Describe a situation where you proposed a way forward and got agreement that enabled a group to overcome a blockage to progress.
3   Describe a situation where you were able to organize people in ways that enabled them to be more effective.
4   Describe a situation where you modelled integrity or taking a principled stance in the face of opposition from, or confusion on the part of, other people.
5   What are your particular strengths in developing other people's leadership? In what ways are you effective in nurturing and developing the leadership of those around you?
6   What positive feedback have you received, directly or indirectly, about your strengths in this area?
7   Of the various functions of a leader described so far, which are the ones that you most need to develop or emphasize in order to be more effective as a leader?

Your vision

8   What is your vision, your dream or your ideal future for your group or organization? How would the future look if you got things right?

9   In what ways have you been successful in sharing this vision with others or in inspiring people with your dream?

10 As a leader, what are the values that are close to your heart?

11 How are these values reflected in the ways you lead or in the strategies you adopt or the steps you take as a leader?

12 To what extent are the core values of your group or organization reflected in its day-to-day functioning?

13 In what ways are you or your group or organization out of step with core values? Where do you not fully "walk the talk"?

14 If you were to change anything about the way you or your group or organization reflects core values, what would you do differently?

3 Leadership, authority and collaboration

INTRODUCTION

So far, we have looked at the role and functions of leadership without making any particular distinction between formal and informal leadership. As it happens, the core functions of a leader are much the same regardless of whether the person plays this role formally or informally. At the same time, it is worth taking a look at what happens when the person occupies a formal position of authority. How does this relate to leadership? Are leadership and authority the same or different? And where does authoritarianism stand in relation to both these concepts?

LEADERSHIP, AUTHORITY AND AUTHORITARIANISM

In practice, there is often great confusion in people's minds about the concepts of authority, authoritarianism and leadership. It is useful to make some clear distinctions between these. Let us look at authority and leadership first. In many settings, particularly where tasks are complicated or the numbers of people are large, it makes sense to delegate particular functions to individuals as a way of allowing the group to operate more efficiently. Heifetz (1994) defines it as "conferred power to perform a service" (p. 57). For example, we delegate to people the authority to speak on behalf of the group, or to make certain decisions, or take certain initiatives on behalf of the group. This is entirely rational and, when this authority is exercised well, it will enhance the functioning of the group. The group, in turn, agrees to accept this person's authority and respect the actions they take within this authority role. An important aspect of this is that authority is essentially something that people are given, or it is a position that they are appointed to or elected to.

Leadership, on the other hand, is not something that people are given. It is essentially something that they take. Taking leadership can be described as a decision we make to see that the things around us work well or that the situations in which we find ourselves are handled effectively. Taking leadership, as it has been described in the previous chapters, does not require any authority. Remember that it is not part of leadership to think for, or impose decisions on, the members of a group. Leadership is an influence relationship rather than an authority one. Rost (1993a, 1993b, 1997) describes it as an influence relationship among leaders and collaborators. It is not something we are given, appointed to or elected to. Essentially, it is a decision to take initiatives to help things go better. From this point of view, leadership and authority are two independent processes. It is not necessary to occupy a formal position of authority in order to take leadership. In practice, the two roles may or may not coincide. There are many people, for example, with no formal authority who regularly take leadership and who make a big difference to the world around them. There are also people we can think of in positions of authority who are, or were, outstanding leaders. Similarly, though, there are people who have authority but who do not take leadership for one reason or another. Because someone is in a position of authority does not automatically mean they will act as a leader.

Authority without leadership

There are three common reasons why people in authority do not exercise leadership. One reason is that they have become scared and have cut themselves off from the people around them. They operate in isolation and do not listen well to the thinking of other people. They do not ask what other people think in case the people actually tell them. They are afraid of hearing something negative. Their approach to the role is a defensive one. They hoard information and power and can sometimes become very territorial-minded. Often, in such cases, they fall back on the trappings of authority and insist on rules and regulations, on their right to command, on their higher status.

Conventional wisdom says that, in situations like this, power has gone to the person's head. We talk about power corrupting people. The process is not as clear-cut or as simplistic as that, however. Power does not always corrupt. In some cases, as we saw in Chapter 2, in the discussion of bossy bosses, research seems to indicate that the opposite may be the case. Powerful people, people who feel powerful, do not always abuse their authority. Powerful people seem to delegate naturally and do not worry much about their high status being recognized. On the other hand, powerless people, people who feel weak and insecure in their position, do become very bossy, rules-minded and authoritarian. Contrary to conventional wisdom, it is sometimes not power that corrupts but powerlessness.

A second source of difficulty is that sometimes people in authority have too much power. In this case, their power is never tempered by alternative viewpoints. In their position of power they have become divorced from the reality experienced by other people. Janis (1982) coined the term "groupthink" to capture this dynamic. Argyris (1986) refers to the "skilled incompetence" of people in leaders who are unable to take on board any perspective that threatens deeply held assumptions or policies. These failures of leader-ship are due in large part to the separation and isolation of leaders from the influence of diverse elements of their constituency. Burns (1978) and Good-win (1978) distinguish between leaders and power wielders, where the latter operate with little regard for the agenda, the needs or the wants, of other parties. In this situation, those in positions of power assume that their own thinking and the thinking of people who share the same social identity, back-ground or status is representative of, or even superior to, the thinking of the group or organization as a whole. In this sense, power that does not involve widespread, open-minded, respectful listening does corrupt. Often, this type of power is linked to being part of a dominant, privileged or oppressor social group. This is a dynamic we shall see more about in Chapter 7.

A third reason why some people in authority do not exercise leadership is that they have become overwhelmed with administration and paperwork. They literally do not have time to think. Sometimes because of pressing demands and lack of resources, sometimes because of failures to prioritize, and often because of a general confusion around the nature of leadership, we are putting some people into formal positions of authority and then making it, practically, very difficult for them to act as leaders. We are confusing the role of administration with the role of leadership. In this situation, day-to-day demands and crises drive out long-term planning and thinking about the bigger picture. The urgent displaces the important. People in authority lose sight of the fact that a key role of leadership is thinking about the big picture over the long term. This can lead to an effective abdication of a leadership role with the person in authority focusing on the minutiae of administration to the detriment of long-term development or falling back on authoritarian-ism in a misguided attempt to get things done more efficiently. In the latter case, the pressure of work leads to an impatience with discussion and con-sultation and an insistence that people simply follow instructions without question. To be effective, leaders need to set aside time to think, to plan, to evaluate. Many leadership teams become less effective over time because of a failure to step back from day-to-day management and look at the bigger, longer-term picture.

Under any of these conditions, authority quickly becomes authoritarian-ism. The difficulties that many people experience with authority – the resist-ance to, the suspicion of or hostility towards people in authority – are, in reality, difficulties with authoritarianism. The authoritarianism they were exposed to left them feeling excluded from information and decision making, feeling treated as inferiors with their own giftedness unappreciated, and feel-ing powerless and hurt. People's bad experiences with authority figures acting in authoritarian ways lead them to view all authority negatively. They come to view all authority as oppressive or abusive when, in fact, it was only the authoritarians that acted in these ways. These negative associations with authority can easily extend to any visible leadership role. In some situations, not only will people become reluctant to allow any member of their group to exercise authority, they will also tend to suppress any individual initiative that does not have the group's formal approval. In this type of situation, the tyranny of authoritarianism is gradually replaced with a different type of tyranny – a tyranny of indecision, fear and distrust.

Authority with leadership

As we have seen, in practice, the two processes of leadership and authority sometimes overlap and in other cases are separate. In theory, however, where authority is exercised in a relaxed and authentic way, it should coincide with leadership, as it has been described here. When a person is *given* a position of authority, they still have to make a personal decision to *take leadership*, to act as a leader. Ideally, everyone in authority would effectively have made this decision. In practice, many have not. McCormack (1996) has commented that authoritarianism is authority that has ceased to struggle to become leadership. Where leadership and authority do actually coincide, we will find that there is very little reliance on the trappings of authority. People do not fall back on an appeal to rules or regulations or insist on the rights conferred by their position. Effectively, the authority aspect becomes low key or invisible. People are led rather than commanded and the relationship becomes a collaborative one rather than an authoritarian one. The functions that have been delegated to this authority role are exercised flexibly and thoughtfully and do not become sources of contention.

IMPLICATIONS

Leadership, from this perspective, what we can call liberation leadership, is something we do, a way of relating to people, not a position we occupy. It enables us to exercise formal authority, when called on, in ways that are experienced as supportive and liberating. At the same time, it does not require that authority in order to act. As well as clarifying the relationship between leadership and authority, this model of leadership has other implications that help to clarify the nature of collaboration in leadership.

Everyone is a potential leader

One implication of liberation leadership is that leadership ability is inherent – everyone is a potential leader. There is a widely held belief that some people are born to lead and others born to follow. However, the process described here has, at its core, a basic human ability of thinking. The potential of being a leader is an essential feature of any human intelligence. Anyone who can think can ultimately take leadership. At any given moment, some people may be in better shape than others to play this role but, potentially, everyone can.

This is often quite noticeable in very young children who, if we have not interfered with their development too much, will naturally take leadership where it is required. Adults who were raised in difficult family circumstances are able to relate how clearly they understood what was going on around them, even in situations where parents or other adults tried to shield them from the difficulties. Children are naturally very sharp and perceptive and will tend to want to act on this awareness if we do not stifle it. It is the case, however, that by the time many of us have reached adulthood, we have lost our ability to lead and to take initiative. As young people, for example, we received the message that it was not our job to think or to take initiative. We were humiliated or punished when we tried to use our thinking or acted on the basis of what we thought made sense. For many of us, the education that we received in the home or in school had the effect of stifling our sense of our power and our ability to take leadership. One of the challenges we face is to assist young people to hang on to this natural leadership ability and not have it taken from them.

This particular challenge has major implications for both child rearing and education. In what ways do we assist young people to practise this natural leadership ability? In general, we tend to act as though they had no such ability and must be instructed and disciplined to instil a sense of responsibility and to ensure proper behaviour. Outside the sports field, or a few limited roles such as prefects or class representatives, what opportunities are provided in schools for the mass of young people to exercise leadership? Where is their thinking sought and listened to about the education process? Where are they encouraged to take initiative to identify and address pressing issues? What is the kind of leadership that we model for young people? If the truth were told, mostly what we model is authoritarianism. Someone once said that employees in a work organization should ideally be treated as though they were volunteers. It is interesting to speculate about what schools might look like if they were not compulsory. If we had to attract young people to schools, what would we have to change? If it is not stifled, young people have a natural curiosity and interest in learning. We might find that we have to listen to their thinking and involve them in decisions that affect them a lot more. We might humbly have to admit that we do not always know better and allow them to lead us. We might have to encourage them to take initiative where they see that things are not right.

The point here is that leadership ability is inherent. With young people, we have to nurture it and provide rewarding opportunities for it to be practised. We also face the challenge, at this point, of assisting adults to reclaim their natural leadership ability that they had stifled along the way. We saw some simple guidelines for doing this in Chapter 2.

The focus on exemplary leadership in much of the recent literature has presented a picture of real leadership as somehow charismatic or exceptional. This has the effect of obscuring the inherent leadership ability and potential of all of us. We are presented with models of leadership who are apparently supremely self-confident and competent, passionately dedicated, convinced of their own correctness, single-minded and fearless. For many people in leadership roles or people who want to make a difference, however, this is not how it feels to lead. They struggle with doubts about their intelligence or their competence, they feel scared, hopeless or powerless at times, they get confused about what makes most sense or they are trying to juggle a number of competing demands on their time and energy while they pursue what they want to achieve. In the midst of all this, it is easy to lose sight of their significance as leaders. The message that comes across is that real leaders do not struggle, that real leaders lead effortlessly. The presence of doubts, fears, confusion, exhaustion or discouragement can be taken to mean someone is not a real leader.

The reality is different. Leadership is not about having no struggles. It is not about finding it easy. Umberto Eco said that the real hero dreams of being an honest coward like everyone else, that they are always a hero by mistake. Leadership is about not letting the struggles stop us. It is not about never making mistakes or having to know it all. It is about giving ourselves permission to get it wrong and learning from what happens. It is not about looking as if we have no difficulties. It is about being able to show our struggle and not pretending to be what we are not. Because we may find it difficult does not mean we are not real leaders. Overcoming the difficulties, the feelings or the blocks in the way is what leadership is about. Everyone has this potential and one of the first steps towards it is realizing we do not have to be perfect before we start.

Leadership is necessary

A further implication of liberation leadership is that leadership is a necessary function in any group. If things are to go well, someone has to think about the individuals and the group as a whole and about where it is going. Someone has to think about the bigger picture. Someone has to take initiative. As we shall see, this does not have to be done only by one person but at least one person must do it. This does not mean, as we saw, that these things are done in an authoritarian or oppressive way. But, they do have to be done. More than just being a necessary function, however, leadership is a highly positive and enriching resource in a group. It is not simply something to be tolerated, it is something to be encouraged.

In contrast to this, from the perspective that all authority and leadership is abusive, some people have experimented with leaderless or structureless groups. Because past authority figures have been abusive, however, does not mean we should not have any leaders. In practice, leaderless groups do not work. Where they have appeared to work, it was the case that informal, individual leaders emerged who took initiatives to make them work. In an influential article in the women's movement, first published in 1970 and later updated (Joreen, 1996), Freeman referred to this as the tyranny of structurelessness (Freeman, 1970). Similarly, Crass (2003), in discussing anti-authoritarian organizing, rejects the notion of leadership as domination and asserts the need for good leadership. As we saw in Chapter 2, rather than designing groups to minimize the role of leadership, a more useful approach would be to design groups to enhance the leadership of each person in the group. Achieving that, in itself, requires leadership. For a group to work effectively, someone has to think about the group and the people in it. Recognizing and embracing this role positively will make a lot more sense than looking for ways to avoid giving it to anyone in case they abuse it. Provided we have a clear understanding of the role of leadership, and when we include the realization that everyone is a potential leader, any fears about abusive leadership can be set aside in favour of a much more positive and exciting set of possibilities.

These difficulties that people have in relation to leaders and authority figures form part of a larger dynamic that is a source of stress and burnout for people in leadership roles. An awareness of how this dynamic operates will make a significant difference to our ability to enhance and develop positive and supportive leadership in any group. This particular dynamic will be the subject of Chapters 5 and 6.

Widespread leadership

Liberation leadership also implies that the more people take leadership, the better things can go. If things are to function well in any setting, *at least one person* must think about the group as a whole and the people in it. However, if more than one person thinks about it then things can go even better. Ideally, everyone would take responsibility for thinking about the group. Everyone in the group would exercise leadership. This is in contrast to the view that there must be only one single leader or that sometimes there can be too many leaders and not enough followers. This model emphasizes the importance of leadership and the need for *at least* one leader. However, it also recognizes the value in having many people exercising leadership. Ideally, everyone in the group would think about its functioning, but at least one person must do it. The challenge here is to develop as widespread a leadership resource as possible.

Having many leaders need not be a recipe for chaos with everyone doing their own thing. This does not mean we will have a large group of leaders competing with each other. Nor does it mean that particular leaders will not take on clearly designated roles and responsibilities. It means that everyone will be encouraged to play a leadership role, taking on whatever responsibility they can manage usefully, that no one person will carry the full burden of leadership even though they may have an overseeing role of some type, and that, over and above any specific responsibility, each person will also be encouraged to think about the group as a whole.

One of the challenges we face is to get as many people as possible to make the decision to take leadership. While we will generally have a limited number of formal positions of authority or leadership, we will always be short of leaders, people who will think about what is happening and take initiatives to make things go well.

Bennis (1997) has touched on something close to this when he talks about "great groups". Rather than emphasizing the role of a single leader, he has begun to focus on the collective efforts of the group. In looking at the experience of very successful projects, he finds that behind every great leader there is a great group and, vice versa, behind every great group is a great leader. In fact, he maintains that, in important ways, it was the groups that made the leaders great. The leaders themselves were rarely the brightest or the best people in the groups. However, they had the ability to surround themselves with talent that helped to push them into greatness. In actual fact, few great accomplishments are the work of a single individual. Part of the skill of the leader is actually bringing together this collective talent to make it possible to achieve their goals. In this view, it is not so much great leaders who achieve things as great groups. So, we can think of the process being described here as in some way being about creating such great groups.

Acting responsibly

Implicit in this model of leadership is a recognition that leaders have to bring other people with them. They cannot act in ways that ignore the thinking or needs of other people. This also implies that leaders, particularly people taking leadership informally, will act responsibly, taking account of other people and the needs of the group as a whole. Having as many people as possible take leadership in a group is balanced by the requirement to act responsibly. Taking leadership entails taking account of other people's thinking and feelings. It does not mean everyone doing their own thing regardless of other people. Treating other people disrespectfully or abusively is not clear thinking. It means we have to become skilled at listening and bringing people with us, at getting agreement and building unity.

Leadership does not need to be visible

There is a perception of leadership that expects leaders to be highly visible, upfront and in formal positions. Much leadership is not actually like this and some of the most effective leadership may not necessarily be visible to others. In discussing servant leadership, for example, Williams (2002) notes that servant leaders tend to avoid the limelight and work behind the scenes. Leadership is often indirect and low key and may not even be called leadership by people in the situation. It may take place in the background, behind the scenes, and may not have the label "leadership" attached to it. It may simply consist of listening to someone who is having a difficulty or making a quiet suggestion to someone or drawing their attention to a problem. It may involve taking an initiative that is not done publicly. Badaracco (2002) talks about what he calls "quiet leaders". These are ordinary people who are not highly visible or seen as public heroes who, day to day, are solving important problems and contributing to a better world. As he sees it, the vast majority of problems that require leadership are everyday situations rather than critical or strategic issues. Quiet leaders are not charismatic and often do not think of themselves as leaders. They simply work behind the scenes to fix the difficulties that arise. For Badaracco, it is this quiet leadership that actually moves and changes the world.

In some cases, people can play a more effective leadership role when they do not occupy the more visible, formal position of leadership. It can happen, in certain situations, that a formal leader will feel less latitude to move or take initiative than the person occupying a more low-key role behind them. In the political sphere, for example, the highly visible public representative may have less room to manoeuvre than the less visible and less well-known advisers and aides around them.

Many people are involved in leadership roles who may not actually think of themselves as leaders. Liberation leadership, as it is described here, is also a model of good parenting or a model of what good teachers will do. Parents, for example, play a key leadership role even though they may not often attach the title of leadership to what they do. Burns (1978) has made the point that true leadership is quite widespread in these kinds of roles.

We do not have to wait until we occupy formal leadership positions before we can exercise leadership. We can decide to play a leadership role in any situation in which we find ourselves. It only requires a decision on our part. With a clear picture of what this role entails and a commitment to treating others as potential leaders, any individual can become a positive force and a resource for the people around them.

COLLABORATIVE OR SHARED LEADERSHIP

This emphasis on recognizing the leadership potential of each individual has led some groups to experiment with alternatives to traditional, hierarchical, authoritarian leadership structures. Increasingly, people are looking for models of leadership that can embody the values of respect for people, empowerment and justice. Attempts to find alternative leadership models, however, have often been frustrated by a lack of clarity about the role of leadership and how it can best be facilitated. This seems to be particularly the case when one looks at the experience of collaborative leadership among various social and religious groups. There is a range of terminology used to describe this type of leadership arrangement – shared leadership, co-responsibility, participative leadership, collaborative leadership and so on. In practice, there are many variations in the models that people adopt but all are based on the desire to move towards a more participative and collaborative type of leadership. What these have in common is an attempt to operate as a group or community without any formally designated leader. Leadership roles are usually divided among the group with different people taking responsibility for different functions and decisions are made on the basis of group consensus. Nygren and Ukeritis (1993) in their study of the future of Roman Catholic religious life in the United States voice their concern about the growth in the use of consensual and team-based approaches to leadership. They point out that, while such approaches are potentially effective, they can often, in practice, lead to mediocre management and paralysis of leadership. In many cases, shared leadership did not deliver all that it promised. While it worked in some cases where people had particularly close relationships, in others it led to a stifling of initiative, to frustration and a loss of a sense of community. So, how can it be made to work as an effective structure? This requires taking account of a number of issues.

Motivation

A useful starting point is to think about the motivation for adopting collaborative or shared leadership. Dislike of authoritarian or abusive leadership is an important but not a sufficient motivation. For some groups this is actually the primary motivation, sometimes stated explicitly and sometimes merely implicit in the steps they take. For collaborative leadership to work, it has to be about moving towards a positive vision of leadership rather than moving away from something negative. In many cases, people are clearer about what they are trying to avoid than what they are trying to achieve. Underlying these particular attempts to set up collaborative leadership has been a deep suspicion about the concept of leadership itself or, at the very least, a lack of clarity about the role of leadership in any setting. People operate with a conception of leadership as inherently oppressive and their aim is to set up structures that ensure that no one person can ever abuse them in the ways they have experienced abuse by authoritarianism in the past. Where this is the case, people end up designing structures and processes around their worst fears of abusive leadership rather than their most positive vision of what is possible. The culture of the group, under these conditions, becomes defensive and stifling. Unless it is rooted in a positive view of the role of leadership, the end result may be very frustrating for the people involved. To be workable, collaborative leadership has to have, as a primary motivation, a positive commitment to enhancing the power and leadership of each individual member of the group.

Collaborative leadership or collaborative administration

Collaborative leadership is often set up by listing out the jobs to be done in a group and allocating responsibility for them to individuals or subgroups. However, a number of difficulties can arise here. One is that dividing up the tasks in the group may lead to collaborative *administration* but not necessarily to collaborative *leadership*. For example, each person looks after their own specific area of responsibility but feels they cannot take any initiative unless they check with the group and get consensus on it. The result can be endless meetings with long agenda of items that should really be dealt with by the responsible individuals. Closely related to this difficulty is a further problem of people being constantly on the alert in case someone gets upset with them for encroaching on their territory. Responsibilities are jealously guarded and people tiptoe around one another in fear of being attacked for interfering in an area that is not their concern. In this situation, people hold back from leadership while they wait for others to take initiative.

Collaborative administration, in the guise of collaborative leadership, can be a confusing and demotivating experience. Some groups have complained about the fact that everything is functioning satisfactorily but that the life or the soul has gone out of the group. Everyone is taking care of their own area of responsibility but there is no sense of excitement or movement or development. Seeing collaborative leadership as simply about dividing up tasks or responsibilities misses the point. Jobs and responsibilities do need to be allocated but this is only a part of the collaborative leadership process.

Individual initiative

For collaborative leadership to be workable, there needs to be an active commitment to nurturing and developing the individual leadership of each person in the group. This means that the group would not routinely check up on or need to "rubber stamp" each decision or initiative that the person takes. We would trust people to act responsibly and assume they would check with the rest of the group on matters that required their input. We would trust them to make informed decisions on routine matters and not require a meeting every time they wanted to do something. Within the broad parameters of their role, they would keep in touch with other people in the group individually, listening to their ideas and concerns, and taking account of these in the decisions they make. They would be expected to consult, at least informally, with the people likely to be affected by initiatives they take or decisions they make. For the larger, non-routine issues that, perhaps, had broader policy implications, they would involve other people more directly in the decision-making process and, in some cases, only act when there is group consensus. The thrust of this process is that individuals would be trusted to act responsibly rather than being routinely scrutinized and overseen by the group. If each person has a clear understanding of the role of a leader, as described in this model, this type of collaborative leadership is possible.

Over and above expecting people to take active leadership within their own area of responsibility, collaborative leadership also assumes they will think about the larger situation. They will be encouraged to think about the group as a whole, in addition to their own immediate area. In doing this, they will be encouraged to take thoughtful and responsible initiative to see that the entire situation works well. This may mean working through other people and coordinating with, influencing, or supporting other leaders in the group to raise issues and propose ways forward.

In evaluating the quality of a collaborative leadership arrangement in any setting, we have to ask what effect it has on the leadership of each individual. It can be very effective if it encourages people to take individual initiative rather than making them reluctant or afraid to do so.

Leaders' support group

It can be useful, in practice, to think of a collaborative leadership group as something like a "leaders' support group". Rather than thinking of a fixed amount of leadership to be distributed or a fixed set of roles and responsibilities to be divided up, it can be helpful to think of it as being a group of leaders who are supporting each other to take full leadership of the environment around themselves. They are not so much sharing leadership as stretching their leadership to the limits. Part of the difficulty with concepts like "shared leadership" or "co-responsibility" is the use of the terms "shared" or "co-", which implies some dilution of leadership. In fact, the challenge for shared or collaborative leadership is how to enhance leadership in the group.

In this sense, collaborative leadership needs to have as its central focus the process of thinking about each individual as a leader and about what will move the person on to the next step in their development as leaders. One way of ensuring this focus is to provide regular opportunities for each person to be listened to as they talk about how their leadership is going and to get encouragement and support from the other leaders. If people are not regularly and explicitly talking about their leadership, they will tend to stop thinking of themselves as leaders and give up some of their initiative. The agenda for such a discussion might consist of each person in the group taking time to talk about: a) what they were pleased with in their leadership over the past period; b) the difficulties and struggles they were having with their leadership; c) their plans for the coming period; and d) the places where they need support. Each person, in turn, would be listened to on these matters before the meeting would conclude. Where the balance was right, we would have a group of people thinking well about each other and about the group as a whole and supporting each other to take initiative to see that everything worked well.

Thinking about everything

The question to be asked with collaborative leadership (having divided up all the different jobs, responsibilities and chores) is who gets the job of *thinking about everything*. Earlier it was stated that at least one person must do this but, ideally, everyone would do it. Having said that, what tends to happen in practice is that, if no one is specifically designated to do it, it falls between the stools and gets neglected. People assume someone else is doing it or that it is not their job to do it. To make collaborative leadership effective, it can be very useful to designate an individual to think about the group (individually and collectively) and its development – a type of "community development leader". The traditional role of religious superior or boss fulfilled this function (however inadequately). In our haste to get rid of hierarchical, authoritarian leadership, we risk throwing the baby out with the bathwater. It is not sufficient to eliminate the role of superior or boss; this central function has to be carried on by an active leadership. Where it happens, the reluctance to give any individual this broad, thinking role highlights the underlying suspicion that is attached to leadership as such. Organizing ourselves so as to avoid giving anyone too much power is not a good motivator and will lead us into creating essentially defensive structures rather than ones that facilitate real growth. In the way that we have been talking about leadership, the role of such a group leader is not to do the thinking for the group or to impose decisions on them, but to *facilitate* the development of the group and of each person's leadership to the fullest. Their job is very much to get as many other people as possible taking leadership. Having such a group leader is not out of step, or in contradiction, with the notion of collaborative leadership. The presence of such a leader need not restrict or counter the initiative or leadership of other members of the group. They exist to serve the group and enhance its functioning and effectiveness.

Decision making

Decision making is one of those areas where people's fears about leadership become apparent. It will not always be possible for groups to operate by consensus as we saw in Chapter 2. It can happen that some groups then become paralysed by this inability to get consensus. There is a real danger of having the lowest common denominator of leadership and a situation where no one will make a decision or take initiative unless everyone agrees to it. In some cases, the group is held back by having to move at the pace of the person with the most distress or painful emotion (fear, suspicion, hurt and so on). People talk about being held to ransom in a group by someone's stubborn intransigence, their silence or their refusal to compromise or look for win–win outcomes. A rigid commitment to acting only by consensus is a recipe for inaction. It makes sense to designate someone to make decisions when action is necessary and, at the same time, when consensus is not possible. This function may be exercised rarely but it is useful to have it designated for those occasions when a decision is required. Mostly, it will be possible to reach agreement within the group but, occasionally, for whatever reason, this may not happen. If the issue is urgent and requiring action, it may be necessary to trust someone to make a decision. Having listened to all the viewpoints on the issue, this person makes the best informed decision they can. The alternative can be paralysis. In some cases, the obvious person to make such a decision is the person with responsibility for that particular area.

It helps to have it clearly understood that this is part of their role and that the group agrees to support their decision. In other cases, where the issue affects the whole group or straddles various areas of responsibility, the "group leader" or the "community development leader" described above would be the obvious person to make the decision.

Rotating leadership

Some groups have experimented with rotating leadership. Sometimes this is done to prevent any one person having too much power. Sometimes it is done to give people the experience of leading. It does present some difficulties, however. One of these is that, every so often, someone may rotate into leadership who is not able for that job at that time. It may be a frustrating experience for the group and a discouraging one for the individual involved. A more important difficulty, however, is that rotating leadership encourages people to think with short-term perspectives and objectives. If leadership is to be effective, the leaders need to think about the group over the longer term and not just for the short periods they rotate into leadership. Someone has to think about the long-term growth and development of the group and not just about the next one- or three- or six-month period. It is helpful to put people into leadership and give them time to grow into the job, think about it, take initiatives and develop their vision.

A more restricted type of rotating leadership occurs where the chairing of meetings is rotated within a group. There is the similar difficulty here of rotating someone into the job who is not ready for it. On the other hand, there is a value in giving people the experience of chairing meetings where this would be a good challenge for them at that time. Within this process, there needs to be a complementary mechanism to allow the group to be thought about over the longer term, independently of, or in conjunction with, the individuals rotating through the role of chairperson.

There is no magic blueprint for collaborative leadership. A key issue is to distinguish between choices that are made based on painful emotions from past experiences and choices based on clear thinking about what makes most sense in the present. The essential factor is having a clear and positive perspective on what leadership is and how it can best function. Where collaborative leadership is approached with such a perspective and where leadership is clearly seen as a resource to be developed, the potential for an energizing, empowering, effective and supportive group is greatly enhanced.

INDIVIDUAL INITIATIVE AND COLLABORATION

Two important aspects of leadership are being balanced in this discussion. On the one hand, leadership is essentially an individual act. It is individuals, not groups, that lead. The functions of leadership that we saw in the previous chapters are carried out by individuals and, at key points in history, for example, particular individuals have played hugely significant roles in changing the world. On the other hand, this leadership is intimately connected to, and in a relationship with, other people. Individuals made a huge difference but they did not change the world on their own. As we saw in Chapter 1, no one person can do the thinking for everyone else. So when we think about leadership, we are trying to release and harness individual initiative while, at the same time, recognizing that it cannot be effective on its own. In this sense, leadership is both an individual and a collective process. To be effective as a leader, I have to think and take initiative and, at the same time, learn from the thinking and initiative of others. As an individual leader, I can figure out many things and take important initiatives but there will also be areas where my thinking is not that clear or where I fail to take initiative. Other leaders around me, however, my collaborators, will have greater clarity in some of these areas where I get confused or will find it easier to take initiative in the places where I get stuck. Together we will fill in the gaps in our understanding of a complex situation or discover effective ways to deal with a challenging situation. In this latter sense, leadership is very much a collective process. Rost (1993b, 1997) and Rost and Barker (2000) make the point that leadership is not what the leader does but rather what the leader and collaborators do together. The challenge I face is to develop my own personal leadership to the fullest, to take complete leadership wherever I can and, at the same time, learn from, work with, support and develop to the fullest the leadership of those around me. In the end, effective leadership requires both of these elements.

SUMMARY

This model of liberation leadership clarifies the distinction between leadership, authority and authoritarianism. It emphasizes that leadership is something we do rather than a position we occupy. And it underlines the fact that everyone is a potential leader. All of this has important implications, as we saw, for how we view and practise collaborative leadership and for the relationship between individual initiative and collaboration. This model has been developed and clarified in working with many different types of groups and organizations. It seems to resonate with a need that people experience for more inclusive and empowering processes that draw on their full potential to take initiative. It is rooted in a deep respect for people's inherent goodness, intelligence and power and a vision of human beings taking complete charge of the world around them.

Liberation leadership acknowledges the difficulties in the way of achieving this vision, however. Having a clear understanding of how such leadership should function is one thing. We also need to take account of practical difficulties and obstacles that have to be surmounted in the course of leading in this way. There are very real dynamics that operate to stifle and subvert the emergence of individual initiative and collaborative, liberation leadership. These will be explored in later chapters. Before that, however, we need to examine other, different conceptions of leadership and how they relate to this particular model.

REFLECTION

Assessing your leadership

1   What are you pleased with, or proud of, about your leadership?
2   What do you enjoy about leading? What do you get a sense of satisfaction from as a leader? What excites you or gives you a thrill as a leader?
3   Where is it a struggle for you as a leader? What do you find hardest about leading?
4   In what ways do you hold back from leading fully or powerfully?
5   In what ways do you lack belief or confidence in yourself as a leader?
6   If you refused to allow any self-doubt or lack of confidence to hold you back, what would you do differently?

Collaborative leadership

Think about situations where you have collaborated with others in a shared project.

7   What worked well about your collaboration?
8   What were the difficulties?
9   Looking back on it, what would you do differently?

4 Leadership: character or competence?

INTRODUCTION

Leadership theory has developed within three broad but overlapping strands or approaches. The first of these, which could loosely be classified as an Academic Psychology Strand, has evolved from an early focus on the traits of leaders (Bass, 1990a), through a focus on leader behaviour or styles (Bass, 1990a; Blake and Mouton, 1964; Halpin, 1966; Lewin, Lippitt and White, 1939), on to a focus on leadership contingencies (Fiedler, 1974) and situational factors affecting leadership styles (Blanchard, Zigarmi and Zigarmi, 2004; Hersey and Blanchard, 1977). As this strand has developed, it is questionable whether or not it actually contains a theory of leadership at all. In many ways, it has the characteristics of a theory of management or, at worst, a theory of compliance. The focus of the research has often been on leadership in business or industrial settings or within the military and its central question has been how to get people (the subordinates) to follow someone else's (the manager's) leadership. It tends to assume that the tasks to be accomplished, or the goals of leadership, are unilaterally set by management, are not open to question and the objective is to figure out how to induce compliance with these goals or with this task. Leadership itself is rarely defined within this strand and it is rarely studied outside the context of management. Trade union leadership, for example, or the leadership of political or social change movements have received very little attention. Leadership within oppressed or marginalized groups has also received little attention. In more recent years, this strand has begun to overlap with a second approach that can be classified as the Organization Development/ Management Theory Strand.

This second strand has evolved largely out of organization development and management theory and has tended to focus largely on the personal characteristics of effective leaders, returning in this to the early trait approach within strand one. Bryman (1996) refers to it as the New Leadership approach. Within this approach, the focus has largely been on the behaviour and attributes of the leaders and chief executives of large business corporations, with a strong tendency to romanticize this leadership and treat the leaders as heroes. In many ways over the last few decades, this has been, and continues to be, the dominant approach to leadership theory. It is exemplified by the works of Adair (2002); Bass (1985, 1990b); Bass and Avolio (1994); Bennis (1989a, 1989b, 1997, 1998, 2000); Block (1993); Conger and Kanungo (1988, 1998); Greenleaf (1977); Kets de Vries (1989, 2001) and Kouzes and Posner (1987, 2002). Works within this strand have built on the thinking of Burns (1978), a political scientist, who straddles both this strand and the third strand that will be examined below. Burns is particularly important because of the distinction he makes between leaders and "power wielders". Under the heading of leaders, he distinguishes between "transforming" and "transactional" leaders. This concept of transforming leadership, which Burns examined as a largely, but not exclusively, political role, has been taken by writers within organization development literature, for example Bass (1990b), and applied, under the heading of "transformational" leadership, to the leadership of work organizations. In doing this, however, they have altered Burns's definition of transforming leadership without any explicit acknowledgement of this fact. Rost (1993a), in particular, has been extremely critical of the way in which Burns's work has been "sanitized" to make it fit within this body of literature. He states that "leadership as transformation has been watered down, bottom-lined, denuded of its moral essence, emotionalized, and to some extent overidealized" (p. 87).

In talking about the development of leadership theory, and he is largely referring to this dominant strand of organization development/management writing, Rost (1993a) maintains that it has largely come to equate leadership with doing what the chief executive says and to see leadership as synonymous with good management. It has evolved into a focus on excellence as defined by the behaviour of very visible chief executives. He refers to it as the "excellence theory of leadership" (p. 18) and maintains that this essentially "industrial paradigm of leadership" (p. 10) has become the dominant approach to leadership in modern times. He believes that leadership must be socially critical and oriented towards social change, yet much of the theory has lost its critical perspective. Barker (1997) is also highly critical of the work in this strand. He believes that leadership has been reduced to slogans and become equated with economic success and the manipulation of people. Theorists and researchers have become obsessed with the rich and the powerful and those who have attained high positions and, in the process, have learned little about actual leadership.

In a similar way to the first, academic strand, this approach to leadership is largely confined to leadership within work organizations and management. While much that has been produced within this strand does have wider implications, these are rarely explored. One small exception to this has been Bennis (1998) who shows signs of recognizing the need for a wider perspective when he discusses his pessimism about the growing crisis facing leadership in the world. He talks there about the growing disparity between rich and poor, the widespread lack of trust in leadership, what he calls the "abandoned other half" (p. 20) (those people made redundant by advances in technology) and the general lack of empowerment of people in work organizations. Unfortunately, this aspect of his work has not been developed and he has reverted to his more traditional approach in later works. Some of his concerns, however, are also echoed by Korten (1995) who maintains that leaders and institutions are not delivering the golden age that they promised. He highlights a global crisis of deepening poverty, social disintegration and environmental destruction.

The third strand of leadership theory, which might be referred to as a Social Change Strand, is more diffuse than the first two but it is important because of the emphasis it places on leadership within non-work organizations and on social change and liberation. The work of Burns (1978), for example, has been used here to understand and develop leadership within social change organizations. This third strand can be classified as a combination of social change literature (social activism, community organizing, development theory, radical or critical psychology, post-colonialism, feminism) (Alinsky, 1989; Archibald, 1978; Baritz, 1960; Brown, 1973, 1974; Fox and Prilleltensky, 1997; Heather, 1976; Hope and Timmel, 1984; Ingleby, 1975; Kirk and Shutte, 2004; Miller, 1986; Moane, 1999; Nord, 1974, 1977; Nord and Durand, 1978; Rost, 1993a, 1993b, 1997; Rost and Barker, 2000; Sedgwick, 1974; Sen, 2003; Wexler, 1983) and counselling/therapy theory (Jackins, 1973, 1978, 1983a, 1987, 1997; Janov, 1977, 1978, 1980, 1990, 2000; Radical Therapist/Rough Times Collective, 1974; Wyckoff, 1976). Much of this literature has been critical of mainstream approaches with their top-down, managerialist perspectives. In particular, the focus within much of this strand has been on leadership as a process of, and resource for, liberation. It has been influenced by a concern with the experience of people in leadership and by an interest in how to develop new leadership. It is within this strand that the approach taken in this book is located. While it acknowledges the importance of particular leadership qualities, it also pays attention to the functions that leadership performs and the socio-political context within which it operates.

In this chapter, we shall take a look at how various theorists, particularly within the second and third strands, have viewed leadership and, in particular, at what they have seen as core characteristics of effective leadership. We try to answer the question as to whether leadership is about character or competence.

CHARACTER OR COMPETENCE

In the early chapters, we focused on leadership as essentially a process of building relationships, listening, thinking and taking initiative. Leadership in this sense is primarily something we do. It is also the case, however, that the personal characteristics or qualities of the individual leader can influence how effective or successful the leader may be. In fact, many theories of leadership place considerable emphasis on these characteristics or qualities, in some cases making them the core of what leadership is about. With liberation leadership, as described here, however, the style of leadership may vary considerably, with each person having their own unique approach. There may be many different ways to achieve the same goal. So which is it? Is leadership a question of possessing certain key qualities or is it a question of the type of relationships we build? Is it about character or about competence? Is it what we are or what we do?

PERSONAL QUALITIES

To begin with, let us think about the personal qualities of leaders? How important are they? In Chapter 1, we saw how participants in workshops were asked to describe the characteristics of individuals who made a difference in their lives or who had a positive effect on them at some point. Essentially, they were asked to think about the characteristics of people who played a leadership role in their lives. These individuals might have been close relations that people remembered in a special way from when they were growing up, or a teacher that inspired them, or people they worked with who stood out in their minds, or friends or acquaintances who, at some point in their lives, made a difference to them. As people reflected on this, they tended to highlight certain qualities more than others. Across a wide range of groups, including different occupational groups, different age groups, different genders, different nationalities, different cultures, different ethnic groups and different religions, there emerged a high degree of consistency in the kinds of qualities that people pointed to as making a difference in their lives (see Table 1.1, p. 4).

The qualities described by people in these workshops are characteristic of effective leaders. As can be seen, some of the most common qualities include having integrity, being caring, approachable, accepting of people, affirming, understanding, positive and being a good listener. People with these qualities make a difference. Having said that, it is also true that no one leader has all of these qualities, no two leaders exhibit the same mix of qualities and many leaders show other qualities not on this list. To say that these qualities are common in effective leaders is not to say that all such leaders have the same style or will handle situations in the same manner. These qualities are important but they are not all there is to effective leadership.

As we also saw in Chapter 1, underpinning these various qualities is the ability of the leader to think well or clearly about people. If there is one overriding quality that is essential for leadership it is probably this ability to think well. In a sense, good leaders are intelligent. We describe them as being "sound". However, they are not intelligent in a purely intellectual or academic way or because they know a lot. Their intelligence is much closer to what people today refer to as emotional intelligence (Goleman, 1996) although I want to broaden the scope of this here. To begin with, good leaders are in touch with their own feelings. They are not numb. They are aware of the feelings thrown up in themselves by their leadership and by the struggles and stresses it entails. They take account of these feelings without being dominated or overwhelmed by them. When it is appropriate, they can show how they feel; they are able to discharge or give vent to these feelings. It is this latter ability that is often overlooked in discussions of emotional intelligence. It is the ability to discharge feelings that enables people to keep thinking clearly and to grow in clarity. They lead as both feeling and thinking persons. Whereas, in the past, rationality was often seen as incompatible with being emotional, it is actually the case that to be unemotional will ultimately lead to irrationality and to rigidity. It is precisely this connection that good leaders have to their own emotions that enables them to stay intelligent and flexible (George, 2000; Jackins, 1978). In the same way, they are also in touch with the feelings of those around them. They are sensitive to another's pain, to their struggle. They are able to listen to other people's feelings, particularly to the expression of painful emotions such as hurt, grief, shame, anger, outrage or fear. They are able to observe, listen and spot the underlying dynamics in a relationship. They are sensitive to subtle cues and the patterns in people's behaviour. Overall they are able to separate what is rational and makes sense in a situation from what is an irrational response based on some painful emotion. They respond thoughtfully rather than with some kind of knee-jerk reaction. They take account of their own and other people's feelings but their responses are not determined solely by them. In the end, they do what makes sense rather than simply what people's feelings demand.

It is this ability to integrate thinking and feelings that gives this type of leadership a quality of wisdom. To be this effective requires self-awareness, awareness of others, the ability to listen, the ability to take account of and deal with feelings and, in the face of emotions that sometimes threaten to overwhelm, the ability to stay thinking.

LEADERSHIP AS WHAT WE ARE

The qualities listed by people in workshops are very similar to the qualities of good leadership that have been proposed by a wide range of writers. In some areas they are identical to what other theorists have written and in other areas they are consistent with, and complement, them. Let's look at what some of these other writers have said.

Bennis (1989a; 1989b, 1997, 1998, 2000) has highlighted a number of qualities that he maintains are central to effective leadership. He holds, rightly I believe, that learning to be a leader is virtually the same process as becoming an integrated and healthy person. In particular, he singles out personal qualities of integrity, dedication, magnanimity, humility, openness and creativity.

He maintains that leadership is often in short supply because people are unwilling to tap into these qualities in themselves.

By *integrity*, Bennis means a commitment to honesty and to acting on principle. At its core it means being honest with ourselves first of all and being able to learn from experience. He places it at the centre of good leadership and sees it as essential if leadership is to stay on track. He notes that the absence of integrity is a central feature of public and national leadership in the United States, for example.

In fact, however, his views on this are borne out by even a cursory examination of leadership scandals in many other countries. In today's world, people are not actively encouraged to act with integrity. Young people, for example, are no longer encouraged to be idealistic in the choices they make about their lives or careers. The focus is on doing whatever it takes to get ahead. The end is more important than the means. Examples of leaders who model true integrity grab our attention precisely because of their rarity. Acting on principle, adhering to values of honesty, justice or fairness are seen as qualities of exceptional, quixotic individuals rather than being expected of everyone. Yet, without integrity, leadership is doomed to become manipulative and exploitative and without it there can be no lasting trust between leaders and their collaborators.

Bennis (1989b, 1998) also highlights the need for *dedication* by which he means a passionate belief in something. True leaders are committed to a cause, a goal, a vocation, a belief, a guiding purpose or a vision and are not simply leading "as a job". This dedication gives them the strength to persist in the face of setbacks or failures. It provides both a sense of direction and the energy to keep going when things get difficult. It also enables them to define reality for people around them, to hold out a perspective or a way of making sense of what is going on. Leaders feel passionately about their vision and this communicates itself to other people. In fact, it is often this passion and dedication that first attracts other people. When leaders speak from the heart about the vision or the values that excite them, and when they speak without any trace of painful emotion, it is difficult not to be moved or inspired.

Interestingly, Davis (1996) concludes from a study of 25 historical leaders that 3 characteristics in particular stood out. The first of these was an unwavering sense of direction based on a deeply held set of values. And it was these values more than a clear sense of vision that guided most of them. The second characteristic of these leaders was their insight into the motives of their followers and their ability to adapt their leadership style accordingly. The third characteristic was their relentless persistence. They never gave up in spite of any setbacks.

Running through Bennis's model of good leadership is a concern with the character of the leader. For Bennis (1989b), the end does not justify the means. Integrity, dedication, *humility* (seeing ourselves accurately) and *magnanimity* (being above revenge or resentment) are core characteristics of many of the leaders he has interviewed. He adds to these an *openness* to conflicting viewpoints, to learning from others, to new ideas and experiences, *curiosity* and a sense of wonder about the world and an eagerness to learn new things and a *creative* approach to getting things done where we are willing to experiment and risk making mistakes. Two additional qualities, a sense of *optimism* and the ability to offer hope and a *bias towards action* complete his picture of essential ingredients of leadership. In the end, the essence of all these qualities is captured by the two concepts, as Bennis puts it, of *virtue* and *vision*. All good leaders display strength of character and a clear sense of direction. The presence of these qualities helps to generate a sense of trust in the leader without which we cannot be effective.

For Bennis (1989b, 2000), the effect of good leadership is to create a sense of empowerment among other people in an organization. This shows up in a variety of ways but in particular in a pervasive feeling that what they are doing has meaning and is significant; a pervasive sense that what matters is learning from mistakes, a pervasive sense of unity, of community, of team; and a pervasive sense of excitement about the work, a sense of challenge, stimulation and fun. This sense of empowerment means that leadership is characterized by a "pulling" rather than a "pushing" style. It is based on enrolling people in the vision and gaining their commitment rather than rewarding or punishing them.

Most of Bennis's research has been on leaders in work organizations, par-ticularly the CEOs and senior executives of large corporations. It is interest-ing to note that in his later works he has expressed a deep concern about what he sees as a leadership crisis in the world. Part of this is due to the lack of integrity that we referred to above and to the lack of any inspiring vision for young people to follow. It is more than this, however. If leadership is to be effective it must address pressing social issues. Bennis (1998) highlights a number of these that were referred to earlier – the growing disparity between rich and poor, the low level of trust in political leaders, those unemployed by advances in technology and the sense of powerlessness that many people in employment feel. Leadership must address these issues. In coming to these conclusions, Bennis is recognizing that true leadership must have a liberating dimension. It is not enough to think about people only as employees. It is not enough to think narrowly about how we can make more money. We have to take account of everything. Leadership has to look at the bigger picture and offer people a direction around those issues that are a threat to their personal or collective integrity.

Robert Greenleaf (1977) echoes much of this approach but from the per-spective of what he calls "servant leadership". For Greenleaf, the essence of true leadership is that the leader is first and foremost a servant to those they lead. True leadership, he states, "emerges from those whose primary motiv-ation is a deep desire to help others" (p. 3). He puts forward two criteria by which servant leadership can be judged. The first of these is whether the people served grow as persons. Does this leadership have the effect of helping them to become "healthier, wiser, freer, more autonomous and more likely themselves to become servants" (p. 13–14)? The other criterion is the extent to which this leadership benefits the least privileged in society. At the very least, they should not be further deprived as a result.

Greenleaf's criteria go right to the heart of true leadership. It could be argued that many of the people put forward by various writers as exemplary leaders would fail Greenleaf's test. Their organizations have become more successful but the effects on the individuals within those organizations and on the least privileged are not at all as clear. The concept of liberation leadership is important, therefore, because it deals directly with these criteria and particularly with the second one. As we shall see in later chapters, the challenging of oppression and inequality are an integral part of thinking clearly about people.

Becoming an effective servant leader requires certain attributes. Like Bennis, Greenleaf (1977) emphasizes the importance of vision. The servant leader is someone who can point the way and generate trust among those who follow their leadership. They can articulate an attractive vision and inspire trust in their values, their competence and their commitment to the vision. In response to this vision and to the trust they generate, other people will choose to support their leadership. According to Williams (2002) the servant leader is "guided by an overarching, prophetic, transforming vision – carefully conceived and simply articulated. By precept and example, the leader guides others toward that vision, converting followers one-by-one through singular acts of bravery, courage, and determination" (p. 67).

Vision and trust are underpinned by the ability of the servant leader to listen to and empathize with people. Central to good communication is the ability to listen and understand. Servant leaders do this automatically and naturally and the effect is that people are more likely to trust them. This emphasizes, once again, the central role of paying good attention to people, putting our finger on the pulse of the situation, and leading from a deep connection to the reality facing people in their lives.

There are particular intellectual abilities that Greenleaf (1977) highlights as important for effective leadership. One of these is having a "sense of the unknowable" (p. 21), which might be described as having an understanding of the deeper issues or underlying processes in any situation. The other ability is to "foresee the unforeseeable" (p. 22), which might be understood as having a sense of the bigger picture and an ability to think in the longer term. In many ways, Greenleaf's description of servant leadership echoes the emphasis in liberation leadership on being able to "think well". The servant leader is very much an "aware" leader, sensitive to the issues and struggles around them and with a sense of the possibilities or potential that might come from change.

Drawing on the work of Greenleaf, Spears (2002) outlines ten characteristics of the servant leader. He emphasizes listening and empathy. The servant leader has a deep commitment to, and is skilled at, listening empathically to others. He also believes that listening, coupled with regular periods of reflection, is essential for the growth of the servant leader. We could add to this that the quality of reflection will be enhanced, as we saw before, by the ability of the leader to tune in regularly to their own feelings and to discharge any painful emotion in the way of thinking clearly.

Spears (2002) includes a commitment to the growth of others as well as healing in his list of characteristics. There is a primary commitment to the growth of each person in the institution and profit should not be the only motive. Beyond this, servant leaders have the potential to heal other people in the places where they have suffered emotionally. In liberation leadership, this healing process is extended not just to individual hurts but also to collective hurts caused by the experience of oppression. The process of discharge that we looked at in Chapter 2 is a powerful tool for healing. As well as assisting people to think more clearly, listening to people and assisting them to discharge also has the effect of healing old hurts. As people discharge, the hurt is let go and people are enabled to rebuild their relationships or overcome divisions that have kept them apart. Separately from its value as a tool for supporting leaders, discharge is also a valuable tool that leaders can use for healing in others.

Awareness, conceptualization and foresight are very similar characteristics that Spears (2002) also includes and, again, these highlight the importance of clear thinking in the role of the leader. The other characteristics on this list are a reliance on persuasion rather than coercion or positional authority, stewardship or a primary commitment to serving the needs of others and a focus on building community among those who are being led. These kinds of characteristics have made the servant leadership model a very attractive one, particularly for people in caring professions. It presents a more humane and more caring picture of leadership than some of the other models in the excellence school.

Various other models of leadership have also highlighted particular traits that are central to effectiveness. Studies of charismatic leadership (Conger, 1989; Conger and Kanungo, 1988, 1998; Robbins, 1998), for example, have produced the following characteristics: self-confidence in judgement and ability; vision; ability to articulate the vision; strong, passionate conviction about the vision; strong commitment and willingness to take on high personal risk, incur high costs and engage in self-sacrifice to achieve the vision; being novel and unconventional; acting as agents of radical change as opposed to caretakers of the status quo; sensitivity to environmental constraints and the resources needed to bring about change; personal power based on expertise, respect and admiration; and likeableness. These are all attractive characteristics. However, the tendency to concentrate on the leadership of work organizations and large corporations means that the interpretation of phrases like "agents of radical change" can have a rather limited meaning. Somewhat related to this point, Burns (2003) questions the whole concept of charismatic leadership. As it is described, he fears that this kind of leadership does not lead to a mutually empowering leader–follower relationship.

The creative leader–follower interaction, in which the leader offers initiatives that followers pick up, amplify, reshape, and direct back onto the leader, is lacking. Just as charismatic leadership fails to empower followers, so leaders are not empowered by subservient followers. . . . At best, charisma is a confusing and undemocratic form of leadership. At worst, it is a type of tyranny.

(p. 27)

Jackins (1987), who has written extensively about issues of leadership and liberation, outlines what he sees as the key aspects of effective leadership. Like others, he places great emphasis on integrity. By this he means honesty, a commitment to doing what is right, the keeping of agreements and promises, the refusal to exploit one person for an advantage, the giving of accurate information and not indulging in pretence. Other important qualities that he emphasizes are the ability to admit mistakes and set about correcting them, commitment to the goals of the group, decisiveness, courage to act rather than play safe, endurance (not giving in to the pull to give up), responsibility, the ability to innovate, flexibility, the ability to encourage and develop other leaders and the ability to furnish confidence and hope.

Building on the work of Jackins, Millman (1978) suggests a similar but expanded set of qualities. She includes a commitment to making things go right, no matter how it feels, the ability to model hopefulness, confidence, taking care of self and fearless action, the ability to listen deeply and communicate a synthesis of the best ideas heard, the ability to make friends with all people and to love them, the expectation of the best in one's self and others, a willingness to correct mistakes and to encourage others to do the same, a vision of reality (being able to see the whole picture as well as the specifics), the capacity to see priorities clearly and to anticipate the next step, respect and loyalty towards others, a sense of humour and the ability to play and keep a balance between taking oneself and the group seriously and lightly, the ability to move forward while seeking unity, the ability to include all people in the process, the ability to see the difference between clear thinking and painful emotion, persistence, skill in training, nurturing and creating safety for leaders and personal integrity.

It is clear as we examine these various writers that there are particular qualities that are seen as central to effective leadership. There is quite a degree of consistency in the picture that emerges. Qualities such as integrity and belief in a vision, for example, are seen as hugely important for leadership. Are these qualities everything, however? Kirkpatrick and Locke (1991), in discussing whether or not traits actually matter, conclude that while they increase the likelihood of success, there are no traits that guarantee success. In this, they echo a theme of this book. Leadership is not just about personality, it is also about relationships and processes of interaction. It is something we do and not just a way that we are.

LEADERSHIP AS WHAT WE DO

Not all writers have emphasized personal traits or qualities. A major influence on the development of leadership theory was the work of Burns (1978, 2003). Unlike most of the other influential theorists on leadership, Burns does not pay much attention to the traits of leaders. Instead, he tries to examine what leadership is and to distinguish between different types of leadership. To begin with, he distinguishes between leadership and what he calls "power wielding". The essential difference between these has to do with whether or not the leader takes account of the needs of the followers. If not, what we are witnessing is merely some form of dictatorship where the only thing that matters is the power wielder's own agenda. For Burns, leadership is defined as inducing followers to pursue goals that represent the wants, needs, aspirations and expectations of both leaders and followers. In this sense, leadership is inseparable from followers' needs and goals. On the other hand, it is not leadership to get followers to do what they would not otherwise do or to do what leaders want them to do. These would be simply power wielding. Within the process of leadership, Burns makes a distinction between "transactional" and "transforming" leadership. In the case of the former, there is a transaction between leader and follower where the follower offers support in return for some form of reward, for example, jobs for votes. Here, leaders take account of the followers' needs and try to meet some of these in order to achieve aspects of their own agenda.

In the case of transforming leadership, however, the leader is committed to elevating the followers to meet their higher-order needs. Not only are the leaders aware of the current wants of the followers, they also look for other potential motives or deeper, unarticulated needs or wants that have the potential to transform and liberate the followers. Transforming leadership leads to a relationship of mutual enhancement where both parties are significantly changed. Leaders and followers raise one another to higher levels of motivation and morality. More significantly, the effect of transforming leadership is to make conscious what lies unconscious among followers. Thus, the essence of transforming leadership is consciousness raising. People become aware of what they feel and connect with their true needs in ways that move them towards purposeful action. Ultimately, transforming leadership raises people's hopes, aspirations and expectations. They come to expect and demand more. As this process unfolds, both leaders and followers are transformed, in some cases to the point where the followers then lead the leaders. Transforming leadership is a process, therefore, that changes people. As it unfolds, they become more aware and more powerful.

At the heart of transforming leadership are a set of end values such as liberty, justice, equality. For Burns (1978), leadership is not just a descriptive term but a prescriptive one that has a strong moral and passionate dimension. The job of a leader is to change the world in response to human wants, particularly liberty, equality, justice, opportunity and the pursuit of happiness

LEADERSHIP AS WHAT WE DO

Not all writers have emphasized personal traits or qualities. A major influence on the development of leadership theory was the work of Burns (1978, 2003). Unlike most of the other influential theorists on leadership, Burns does not pay much attention to the traits of leaders. Instead, he tries to examine what leadership is and to distinguish between different types of leadership. To begin with, he distinguishes between leadership and what he calls "power wielding". The essential difference between these has to do with whether or not the leader takes account of the needs of the followers. If not, what we are witnessing is merely some form of dictatorship where the only thing that matters is the power wielder's own agenda. For Burns, leadership is defined as inducing followers to pursue goals that represent the wants, needs, aspirations and expectations of both leaders and followers. In this sense, leadership is inseparable from followers' needs and goals. On the other hand, it is not leadership to get followers to do what they would not otherwise do or to do what leaders want them to do. These would be simply power wielding. Within the process of leadership, Burns makes a distinction between "transactional" and "transforming" leadership. In the case of the former, there is a transaction between leader and follower where the follower offers support in return for some form of reward, for example, jobs for votes. Here, leaders take account of the followers' needs and try to meet some of these in order to achieve aspects of their own agenda.

In the case of transforming leadership, however, the leader is committed to elevating the followers to meet their higher-order needs. Not only are the leaders aware of the current wants of the followers, they also look for other potential motives or deeper, unarticulated needs or wants that have the potential to transform and liberate the followers. Transforming leadership leads to a relationship of mutual enhancement where both parties are significantly changed. Leaders and followers raise one another to higher levels of motivation and morality. More significantly, the effect of transforming leadership is to make conscious what lies unconscious among followers. Thus, the essence of transforming leadership is consciousness raising. People become aware of what they feel and connect with their true needs in ways that move them towards purposeful action. Ultimately, transforming leadership raises people's hopes, aspirations and expectations. They come to expect and demand more. As this process unfolds, both leaders and followers are transformed, in some cases to the point where the followers then lead the leaders. Transforming leadership is a process, therefore, that changes people. As it unfolds, they become more aware and more powerful.

At the heart of transforming leadership are a set of end values such as liberty, justice, equality. For Burns (1978), leadership is not just a descriptive term but a prescriptive one that has a strong moral and passionate dimension. The job of a leader is to change the world in response to human wants, particularly liberty, equality, justice, opportunity and the pursuit of happiness

The creative leader–follower interaction, in which the leader offers initiatives that followers pick up, amplify, reshape, and direct back onto the leader, is lacking. Just as charismatic leadership fails to empower followers, so leaders are not empowered by subservient followers. . . . At best, charisma is a confusing and undemocratic form of leadership. At worst, it is a type of tyranny.

(p. 27)

Jackins (1987), who has written extensively about issues of leadership and liberation, outlines what he sees as the key aspects of effective leadership. Like others, he places great emphasis on integrity. By this he means honesty, a commitment to doing what is right, the keeping of agreements and promises, the refusal to exploit one person for an advantage, the giving of accurate information and not indulging in pretence. Other important qualities that he emphasizes are the ability to admit mistakes and set about correcting them, commitment to the goals of the group, decisiveness, courage to act rather than play safe, endurance (not giving in to the pull to give up), responsibility, the ability to innovate, flexibility, the ability to encourage and develop other leaders and the ability to furnish confidence and hope.

Building on the work of Jackins, Millman (1978) suggests a similar but expanded set of qualities. She includes a commitment to making things go right, no matter how it feels, the ability to model hopefulness, confidence, taking care of self and fearless action, the ability to listen deeply and communicate a synthesis of the best ideas heard, the ability to make friends with all people and to love them, the expectation of the best in one's self and others, a willingness to correct mistakes and to encourage others to do the same, a vision of reality (being able to see the whole picture as well as the specifics), the capacity to see priorities clearly and to anticipate the next step, respect and loyalty towards others, a sense of humour and the ability to play and keep a balance between taking oneself and the group seriously and lightly, the ability to move forward while seeking unity, the ability to include all people in the process, the ability to see the difference between clear thinking and painful emotion, persistence, skill in training, nurturing and creating safety for leaders and personal integrity.

It is clear as we examine these various writers that there are particular qualities that are seen as central to effective leadership. There is quite a degree of consistency in the picture that emerges. Qualities such as integrity and belief in a vision, for example, are seen as hugely important for leadership. Are these qualities everything, however? Kirkpatrick and Locke (1991), in discussing whether or not traits actually matter, conclude that while they increase the likelihood of success, there are no traits that guarantee success. In this, they echo a theme of this book. Leadership is not just about personality, it is also about relationships and processes of interaction. It is something we do and not just a way that we are.

transformational leader. Having said that, as we shall see, there is a real question as to whether what they describe is truly transforming in the sense that Burns describes. By applying it to work organizations they have put limits on the scope of this leadership. It has lost its revolutionary core.

In contrast to the focus on character and traits, Boyett and Boyett (1998) maintain that leadership has less to do with character than with relationships. For them, the one thing that all leaders have in common is that they have followers and this means that the central task of the leader is to build solid working relationships with other people. Here again we can see a parallel with a core aspect of liberation leadership. Boyett and Boyett stress that leadership is about what you do more than about who you are. Precisely the same point is made by Kouzes and Posner (1987, 2001, 2002). They also believe that leadership is primarily a relationship based on mutual respect and caring. To achieve this relationship, Kouzes and Posner (1987, 2002) point to five practices that are central to effective leadership. The first is *Challenging the Process* – leaders search for challenging opportunities to change, grow, innovate and improve and they experiment, take risks and learn from the accompanying mistakes. These challenging opportunities commonly emerge from the listening that the leader does. In the context of liberation leadership, challenging the process would also include questioning fundamental values and social institutions and looking for structures and processes that are liberating for both individuals and oppressed groups. *Inspiring a Shared Vision* – leaders envision an uplifting and ennobling future and they enlist others in a common vision by appealing to their values, interests, hopes and dreams. *Enabling Others to Act* – leaders foster collaboration by promoting cooperative goals and building trust and they strengthen others by sharing information and power and by increasing their discretion and visibility. *Modelling the Way* – leaders set an example for others by behaving in ways that are consistent with their stated values and plan small wins that promote consistent progress and build commitment. *Encouraging the Heart* – leaders recognize individual contributions to the success of every project and celebrate team accomplishments regularly. This focus on relationships is also emphasized by Wheatley (2005) and by Binney, Wilke and Williams (2005) who maintain that it is the quality of the relationship between the leader and the group that leads to results. They state that "people work for people – not for visions or strategies or targets – and give their best when they feel connected to the leader and the leader feels connected to them" (p. 38).

Adair (2002) adopts a functional approach to leadership. He sees leadership as a set of broad tasks that must be completed and within these there are some specific functions that must be carried out. At the core of the process are the three interrelated tasks of achieving the common task, building and maintaining a team and motivating and developing the individual. (The nature of this common task, however, can be problematic. Adair's model seems to take it as already established and agreed. In fact, however, a key role of leadership is to question whether the established task is actually rational and, in that context, to respond particularly to the billions of the world's people who are lacking in the most basic of human wants. He calls for "the protection and nourishment of happiness, for extending the opportunity to pursue happiness to all people, as the core agenda of transforming leadership" (Burns, 2003, p. 3). This emphasis on end values makes transforming leadership a deeply revolutionary type of leadership and this is reflected in some of the examples of such leadership that Burns describes, such as that of Gandhi.

There are particular characteristics that are central to the process of leadership. These are not characteristics of the people but of the relationship. For Burns (1978), leadership is a *collective* process. Of necessity, leadership involves responding to and building on the needs and wants of both leaders and followers. Leadership is also *dissensual*. In the interaction between leaders and followers, differences and conflicts emerge that have to be worked through and cannot be ignored. The working through of disagreements and conflicts produces greater clarity both about issues and about direction. Leadership is *causative*. The result of the interaction between leaders and followers is a change in social relations and political institutions, ultimately the creation of new institutions and paradigm-changing ideas. Leadership is *morally purposeful*, it points a direction. Leadership is morally *elevating* and in the process asks for sacrifices from followers rather than simply promising them rewards.

Bass (1990a, 1990b) and Bass and Avolio (1994) have adapted the work of Burns and applied it to leadership in work organizations. They use the concept of transformational leadership to describe effective organizational leadership and isolate some core characteristics of this approach. Transformational leaders increase subordinates' awareness of the importance of their tasks and the importance of performing them well. Transformational leaders make subordinates aware of their needs for personal growth, development and accomplishment. Transformational leaders motivate subordinates to work for the good of the organization rather than exclusively for their own personal gain or benefit. In achieving these effects, transformational leaders manifest what they refer to as the "four I's": *Idealized influence* – they are role models (they are considerate; they share risks; they are consistent; they can be counted on to do the right thing; they have high ethical standards); *Inspirational motivation* – they motivate by providing meaning and challenge (they build team spirit; they display enthusiasm and optimism; they involve people in envisioning attractive future states; they are committed to the goals and shared vision); *Intellectual stimulation* – they make people think (they question assumptions; they reframe problems; they approach old situations in new ways; they encourage creativity; they ensure no public criticism of mistakes or ideas); *Individualized consideration* – they pay attention to each individual's needs for achievement and growth (they act as coach and mentor; they listen effectively; they delegate as a means of developing people). Bass and Avolio help to itemize some of the steps involved in being a and in the best interests of the group and its members.) As described by Adair, leadership is thus very much something we do. However, he does not ignore the importance of particular qualities in carrying out this role effectively. Apart from personal qualities such as enthusiasm or fairness, he singles out a number of other qualities that are directly related to leadership effectiveness. These include intelligence, imagination (creativity, ingenuity, inventiveness, originality, resourcefulness), humility and wisdom (a combination of intelligence, experience and goodness).

Davidson (1995) sees the role of the leader as managing the mission of the organization. The leader spends a lot of time keeping people focused on and enthusiastic about core values. They also help the organization to clarify what its purposes are and to ensure that these are understood and shared by everyone. The purposes are those unique or special things it offers the various groups or institutions with which it interacts. By having a shared value system and clear purposes, the members of the organization are free to operate without strict supervision and the leader is free to think about the bigger and longer-term picture. This is a useful perspective because it clearly separates leadership from management and puts the emphasis on the thinking role of leadership.

Separately from particular qualities or characteristics of individual leaders, we can see here that leadership is also a process that has important functions at its core. At the same time, it is not always clear in these writings what the role of leadership is or how it is defined. This problem has been discussed in some depth by Rost (1993a, 1993b, 1997).

LEADERSHIP AS GOOD MANAGEMENT

Rost (1993a, 1997) and Rost and Barker (2000) have been particularly critical of much of the writing about leadership. Rather than seeing leadership as a process and a relationship, many scholars have emphasized what Rost sees as peripheral aspects, including the content of leadership. In particular, he believes that the "industrial paradigm of leadership", which is based almost exclusively on the writings of management scholars in business and educational management, puts forward a view that leaders are great executives with certain traits (energy, trustworthiness, charisma, vision and so on) who behave in certain characteristic ways (for example by challenging the process, modelling the way, managing by walking around) and facilitate the work democratically but forcefully. One of the problems about this, for Rost, is that much of these writings are very management oriented and, in effect, they equate leadership with good management. Whereas Burns used examples such as Roosevelt or Gandhi to illustrate transforming leadership, most current writers on leadership use the CEOs of large profit-making corporations. For Rost (Rost and Barker, 2000), the industrial paradigm of leadership presumes a top-down, hierarchical structure. It is goal oriented (with the goal defined in terms of organizational performance). It is focused on efficiency, self-interest and materialism. It highlights male characteristics of leadership, uses utilitarian ethics and uses quantitative methods to solve what it sees as rational/technocratic problems. This has been a profitable approach but it is not adequate to meet the challenges of environmental change, alienation, drug abuse, anomie, social "misfits" and the falling number of consumers that are the consequences of our current economic system. In other words, this model serves the economic needs of work organizations but does not serve the social needs of society. Commenting on the concept of transformational leadership, Rost notes how Burns's original notion was watered down, sanitized and robbed of its moral dimension. Essentially the management writers removed its truly revolutionary elements and identified it with any significant change in an organization. Unlike management theorists, more recent critical theorists see leadership as being fundamentally about social change and human emancipation and not just about organizational goals. They see it as having a socially critical role and as residing in a relationship rather than in a person. For Rost and other critics of the excellence theory of leadership, the emphasis on traits distorts our understanding of the role and reinforces the notion that leadership resides in a person rather than in a relationship. In this sense, leadership is the ability to get people to do what you want. Leaders then become great people with special traits who influence followers to do what they (the leaders) wish in order to achieve the goals of the organization (defined in terms of excellence and effectiveness).

Looking at many of the recent theories of leadership, there is a clear underlying focus on getting people to buy into the leader's vision and achieve the leader's goals. In fact, many of these theories are not, strictly speaking, theories of leadership at all. They are actually theories of compliance. At best, to use Burns's conception, they are forms of transactional leadership. At worst and not uncommonly, they are mere exercises in power wielding. According to Rost, transformation came to mean doing the leader's wishes as the transformational leader took charge and did the right thing. This, however, is not really what true leadership is about.

LEADERSHIP AS INFLUENCE

In contrast to the excellence theories of leadership, which he criticizes for either not clearly defining what leadership is or else making no attempt to define it, Rost produces a very useful definition of leadership as "an influence relationship among leaders and their collaborators who intend real changes that reflect their mutual purposes" (1993b, p. 99). This has a number of elements. It means that leadership is based on mutual, non-coercive influence. The influence is multidirectional and it is based on persuasion. It means that followers/collaborators play an active role in the relationship. For Rost, there is no such thing as followership. Both collaborators and leaders are all doing the leadership even though not all of them are equal in influence at any given time. Thus leadership is not what the leader does but rather what leaders and collaborators do together. "Postindustrial leadership", as he describes it (Rost and Barker, 2000, p. 5), will be based on the assumption that leadership is a collaborative exercise rather than the result of one individual's intentions or actions. It means that leaders and collaborators develop mutual purposes that reflect both what the leader wants and what the collaborators want and they intend change that is substantive and transforming, not trivial or insignificant. He summarizes the main elements by saying that leadership is:

1   A relationship rather than an individual.
2   A process entirely distinct from management.
3   A relationship in which other people besides managers can be leaders.
4   A relationship in which the focus is on the interaction of both leaders and collaborators instead of focusing only on the behaviors and/or traits of the leader.
5   A relationship that aims at mutual purposes rather than just the wishes of the leader.
6   A process in which people intend significant changes as opposed to a process in which they achieve any goal.
7   A relationship in which only influence behaviors are acceptable rather than one wherein all legitimate behaviors (authority and other forms of coercion included) are acceptable. (Rost, 1997, p. 14)

According to Rost, all of these elements are central to leadership. Without these, it is not a true leadership relationship. This is very helpful in allowing us to think about our own behaviour and relationships and assessing whether these actually represent true leadership or not.

From a less academic perspective, Jackins (1987, 1997) has offered a number of related definitions of leadership. Rather than focusing on leadership in the abstract in these cases, he focuses on what leadership means from the perspective of the individual leader. Very simply, he defines leadership as thinking about the well-being of the group and its individual members. He also describes it as choosing to act in a way that makes things go well. Implicit in these simple definitions is the idea of leadership as a choice and a decision. In a more detailed way, he defines it as organizing other intelligences to act jointly with the leader's own intelligence for common goals. Elaborating on this and drawing in the wider social context, he says that leadership is "organizing other human intelligences with one's own, for the purposes of human liberation, social justice, and other concerted activities to make things go well in the world" (1997, p. 131). As part of this broad liberating role, he sees the tasks of the leader as "initiating proposals and actions, securing agreement within the acting group, keeping a long-range perspective, noticing the results and implications of present and immediate actions on long-range results and actions, modelling correct attitudes and behaviour, and modelling courageous initiative" (1997, p. 131). In this, he notes that correct attitudes include particularly a modelling of integrity. These various definitions that Jackins offers capture the functions of the leader in thinking about the group in both the short and long term, in thinking together with other people and in thinking about, and trying to achieve, common, liberating goals. They also capture the proactive role the leader plays in organizing people to do all this, in taking practical initiatives, in learning from experience and in modelling particular attitudes and behaviour. He describes all this not from an exclusive point of view of a single, formal leader but from the point of view of any individual member of a group choosing to take leadership and in a context where the aim is to have as many people as possible exercise leadership.

TRADE UNION LEADERSHIP

While the study of leadership in psychology has focused largely on the leadership of work or military organizations, within the study of industrial relations efforts have been made to examine trade union leadership. Rather than examining the particular qualities of these leaders, this research has mainly focused on their behaviour and relationships. Darlington (2001) points to the importance of leadership in a trade union context when he states that "Leadership is central to the fundamental problem of how individual workers are transformed into collective actors, willing and able to create and sustain collective organization, and to engage in collective action against their employers" (p. 2).

He refers to the pioneering studies of Batstone, Boraston and Frenkel (1977, 1978) where a typology of shop steward leadership was developed. This typology was later modified by Marchington and Armstrong (1983). In the original studies, Batstone *et al.* categorized leaders along two dimensions: the extent to which they pursued union principles (for example, the maintenance of unity, fairness and equality, protection from managerial whim, looking after each other, helping the less fortunate) and the degree to which they played a representative or a delegate role. Stewards were classified as the former if they shaped the majority of issues that they dealt with (initiating issues, amending issues, squashing issues raised by others) and if they tended to handle issues themselves without resort to other stewards or officials. They were classified as the latter if they deferred to the members' wishes without taking an independent stance on issues or being an opinion leader. These two dimensions gave four categories of leadership: leader; nascent leader; cowboy; and populist. The "leader" was a shop steward who was able to play a representative role in relation to their members while attempting to implement union principles. The "nascent leader" was a shop steward who was often sponsored by a leader. They were committed to union principles but were unable to play a representative role on their own, without the support of other stewards. The "cowboy" was able to play a representative role, at least in the short term, but was not committed to broader union principles. They typically were concerned with maximizing the short-term earnings of their own members. The "populist" lacked both a commitment to union principles and the ability or desire to be a representative and simply acted as a delegate, following the expressed wishes of their members. Although they accepted that their findings might not be typical, Batstone *et al.* found that both cowboys and nascent leaders were not very common nor long-lasting in those roles. Nascent leaders either developed into full leaders or reverted to being mere populists. Cowboys only received support for as long as they could deliver gains. When that stopped they were quickly replaced in the role.

Marchington and Armstrong (1983) modified this typology in response to various criticisms of and perceived weaknesses in it. They renamed the union principles dimension "orientation to unionism" and defined it in terms of seeing the importance of collective organization and unity and the value of local union activity. Those low on this dimension conceived of unionism merely at the level of their own constituencies and their priority was their own immediate members rather than any wider group. For them, the "leader" was highly committed to unionism and was willing and able to lead all the union membership with their commitment being to the collectivity. Many had wider political aims – for example, socialism or workers' control – but that did not mean that they were any less committed to their own members. They believed in being proactive and taking the initiative in relation to their members and in both raising and squashing issues when they felt necessary. One thing they did not do was to court popularity.

The "populist" was almost the exact opposite of the leader. They were neither committed to unionism nor to representing their members. They saw their role very much as the mouthpiece or the spokesperson for the group. Usually, the populist would ask the membership which way they wanted them to vote or how they wanted them to deal with an issue. Quite a few of the populists only remained in the job because no one else would do it. Politically, they were more conservative than the other types, and some strongly disagreed with many of the activities they felt unions pursued.

In this schema, cowboys were renamed as "work group leaders". Some work group leaders were anxious to lead their own groups or constituents but were not interested in being involved in any wider leadership group. Their primary concern was to protect their own members' interests. In this they were similar to the cowboy. However, Marchington and Armstrong found that these stewards were much less sectionalist, militant and disruptive than the classification of cowboy would imply. Although they were not particularly concerned about others, they were not particularly disruptive and, on many occasions, they seemed to control their sections and prevent them from taking action. Their key features were strong leadership over their members and a very active concern to look after the interests of those members. Some of them were also very conservative about their role as trade unionists. They were not particularly anxious to challenge managerial prerogatives nor were they committed to a wider orientation of the union. At the same time, they were very active within their own constituencies and hugely aware of unity at that level. Because they were willing and able to squash some grievances rather than progress them, they were categorized as group leaders.

Many of the next category, "cautious supporter", were young, inexperienced stewards who were being supported and developed by their more senior colleagues. They were committed to the wider union movement but felt that they lacked both the experience and the ability to lead their members in a representative way. For people like this, the original term "nascent leader" would be appropriate in that this was merely a temporary stage in their development before moving on to be a leader or reverting to being a populist. However, there were others in this category to whom this would not apply. Some were not young and inexperienced but they were dependent on their members and not in a position to act independently of them by squashing or initiating issues. Their union principles were too high to be either populists or work group leaders, and they were too willing to follow their own members to be a representative.

Both of these typologies are very interesting and useful perspectives on trade union leadership. They also highlight some of the broader leadership principles and characteristics that we have been looking at here. Their focus is largely on leadership as something we do. Unlike some of the other approaches above, they pay little attention to particular personality characteristics of the leaders. They also highlight the role of leadership in thinking and acting independently of the members and not just following them unquestioningly. In addition, they emphasize the role of leadership in thinking about the longer-term and bigger picture. Rather than thinking in terms of narrow self-interest, the leader thinks about the broader implications for the group as a whole. Although less explicit but nevertheless relevant, these typologies also highlight the importance of relationships with leaders, in particular, having a strong network of relationships with members, with other stewards and with management. This latter aspect of trade union leadership was found to be one of the most important factors in effective trade union leadership by Roby (1998) in a study she conducted of trade union shop stewards. Ongoing, one-to-one contact that was characterized by respect and validation was seen to be highly significant in influencing members to become shop stewards.

SUMMARY

This chapter has drawn attention to many of the qualities required to be an effective leader. It underlines the importance of character and soundness as general qualities to be looked for in a leader. It also reminds us that true leadership adopts a large and visionary perspective. In particular, true leadership has a central transforming or liberating role. Whether we call it transforming leadership, servant leadership or liberation leadership, we are describing a relationship where there is a commitment to the growth, development and complete liberation of both leaders and their collaborators. Anything less is selling people short and settling for a very restricted view of leadership. At the same time, we also see here that leadership is an active role that people play. It is not just about character. It is about a certain kind of relationship between leaders and their collaborators. It is about ways leaders act and the effects they achieve. What we see in this chapter is that leadership has very definite goals, purposes and functions but also very definite qualities that make it more likely to achieve these goals and purposes and be more effective in the functions it performs. Whatever the theoretical or other shortcomings of these various approaches, between them they do clarify essential aspects of the nature of leadership. In particular, they make it clear that leadership is both character *and* competence.

REFLECTION

1   Make a list of leaders who, in your view, model the ability to think clearly, listen deeply and build effective relationships.
2   Give examples of leaders who, in your view, have modelled decisiveness, the ability to bring people with them, the taking of principled stances and the ability to develop new leaders.
3   Give examples of people who, for you, exemplify transforming leadership.
4   Which of the various perspectives on leadership outlined in this chapter make particular sense to you or strike a chord with you?
5   What particular leaders (in your own lifetime or historically) have inspired you?
6   Tell the story of people who made a difference to you personally in your life. What was it about these people that enabled them to make this difference? What was special about them? What were the qualities or characteristics that stood out about them?
7   Have you actively made a decision to lead or to be a leader? Is your leadership actively chosen by you or simply the result of circumstances or the decisions of other people? Have you fully owned or acknowledged the fact that you are a leader?
8   Complete this sentence: If I took full responsibility for my leadership in this group or organization, if I saw myself as a key leader, in the coming period I would . . .

Leadership goals

9   List three long-term goals (five to ten years) for your leadership.
10   List three medium-term goals (two to five years) for your leadership.
11   List three short-term goals or next steps for your leadership.

5 Destructive reactions to leaders
The isolation-attack dynamic

INTRODUCTION

So far we have looked at the content of leadership and what makes for good leadership. We also need to understand, however, what happens when people take on such roles. One of the interesting things about leadership is that in many situations people are reluctant to take it on in any formal way. It is sometimes seen as a burden or a threat. For people who have already been in leadership roles, the experience may be one that has left them drained, wounded or completely burnt out. They may have found that when they took on the role, the people around them seemed to change, "go funny" or act differently. Why should this be? It turns out that there are a number of processes that operate around the *role* of leadership, that may have little or nothing to do with the person in that role and that have the effect of getting in the way of the most effective functioning of that person and that role. They have the additional effect of making leadership seem like an unattractive job to take on. While it is of huge assistance in staying on track to have a clear picture of the role, the functions and the qualities of leadership, we also need to understand these particular dynamics and the way they operate to distort and undermine effective leadership. The broad process described in this chapter has received very little attention in the literature on leadership, mostly arising anecdotally or in non-academic sources. Interviews with people in leadership roles, however, confirm that this is a major aspect of the leadership experience.

Putting it in its barest form, faced with someone else taking leadership, there is a pull for people, particularly but not only when a leader gets into difficulty, to isolate, abandon, attack or undermine that person. Mostly these reactions operate unconsciously and without any deliberate intention to cause difficulties. Their effect, however, is to weaken leadership and to increase the stress associated with the role. If we are to stay effective around leadership, it helps enormously to have a full understanding of this dynamic. Failure to understand this, and failure to take steps to deal with it, have had a hugely detrimental effect in many groups and organizations. The origins of these reactions lie partly in our early experiences, particularly as young people, so let us look at these before examining in more detail how this process works itself out.

EARLY EXPERIENCES AROUND LEADERSHIP

Our early experiences around leadership, both our own and other people's, tend to leave us conditioned to act in very rigid ways when faced with someone in a leadership role. As young people we may have found that, when we tried to take initiative, it was stifled by the adults around us or resulted in us being punished or humiliated. Faced with a young person unilaterally taking initiative, adults may respond by criticizing or attacking the young person for not getting their permission – "who told you that you could do that?", "how dare you speak to me like that", "you are not to do anything without asking me first". Or, the young person may find that, instead of being praised for their efforts or initiative, their shortcomings or failures are highlighted – "that's not the way to do it", "you didn't do that right", "if you are not going to do it properly then don't do it at all", "you are only making more work for me if you do it like that". Thus, the young person's early attempts to take leadership are squashed and suppressed. Some of us learned over time not to bother taking initiative because we got hurt whenever we did.

At other times, young people may find themselves being embarrassed or humiliated for their initiative or their "precociousness". We may laugh at the young person who uses language in a more advanced way than we expect for that age or who, in an attempt to experiment with language, uses words inappropriately with unintended effects. Sometimes, the achievements or talents of young people are used by admiring adults to impress others to the great embarrassment of the young person. They may be required to perform their party pieces not because they themselves will enjoy it but because their parents will get some satisfaction from it. Gradually, being visible, displaying talent or being different come to have an association with feeling humiliated.

Alternatively, it can happen that the attempts by young people to take initiative are greeted with apathy and lack of interest by adults. The young person who bounds into a room full of excitement about the possibility of a game or an adventure is met with the exhausted yawns of a parent who just wants to relax at that point. The interest, the enthusiasm, the excitement, the curiosity and the creativity of the young person receive little or no encouragement from the adults around them.

What we are seeing here in all these various reactions to young people are implicit models for how initiative and leadership should be treated. The young person experiences hurt, embarrassment, humiliation, disappointment or other painful emotions as a result of the reactions of the people around them to their ability, initiative and leadership. Although this has received little systematic study, where these reactions form a pattern in our early lives they seem to affect the ways that we ourselves, as adults, react to other people's leadership.

The other side of this story is that, in all of these encounters, we are also seeing a particular kind of leadership being modelled by the people around us. This leadership was sometimes experienced as authoritarian if not downright oppressive, abusive and hurtful. Parents and other authority figures were people to be obeyed unquestioningly. They did not ask for our opinions or suggestions. They did not admit to mistakes or apologize when they got things wrong. They had a hard time listening to us, trusting us or being influenced by us. They assumed that they knew best. They punished us when we did not cooperate with them. We were encouraged to look up to and admire them uncritically, even when they were flawed. If we think of our lives as young people, we may actually find few examples or models of non-authoritarian and non-oppressive leadership. Thus, not only were we learning how to treat other people's attempts at leadership, we were also learning how leaders themselves should behave.

In addition to these personal experiences around leadership, it is also the case that, historically, on a much larger scale, we also have had few models of non-oppressive leadership. Our histories are the histories of dictators, despots, emperors and empresses, kings and queens, conquerors and colonizers. What was happening in the home and in school was being reflected in, and reinforced by, society at large. A similar point was made by Wilhelm Reich (1946–1972) in his discussion of how fascism was able to take hold of people. He maintained that the authoritarian family was actually the training ground for the authoritarian state.

The processes described here are complex and people's experiences are varied. The link between these early experiences and our later responses to leadership are not simple or absolute. There may have been positive, balancing experiences where we got great encouragement and support for our initiative. In fact, those relatives or teachers, for example, who were able to model a different, more affirming type of leadership are often the people who stand out in our memories as special. They stand out precisely because they were not the norm. The point is, however, that where we experienced hurtful, negative reactions as young people, the emotional effects that we still carry from these may leave us predisposed, as adults, to direct very similar reactions to the leadership and initiative of others. In outlining the theory behind the FIRO-B personality test, Schutz (1966) made a similar link between childhood experiences and later adult behaviour in relationships. One of the elements of this test is *control behaviour*, which is related to initiative, and Schutz sees people's reactions in this area as a reflection of childhood experiences around control. The strength and rigidity of this predisposition to re-enact early experience will depend on the depth of the hurt we received as young people and on the extent to which we have been able to heal that hurt. It will also be influenced by the presence of positive role models in our early lives. While this area has not received much research attention, it seems to be the case, in listening to people's leadership stories, that very few of us escaped without some hurt in this area and, as adults, we still carry the residue of that hurt into our relationship with other leaders.

Finally, before leaving this section, it is also important to note that broader experiences of systematic oppression within society also play their part in conditioning us to respond negatively to leadership. The hurts we endure as part of being oppressed are also instrumental in shaping our own ability to lead and our reactions to the leadership of others. We shall see more about this in later chapters

THE ISOLATION-ATTACK DYNAMIC

The effect of these early, oppressive and historical experiences appears to be that there is a strong pull for us to respond to someone else's leadership in ways that reproduce what we saw modelled by the adults around us. Essentially, we tend to treat leaders in a similar way to what we experienced growing up. In practice, this means that faced with someone else visibly taking on a leadership role, we may (awarely or unawarely) adopt a distorted view of their leadership and react to it in particular negative, destructive and rigid ways (Figure 5.1). These rigid, negative reactions can be classed as either passive or active. Passive negative reactions tend to be experienced by the leader as isolation. Active negative reactions tend to be experienced by the leader as an attack.

Isolation of leaders

One response to leadership is to isolate it. We adopt an attitude that "it is the leader's job to get things right" and we, effectively, abdicate responsibility to them. We ignore them, abandon them, give them little or no feedback, encouragement or support and basically leave them isolated. These are essentially passive negative reactions. When times are good this can represent a simple type of "benevolent ignorance" – we just forget to think about the person in the leadership role. On the other hand, if problems arise with their leadership, this process can become more active, more intense and extreme – we may deliberately isolate them and obstruct them. Conversations are changed when they join a group. They may be ostracized from friendly, informal interactions, or they may notice the atmosphere change when they enter a room. Social groups that they were once part of may now actively exclude them. In this type of situation, people who were once relaxed and open around them now become distant and awkward when the person has taken on the role of leader. We often hear people in leadership talk about the "loneliness at the top". Part of this refers to the isolation that seems to go with the role. I worked, on one occasion, with what had been a very close-knit group where the members had decided actively to ignore and exclude, at a

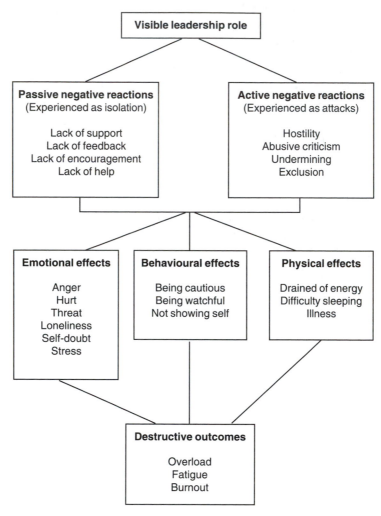

Figure 5.1 Destructive Reactions to Leaders.

social level, the person in charge in the hope that they could force this person to accept their point of view. This meant keeping contact to the minimum required by the work, not having "chit-chats", not saying good morning or goodbye, not offering help, and, in general, trying to "freeze the person out". They had adopted this strategy as a result of deep frustration with the refusal of the leader to take on board their concerns. Their reaction was understandable but not at all helpful in producing the effect they desired. It simply left the leader more isolated, more defensive and less open to their ideas.

One variation on this occurs where we put leaders on a pedestal and assume they can do no wrong. We look up to, admire and have high expectations of the leader. We expect them to work miracles or transform the situation facing us without any active help from us. We assume they do not need our help and there is nothing we can contribute to their leadership. This can be just as isolating as ignoring them. In some cases, this may characterize the early stages of the relationship between the leader and others in the group or organization. It is certainly less painful than dealing with hostility or suspicion although it can sometimes cause the leader to cringe inwardly with embarrassment at the unrealistically rosy picture held by other people. Sometimes, leaders may be seduced by it and agree to try to play the role of benevolent and superior expert. In doing this, they effectively come to usurp leadership and assume they must be the only one to play that role. If, as leaders, on the one hand, we can avoid being seduced by this tendency, and, on the other hand, avoid abdicating leadership altogether in an attempt to escape it, we can see this process as the early stage of a relationship that is committed to empowering the people around us to assume their own leadership.

Attacks on leaders

Isolating the leader is one type of response. We can also respond in a more actively negative way. We may criticize, act with hostility or suspicion towards, or undermine people in leadership. We try to deal with problems and correct mistakes by attacking or "having a go" at the person in leadership. Jamison (1984) refers to this as the "nibble" theory of leadership. Sometimes these attacks are direct and upfront. We tell the person to their face that they are useless and incompetent without offering any constructive alternative. Or we question every decision they make and act in a hostile or non-cooperative manner. Often the attacks are indirect and take the form of bad-mouthing the leader or gossiping about them in ways that are undermining or destructive. We criticize and complain about them to the people around us. We point out their failings, their mistakes and their shortcomings. In some groups, or with some individuals, conversations are dominated by endless, animated and repetitive discussions of what is wrong with the leader. It can be quite difficult to have a conversation that does not, at some point, come around to an attack on the leader.

Attacks on leaders are often rationalized or legitimized as an attempt to correct their mistakes. In practice, there is often very little that is constructive about them and they may bear little or no relationship to the actual competence of the leader. (We shall see more about this in the next chapter.) As a rule, attacks simply don't work as a way of correcting leadership. Sometimes, they are merely the venting of anger or frustration but in ways that actually make leadership even more difficult. On the receiving end, many of these attacks are experienced as "personal". At other times, they seem to be designed (often unconsciously) to upset other people and turn them against the leader. Rather than assisting people to think more clearly about the leader or the difficulties facing the group, they focus on triggering emotive reactions that leave people less able to think rationally about what makes sense. Attacks, in this sense, are the acting out of painful emotion. They may masquerade as "thinking" about the leader but they are much more about the expression of the attacker's anger, fear, frustration, hurt or worry.

In describing the destructive nature of attacks, this is not to suggest that leaders do not make mistakes or that such mistakes do not need to be corrected. What it is suggesting is that we are not very skilled at responding constructively to such difficulties. So where does this leave criticism? Is it ever valid to criticize a leader's behaviour? This is not a simple question. Glasser (1994) takes a very definite view on it. He maintains that there is no such thing as constructive criticism. When we are criticized we feel as though we have lost power, lost friendship and lost the freedom to act as we think best. For Glasser, criticism simply does not work and the aim should be to eliminate it from all our relationships. Coaching rather than criticism should be the goal. We sometimes say that criticism should be directed at policies and practices but not at the person. It seems, however, that in effect, once painful emotion is involved, we have great difficulty making this distinction. Feelings seem to take over and cloud our judgement about what is helpful or constructive. Because of this, criticism that is motivated or directed by painful emotion rather than by rational thinking becomes, in effect, an attack on the leader. In a similar way, criticism that has the effect of pushing other people to act out their painful emotion or to organize against the leader will be experienced as an attack. At some point, the leader becomes identified as the problem and getting rid of the leader as the solution. (Complicating things even further is the difficulty that the leader's painful emotion may distort their perception of whether what is happening is an attack or a legitimate disagreement over policy or practices.) In contrast to this, there is a way in which leadership difficulties can usefully be thought of as collective difficulties. If a leader is not functioning properly we can ask about the particular difficulties the leader is having; we can also ask about the difficulties other people in the group are having in trying to respond constructively to the leader's difficulties. Seeing the leader alone as the problem is often an oversimplification of the difficulty. For now, we can say that criticism is only valid when it encourages people to think more clearly and more rationally, when it encourages people to take constructive initiative rather than simply be upset, and when it does not simplistically reduce the problem to the person of the leader. Little of what passes for constructive criticism in practice meets these standards.

We sometimes talk to other people about our upsets with the leader as a way of trying to "get it off our chest" or clarify our own thinking. If this is done thoughtfully, it can be very helpful. But when does it simply become destructive gossip? How do we distinguish between destructive gossip and using other people as a resource to think about the leader or to deal with our own painful emotion? For a start, in a constructive effort to discharge our own painful emotion (rather than act it out) and to heal the hurts we carry that get in the way of thinking clearly about the situation, the focus and the emphasis would be on ourselves and not on the leader. We would be talking about how we are feeling rather than what's wrong with the leader. We would be talking about where we are stuck rather than where the leader is stuck. We would be talking about what we need to do rather than what the leader needs to do. In fact, if we were getting the balance right, there would probably be very little reference to the leader at all. It would not even be necessary to identify with whom we are having the difficulty. It would also be the case that, if we were handling this well, nothing that we say would have the effect of confusing the person listening to us about their relationship with the leader. The aim of the conversation would not be to turn them against the leader or to get them on our side. In fact, if we did not think that they could stay detached, we might decide not to voice our feelings to them and instead find someone else who could listen without having their own painful emotion get in their way. A possible tell-tale sign of destructive gossip may be when we specifically voice our criticisms or upsets to someone we suspect shares the same upsets or has their own doubts about the leader, someone we know will not be able to listen to us in a detached way. Another tell-tale sign occurs when our goal is to mobilize people *against* the leader rather than *for* some constructive action. Our goal is to spread the upset at the leader rather than empower other people to think rationally about the leader and to take constructive steps to resolve the difficulties. The effect of an attack is to lower other people's estimation of the leader or undermine the leader's relationship with these people or create divisive feelings that get in the way of listening and working together to resolve problems.

In the way we are describing it here, an attack is any critical, contentious, blaming, destructive or undermining behaviour that is largely a dramatizing or acting out of painful emotion or that has the effect of causing other people to dramatize or act out their painful emotion, or that is, in that particular context, inappropriate, unhelpful or irrational. We can think of a continuum of behaviour stretching from, at one end, totally relaxed, thoughtful, rational, open-minded and unemotive disagreement. It would move through a stage of largely thoughtful and rational and perhaps more animated disagreement but also with some painful emotion involved. At the other end, it would involve disagreement that is rigid, inflexible, closed, thoughtless, hurtful and suffused with painful emotion. There is no sharp dividing line here. At some point, the painful emotion comes to dominate and legitimate disagreement becomes a destructive attack. At this point, the "attacker" is no longer thinking well or clearly about the leader and doing what it takes to resolve the difficulty but is mainly being driven by the painful feelings that have taken hold whether or not these are useful or appropriate in the situation. The behaviour has now become largely counterproductive.

From this perspective, it is only in extreme situations, or after all other attempts to resolve difficulties have failed, that we would "go public" with our criticisms or actively organize an opposition to a leader. In such cases, the crucial test is the degree to which our actions are rationally thought out and appropriate as opposed to being motivated by feelings of powerlessness, desperation, hopelessness, frustration or other painful emotion.

This discussion of attacks has concentrated on it as a one-to-one process. It need not always be so, however. Unremitting criticism from across a group or organization, where no one individual is necessarily caught up in heavy painful emotion, but where, at the same time, no one is able step back and think about how the leader is coping with all the criticism or monitor whether it is achieving anything useful, could function as an attack. In this situation, no one piece of criticism is that destructive on its own, but all together and over time the discussion becomes inappropriate. The group, as a whole, has become so preoccupied with delivering the criticism that no one is thinking rationally about whether this makes sense or whether it is achieving any useful result. The leader here has been attacked by the group rather than by any one person.

The process being described here damages the person in the leadership role. But this is not all. Quite apart from whether or not it changes the leader's behaviour, this process tends to have the effect of making it very difficult for other people to think clearly. Over time, it has the wider effect of making people in general very reluctant to take on leadership roles – "There is no way I want that job, I saw what happened to the last person who took it!" "No amount of money would pay me to put up with that kind of abuse." In some organizations, the habit of attacking of leaders has become institutionalized as the only way to deal with leadership difficulties. In such organizations, leaders who make mistakes or who do not keep people happy are routinely attacked and "done in". Some organizations regularly oust leaders who do not live up to expectations and, in the process, create a climate that guarantees that successive leaders will act defensively and direct their energies into surviving rather than excelling. Political organizations are one example of this.

No news is good news

The role of leadership seems to attract these fairly unthinking responses of isolation or attacks. It is difficult to find leadership situations where there is not some element of rigidity and irrationality in the ways people react to that leadership. In the more extreme situations, the isolation is intense or the attacks are constant. Sometimes, the process can oscillate between these extremes. Periods of isolation may be interspersed with periods of attack. It can get to the point where leaders dread meetings or dread occasions when someone wants to talk to them. Eventually it can feel like no news is good news. If someone wants to see them, it is probably because they are upset, or have a problem, or have some demands to make. It is unlikely, or so it can feel, that, for example, the person simply wants to thank them or affirm them for their leadership.

Our efforts to correct mistakes by attacking leaders are counterproductive and rarely work as a useful strategy. Mostly they are a reflection of people's powerlessness rather than any rationally thought-out strategy. In that sense, the attack may sometimes tell us more about the attacker than it does about the person being attacked. The effect, however, is often destructive of the person in the leadership role and, over time, of the group or organization as a whole.

This dynamic is pervasive. Few people in leadership roles are completely untouched by it. Few people around leaders manage to behave fully rationally, appropriately and supportively all the time. Because of the kinds of conditioning I described earlier, we all tend to get pulled into the isolation-attack dynamic to one degree or another.

Unrealistic expectations

The early conditioning around leadership and the processes described above lead to a number of knock-on effects. The first of these is that people can develop very unrealistic expectations about what leadership can do (Table 5.1). These expectations may be held (often unawarely) by the person in leadership or by the people around them. They include such beliefs as that it is the leader's job to have all the answers, or that leaders must never make mistakes, or that leaders must always appear strong and on top of things, or that it is the leader's job to keep everyone happy and so on. These, and others like them, are impossible expectations to live up to but, where they are held by people, they impose additional stress on the person in leadership. In one particular study, Leader and Boldt (1994) reported that school principals found the high expectations from staff, parents and the media to be "daunting and disconcerting". It is not possible to lead without making mistakes. It is not possible to know always what to do or never to feel stuck or overwhelmed by the demands. In some cases, leaders, as a result of the isolation-attack dynamic, get pulled into trying to meet such expectations in an attempt to avoid being attacked or isolated. In other cases, the unresolved disappointment with past leaders causes other people to impose these expectations on the current leader.

Whatever the source, we need to recognize when these expectations are

Table 5.1 Expectations of Leaders

- Keep everyone happy
- Make no mistakes
- Always know what to say or do
- Take responsibility for everything
- Do not require praise or encouragement
- Cope easily with criticism
- Function well in isolation

operating and give up any requirement that they be met either by ourselves or others. In fact, it is precisely by coming to terms with these expectations that our leadership improves and grows. By giving ourselves permission to make mistakes, we are then free to learn from them. By admitting that we do not always know what to do, we can be open to the help or leadership of other people. By being honest about when we feel weak or vulnerable, we can lean on other people for support and avoid slipping into the pretence of strength.

Effects

This dynamic has a range of effects – emotional, behavioural and physical. On the receiving end of these reactions, leaders can feel hurt, angry, threatened, lonely or self-doubting. For some leaders, this is a highly emotional situation that creates huge stress. They may be carrying lots of painful feelings with nowhere to release them. It can cause them to become very watchful and cautious. They lose their spontaneity and learn not to show themselves or expose themselves to further negative reactions. Some leaders have difficulty sleeping at night as they anticipate the demands of the following day or go back over the hurtful incidents of the previous one. Over time, their energy gets drained and they struggle with tiredness or exhaustion. Their immune systems may be affected and they find it harder to shake off illness.

Overload

Under the conditions described here, over time the person in the leadership role can become overloaded. Either because of the isolation and lack of help or in an attempt to avoid being attacked, or because they have unawarely imposed impossible expectations on themselves, leaders take on more responsibility than they can handle effectively. Leaders sometimes feel that "if I don't think about it, no one else will". Every minor detail becomes the leader's responsibility. There are many situations where the leadership role has become so overloaded with administrative and other functions that it is virtually impossible for the individual involved to lead effectively. The leader ends up trying to be all things to all people. Not only are people expected to play the role of leader, they are also, in many situations, expected to carry heavy loads of administration or to look after petty, minor details that should really be carried by someone else. Bennis (1989b) tells the story of how, when he became President of the University of Cincinnati, a member of staff wrote him a note to complain about the temperature in his classroom and another phoned to complain that the squash court was closed at 7 p.m. when he wanted to use it!

Fatigue

As the pressure mounts on leaders, they become fatigued and begin to wear out. Many people in leadership roles operate on top of heavy layers of fatigue. This is particularly noticeable in caring or helping professions where there is a very personal commitment to the work. Often they are reluctant to rest or take time off because it would feel selfish or unreasonable or because they cannot depend on others to take over. Usually, it does not feel very safe to admit to or talk about these difficulties with the people they are leading because of the unrealistic expectations described above and the fear of the isolation-attack dynamic. If we listen carefully, however, we may hear clues being dropped, often in casual, throwaway remarks. We may hear people talk about needing a holiday or a sabbatical or about getting "too old for this". What is noticeable, however, is that if the person ever gets the holiday, they are almost as tired on the first day back as they were on the day before they left. The fatigue is not just physical; it is also emotional. It is related to the stress of the job and will not be eliminated simply with an occasional rest or relaxation (though these may help). It is held in place by the isolation of the job and the lack of any safe place to be listened to talking about how it is for them in leadership. A relatively short period of good listening where the leader feels safe enough to talk about how they feel and actually to discharge their feelings can be worth a much, much longer period of purely physical resting. We have to become skilled at recognizing the signs of leadership exhaustion and finding useful ways to support people at this point. Unfortunately, the tendency is to miss these signs and to leave the leader isolated within their exhaustion.

Burnout

Over time, the combination of isolation and/or attack, overload and fatigue can lead to a gradual lessening of the leader's enthusiasm for the job. What began as an exciting challenge then becomes much more of a chore and a burden. Cynicism creeps in. The original vision is lost sight of and the passion and commitment fade. Unchecked, this process can lead to leader burnout where the individual either becomes ill (physically or emotionally) and has to stop, or else turns to some type of addiction such as alcohol in order to keep going. Alternatively, some individuals simply give up and either resign or else retire "on the job". The effect is that someone who started out with great potential has now become, at best, ineffective, and, at worst, destructive and a liability to the organization. There can be a huge wastage of resources in this process. It is remarkable that we seem to be very proficient at spotting and selecting potentially good leaders but we are extremely inept at ensuring they survive, thrive and develop in their leadership roles. In some cases, there are elaborate consultation procedures and detailed selection processes to get the right person for the job. However, having carefully selected them, it is as though we then abandon them and expect them to sink or swim with little or no support. The resources that go into making sure we get the right person are sometimes huge compared to the resources that go into making sure this person is able to function effectively once they take on the job.

Ultimately, the effect of this dynamic is to reinforce leadership difficulties and cause leaders to become more defensive, more distant, more authoritarian and more rigid. This, in turn, provokes a further cycle of the isolation-attack dynamic and the process becomes self-reinforcing.

RATIONAL RESPONSES TO LEADERSHIP

Faced with these processes, it becomes important to think about how we can rationally respond to other people's leadership (Table 5.2). What makes sense in terms of getting the best from leaders? How can we set things up so that leaders function most effectively? How can we avoid the problem of burnout?

Based on what we know of leadership and of the places where it can get difficult, the starting-point for getting it right is that someone has to think clearly and rationally about the person in leadership. When leadership gets into difficulties there is a strong tendency for people to substitute *getting upset at* the leader for actually *thinking about* the leader. When leadership gets stuck, someone else around the leader must take leadership. We have to think about what is happening, where people are getting stuck or confused, and what might work to move things on. In practice this will mean separating our *feelings* about the leader from our *best thinking* about what will make a difference in the situation.

It is important to recognize the pressures that operate on leaders and, in particular, the isolation-attack dynamic described above. It can help to notice how other people are reacting to, and treating, the leader. Notice where their reactions have become rigid or inflexible. Notice where they have stopped thinking clearly. Notice the effects on the leader and on other people and whether or not the situation is improving. If what is happening is not working

Table 5.2 Rational Responses to Leadership

- Think rationally
- Recognize the pressures
- Notice other people's reactions
- Spot the rigidity or inflexibility
- Do something different
- Ensure that the leader does not become isolated
- Take responsibility for building and maintaining a close relationship with the leader
- Do not use public attacks
- Interrupt attacks

---

or is not having any useful effects, do something different. We need to take a positive initiative around leadership that is in difficulty.

One implication of what has been described here is that it will be important to ensure that the leader does not become isolated. This will mean that someone must take responsibility for building and maintaining a close relationship with the person in leadership. This can be done in a number of ways: keeping regular contact with the person in the leadership role; giving positive feedback to the person; listening to them; and offering practical help. The latter suggestion, offering practical help, is a much undervalued support. While it is often nice to hear appreciations and affirmations of our leadership, there are times when it makes such a difference to have someone simply offer practical help. When someone offers to take on a piece of the work for us, we truly get to notice we are not on our own. Sometimes, a leader will go to do something and discover that someone has already taken care of it. On such occasions, we may notice a deep sigh of relief as the leader realizes they are not the only one thinking about what needs to be done.

All of this, of course, may be misinterpreted by those around us. They may see us as trying to curry favour with the leader or of being a naive lackey. We may have to risk such misperceptions in order to ensure that leadership is able to function effectively. If we can avoid isolating ourselves from the people around us, while we move in on the person in leadership, we can actually balance these different relationships without risking too negative a reaction from other people. They may worry about our close relationship with the leader but their own close relationship with us will enable them to judge whether we have really "sold out" or become unthinking sycophants.

Within the relationship that we build with the person in leadership, a key role we can play is that of listening (with "no strings attached"). This means making it safe enough for that person to talk openly about themselves and their leadership. The safety comes from showing them that they will not be attacked by us, that we will not give up on them, that we will not breach confidentiality or gossip about them, that we will not lose sight of them as a person and that we will not use the relationship for some personal gain or manipulative purpose. Under these conditions, the leader can use our listening as a resource to break the isolation, think out loud about difficulties, ask for help, or discharge exhaustion or other painful emotion in the way of leading effectively. In the face of impatience, frustration or desperation the leader will often become defensive and more distant. If we can keep these in check and listen relaxedly we may find that, in fact, we have more rather than less influence.

One way we can help create this kind of safety is to give up the habit of using public attacks or criticisms of their leadership as a way of changing the leader. Any difficulties we have with the leader will be dealt with privately with them and not made public and will not involve any form of attack. One of the fears that people sometimes have about this suggestion is that it appears to give leaders a "blank cheque" to do anything they like. If we are never going to criticize them, they are free to do what they wish. One consolation I offer them about this is that, given the pervasiveness of the isolation-attack dynamic, they can rest assured that, even if they personally give up public criticism of leaders, many others will continue to attack. Their particular attack will not be missed! However, there is a very real possibility that the alternative steps they take to influence the leader may make a significant difference to the resolution of difficulties.

Just as we can decide to give up attacking leaders, it can also make a big difference to decide to interrupt any attacks on the leader by other people. I do not mean interrupt in a crass, hurtful or attacking way, although in very extreme situations there might not be any easy alternative. It can help a lot, for example, to find ways to redirect the energy into looking at constructive ways forward rather than arguing over who is to blame. Sometimes, we can ease the situation by injecting some humour that releases tension and allows people to think more clearly about what makes sense. We might suggest taking a break where we see the discussion becoming destructive. There may be times when it makes sense to point out that what's happening is not helpful and ask people to stop. In general, it is not useful to abandon a leader when they get attacked. It can be very hard to think straight when under attack and it is precisely at that point that some clear thinking from someone else can make a decisive difference.

There are many ways we can respond rationally to leadership, particularly leadership that is in difficulty. The key piece is that we decide to keep thinking and not just settle for being upset. When a leader gets into difficulty, someone, metaphorically, has to take that person by the hand and lead them. Doing this effectively and making a real difference in the situation is not necessarily easy or straightforward. Not doing it, or not even trying to do it, however, is to settle for some degree of powerlessness. Our failure to respond rationally to leadership that is struggling makes us, in effect, part of the problem.

STAYING EFFECTIVE

Just as the people around the leader can play an important role in ensuring that the leader continues to function effectively, it is also important that the person in the leadership role also takes steps to stay effective. Various strategies are detailed in Table 5.3. Essentially, as leaders we need to build close relationships with the people around us and to resist the pull to distance or isolate ourselves. We have to continue to keep listening to other people. Apart from building informal contacts, it is possible to structure regular opportunities for feedback that allow people to articulate their best thinking but without encouraging them to blame or to attack anyone in the process. In general, as leaders, we can play an important role in modelling the type of relationship we would like people to have with us – listening, encouraging, appreciating,

Table 5.3 Staying Effective in Leadership

- Build a support network
- Find someone who will listen
- Take pride
- Remake the decision to lead
- Connect with your vision
- Review and reset your goals
- Act decisively
- Have closeness
- Have fun
- Rest
- Exercise
- Have a healthy diet

affirming and so on. By building up a support network around ourselves, we can ensure that there are places where we can be listened to as we work through any difficulties we are encountering, places where we can get helpful feedback and encouragement and places where we can turn to for help.

Many of the blocks around leadership, for both leaders and those around the leader, are actually emotional. Because of this, a powerful tool for effective leadership is the use of counselling that allows people to discharge any painful emotion getting in the way of their thinking clearly. We can improve our effectiveness enormously by ensuring that, as leaders for example, we have regular access to someone who has agreed to listen to us while we talk about where it gets hard for us in our leadership and who will assist us to stay connected to our strengths and to our vision.

To continue to be an effective resource for people, it is important that leaders are able to think positively about themselves as leaders. This means not losing sight of and being able to take pride in our own strengths, talents and achievements. Being able to stay pleased with ourselves while we lead is an important aspect of managing the stresses associated with the role.

Since leadership, at base, is a decision we make to see that things go well, it is helpful for leaders to remake the decision to lead consciously and repeatedly. Recommitting ourselves to this decision helps to reconnect us with our goals and allows us to keep a clearer perspective on what is happening around us. Part of remaking the decision to lead is also reconnecting with our own personal vision. Remembering why we do this work, what first attracted us to it, what excites us about it, why we feel passionately about it, and what it is about the work that is close to our heart are important aspects of maintaining clarity. While we are connected to our vision, it is difficult for us to be overwhelmed by minor details or short-term crises.

As we remake the decision to lead and as we reconnect with our vision, we also get to reset our goals. It is helpful for leaders periodically to revisit their goals and reset them in the context of their long-term vision. Within this we can first reset our long-term goals and from there set shorter-term goals or objectives. Having the vision and a set of closely related goals allows us to stay on track and avoid becoming bogged down in unimportant distractions. With a clear connection to the vision and a clear set of goals, leaders are then able to act decisively. Doing nothing, dithering or postponing action will ultimately drain us of energy. Making the decision to take decisive action will help to maintain our energy and will throw up new challenges to our thinking and our direction.

Staying on track like this requires stepping back from the work and setting aside regular time to reflect, to reconnect, to plan and to heal. Heifetz and Linsky (2002a) talk about the importance of leaders having a "sanctuary" where they get to reflect and renew themselves. Some leaders undermine their own effectiveness by not insisting on having this time for themselves. They treat it as a luxury rather than a necessity for good leadership. The result is that they become overloaded and too busy to stop and think. It would, in fact, be difficult to overestimate the importance of having this time for leaders. The effort it takes to establish it will be more than made up by the quality of leadership that follows from it.

There are also a number of more personal factors that are important in maintaining effectiveness. If we are to stay effective it helps to have some closeness or intimacy in our lives. There needs to be a place where we get to make close, human contact with another person that is nourishing for us personally. This counteracts any of the isolation attached to the role of leadership, helps us to reconnect with those aspects of our own goodness and humanity that we may have lost sight of, prevents us going numb to our feelings in order to survive and provides a safe place to heal some of the hurts we accumulate as we lead.

Similarly, it is important for leaders to have fun in their lives. One of the things we sometimes sacrifice in our commitment to the leadership role is fun. A characteristic of the lives of many leaders is the seriousness and the weight of concern that they carry. A challenge for many of us is to figure out how to introduce some light relief. Someone once said about leadership that if we are not having fun, there is something wrong with the way we are doing it. Having fun in our lives allows us to keep a clearer perspective and, at the same time, makes a difference to our general health. Particular organizations evolve a culture of seriousness, formality or hard work that rules out the opportunity for, or encouragement to have, fun. Apart from the additional stress this imposes, people are simply not as effective under these conditions. Having fun is not a luxury and, as leaders, we have to ask ourselves what we need to change in our lives so as to build in the opportunity for more enjoyment.

Also significant for our health and effectiveness is the importance of having sufficient rest and exercise. We are not of much use to people in the long term if we try to lead while abusing our bodies with overload. Our effectiveness will increase as we become well rested and well exercised. If we can also maintain a healthy diet while we do this it will assist us even more to hang on to our energy and our clarity. So, making a difference in leadership means looking after the whole person and all aspects of our being – physically, emotionally, mentally and spiritually.

These factors are important in maintaining the effectiveness of leaders. They require us, as leaders, to take the initiative in seeing that the conditions of our lives are such as to enhance our well-being. Contrary to how it can sometimes feel, there is no inherent conflict between being effective and looking after ourselves well. In fact, not only does it make sense for us, as leaders, to take the steps to ensure we stay in good shape, it also makes sense for us to model how to do this for other people. In general, we do not have many models of leaders who look after themselves well. Providing such a model of thoughtful, self-caring leadership is an important part of the process of training new leaders.

SUMMARY

Effective leadership can be seriously undermined by the kinds of processes described by the isolation-attack dynamic. Counteracting these is not solely the responsibility of the leader. Making leadership work is a collective process. It requires a clear understanding of what is required in order to enable people to think well and function effectively. It also requires a clear understanding of how effectiveness can be hindered. It requires a commitment to combating any rigidities that have crept into the relationship between leaders and those around them and a commitment to nurturing, supporting and thinking about leaders. A leader cannot do all this on their own. It requires as many people as possible thinking clearly about what is going on in the situation and taking initiative to create the conditions for everyone to function at their most effective at all times. In this chapter, we have looked at the isolation-attack dynamic broadly. In the next chapter, we shall look at this in more detail, particularly at the ways leaders can get attacked. And we shall examine what other writers have had to say about these processes.

REFLECTION

Leadership difficulties

Think about your experiences in a visible, leadership role.

1 What was hard about being in a leadership role? Where was it a struggle for you?
2 In what ways did people react negatively or unhelpfully to you as a leader?

3   What was the effect on you emotionally? What painful or negative emotions did the difficulties stir up?
4   What was the effect on you physically?
5   What was the effect on the way you acted?
6   What was the effect on the way you thought about things?
7   Are there any ways that those difficult experiences still affect you?
8   Tell the story of leadership in your life. What are your earliest memories around taking initiative or leadership? What were good experiences? What were difficult experiences? How has your early experience of taking initiative or leadership left you feeling about yourself and about leadership?
9   What were the models of leadership that you were exposed to growing up (e.g. in the home, at school and so on)? How have these affected your relationship with people in authority or in formal leadership roles?
10 What expectations do you attach to the role of leader? What assumptions do you make about how you as a leader, or other leaders, should function in this role? Are any of these expectations unrealistic?

6 Handling attacks on leaders

INTRODUCTION

The isolation-attack dynamic described in some detail the rigid, destructive processes that can operate around the role of leadership and which make little sense in any rational way. Often, these processes are taken for granted as either normal or inevitable aspects of the job and people are encouraged to learn to live with them – "if you can't take the heat, get out of the kitchen". The effects, however, as we saw in the last chapter, can damage leaders and leave them much less effective than they would otherwise be. Attacks on the leader, especially, can be extremely stressful and draining. Although pervasive and a major factor in determining how successful leadership will be, these dynamics have not received a huge amount of attention in the literature and certainly not within the mainstream writings on leadership. In this chapter, I want to examine in more detail the way leaders get attacked and how these attacks can be handled. Before looking at this, however, let us see what has been written generally about these processes.

ATTACKS AND ISOLATION

Heifetz (1994) and Heifetz and Linsky (2002a, 2002b) talk about leadership being dangerous, particularly in situations that require what they call adaptive change. Adaptive change occurs where old solutions or variations on existing approaches are no longer adequate and people are required to invent new, creative approaches that call into question taken-for-granted assumptions or norms. In situations that call for adaptive change, people look to leaders for easy answers and impose a variety of unrealistic expectations on the leader. The result is that leaders end up pretending to have the answers and disappointing people or else they get replaced. The greater the amount of change and the amount of new approaches required, the more resistance there will be and this creates greater danger for those in leadership. They go on to describe four types of danger facing leaders: getting marginalized, getting diverted, getting attacked or getting seduced. Regardless of what form it takes, the aim here is "to shut down those who exercise leadership" (Heifetz and Linsky, 2002a, p. 31). While adaptive change is certainly one of the conditions that cause leaders to be attacked, I have found, in interviews with people in leadership roles, that the attacking of leaders does not occur only under conditions of adaptive change. Many other circumstances apart from adaptive change might lead to this happening, such as, for example, when someone is an unexpected choice for the leadership role or when they have an oppressed identity relative to the group they lead. In the latter case, for example, a woman taking leadership in a traditionally male context may find herself under attack from men in that situation. When attacks do come, however, Heifetz and Linsky see most of the dangers as subtle. Leaders are taken by surprise by them and in many cases do not see the danger until it is too late. Certainly, for many of the leaders I have spoken to over the years, part of the hurt caused by the destructive reactions they experienced was due to their unexpected nature.

Within psychoanalysis, the concept of transference is also relevant to the process of attacking leaders. According to psychoanalytic theory, the process of transference means that people attach to leaders various unresolved feelings from childhood that refer to their relationship with authority figures such as parents, teachers and so on (de Board, 1978). This means that people will either idealize leaders or treat them with suspicion, as though they were these earlier figures. Kets de Vries and Miller (1984) describe how transference occurs when people react to a current relationship as though it were a significant and intense relationship from the past (usually involving parents or siblings). Kets de Vries (1989, 2001) stresses the importance of this dynamic and its resolution for effective leadership. He states that "employees may consciously or unconsciously perceive and respond to their leaders not according to objective reality, but as though the leader were a significant authority figure from their past" (1989, p. 9). This can lead to great isolation and loneliness but also to hostility. "Employees may subconsciously blame their leaders for failing to live up to their own exaggerated expectations. Angry about this . . . these employees may find their attitudes quickly turning from admiration to hostility and rebellion" (1989, p. 10).

This transference process usually happens unconsciously. The person tries to deal with unresolved conflict from an earlier relationship in a more satisfactory way by re-living it in the present relationship. Because it arises out of a past conflictual relationship, the behaviour in the present is inevitably inappropriate. The person is reacting to the other as though they were a parent, sibling or other significant figure from the past. Kets de Vries and Miller (1984) see this process as universal and, in particular, as arising in the context of relationships in which power is a key aspect such as superior/ subordinate relationships. The transference behaviour can appear as an "overreaction or underreaction or as a bizarre response" (Kets de Vries and Miller, 1984, p. 75). As part of this process, hostility is seen by them to be a feature of many leadership situations. It can take various forms and go in different directions (upwards, downwards, laterally) but it is, in their view, one of the most destructive aspects of leadership. In the case of subordinates, "transference hostility" (p. 90) leads them to become uncooperative, mistrustful, suspicious and vindictive. The confusion with an earlier parent causes them to try to punish the person in authority. These behaviours can have a resultant effect on how the leader behaves and cause them to make decisions for defensive or protective reasons rather than rational reasons.

According to Jackins (1973, 1984, 1987, 1997) being attacked is almost an inevitable part of being a leader. In this, he takes a much broader view than that of Heifetz and Linsky (2002a, 2002b). One example of this is treating the leader as though they were the enemy because of resentment against past oppressive leaders (Jackins, 1973). Doing this makes their leadership impossible and destroys them as leaders. He describes various different kinds of attacks that might happen (Jackins, 1984, 1987) and we shall look at these and their implications in more detail further on.

For a number of writers, this dynamic is linked to the experience of oppression. Lipsky (1979) describes this process in the context of the struggle to eliminate white racism and talks about the pull for Black leaders to be attacked by their own constituency. Memmi (1957/1990), in his analysis of post-colonialism, describes a similar process and Allport (1954/1979) touches on a related dynamic in talking about the workings of prejudice. One effect of the latter was in-group hostility or aggression towards members of their own group. Allport describes how members of a group may be viewed with hostility by other members of the group. This may lead to blaming people, looking down on them, acting aggressively towards them, being angry with them, rejecting them, being hostile towards them or bickering with them. The contention here is that much of this negativity will be directed at those in leadership roles. Within internalized oppression, the process of attacking leaders seems to co-vary with the depth of the oppression and the degree of powerlessness felt by people. In other words, the heavier, deeper or more institutionalized the oppression, the more likely leaders are to be attacked. Having said that, while agreeing that internalized oppression seems to reinforce the process, Jackins (1983b, 1984, 1987) sees it very much as a dynamic around all types of leadership.

Although much less comprehensive than the above authors in their treatment of this process, other writers have touched on the type of dynamic being described here. Sadler (2003) notes that the challenges that leaders face are not usually direct and confrontational. They may involve indirect resistance and non-cooperation and can be justified with all kinds of plausible reasons. They do, however, have serious implications for the credibility of the leader and, if successful and allowed to continue, can give rise to further challenges. Jamison (1984) describes how anyone who stands out and becomes visible in a leadership role can have their leadership gradually "nibbled" away to the point where they take no more initiative than anyone else. This is usually achieved through ongoing and continuous criticism.

Mouly and Sankaran (2000) have conducted an exploratory study of the "tall poppy syndrome" in New Zealand. While this focused mainly on high achievers rather than leaders as such, it does recognize the tendency for highly visible or successful people to attract envy, jealousy or hostility. This reference to a fairly commonly used phrase, the tall poppy syndrome, reminds us that this process is one that is widely known about even though it has been little studied.

Hestenes (1999) highlights a number of symptoms of a leadership crisis that she perceives. She points to the poisoned atmosphere for leadership – the way in which leaders have learned through a variety of experiences and observations that it is a dangerous thing to be in leadership and therefore leaders need to be self-protective. At the same time, however, self-protection and leadership are contradictory impulses and they collide with each other. She notes that it is difficult for someone to lead when they are trying to protect themselves in an environment that is often very poisoned and full of distrust. In the same context she also refers to the tall poppy syndrome where anyone who becomes visible as a named leader risks, as it were, having their head chopped off.

Harvey (1999) describes the process of "backstabbing" which he defines as "an attempt to discredit by underhanded means, such as innuendo, accusation or the like" (p. 19). He suggests that it is prevalent in all kinds of organizations, including families, churches, businesses, governmental agencies, academic institutions and voluntary associations. He notes that managers in particular seem to complain about it a lot. He also states that he knows of no literature that deals with the underlying dynamics of backstabbing. In fact, what he describes is very similar to what is being discussed here and, while the literature is sparse, it is by no means non-existent.

Separately from academic writers and theorists, references to attacks are also found in various comments from people in leadership roles. Heer (2003), in talking about leadership in a Christian church, states:

> In America, the criticism of leaders has always seemed to be a national past-time. We want leaders who will really lead, so we put them into positions of leadership, issue them a combat jacket with a target painted on the back, push them out in front of us, and then take steady aim so we can shoot at the first sign of decision-making that does not particularly suit us. We love to criticize people in leadership positions who do not lead, and people who lead, but not to our fancy. We have always been quick to critique the performance of our leaders. But I have observed a sinister change take place over time – a change that has accelerated over the past five years. Incivility has invaded the chatter of our armchair quarterbacking. It is now the person, not performance, that we are quick to criticize.
>
> (para. 3)

He notes that, in the past, the criticism would have been of the leader's judgement or their decisions. Now, however, people attack leaders themselves and question both their integrity and their character. In doing this, those attacking seem to assume that the attacks will have no effect on the person being attacked. Heer complains that leaders have become fair game for hunting and that it is considered okay to humble and humiliate them.

Similarly, still in the context of conflict between Christians, Wimber (1992) states that appropriate criticism of leaders is often delivered in an inappropriate way. To correct a person in a leadership role properly requires a number of steps, beginning with a private conversation, phone call or letter. Public forums should only be used after private approaches have been tried and have failed. He believes that this process is exhausting for the person trying to bring about change and this is probably why it is rarely followed.

One area that has come close to describing the type of dynamic being studied here is that of horizontal violence. Hastie (n.d.) describes horizontal violence as "hostile and aggressive behaviour by individual or group members towards another member or groups of members of the larger group" (para. 1). She sees this as endemic in the workplace and includes among its manifestations belittling gestures, verbal abuse, gossiping, backbiting and fault finding. Farrell (2001) notes that horizontal violence can be seen as a reaction to, and reflection of, being oppressed. The examples described above, of course, are very similar to the kinds of hostility faced by people in leadership. The study of horizontal violence, however, tends to focus on lateral or downward violence and seems not to recognize the capacity for group members to attack those who take leadership, which was highlighted by Lipsky (1979).

Separately from the issue of attacks on people in leadership roles, the isolation of leaders is also explored. Gronn (2003), in a study of school leadership, quotes one leading teacher in an Australian school:

> You don't get too many thanks from the staff members, they, they sort of come and complain when things aren't going their way but, you, they expect it all to work properly and they've got their classes in the rooms that they want, and so you usually only hear the complaints rather than anything positive, but, but I would now take the fact that if, the less people come and complain the better it is.

(p. 271)

Horton (1992) draws attention to the loneliness of leadership. He sees leadership at all levels experiencing pressure and the resultant loneliness. He notes that women executives are more likely to experience loneliness than men because of being shut out and that loneliness is a particular hazard for the heads of colleges and universities. He quotes William Harper, the first president of the University of Chicago, who wrote in 1904:

Another feeling which gradually grows upon the occupant of the presidential chair is that of great loneliness . . . the feeling of separation from all his fellows. At certain times he realizes that in all truth he is alone; for those who are ordinarily close to him seem to be, and in fact are, far away. . . . The college presidency means the giving up of many things, and not least among them, one's most intimate friendships. Moreover, this feeling of separation, of isolation, increases with each recurring year, and, in spite of the most vigorous effort, it comes to be a thing of permanence. This is inevitable, and it is as sad as it is inevitable.

(p. 38)

At the top of an organization, he maintains, the spotlight is always on the leader. Because of this, not only is the job lonely it is also exhausting both physically and spiritually. In a similar vein, Lockwood (n.d.) also looks at isolation, focusing particularly on the isolation of the CEO. He refers to the toll this takes in terms of stress, damage to relationships and distraction from important responsibilities. Napier and Sanaghan (1998) also address this issue and state that the question is not *whether* leaders become isolated but rather how they can learn to reduce the isolation and minimize its consequences. For them, the isolation results from leaders who cut themselves off and people below the leader who distance themselves from the leader. This dynamic of the isolation of top executives is alluded to also by Goleman, Boyatzis and McKee (2002) when they talk about what they call the CEO disease. In this particular case, the focus is on the difficulty that leaders have in getting feedback from people. This theme of leader isolation is evident in a search of many websites dealing with leadership. For example, Yalom (1998) describes what he found as a therapist working with leaders. Among the issues are the lack of any peers, the loneliness, and also the fear of being found to be an imposter. These affected both leaders' work and their family lives. A survey compiled for the Leadership Summit Leaders (Business-europe.com, 2004) found that 43 per cent of business chiefs think backbiting and bitchiness are the worst aspects of their job. Also, however, 31 per cent reported that loneliness was the worst thing about being a leader.

Studies of stress and burnout have highlighted the role of isolation in contributing to exhaustion and burnout among leaders and also the difficulties caused by poor relationships. Dworkin (1987) defines burnout as

an extreme form of role-specific alienation characterized by a sense that one's work is meaningless and that one is powerless to effect changes which could make the work more meaningful. This sense of meaninglessness and powerlessness is heightened by a belief that the norms associated with the role and the setting are absent, conflicting, or inoperative, and *that one is alone and isolated among one's colleagues and clients.*

(Italics added.) (p. 28)

In a study of school principals, for example, Leader and Boldt (1994) list among their difficulties and concerns the isolation and loneliness that seem to go with the job. Levinson (1981) includes among the causes of executive burn-out the exposure of managers to risk of attacks for doing their jobs, without providing a way for them to fight back. Burnout, then, seems to be one possible outcome of this dynamic and conversations I have had with former leaders do indicate that the destructiveness of the treatment they received was a factor in their eventual decision to relinquish leadership.

Cooper and Quick (2003) note that loneliness and disconnection from the rest of the organization are very common and can lead to self-defeating behaviour. Cubitt and Burt (2002) found that professional isolation (loneliness) and work overload were the most significant predictors of stress in primary school principals. Similarly, Read (2000) found significant feelings of under-appreciation and isolation among school leaders. Eykman (1991) discussed the necessity for leaders of a therapeutic community to endure loneliness as a necessary part of the role. Murray and Keenan (1992) found that women leaders often encountered isolation and restricted opportunities for advancement. Similarly, Fielden and Davidson (2001) state that, among other pressures, women managers face the possibility of direct and indirect exclusion, especially in organizational cultures that perpetuate the " 'manager = white, middle class, male' myth" (p. 124). They also note that isolation and tokenism, particularly of ethnic women, can lead to bullying and harassment in the workplace.

Welch, Meideros and Tate (1982) identified a number of sources of stress as contributing to school principal burnout and included among these the isolation inherent in the role as reflected in poor relations with teachers and/ or students. Gmelch and Burns (1993) included confrontations with colleagues among the sources of stress for departmental academic chairs. Chaplain (2001) included managing others (unsupportive people, the need to keep everybody happy) in his list of stressors faced by primary school head teachers. Sarros (1988) found interpersonal relations (with colleagues, parents and others) were one of the two main factors contributing to principal burn-out.

In one of the more interesting studies, Friedman (2002) found that the main stressors to which the school principal is subject come from four main sources: (1) stressors stemming from unreasonable demands from parents, parents' rude behaviour, and the overload that parents inflict upon the principal; (2) stressors stemming from weak teacher performance, which includes lack of discipline, unresponsiveness to the principal's requests, poor motivation to work and achieve, and overall, a demonstrable non-recognition of the principal's authority to tell them what to do, in professional, administrative and organizational terms; (3) stressors stemming from overload; and (4) stressors stemming from inadequate performance on the part of school support staff (i.e. the school secretary and service staff). Of these four factors, Friedman found that the teachers carry the highest impact on the principal's burnout. They are followed by parents and lastly by overload. He states that

> . . . teachers behave in an undisciplined manner . . .; they turn down positions of responsibility at school offered to them by the principal . . .; they directly resist the principal's efforts at introducing change . . ., fail to cooperate and refuse to accept the principal's decisions . . ., and treat the principal disrespectfully. . . . From the principal's point of view, the behaviours involving lack of discipline, excessive demands, and overload resulting from teachers' and parents' actions indicate a refusal to accept the authority and command of the principal, and reflect a lack of trust and non-recognition of the principal's status.   (p. 246)

He goes on to note that school principals expect that everyone associated with the school will respect the role of principal, the principal's instructions, leadership and their plans for the future. Instead, however, the principal discovers that teachers are disobedient and unmotivated and they show a reluctance to accept the principal's authority without questioning. Parents also place excessive burdens on the principal. These patterns of behaviour from teachers and parents along with work overload give rise to a discrepancy between the principal's initial beliefs about what he or she would have to cope with and the reality on the ground. This discrepancy places the principal under severe pressure and ultimately leads to burnout.

Maslach (2003), in discussing interventions to deal with burnout, notes that most approaches to burnout intervention focus mainly on individual-centred strategies rather than on organizational approaches. This is paradoxical given that organizational factors seem to play a bigger role in burnout than do individual factors. By extension, we could also say that the stresses around leadership are part of an organizational dynamic rather than being due to individual factors. In the present context, for example, the isolation and attacking of leaders are not due simply to incompetence, individual difficulties or personality factors but are actually part of a much larger dynamic and may well be reinforced or supported by the culture and traditions of the organization or group.

The issue of isolation is also recognized among activists. Westerling (n.d.) sees this as a major challenge to leaders in groups that are traditionally under-represented (e.g. people of colour, gay/lesbian, etc.) and comments that it is difficult to create and develop a liberation movement in a situation where leaders are isolated and unsupported. Coping with the stresses and demands of the role can leave people exhausted and reactive in the way they lead.

NEGLECT OF THIS ISSUE

At this stage, it is clear that the attacking and isolation of leaders is a widely recognized phenomenon with much experiential and anecdotal evidence. However, it is also one that has received little systematic attention or research within the leadership literature. Over the past 70 years research on leadership has focused primarily on the effects of leadership style and behaviour on followers and on the particular conditions that lead to stress and burnout among those in leadership positions. Very few studies have examined the effects of follower behaviour on leaders, particularly negative or destructive follower behaviour. Conflict between leaders and followers has been noted either as an outcome of particular leadership styles or as a contributing factor to the stress of leadership. It has seldom, however, been the main focus of research and has rarely been identified as a significant aspect of the leader–follower relationship. Its occurrence is seen more as an unusual aberration rather than a common feature of the relationship. In the research, followers are primarily seen as figures to be acted on by the leader rather than as people who might have a profound influence on the well-being and effectiveness of that leader. Leader–member exchange (LMX) theory, for example, which has been a major focus of research over the past 30 years, suggests that leaders develop differential relationships with followers that lead to the formation of high-quality relationships with some of these (the in-group) and lower-quality relationships with the rest (the out-group). At first glance, this would seem to offer the promise of throwing light on negative or destructive aspects of leader–follower relations. However, most of the research has focused on the effects of high LMX relationships on followers (Gerstner and Day, 1997; Judge and Ferris, 1993; Sherman, 2002; Turban and Jones, 1988; Whittington, Goodwin and Murray, 2004). Howell and Shamir (2005) point out that the effects that followers have on leaders has been relatively under-developed and less researched in LMX theory. While it suggests that followers' motivation and abilities contribute to the quality of the leader–member relationship, LMX theory offers very little insight into the manner in which followers influence the nature of the relationship. It is important to explore, therefore, why there has been such a neglect of this issue. There are many references in passing to the processes of isolation and attack but few, with the exception of some of the writers already mentioned, seem to have considered them a key issue facing leaders. Why should this be?

One possible answer to this lies in the work of Rost (1993a, 1993b) in particular, and of Barker (1997). They highlight a range of problems with the state of leadership theory as it has developed over the past century. To begin with, in much of the writing, the study of *leadership* has come to be equated with the study of *leaders*. Leadership itself is often not defined clearly and it is assumed to be simply what people in leadership roles do. Rather than looking at leadership as a process, writers have focused on leaders as people. As we saw in Chapter 4, over the last 25 years, in particular, much of the focus has been on excellent, highly effective leaders (at least as defined by the authors or based on the economic or financial success of their enterprises)-(Bennis, 1998, 2000; Bennis and Thomas, 2002; Kouzes and Posner, 2002). Rost (1993a) refers to this as the excellence approach and sees it as part of what he calls the industrial paradigm of leadership. In this approach the leader is seen as a hero, reminiscent of the "Great Man" approach to leadership in the very early years of thinking about this subject. Within this focus on successful, excellent leaders, researchers have concentrated on their successes and their characteristic traits and styles rather than on their difficulties and struggles. Difficulties, as such, are opportunities for great leaders to show what they are made of. They are of no particular interest in and of themselves. The aim has been to pinpoint what it is that makes someone an effective leader rather than understanding the leadership dynamic. Thus the focus has been on the leader as a person rather than on leadership as a process. Similarly, there has tended to be more of a focus on the leader as a person rather than on leadership as a relationship. To the extent that this relationship is considered, it is a one-way relationship. Writers describe what leaders do to build effective relationships rather than describe the actual relationship dynamic. The other people in the relationship are simply there to be led and to be acted on rather than being seen to have any active role themselves in the relationship or in the ultimate success of the leader. The relationship itself, separately from the behaviour of the leader in that relationship, is rarely explored fully. In particular, the dynamics of that relationship tend to be examined only from the perspective of how leaders exert influence on their followers or collaborators.

Building on the work of Burns (1978), Rost is at pains to stress the process nature of leadership. In doing this, he places important emphasis on the role of followers (Rost 1993a) or more correctly "collaborators" (Rost 1993b). These have received little or no attention in most of the leadership literature. Given all this, it is understandable that the reactions of followers/collaborators to those in leadership roles have been neglected. Any destructive reactions on their part are thus not seen as part of a process or dynamic. They are minor obstacles to be overcome by transformational superheros. They are incidental and represent "difficult people", people with personality problems, rather than being part of any systematic process. They say more about the personalities of those who manifest them than they do about the nature of leadership as a process. What Rost is describing helps explain the neglect of this topic. At the same time, as we saw in Chapter 4, the issues he highlights around the nature of collaborative leadership underline the importance of examining this process in great detail.

THE ATTACKING OF LEADERS

Given the apparently pervasive nature of this dynamic, what strategies are available to counteract it? In Chapter 5, we saw a number of possible ways that leaders and those around them can lessen the impact of these processes. Over and above these ongoing and longer-term strategies, however, if we focus particularly on the active and often direct attacks on leaders, how can these be handled, particularly in the short term? What steps can we take to ensure that we stay effective in a leadership role or that we do not begin to burn out when faced with attack?

Learning how to deal with this dynamic involves giving up the assumption that isolation and attacks are a necessary, inherent or inevitable part of the job or that they are somehow beyond our control. It means taking a systematic look at the different kinds of attacks that come at people and understanding how they operate. Jackins (1984, 1987) is very useful in this regard as he details a range of different ways that leaders get attacked. Although his account of these varies somewhat, we can build on his analysis to describe the various types of attack in the following way.

Correcting a mistake

The first, and most obvious, reason why someone may be attacked is if they make a mistake. In this case, the leader says or does the wrong thing, misjudges a situation, handles a situation badly, adopts a poor policy, overlooks a problem, forgets to do something or makes any of a myriad of other errors. Because of the ways we have been conditioned to deal with leaders in situations like these, it tends to be unlikely that people relaxedly approach the person to point out the difficulty. In general, we are not skilled at presenting criticism in ways that enable people to keep listening and to learn from what we have to say. We do not politely and pleasantly go to the leader and ask if we can draw their attention to a problem we have noticed. More commonly, we communicate blame, disapproval, dislike, impatience, disappointment, resentment, frustration or some other painful emotion. On a bad day, the language or the tone of voice used causes the leader to become defensive. In fact, it is fairly rare to witness leaders openly admit mistakes without any defensiveness. Many leaders seem to view it as a sign of weakness to do this. Instead, they either defend their mistakes, deny that any mistakes were made or try to shift the blame to someone else. In some organizations this has become institutionalized as the normal way of responding to complaints. This, of course, then generates further dissatisfaction among those who have seen the mistakes and reduces the credibility of the leader. It can lead to an ongoing cycle of attack and defence where attitudes polarize and little progress is made.

In contrast to a defensive approach, an attack of this kind can be handled relatively simply on the part of a leader by listening relaxedly and non-defensively to the criticism, ignoring the abusive language or tone of voice, thanking the person for pointing out the mistake, admitting it, trying to correct it if at all possible and promising not to repeat it. The attack can be put to rest and not allowed to become the basis for a deteriorating relationship. In the process, the open admission of mistakes can actually enhance the leader's credibility in the eyes of those involved.

Handling such an attack, and others that we will come to, in this way is not necessarily easy for a leader. There may be all kinds of feelings bubbling beneath the surface as they listen to the complaint. They may feel scared, embarrassed, ashamed, inadequate, hurt, let down, angry or any of a wide range of upsets. The challenge, however, is to stay thinking rather than sink into the upset feeling. The priority is to deal with the attack and sort it out rather than act out our own painful emotion. If we can keep our own feelings in check, keep our attention off our own upsets, focus on the other person and think about what is going on, we can stop the attack and come out with a positive result.

The feelings we struggle with in the situation can be dealt with afterwards when the situation has been handled. To dramatize or act out these feelings at the person who is attacking us will not, in general, be helpful since this person is already caught up in their own painful emotion. Instead, we can talk to someone close to us about hard it was or how scared we felt. We can release the hurt or the tension with someone who has the slack to listen to us, who is not preoccupied with being upset with us.

Getting attention

The problem for leaders, however, is that, even if they make no mistakes, they may still be attacked. There is a second type of attack where leaders have not done anything wrong but still find themselves being criticized in ways that feel very hurtful and unfair. It may involve what looks like an over-reaction to an innocent remark or gesture or action on the part of the leader. Or it may involve some criticism of the leader's style or personality. Sometimes, it has a personal edge to it that makes it hard to listen to. For example, someone may criticize the way the leader "acts as though they know it all" or the way they "adopt a very superior attitude to everyone". Sometimes, the criticism will be of how the leader looks or sounds. On the receiving end, it can feel very abusive or insulting. In practice, what often happens is that the leader reacts against this attack and gets defensive. Feeling treated unfairly or disrespectfully, they may refuse to listen further – "I don't have to take this kind of abuse from anyone". Or else they may attack back – "who do you think you are talking to me like that?" In either case, an impasse is quickly reached and both parties go away feeling bruised or angry.

If this kind of attack is handled differently, some interesting things may be observed. Instead of getting defensive, the leader now stays relaxed (or, at least, tries to look relaxed!), lets the person talk without interruption, listens respectfully and, when the person has had their say, tries to draw them out further. Instead of making a statement, the leader asks a question. When the person has finished offloading their annoyance, or at some appropriate pause in the invective, the leader can ask, for example, "Is there anything else you don't like about the way I am doing things?" They can ask the person to "tell me more". If the leader can communicate a non-defensive openness to what the person is saying, and a genuine concern to understand their upset, after a while the focus of the attack will shift. The leader may hear the person say, "Look, I don't mean to be getting at you personally. It's just that if you had to put up with what I had to deal with all last week, you would be upset also." At this point, it is clear that there is another issue bothering the person that is actually much more relevant than the upset with the leader. Now, the leader can focus on this deeper issue and offer the person an understanding ear. In a sense, the leader adopts a counselling role. If this is done sensitively, the person may well finish the conversation by apologizing again for their earlier comments about the leader and thanking them for being so understanding. Essentially, this kind of attack is coming from someone who is upset and simply wants attention. They have a problem and instead of going up to the leader and relaxedly saying, "Excuse me, I have a problem; would you be willing to listen to me while I tell you about it?", they go up and attack in the hope that the leader will notice something is bothering them and ask them about it.

As with the first kind of attack, if we can keep our own feelings out of it and respond thoughtfully, we can bring it to a useful conclusion. The feelings we have set aside can be dealt with afterwards in a safe, appropriate context.

Testing the leader

The third type of attack tends to occur in situations where the leader is new and people have not yet made up their minds as to where they stand with this person. It can also occur in situations where the leader is challenging a group to take a new, possibly risky, direction, or adopt a very new policy, or is holding out a new, hopeful vision. Under these conditions, people may attack the leader as a test. In saying it is a test, this is not to imply that it is deliberately, awarely or consciously done. As with other types of attack it may actually be quite unconscious on the part of those attacking. However, people want to know whether they can trust the leader. They may not be sure of the leader's integrity. They may be worried about the leader having motives or a hidden agenda that is not in their best interests. They want to know if there is more to the leader than meets the eye. They want to know whether the leader is dependable and to be trusted if the situation becomes threatening. They want to know what they can expect from this person. Essentially, they want to know whether the leader is "sound" and worth following. This type of attack will often take the form of a sceptical, suspicious or cynical questioning or interrogation of the leader's motives, qualifications, integrity or intentions.

Or it may consist of telling the leader their ideas are useless, out of touch with reality or doomed to failure. At times, it may get heated or quite personal and the leader may feel very challenged by it all. Sometimes, they get defensive and refuse to have their motives or integrity questioned like this – "Look, I don't have to justify or explain myself to you." They may insist that people respect their role or position. They may demand that people give them the support they feel entitled to or they may insist on people according them the respect they think they deserve.

Because this attack, however, is primarily a test, if the leader gets defensive or attacks back, they fail the test. If they appear rattled, thrown or upset by the attack, it puts a question mark over their credibility, dependability, integrity, commitment, transparency or whatever other doubts people were raising. On the other hand, if the person stays relaxed, listens, acknowledges the difficulties, answers the questions and gives people all the information they need in order to make up their minds, people will satisfy their doubts and may well decide to follow the leader.

In some kinds of very conflictual or emotive situations, leaders may find that they have to undergo a sequence of such tests as people's fears repeatedly intensify and recede. They face an initial challenge, and, after calmly and relaxedly answering this challenge, they are allowed to proceed for now. Some time later, for whatever reason, people's fears or suspicions are aroused again and a further challenge ensues. Once again, the leader addresses the concerns and the challenge recedes. Gradually, as people check out the leader like this, the attacks become less intense and fewer and further between. Over time, people's trust in, support for, and commitment to, the leader grow and the attacks disappear. In essence, these attacks can be put to rest by listening to the underlying concerns and addressing these in an open, honest and relaxed manner.

A variation on this type of attack can occur when a new leader finds themselves being met with non-cooperation or non-acceptance of their leadership. It may take the form of openly defying them, ignoring them or undermining them with others. Depending on the actual context, this may be dealt with, in the ways described above, by explaining clearly what is required. Or, it may require the leader to assert themselves and insist that people follow their instructions or not act in ways that undermine them. If this is done firmly but relaxedly it may increase the leader's credibility. In some cases, however, this type of attack may more accurately fit into the next category and should be dealt with accordingly.

For each of the above three types of attack, the way we can usefully handle them is much the same. Basically, these attacks can be listened away. In each case, the leader listens until they can identify the issue at the heart of the attack – a mistake on the leader's part, an underlying upset, or a testing of the leader. The leader then responds appropriately in a relaxed way by apologizing, listening, giving information and so on. The fourth kind of attack, however, is different.

Acting out accumulated hurt

This type of attack is quite different both in its source and in how it can be handled. It can often happen that a group or organization contains an individual or individuals who, over time, have been badly hurt by their experiences in that group or organization. Sometimes they were hurt previously and have brought this old hurt into the current group or organization. Whatever its source, at this point, these individuals carry a deep well of hurt or pain that has accumulated, perhaps over many years. The hurt is often very close to the surface for them and is easily triggered. It is something they have difficulty ignoring or taking their attention off for any lengthy period. It preoccupies them. One example of this would be people who are identified as having a "chip on their shoulder". Another would be people who are chronically negative and critical. In many cases, they have become progressively isolated over the years and now have few people who are comfortable with them or who can easily work or live with them. They tend to alienate the people around them. They may be seen as "difficult" people with stubborn or domineering personalities. In some cases, they will be described as "born troublemakers".

These are the kind of people around whom, when they go to speak at meetings for example, everyone else freezes or starts to fidget and become uncomfortable. The rest of the people at the meeting know, from past experience, what is coming. It is like a broken record and is very predictable. The tone of the attack will tend to be angry, bitter, tight, blaming, whingeing, unyielding and inflexible. It is a tone that is very hard to listen to. The hurt or pain that these individuals carry tends to spill out relatively easily and, in particular, will often attach itself to anyone in a visible leadership role. Thus, leaders are often the focus for attacks from these individuals as they dramatize or act out how hurt they feel inside. It will tend to be difficult for them to continue to see the person they are attacking separately from the issues that concern them and the leader then becomes the problem in their eyes.

This type of attack is different in a number of ways. First, it is fairly predictable. We know these individuals from past experience. Their attacking is part of a deeply ingrained habit at this point. They do it a lot. Other attacks may be sporadic, come from a variety of directions and be much less predictable but these ones we can expect. In addition, no amount of listening and drawing out the issues will drain this attack. It is like a bottomless pit to all intents and purposes. (Theoretically, this is not the case but in practice it is effectively so.) In general, this person carries so much hurt and bitterness that they are beyond the resources of the group (in terms of time, energy, skill and commitment) to cope with. In some situations, they require ongoing, skilled help to deal with their pain.

Unlike the earlier cases, this attack cannot be listened away or even usefully listened to for any great length. This leaves a limited number of other options. Mostly, it has to be either avoided, prevented, or interrupted and stopped when it occurs. Because it is predictable, we can sometimes avoid situations where it is likely to occur. We can excuse ourselves or not join in a discussion that we know will lead to an attack. Alternatively, we can structure situations so that it does not get too much opportunity to be disruptive. If this person stands up at a meeting and attacks the leader, for example, the response can be to thank the person politely for their contribution and then, without further addressing the person or the issue, invite contributions from other people or move on to other matters. A simple strategy is to have an agreement that no one at a meeting speaks twice until everyone has spoken at least once. That way, no one can take over and dominate the meeting. Occasionally, if the attack continues, the person may need to be interrupted and firmly required to stop or to leave if they persist. This does not have to be done harshly but it does require firmness. The point here is that the habit of attacking in this way is destructive not only of the leader and the group but also of the individual attacker themselves. The effect for the latter is to reinforce their pain and the rigid, counter-productive strategy they have evolved for handling it.

Because of its intensity, other people tend to feel powerless around this attack. Unfortunately for the leader, when the attack comes, people tend to go silent and not intervene. They may come to the leader in private afterwards to express their regret or horror at what took place but, at the time, they are unable to come to the aid of the person being attacked. As we saw in the previous chapter, however, people around the leader can play a key role here in helping to handle this attack. Rather than leaving a leader to deal with it on their own, others can step in, point out that it is inappropriate or unhelpful and insist that the person stop. Even if they do not succeed in preventing it at that point, their intervention will at least give the leader some useful breathing space and a reminder that they are not on their own. In the middle of an attack like this, it can be hard for the leader to tell that there is anyone on their side and another intervention, even if it does not work, can help the leader to stay thinking and prevent them getting confused or lost in their own feelings.

One important consideration in thinking about this and other attacks is that there is a distinction to be made between the content of the attack (the complaints or accusations, for example) and the actual process of attacking. These have to be thought about independently. The process of attacking is often destructive in itself, regardless of the content of the attack. Before the issues can be dealt with, the attack itself has to be stopped. This sometimes confuses people who allow attacks to continue because the content or the excuse seems justified – because the leader actually made a mistake, it is okay to attack. This could be seen in the case of the attempts to impeach former president Clinton in the US. People become so caught up in wondering whether the leader did or did not do what is alleged that they miss the underlying process of a leader being attacked. Attacking, however, as a way of dealing with issues is a destructive process whether or not the leader is at fault. The usual effect on leaders is to make them more defensive, to scare them and to make it difficult for them to keep thinking clearly. The challenge we face is to learn how to address issues without needing to attack anyone.

There is one other strategy the leader can adopt that may help to reduce or take the edge off this kind of attack. As was pointed out above, attackers such as this have often become progressively more isolated as time goes on. This isolation can be one of the factors propelling them into desperate attempts to attack. Recognizing this isolation, the leader can take steps to build a closer relationship with this individual, *in between attacks*. The leader can go after making relaxed, sociable contact with the person when they are not engaged in an attack or preoccupied with painful emotion. They can greet them in a friendly or respectful way, spend time in relaxed, non-contentious conversation over a work break, or spend time listening to them about topics or interests that are not the source of distress or pain for them. There may be limits to how close a relationship the leader can build like this, but, to the extent that it can be achieved, it can make it less likely that the attack will be directed at the leader or that it will be so destructive. Because of the closer relationship outside the conflict situation, the attacker will have more of a connection with the leader as a person and not just as an anonymous role. They are somewhat less likely to lose this connection when painful emotion takes hold and this will help the attacker to moderate the intensity, duration or frequency of their attacks. It may not be possible to eliminate these attacks completely (short of requiring the person to leave the group or organization) but we can make it less likely that they will spill over onto us. Other people may still have great difficulty handling these attackers but we will seem to escape the more extreme outpourings because of our efforts to reach out.

We shall see some further perspectives on this type of attack in later chapters where we look at the processes of conflict, change and influence. These will suggest some additional strategies for managing this kind of attack situation. One strategy in particular is worth describing at this point also. A characteristic of many attacks is that the person attacking loses a sense of connection to the leader *as a person*. In the absence of this connection, it is difficult for the person to judge what is appropriate and very easy to misinterpret the reactions, motives or concerns of the leader. Depending on the type of relationship they have, it may sometimes make a big difference for the leader to let the other person see the personal effects on them, and the struggle they are having in the face of the attack. Without in any way blaming or hitting back at the person, the leader can show where they are hurting or having a hard time, they can show how much they care and how much it matters to them to get this relationship right. By taking a risk and exposing their own vulnerability, they can re-establish the personal connection and create a constructive climate for resolving the difficulty. This can be a workable way to deal with some attacks, particularly where there is an initial bond of caring or a commitment to an ongoing relationship.

These different categories of attack are not entirely mutually exclusive. The fourth type of attack, for example, may attach itself to a mistake by the leader or a proposal to introduce change. However, the tone of the attack and the habitual nature of it will distinguish it from the other types. Usually, if an apology or an attempt to listen sympathetically or give information does not put an end to the attack, then we may be dealing with this fourth type and the need to adopt an alternative strategy. In some cases, what begins as an attack of Type 1, 2 or 3 may evolve into an attack of Type 4 as the individual becomes increasingly inflexible and destructive. In this scenario, it is not that the individual involved necessarily conforms to the pattern of a chronically distressed person. However, the depth of feeling in the situation overwhelms clear thinking and clouds their judgement about what is appropriate at that point. At some stage, the painful emotion takes over to the point where listening or attempts at rational discussion become futile. The challenge for the leader is to keep thinking and figure out what response makes sense under the circumstances. Brown and Mazza (2005) make the point that being permissive and allowing negativity to continue can bring the work of a group to a halt. At the same time, going to the other extreme, being rigidly authoritarian and refusing to listen to people's concerns can lead to rebellion and thus also to a disruption of the work. The challenge is to strike a balance between these extremes while recognizing that we have the right to expect support for our leadership.

There are a couple of other variations on these attacks. One of these is what could be described as a *collective pattern of attacking*. Rather than classifying it as a separate type of attack it is more useful to see it as falling within and between the existing types. In this case, attacking can be seen as a bad habit that has evolved and been institutionalized in a group or organization. It has become part of the culture. People attack because that is the way conflict or leaders have always been handled and they know of no other way to deal with them. They are not particularly trying to be destructive or hurtful and the problem is not just with one or a small number of individuals. Everybody, or nearly everybody, does it. Here again, it is not that everyone is chronically overwhelmed with painful emotion, it is simply a bad, thoughtless habit. The strategies we have already looked at will be useful here some of the time. In addition, however, there comes a point where someone needs to draw attention to the pattern in the way the group handles conflict. People need to become aware that there is an inflexible pattern in the way they react that is separate from, and independent of, the issue or the leader involved. Without blaming or attacking back, we can invite people to notice what the group is doing and the effects it is having. The pattern needs to be interrupted and alternative strategies, structures or procedures offered to people as a way of addressing difficulties.

The other variation on this kind of attack is from people who have been so badly hurt, particularly in childhood, that they are pulled to find someone to hit back at, sometimes violently. They attack because the leader is identified as being too idealistic or naive or as a "do-gooder". Such an attack was made on Martin Luther King on one occasion when he was stabbed by a complete stranger, a very disturbed woman, during a book-signing event. Jackins (1987) maintains that with these attacks we just have to organize protection for ourselves or learn self-defence. It is not a situation where we should try to use reaching out or listening as a way to stop the attack.

Removing threats to the system

The final type of attack is also quite different from the earlier examples. This final type of attack will be directed at any leader who threatens cherished, core values or vested interests of the status quo. In this case, the attack will come from the system that is being threatened and, indirectly, is an indication of the significant influence of that leader. In a loose sense, the attack here comes from outside or above as opposed to within or below. Leaders, for example, who are a threat to a political system, may find themselves on the receiving end of attempts to discredit or smear them. Often, these kinds of attacks will involve imputations of irregularities in their behaviour of a financial, criminal or sexual nature. Martin Luther King, for example, was systematically targeted by the FBI in order to discredit him sexually. The attacks are designed to generate an emotional backlash against the leader from those who might be followers. Their aim is to stir up painful emotion that makes it difficult for people to think clearly or objectively about, or to stay committed to, the leader. Ultimately, the aim of this attack is to destroy this person's leadership and influence. In extreme cases, where the system fails to discredit the leader, it may actually attempt to eliminate them. Some well-known examples of this have emerged over the years, such as the death of Karen Silkwood, the anti-nuclear activist in the US, or of Ken Saro-Wiwa of the Ogoni people in Nigeria.

By its nature, this kind of attack has a degree of predictability. The greater the threat we become, the more likely we are to be attacked. For this reason, however, it also means we can take steps to protect ourselves from it. We can see to it that we do not place ourselves in potentially compromising situations or leave ourselves open to false accusations of impropriety. We can also adopt strategies that avoid unnecessarily "scaring" the system we are trying to change and thus attracting an attack. Using violence, for example as a way of bringing about social change, tends to have the effect of generating further violence in retaliation.

Once this attack comes, various suggestions have been made as to how it should be handled. Jackins (1987), for example, maintains that it is pointless to try to discuss or debate or even to deny the substance of this attack. Instead, the group must unite around the leader and they must counter-attack without hesitation and indignantly. Discussing the attack has the effect of spreading it and leaving even more people confused. Any mistakes or weaknesses on the part of the leader that are offered as excuses for the attack should be dealt with within the group privately and *after* the attack has been defeated.

There are a number of factors involved here, however. The first is the challenge of distinguishing between attacks of this sort and the first type of attack (attempts to correct actual mistakes). It could easily happen that a leader under attack would see it not as someone genuinely but inappropriately trying to correct a mistake but as someone out to destroy their influence or leadership. This particular difficulty is evident in some of the responses of the Roman Catholic Church to allegations of clerical child abuse. Some leaders in the Church, for example, saw these allegations as media attempts to discredit the institution and this then dictated the kind of response they adopted. Accurately judging the source of the attack is vital. A second factor is that success in dealing with this attack depends, crucially, on having a united front or strong allies. The work of building this unity or winning these allies cannot wait until the attacks come but rather has to be an ongoing part of the work of leadership. Where people have a solid relationship with the leader, it is difficult for attacks to take hold. Any false allegations in the attacks do not square with what people know of the leader and will be dismissed as outlandish.

However, where the attack builds on actual mistakes or weaknesses of the leader, not to deal with these until after the attack has been defeated may put a huge strain on the loyalty of supporters and may lead to feelings of confusion, disappointment or distrust as some of the real problems are revealed. Supporters may need explanations, admissions, apologies or corrections if they are to stay clear in their own thinking and maintain their commitment to the leader. A policy of silence or of defiant counter-attack has the potential to lose good people who are left confused by the apparent substance to the content of the attack. It can also lose potential allies who have not yet been won over to support the leader.

Where the accusations or allegations contained in an attack are clearly without substance, they can either be ignored or the attacker can be required to withdraw them or accused of underhand tactics. However, where these do have some substance, and/or as the attacks mount and spread, there comes a point where they must be dealt with. In public, the strategy may be to draw attention to the attempts to destroy the leader or weaken the organization without debating the allegations. In other words, publicly the focus would be on the *process* taking place. Privately, however, bearing in mind that the primary purpose of this attack is to destroy the leader, the substance or *content* of the attack, the alleged weaknesses or mistakes, have to be addressed – not with the aim of convincing attackers but with the aim of strengthening, or not losing, allies or supporters. Vigorous steps may need to be taken internally to address the mistakes or weaknesses while continuing to defend against the attacks publicly. If people are to stand by the leader or speak out publicly on behalf of the leader, they need to know the truth and what actions are being taken to correct the mistakes.

Applying this reasoning to the case of Martin Luther King and attacks from the FBI would have suggested a two-pronged strategy on King's part: public indignation and counter-attacks on the FBI and private admissions of mistakes, and promises to correct these, with close supporters or others who were prepared to listen.

Intimidation rituals

This fifth type of attack is not confined to political systems. An insightful account of how it can operate within the context of work organizations has been provided by O'Day (1974). He talks about the phases that an attack process will move through in an organization where it is attempting to confront "reform-minded subordinates". A reformer is any person in an organization who acts to alter the structure or the functioning of the organization when they have *not* been formally given authority to bring about change. He describes the process as a series of intimidation rituals and points out that organizations will prefer to intimidate reform-minded individuals rather than put energy into the structural or personnel changes that might be required to win these people over.

The first phase of this process is *indirect intimidation* and this has two steps, *nullification* and *isolation*. Nullification involves telling the person that their accusations or suggestions are invalid. The person is told they have misunderstood or misperceived the situation. The hope is that the person will take the word of those in authority and give up at this point. If the reformer insists, further investigation may be conducted but the results will be used to prove that the reformer's ideas have been taken seriously but that the concerns are groundless. Repeated exposure to this ritual of nullification should convey the message that it is pointless to pursue reform.

If the reformer continues to raise issues, the next step will be to isolate the person. This can include closing communication links, not responding to communications, restricting access, transfers to less visible areas and reducing resources. In some cases, frustration with this isolation process can lead reformers to overreact in order to get some response from those in authority and this can trigger phase two of the process.

If the reformer refuses to stay silent and, in addition, tries to mobilize support from others, the second phase of the process begins. This is the phase of *direct intimidation*, involving two steps, *defamation* and *expulsion*. Defamation attempts to call into question the motives and character of the reformer and thus cut them off from potential supporters and allies. Questions may be raised about debatable motives, psychological problems or gross incompetence. Events may be distorted or instances of misconduct fabricated. The aim is to blackmail the reformer into giving up and to trigger negative reactions among possible sympathizers.

Finally, when neither nullification, nor isolation nor defamation are successful in silencing the reformer, or in inducing them to leave voluntarily, the organization will attempt to expel them. Formal dismissal procedures will be set in motion based on allegations of incompetence or psychological problems and the person will be forced to leave.

O'Day is not the only writer to describe the tactics used to silence dissent in the workplace. Weinstein (1979), for example, listed specific ways that organizations deal with "oppositionists". These include being ignored, being victimized, being forced to resign, being sacked, being labelled a "troublemaker" and discredited, being transferred to undesirable locations, being denied promotion or salary increases, being prevented from doing meaningful work, being labelled mentally ill, being ostracized, being blacklisted and, in extreme cases, being killed. Although the focus here is on work organizations, it is clear that these same processes could be applied to many other types of system.

SUMMARY

As we saw in the last chapter, we need a more sophisticated approach to dealing with leadership difficulties instead of just attacking leaders. We need to talk directly to leaders about any difficulties rather than gossiping or giving out about them behind their backs. We need to resist the pull to make a public issue of the difficulties until all other possible solutions have been explored. We have to learn how to keep painful emotion from taking over when we approach leaders with our difficulties.

Having a clear picture of how attack processes operate can enable people in leadership to think more clearly about how best to handle them. They can take steps to protect themselves where necessary. It also gives people a way to depersonalize the attack and retain some distance from it so that they can continue to function flexibly and creatively in the situation. In many cases, and in spite of appearances, the attack is not personal. It is simply someone caught up in painful emotion that has left them hurting and confused. We just happen to be the target for that.

Even though we can come to understand what is really behind attacks of these kinds, they can still be distressing to have to handle. There is one small consolation that may be of help if we can remember it at the time. This is that people sometimes attack when they feel some safety. They do not always attack the person they are most scared of or most upset with. Instead, they may attack someone with whom they have felt some safety or some hope or some connection. In other words, the fact that someone attacks us may actually be an indication that we have got something right. Otherwise, they would not have attacked. This is a very small consolation but when we are being attacked anything that enables us to maintain our perspective helps!

Very little has been written specifically about the attack process and there is a need for even greater clarity about it. The experiences of individual leaders will vary enormously and the processes described here are oversimplified to some extent. However, these basic tendencies in the relationship with people in leadership are very common even though they vary in intensity from situation to situation. Being clear about these processes and their knock-on effects can be very useful in thinking about how to enable leaders to play an effective role. The strategies suggested here are not magic solutions that will always work nor are they the only possible ways to handle attacks. There are many exceptions to these guidelines. Underlying all of them, however, is the need to stay thinking in the face of attacks and not allow our own painful emotion to determine what we do. Finally, as the workings and effects of these dynamics become clearer, the individual responses to attacks described here can be supported and enhanced by the development of agreed policies in the group or organization as to what are and are not acceptable ways to deal with leadership difficulties.

REFLECTION

1   Describe times when you have felt isolated as a leader.
2   How did you cope with the isolation? Did you turn to anyone for support?
3   Describe times when you have felt attacked as a leader.
4   How did you react to being attacked?
5   Applying the analysis from this chapter, why do you think these attacks took place?
6   What do you think helped you to survive in these situations?
7   What kinds of help or support from others would have made a difference to you in these situations?
8   Looking back on how you handled these situations, what would you do differently with the benefit of hindsight?
9   In what ways have you seen other leaders handle attacks successfully?
10 In what ways have you seen other leaders handle attacks unsuccessfully?

Part II
The leadership context

7 Oppression and leadership

INTRODUCTION

In the early part of this book, we saw that leadership consists of a process of building close relationships with people within which we get to listen deeply to them so that we can think clearly about them. The focus there was on the *content* of leadership, what it is that leaders do. To have a full picture of what is involved in this process, however, we also have to look at the leadership *context*. Leadership does not take place in a social vacuum. It is not just an interaction between individuals with no history to their relationships, no feelings about their experiences, no differences in access to power and resources, or no learned or conditioned responses to their environment. The people involved have a shared history and an ongoing dynamic to their relationship. In other words, leadership has a social context. Since we have defined leadership as a process of thinking about people, we need to take account of this social context and of all the factors that influence the ways they think, feel and behave.

At the heart of this social context are the processes of oppression and liberation. We are trying to lead people who bring with them their experiences of hurt, mistreatment, inequality and injustice, whether as women, as workers, as poor, as ethnic minorities, as men, as Jews, as young people, as elders, as disabled, as gay people, as people of colour, as religious groups or as any number of other significant identities. For some people the feelings left by these experiences are raw and close to the surface. Their lives are grim and a constant, painful struggle. For others, the feelings are distant, disconnected or difficult to access. The day-to-day struggle is less intense and consuming but the residue of past mistreatment nevertheless shapes their decisions, priorities, actions and feelings. Some people are deeply aware of, and able to name, their experiences of oppression; others have not looked much at this aspect of their lives. What is clear is that everyone carries with them the effects of earlier, and in many cases, current ongoing experiences of oppression. If we are to think clearly about people, we need to understand this process and how the residue, or "baggage", left by oppression distorts the ways people think, feel and act. Ultimately, our goal is to liberate humans from oppression and its effects and in doing this to free up people to exercise their full potential as leaders. In this chapter, we shall focus particularly on the broad process of oppression before looking in later chapters at more specific aspects of this dynamic and at the process of liberation.

DEFINITION

Oppression can be defined in several ways. A very simple definition is the following: *oppression exists where people do not get equal treatment, or do not get treated with respect because they belong to a certain group or category of people.* This definition highlights the fact that oppression is a social phenomenon. It occurs because people belong to, or are seen to belong to, particular groups or categories. They get mistreated as members of these particular groups. As Mullaly (2002) describes it,

> What determines oppression is when a person is blocked from opportunities to self-development, is excluded from full participation in society, does not have certain rights that the dominant group takes for granted, or is assigned a second-class citizenship, not because of individual talent, merit, or failure, but because of his or her membership in a particular group or category of people.
>
> (p. 28)

A somewhat more technical, but complementary, definition is that oppression is *the systematic, one-way, institutionalized mistreatment of the members of one group by those of another group or by the society as a whole.* This definition emphasizes a number of additional characteristics of oppression. In particular, it highlights the systematic nature of oppression, which distinguishes it from simple interpersonal mistreatment. People may be mistreated without necessarily being oppressed. Unlike simple mistreatment, oppression is built into the social system around us. It is not accidental or random (Mullaly, 2002). It is, in fact, quite predictable and, again, comes to people by virtue of their belonging to, or being seen to belong to, particular groups. If we know that someone has been born into a particular oppressed group, without knowing anything about the individual, we already know a lot about what this person will have to deal with as they move through life. For example, if someone is born female, we can say a lot about what she is likely to experience as she grows up even though we know little about that particular individual female. Similarly, we can say a lot about the likely experiences of a person of colour, or of a person raised poor, or of members of many other oppressed groups. The mistreatment is systematic and predictable.

In the same way, the mistreatment is one-way. It goes from those with power and privilege towards those without power or privilege. The oppressive system reinforces, condones, facilitates, encourages or legitimizes the mistreatment of the one group by the other. Mistreatment in the other direction is judged to be illegitimate or unacceptable and few resources and opportunities are available to embed this mistreatment systematically in social structures and processes. The one-way nature of oppression is sometimes a source of confusion for people when they look at the mistreatment of members of dominant or oppressor groups by members of oppressed groups. For example, there probably is not any man who has not, at some point, been hurt or mistreated by a woman. This, however, does not mean that men are oppressed *by women*. This mistreatment of men by women is generally not systematically reinforced and socially sanctioned. On the other hand, the mistreatment of women by men is systematic, reflected in formal and informal social structures and processes and, at various times and places, backed up by the rule of law. Both mistreatments may *feel* equally hurtful to the individual on the receiving end but there is a real difference in the context within which the mistreatment takes place. (This is not to suggest that men, as a group, are not oppressed but merely that women are not their oppressors.) This kind of confusion is evident in Liu *et al.* (2004) and Liu and Rasheed Ali (2005) where they talk about different kinds of classism, including upward classism. In a similar way, the backlash from an oppressed group against their oppression is sometimes described as oppressive of the dominant group. While it may be very hurtful and even destructive we have to see it as conceptually different. Freire (1972) touches on this distinction when he states that "Behaviour which prevents the restoration of the oppressive regime cannot be compared with acts which create and maintain it" (p. 33). He maintains that any restriction on the right of the oppressor to oppress others, or to act without any limitations on their privileged way of life, will feel like an oppression of those oppressors or as a violation of their individual rights. Feelings, on their own, however, are not a sufficient indicator of what is rational or appropriate. It is neither useful nor appropriate to equate this mistreatment of the oppressor with the original oppression or to see it as a separate, unrelated oppression. It has to be looked at, thought about and understood in the context of the original oppression. Apart from the mistreatment of members of the oppressor group, it is not uncommon to hear people speak about members of an oppressed group "oppressing" each other. Here again, there is a confusion between mistreatment and systematic oppression. The mistreatment in this case, as we shall see in more detail in the next chapter, is actually a reflection of the way in which the external oppression has been internalized by the oppressed group and is not an example of people oppressing themselves. To use language loosely in describing these different situations is to obscure the basic nature of the underlying dynamic and to downplay the essentially one-way direction in which oppression operates.

The above definition of oppression also draws attention to the fact that, sometimes, there is no one group that is the agent of the oppression. In some cases, we can point to obvious groups that participate as agents of a particular oppression, playing a prominent role in mistreating the target, oppressed group. In other cases, however, there is no one, obvious, agent group and it is easier to see the oppression as embedded in, and carried out by, the society as a whole. Thus, while it is not accurate to state that men are oppressed by women, it is true that they are an oppressed group. This oppression, in the form of a very vicious conditioning of young boys and men into very limited gender roles and into being agents of women's oppression, is built into the fabric of society but does not depend on any one group acting as its agent. This particular focus on oppression at societal level is also helpful, in some ways, in moving us away from seeing particular groups as "the enemy". The oppression resides primarily in the system rather than in the people who act as its agents. It is the oppressive system rather than oppressive people that has to be eliminated. This is a point that I shall return to later in this chapter.

Over time, the mistreatment of people becomes institutionalized and is reflected in the various aspects of the system, for example, the education system, the legal system, the economic system, language and discourse, religion, or the mass media (Moane, 1999; Schwalbe *et al.*, 2000; Mullaly, 2002). This mistreatment has major effects, as we shall see, on how people think, feel and act. Being sensitive to, and aware of, how the process of oppression operates are vital in the context of leadership. In order to lead effectively we need to understand the dynamics of oppression and the ways in which it affects people. Understanding these dynamics gives us a way of thinking about people, individually and collectively, and how they can be supported effectively. It gives us a way of thinking about how we can be a resource for people. It gives us a way of clarifying what we are trying to achieve as leaders. To do this successfully, we need to understand in more detail how this process operates.

HOW OPPRESSION OPERATES

Moane (2003) makes the point that liberation involves transforming not only the social conditions associated with oppression but also the psychological patterns associated with it. We can think about the effects of oppression in terms of their material, economic or physical outcomes for an oppressed person or group. We can also think about the psychological effects and it is useful to look at these in some depth (Table 7.1). The process of oppression can be thought of as a sequence of experiences starting with the existence of prejudice towards a particular group. In some cases, with some groups, we might not even describe the problem as, or associate it with, prejudice. We might talk about groups around which there tend to be a lot of misinformation or misunderstanding. Perhaps people make inaccurate assumptions about these groups or there are various myths about them. Maybe they get stereotyped a lot. We might even think in terms of groups that other people feel uneasy with, awkward around, or uncomfortable with. Several possible

Table 7.1 Effects of Oppression

Prejudice; Misinformation; Misunderstanding; Stereotyping
•
Active mistreatment
•
Negative messages
•
Negative self-image
•
Acting out of negative self-Image
(Internalised oppression)

groups can fall under these headings. Some of the groups that could fit these descriptions are very commonly thought of as oppressed groups and some might just be thought of as "different". There are some groups that people can readily accept as being the targets of prejudice while there are others to which they would be reluctant to apply such an extreme description. The point is that the dynamic I want to describe here applied both to obviously oppressed groups and to groups to which people might not readily attach the word "oppressed". We use a variety of terms to describe many of these groups, for example, out-groups, marginalized, underprivileged, disadvantaged, subordinate, minority or oppressed. What they all have in common is that they evoke some degree of negative feelings or painful emotions among other people ranging from extreme prejudice to discomfort, unease or awkwardness.

Mistreatment

What effects do these negative feelings have? Typically, the prejudice, the misinformation, the misunderstanding, the stereotyping, the unease, discomfort or awkwardness attached to these groups translates itself into some kind of mistreatment. It does not just stay as a negative attitude. It gets acted out. For example, someone may find themselves turned down for a job because of the address they put on their application form. Or, they may find that they have to endure put-downs or jokes because they belong to a particular category of people. Or, they may find themselves under close scrutiny by the police or security services because of the ethnic or religious group to which they belong. The important thing to realize is that, while the intensity and type of mistreatment varies from group to group, the underlying process remains the same.

The mistreatment can take many forms. These could be ranged on a continuum from heavy, overt and aware mistreatment at one extreme to subtle, covert and unaware mistreatment at the other extreme. At the one extreme, they may include physical violence, verbal attacks or abuse, discrimination, demeaning people, acting arrogantly or acting in a superior manner towards them. At a less extreme level, but still extremely hurtful, they may include rejecting, excluding or ignoring people, telling offensive jokes about them or ridiculing them. Towards the other extreme, they may include acting overly politely or "nice" towards people, "walking on egg shells" or acting timidly around them, adopting condescending attitudes, using unaware, disrespectful language, having low expectations of them or being over-eager (or even simply eager) to prove to them that we are not prejudiced. In very subtle ways it includes a lack of any real connection with them on a human level, the pretence that everything is okay and that we, as members of an oppressor group, have no difficulties or struggles. For example, oppressor groups some-times assume that "niceness" cannot be oppressive. However, one of the things that members of oppressed groups have little time for is pretence, a superficial niceness that is not based on any real connection to people. I have often heard people say that they would prefer to deal with someone who is openly negative towards them than someone who pretends to like them but is not there for them when it counts. Pretence can also include an attitude or assumption that the oppressor group has no problems or struggles of its own. Simply to be in the company of people who act as if they have no problems, who show great confidence all the time and who do not show any of their vulnerabilities or their struggles can, in itself, be experienced as oppressive. In this type of situation, the oppressor group only has to look and sound a particular way for it to be experienced as oppressive. This is very confusing both for the oppressed and the oppressor. The confusion for the oppressed person has to do with the fact of feeling bad in a situation where the other person does not appear to have done anything that was obviously oppressive. The confusion for the oppressor person is that their intentions may be good and they may have been careful not to say or do the wrong thing but the other person still feels oppressed. It may help here to realize that it is the total situation that is oppressive and not just the individual people.

As an Irish person, for example, I have found myself in situations abroad where, on reflection, each individual treated me in a positive or welcoming way, but where the pervasive air of self-confidence, certainty, self-satisfaction and "okayness" was enough to trigger all of my own internalized self-doubt and feelings of unease and lack of safety. No one else around me looked as if they had any doubts or struggles in the situation. No one acted as if they felt insecure, uncertain, embarrassed, scared or ashamed. No one showed any vulnerability or evidence of having a hard time. For someone who struggles a lot of the time with feelings like these, to be around people who did not seem to show any struggle that I could see was very difficult. It felt that I rarely got to see the full person. And it was not only that they did not show their struggles. Much of the time, I also could not see their real humanity. It was like being with someone who was being careful to behave correctly but was not able to do this spontaneously or someone who behaved in a superficially nice or programmed manner rather than relating sincerely or genuinely "from the heart". All of this was enough to leave me feeling bad about myself. None of these individuals was to blame but, at the same time, they were part of an oppressive situation. The point is not that they should be blamed or that they should feel guilty but simply that oppression often takes subtle, complicated forms and these need to be thought about in all their complexity. In this sense, eliminating oppression has change implications not just for the oppressed but also for the person who wishes to be an ally. Liberation, as we shall see, does not mean simply changing the oppressed but also changing the ally and the oppressor.

In this context, Jackins (1997) maintains that any acting out of distress or painful emotion (for example, fear, embarrassment, awkwardness, isolation) by a person who is a member of an oppressor group may be experienced by members of the oppressed group as oppression directed at them, regardless of our intentions. This point is important because often people think of oppression only in terms of extreme forms of mistreatment. Sometimes, however, it is the subtle, indirect forms of mistreatment that are the most difficult for the oppressed person to deal with. In the same way, we tend to think about oppression as something that is consciously or deliberately intended. However, most oppression happens involuntarily and our intentions are not a good guide to whether or not we have acted oppressively in a situation. The fact that we did not mean to hurt someone does not mean we have acted non-oppressively. In discussing racism, Feagin and Sikes (1994) make the point that

> Contrary to a common white view, modern racism does not consist mainly of the isolated acts of scattered white bigots, but rather, has been inescapable in the everyday worlds of African Americans. Almost any encounter with whites, in workplaces, schools, neighbourhoods, and public places, can mean a confrontation with racism.
>
> (p. 4)

In the same vein, Sue (2003) states that it is the more subtle forms of racism, perpetrated by well-intentioned people, that actually do the most harm to people of colour. Weinrach (2002), in discussing anti-Semitism, stresses that it is behaviour rather than the motivation behind it that counts and points to many examples of unaware behaviour that are experienced as oppressive by Jews. Mullaly (2002) makes a distinction between "conscious acts of aggression and/or hatred" (p. 54) and "unconscious acts of aversion and avoidance" (p. 55). He maintains that many, if not most, oppressive acts at the personal level are of the covert, aversive type rather than being overtly and openly aggressive. He sees feelings of hostility, fear, avoidance and superiority being expressed covertly in ordinary, mundane interactions at the level of gestures, speech, tone of voice and body language. For some very oppressed groups this is probably an overstatement but the distinction between overt and covert acts is still an important one. As regards an oppressed person, therefore, the mistreatment is often pervasive and difficult to escape. Dominant or oppressor groups think only in terms of extreme forms of mistreatment and ignore or miss the impact that more subtle forms have on people. One of the challenges we face in overcoming oppression is to become aware of all of the less than obvious ways in which our negative feelings and our behaviour interfere with having a relaxed, human connection with people who are different from us. In order to build solid relationships we need to clean out the unaware oppressiveness that cuts us off from people and makes the relationship unsafe for them.

In particular, as leaders, we need to become aware of the ways in which any negative feelings we have interfere with our ability to build close, solid, aware relationships with, and to think clearly about, people who are different from us. Separately from what we intellectually believe or think about particular groups, we need to look at the feelings we have about and around them that may make it difficult for us to have a relaxed, clear-thinking and deeply connected relationship with them. White people, for example, who are committed to eliminating racism and are active in groups or organizations to bring this about, still need to look at and discharge the racist feelings they still carry in spite of this commitment. Their active commitment does not mean that, at a personal level, they are free of racism. So, as leaders, in terms of our own personal development, we may have quite a lot of work to do to free ourselves from unconscious oppressive feelings, thoughts and behaviour. Doing this work is a key part of leadership development.

Negative messages

What are the effects of the mistreatment in whatever form it takes? Contained in the mistreatment is a set of negative messages that operate on two levels. First, every time the person experiences mistreatment, they are hearing something about themselves personally, as an individual. They hear that there is something wrong with themselves personally – that they are worthless, insignificant, undesirable, second-class, stupid, ugly and so on. Secondly, however, they also hear that there is something wrong with the group they belong to; there is something wrong with their people. The same negative messages they get about themselves are also attached to their whole group. Because the mistreatment is systematic rather than accidental or random, it is likely to be experienced repeatedly in one form or another. People may experience hurtful, abusive or disrespectful treatment on many occasions and in a variety of ways and, with this, the consistent repetition of these messages. Their day-to-day experiences in school, at work, in church, with government agencies or social services, in the mass media, and in the culture generally all tend to reinforce the same messages. The impact of these messages may be moderated to some extent by the level of awareness or critical consciousness around the oppression. Very blatant instances of mistreatment may not be at all confusing to people as incidents of oppression, at least intellectually, although they may still install or reinforce feelings of fear, inadequacy, shame and so on that are difficult to ignore. More subtle instances may leave people confused about what exactly occurred or who was at fault and, at the same time, on a feelings level, reinforce a sense that there is something wrong with themselves. Regardless of the level of awareness or critical consciousness, however, it is difficult to escape these negative messages in an oppressive society, culture or context.

Negative self-image

Over time, these repeated negative messages shape the person's image of themselves personally *and* their image of their group as a whole. The effect operates on both levels. At a personal level, the negative messages now become part of a negative self-image. If someone is told often enough, directly and/or indirectly, that they are inferior then, eventually, they begin to think of themselves (and their people) as inferior. If someone is repeatedly told in different ways that they are ugly, or stupid, or unimportant, it will be difficult to remain detached from and untouched by these messages, particularly when there are few contradictory messages. Gradually, they will distort the way the person actually feels at a personal level and about their own group. If these messages are socially condoned and reinforced through important social and cultural institutions and channels of communication, the impact is even greater.

These same negative feelings, at a personal level, also become attached to people's identity as members of particular groups. In this sense, not only do I feel insignificant as an individual person but I also, and in particular, feel insignificant as an Irish person, or as a woman, or as a working-class person and so on. If enough individuals consistently get similar negative messages, these then can be said to shape the self-image of the group as a whole. The group begins to develop a stereotype of itself based on these messages. As we spend time with the group and get to know them, we see a pattern emerge in the characteristic ways they think and feel about themselves. These negative feelings and thoughts begin to form a recognizable pattern within the group. Many of the stereotypes of particular groups are simply a reflection of these pervasive ways of thinking and feeling that characterize a significant number of individuals in the group. It is not that members of this group are in some way inherently like this by virtue of belonging to the group. It is rather that their feelings and way of thinking have been shaped from the outside by the oppression.

This is not to say that groups internalize only a negative self-image. There will be many positive things about their culture that people will manage to notice and be proud of. There will also be individual differences within the group in terms of the balance of negative and positive images they hold (Moane, 2003). However, within an oppressive system, whatever messages about the positive images that exist, there is a constant struggle with the negative messages surrounding the oppressed group and the effects that these have on people's self-image. We shall see more about this when we look at the issue of identity and liberation in Chapter 10.

Acting out of negative self-image

Finally, as these messages become part of the individual's and group's self-image, this self-image begins to be acted out. Now, not only do the people in the group *feel* inferior, for example, they also *act* inferior. Not only do they feel bad about themselves in whatever way the society projected at them, they also act that way. They may lose confidence in themselves and act in ways that are consistent with the messages they have got. We may see this reflected in their body language, their tone of voice, their eye contact or in the strategies they adopt to deal with the world around them. They may become invisible and anonymous, stop having high expectations for themselves, stop making demands, stop making direct eye contact, become hopeless and give up trying, attempt to pass as members of the dominant group, develop indirect, apparently "devious" or predatory or anti-social ways of achieving their ends, along with many other possible responses.

This, of course, can then seem to be "proof" that the original prejudice was well founded. Social scientists have long recognized this in the phenomenon of "blaming the victim". The acting out of the negative self-image becomes a noticeable pattern in the way that a group behaves and is sometimes identified as part of the culture of that group. As leaders, we need to understand clearly that this is a reflection of the experience of oppression and not some natural or inherent characteristic of those people.

This process was very clearly highlighted for me, a number of years ago, when I answered a knock on my front door one morning. There was a Traveller woman standing there along with a four-year-old little girl, her daughter. (In Ireland, Travellers are an ethnic, historically nomadic group who are highly oppressed.) As soon as I opened the door, the woman said, "I'm not a Traveller, but I'm married to one." This was all she said and one can imagine the unspoken piece, for example, ". . . so don't slam the door in my face" or ". . . so treat me with some respect". This woman had learned to accommodate to the mistreatment of Travellers by slightly distancing herself from them. She was not actually a Traveller herself, only married to one. The effects of the oppression on the mother were pretty clear but what effects must this have had on her daughter who hears her mother make this kind of statement at every door? What questions does this raise for her about her own identity; what messages does it convey? Already, by the age of four, this little one is getting very definite messages about what it means to be a Traveller. Already, by this age, she is getting the message that there is something wrong with being a Traveller; that being a Traveller is not something her people can proudly proclaim. Notice, also that she gets these messages even if I, as an individual settled person, treat her mother with complete respect. The messages have been internalized to one degree or another within the Travelling community and she will pick them up from within her own culture, in this case, through her mother. It only needs a minimum of external mistreatment to keep these messages alive and internalized. In the case of Travellers, of course, as with many other oppressed groups, there is much more than a minimum of such mistreatment.

IMPLICATIONS FOR LEADERS

In workshops with people, I have regularly asked them to make a list of all the groups that they think of as oppressed, marginalized or disadvantaged. A number of things emerge from this exercise. It quickly becomes apparent that this list is very long – there are a lot of oppressed groups. More importantly, it becomes clear that everybody in society is a member of at least one oppressed group. In fact, when people look at this in more detail, it is clear that they are all members of a number of oppressed groups.

This raises some important questions, particularly for leaders. For example, what has been the effect on us of our own experience of oppression? How has this affected how we feel about ourselves and about people who share our identity? In particular, what painful emotion has it left us with that is attached to our identity? How has it affected our relationships with people who share this identity with us? Can we be pleased with and proud of them or are there places where we feel ashamed of them, disappointed in them, dislike of them, rejection of them, anger towards them, isolation from them and so on? How has it affected our relationship with people who are different from us? Are we completely relaxed and at ease with them or are there places where we feel intimidated, inferior, embarrassed, less attractive, insignificant and so on? How has it affected our self-image and self-esteem? How has it affected our confidence and our belief in ourselves? Can we be pleased and proud of ourselves or are there places where we struggle with self-doubt and feelings of inadequacy? How has it affected our sense of our power? How has it affected our ability to take initiative or leadership? Do we feel powerful and comfortable being visible and at ease taking initiative? Overall, how has our experience of oppression affected the various ways we think, feel and act?

There are also some overarching questions that are raised. First, do we know the answers to all these other questions? Do we know what effects our experience has had on us and what "baggage" it has left us with? How aware are we of our own oppression? Secondly, where do we do the work of finding the answers to these questions and healing the effects of our oppression? Where do we work on our own liberation? And, are we actually doing this work on our own oppression and on eliminating this baggage? Or is our focus mostly on other people's oppression? These have implications for the kinds of relationships we build with people. For many people in what are called the "helping" professions, there can be a strong tendency to focus on the other person's oppression exclusively. They can identify the other person as oppressed, needing help, carrying a lot of baggage from the past and so on without any awareness of the baggage they themselves bring into the relationship. If this is the case, the relationship may well be experienced by the other person as unequal, patronizing, disempowering and unsafe. We are preoccupied with their oppression while appearing to be unaware of, or downplaying, the relevance of our own oppression. We are asking them to do something (i.e. work towards their own liberation) that we are not able to model for ourselves. We communicate that the problem is with them rather than with us.

The Aboriginal Australian poet and artist, Lilla Watson, captured this dilemma very sharply when she said: "If you have come to help me, you are wasting your time. But, if you have come because your liberation is bound up with mine, then let us work together." As leaders, we have to be actively involved in the process of our own liberation in order to be able to be an effective resource for other people. I don't think we can fully understand any other person's oppression unless we are doing this work on ourselves and I don't think we, as leaders, will be able to stay thinking clearly about other people unless we are doing this work. Our own internalized oppression will leave us confused in important ways unless we do this work.

This, however, is only part of the story. In workshops, I have also asked people to make a list of all the oppressor or dominant groups they can think of in society. This can be a more difficult exercise for people with significant groups surprisingly being overlooked sometimes. Gradually, however, they do produce another long list. As they do, it becomes apparent again that they are all members of at least one of these oppressor groups. In fact, it is probably the case that everybody is a member of a number of oppressor as well as oppressed groups. They may be targeted with oppression under one identity and agents of oppression under another. Here again, there is a similar set of questions facing us about the effects of our experience either currently or in the past.

How has our experience as a member of an oppressor or dominant group affected how we feel about ourselves? In particular, what painful emotions such as guilt, fear, shame has it left us with? How has it affected our relationships with people who are similar to us and people who are different from us? Where do we struggle with feelings of prejudice, rejection, isolation, hatred, awkwardness, shame, superiority and so on? How has it affected our confidence and our belief in ourselves? Where do we assume our thinking or ideas are better than other people's? Where does arrogance or superiority creep into our self-image? How has it affected our sense of power and our ability to take initiative and leadership? In what ways do we assume leadership, take charge of situations, impose our views and so on? How comfortable are we following other people's lead? Overall, how has this experience of dominance or privilege affected the various ways we think, feel and act?

In general, there is much less awareness about these effects than there is about the effects of being oppressed. People tend to be that bit more aware of their oppressed identities than they are of their oppressor identities. From the point of view of leadership, however, we need to know how these experiences have interfered with our ability to build solid, equal, respectful, supportive relationships that are experienced as empowering and liberating. While it is often the case that members of the helping professions have not done enough work on their own liberation from oppression, it is even more commonly the case that they have done little to become aware of, and free themselves from, oppressive attitudes and feelings. Because we do not intend to be oppressive and because we are working closely with members of an oppressed group, we can fool ourselves into believing that we do not act oppressively in the relationship.

Freire (1972) drew attention to this difficulty in the relationship between oppressors and oppressed:

> It happens, however, that as they cease to be exploiters or indifferent spectators or simply the heirs of exploitation and move to the side of the exploited they almost always bring with them the marks of their origin: their prejudices and their deformations, which include a lack of confidence in the people's ability to think, to want, and to know. Accordingly, these adherents to the people's cause constantly run the risk of falling into a type of generosity as harmful as that of the oppressors.
>
> (p. 36)

He believed that while they might want to eliminate the injustice, their own conditioning would lead them to believe that they must be in charge of this process. It would be difficult for them to trust the oppressed in spite of any intention to do so. And yet, trusting the oppressed is absolutely essential if change is to take place. This might explain a relatively common occurrence whereby the leadership of various advocacy and social change organizations remains in the hands of members of dominant groups rather than of the oppressed groups. It seems to be the case that members of oppressor groups have difficulty getting behind the leadership of members of oppressed groups and are constantly pulled to usurp that leadership themselves, however unintentionally and however much in good faith they do it.

INTERNALIZED OPPRESSION

As the above dynamic illustrates, there is a way in which the external oppression experienced by groups becomes internalized over time. The patterns of this *internalized oppression* give us many clues to how we can be allies for groups that are marginalized, disadvantaged or oppressed in one way or another and how we can play an effective and liberating role as leaders. Understanding the concept of internalized oppression is essential for effective leadership. What began as an external mistreatment has been internalized, over time, by the person and the group. In one sense, although it oversimplifies the process, it can be said that the group now mistreats itself and holds itself in check. It is no longer the outside barriers alone that hold it back, so much as the voice in the person's own head that says, "I have no right to . . .", or "I'm not good enough . . .". If not the voice in the person's own head, it will be the voices of other members of that person's group saying, "Who does she think she is?" or "Who asked him to do anything?" As we saw earlier, we sometimes describe this as people "oppressing themselves" although this is not really an accurate description of the process. The oppression originates outside the person and the group and it is more accurate to call this *internalized oppression*.

A key part of effective social change, as well as a key role of leadership, is assisting people to counteract their internalized oppression. It is often not clearly understood that most of the damage done by oppression is done by its internalized forms. If people did not internalize the oppression, that oppression could not be maintained for very long. Memmi (1968) talks about the "spiritual ruin" (p. 20) wherein the oppressed consent to their own abasement. The process described here is one of the reasons why groups that have themselves experienced oppression can, in turn, when they manage to get power, become almost as oppressive as the groups they have replaced. Internalized oppression pulls people to seek relief from the oppression by switching roles and playing an oppressor role in relation to some other group. Many social change movements have been unsuccessful, ultimately because they viewed change as being, solely, about the removal of the external barriers or oppression. In the process they neglected to notice or to tackle the internalized oppression that locked people into the oppressed position. We can see this happen in the case of some national liberation movements, where, following a revolution, the formerly oppressed, but now powerful, group proceeded to replicate the oppressiveness of the old regime. The problem was that while they had succeeded in removing the external forms of oppression that they faced, they left their own internalized oppression largely untouched. This then became acted out once they were in power. Such a preoccupation with external forms of oppression, while ignoring or minimizing the internalized oppression, has been a characteristic of various social change movements. In fact, as we shall see, the liberation process is not actually complete until *both* the external oppression and its internalized forms have been eliminated.

Confusion around the nature of liberation emerges in discussions of the issue of power and where power resides in an oppressive society. Gorz (1982) takes a very clear position on this. For Gorz, the key thing we need to understand is that in any large-scale bureaucracy or military machine, *no one holds power*. Instead, what we find are people, simply as agents of the system, obeying the logic of that system. Essentially, power resides in the system, not in the office holders. As long as the oppression exists, it does not matter who holds the positions of power. For this reason, it is also an illusion to believe that liberation consists of taking over the machinery of domination. All that would be achieved would be to replace one oppressive group with another. Liberation means changing the system and the relationships and not just changing the actors.

The model of leadership described in the early part of this book emphasizes the building of relationships, listening closely and thinking clearly about people. Because of the pervasiveness of oppression and internalized oppression in people's lives, we will not be effective in leadership and will not be able to hold out a liberating vision unless we have a deep awareness of these dynamics and a commitment in practice to assisting people to overcome their destructive effects.

CIRCLES OF OPPRESSION

Various models have been proposed to illustrate how oppression is installed and kept in place (Chafe, 1977; Harro, 2000a; Moane, 1999, 2003; Mullaly, 2002; Ruth, 1988, 2005; Schwalbe *et al.*, 2000; Watts, Griffith and Abdul-Adil, 1999; Young, 1990). Mullaly (2002), for example, sees the process as operating on a personal, cultural and structural level and the effects at all of these levels have to be addressed. At a personal or individual level, oppression consists of negative thoughts, attitudes and behaviour towards particular subordinate groups. At a cultural level, it consists of the values, norms, assumptions, and particular ways of thinking and seeing and acting that are reflected in history, literature, the mass media, stories, movies, humour, stereotypes and popular culture and that together operate to maintain a belief in the superiority of one culture over another. Mullaly sees it as the cement that legitimizes and holds personal and structural oppression in place. At a structural or institutional level, oppression consists of social institutions, laws, policies, social processes and practices, economic and political systems that operate in favour of the dominant group. In an oppressive system, these levels overlap and reinforce one another and each has to be transformed as part of the process of liberation. Since change ultimately requires individual initiative as one step in the liberation process and since, as we have seen, leadership operates to a large extent through individual action, an important focus of the present book is on the personal effects of oppression and the way in which personal liberation is central to the elimination of cultural and structural oppression. (This, of course, is not to downplay the importance of organization and collective action but merely to recognize that these require individual initiative and leadership to make them happen.)

A particularly useful model here is to think in terms of four "circles of oppression" that surround the individual. (This is adapted from the four "circles of control" described by Chafe (1977) in his discussion of racism and sexism.) These are the mechanisms that ensure people accept their victim status and, in a sense, "agree" to be oppressed. The outermost circle of oppression is *physical oppression*. At the base of many oppressions lies the use of physical violence or the threat of it to ensure cooperation from the oppressed. People are coerced, intimidated, imprisoned, beaten or otherwise physically forced to endure the oppression. At the extreme, it involves the threat of death or the actual killing of people. Physical oppression on its own, however, is not particularly effective or efficient as a means of domination. Where possible, people will resist it either directly or indirectly. It also requires ongoing repetition, reinforcement, vigilance and energy from the oppressor to ensure that it continues to have an effect. Often, it requires a very large army of oppressors to ensure there is compliance. Because of this, therefore, physical oppression tends to operate in conjunction with other mechanisms.

In general, this form of oppression is reinforced by *economic oppression* where members of oppressed groups are rendered powerless by keeping them in the low-paid, low-status jobs or in unemployment and poverty. They may find themselves, individually and collectively, with little power or few resources and subject to ongoing discrimination. They may also be denied access, either deliberately and systematically or indirectly by dint of circumstances, to education or training that would enable them to break out of this economic oppression. The day-to-day demands of survival, of putting food on the table, of providing the basic necessities for living become the major focus of people's lives. Their energy goes into managing their debt. In extreme circumstances, just as people manage to get their head above water and clear one piece of debt, another financial crisis comes crashing down on them. The cycle of poverty makes it difficult for people to have the additional energy for mobilizing and organizing for change. Even in the less extreme economic circumstances, the system will tend to preoccupy people with worries and concerns about financial security and comfort. They will be encouraged to put their energy into trying to climb the ladder out of the oppression rather than working to change the system. The dominant economic system today tends to institutionalize greed as a preoccupying value and distracts people with promises of wealth, comfort and financial security that are ultimately available only to a minority. The effect is to leave economic oppression intact.

Economic oppression, reinforced occasionally by physical oppression, is a powerful way of ensuring people stay oppressed. Having said that, there is a long history of individuals and groups who rose above this oppression, who were able to see clearly how the system operated and who organized and resisted in whatever ways they could. There is a third mechanism of oppression that operates to obscure the reality of the world around us and make it less likely that people will resist. This is *psychological oppression*. Underlying the economic oppression is psychological oppression where the dominant group, through its control of education, religion, science, the mental health system, the mass media and so on, comes to define what is "natural" or "normal" for members of the oppressed group and to set limits on what the oppressed group can legitimately and realistically aspire to. Psychology and other social and natural sciences, for example, have been used to justify and legitimize the oppression of many groups. The supposedly impartial research and findings from these areas have been taken at various times to prove the inherent inferiority of oppressed groups or the inevitability and legitimacy of the inequalities they faced. Anyone who then questions the status quo has to go against the weight of this authority and challenge what everyone else seems to take for granted. Watts, Williams and Jagers (2003) see this kind of "ideological violence" as at the core of all oppression. Members of the oppressed group are systematically exposed to prejudices, stereotypes, myths and misinformation about what they are supposed to be like. There is little awareness around them of the reality they face. It requires great insight, courage and perseverance to question and resist. In certain cases, the mental health system has been used as a weapon against dissidents who were too controversial or outspoken in their opposition to the system. The dissatisfaction with the system was interpreted as a symptom of mental illness and individuals found themselves being drugged or incarcerated as a result.

The key to the maintenance of oppression, however, is the fourth mechanism, which we can call *internalized oppression*. This is where people come to believe in their own inferiority and their powerlessness to change things. They buy into the kinds of stereotypes that are directed at them. The result is that the person essentially "agrees" to be oppressed. This means that members of the oppressed group come to "police" themselves and the dominant group can take a more subtle and less visible role for themselves. The oppressed person now blames themselves for their disadvantaged status. The problem is a personal failing rather than a systematically maintained inequality. The combination of economic, psychological and internalized oppression, with or without active violence, is a powerful means of maintaining oppression. Together, they render the oppression obscure and confusing and make it difficult to name what is happening or organize to change it. Understanding what internalized oppression does to people is central to being able to think clearly and lead effectively and is central to the process of liberation. For this reason, it will be explored in much more detail in the following chapter. Before doing that, however, there are other descriptions of the process of oppression that underline many of the mechanisms described here.

MECHANISMS OF DOMINATION

A somewhat similar description to the four circles of oppression, but, in this case, highlighting six mechanisms of domination has been presented by Moane (1994, 1999, 2003) in her discussion of colonial oppression. Drawing on feminist perspectives she begins with *violence* or *physical coercion* and includes in this the use of military and police violence, battery, rape, incest and sexual harassment, as well as the promotion of drugs and the creation of drug dependency. We could add to this the use of alcohol as a specific drug to keep people powerless and dependent. This has played a particularly devastating role in the context of various indigenous peoples, for example. Next, under *economic exploitation*, she includes the seizure of land and goods, destruction and appropriation of industries, trade limitations, vertical and horizontal segregation, biases in evaluation and exploitation of unpaid labour in the home and community. She goes on to note that *sexual exploitation* through rape, prostitution and regulation of birth control has been a feature of patriarchy but has tended to be neglected in discussions of colonialism. A fourth mechanism of domination is *exclusion from power*, particularly political power. This is reinforced by the *control of ideology and culture*, where the dominant groups, through their control of education, religion, language and other symbolic aspects of life, are able to suppress history and put forward negative stereotypes of the inferiority of the colonized. Lastly, through *fragmentation*, the colonized are kept divided from one another by various means, such as promoting a select few of the subordinate group, that create competition and envy. Underpinning the effectiveness of these mechanisms of domination, however, is the process of internalized oppression. The internalization of the oppression allows these mechanisms to go unchallenged, renders challenges, when they do come, ineffective and keeps oppressed groups from being able to mobilize their full power effectively against the oppression. We shall return to some of the processes described here when we look at the specific characteristics of internalized oppression in the next chapter.

GENERIC PROCESSES

Schwalbe *et al.* (2000) describe the process of oppression in terms of four generic processes that operate to reproduce inequality. "Othering" (p. 423) refers to the process by which a dominant group defines an inferior group. It can take three forms: oppressive, implicit and defensive. Oppressive othering occurs when the dominant group defines another group as morally and/or intellectually inferior. In doing this it defines differences as deficits. Implicit othering manufactures the impression that members of the dominant group are powerful, superior and worthy, regardless of reality. These impressions help to create feelings of trust, awe or fear that, in turn, legitimate the inequality and make people less likely to resist. Defensive othering occurs where members of oppressed groups differentiate themselves from other members of their group in an attempt to avoid the stigma or worst excesses of the oppression.

"Subordinate adaptation" (p. 426), the second generic process, refers to the strategies people adopt in order to cope with the oppression that ultimately have the effect of reproducing that oppression. Not all forms of these adaptations might lead to a reproduction of inequality but many do. These include giving up power in return for patronage (which, while benefiting the individual in the short term, disadvantages the group in the longer term), forming alternative subcultures that give people status or success not available in the dominant culture (for example, the drug trade), "hustling", which involves some form of illegal or dishonest activity usually directed at exploiting other disadvantaged people, and individual "dropping out", which involves dropping out of school or of political involvement.

"Boundary maintenance" (p. 429) operates to limit the access of oppressed people to important or valuable resources. Most of this is accomplished institutionally through families and schools where significant processes of socialization take place and where people get access to "cultural capital" (p. 431). In addition, boundary maintenance is achieved through the restriction of access to key influence networks. In extreme situations, the dominant group will use violence or the threat of it to maintain the boundaries and keep the oppressed out.

The final generic process is "emotion management" (p. 434). This becomes a key task in maintaining a system of inequality. Feelings of superiority or inferiority, of fear, of complacency or resignation, of anger or resentment and so on must all be regulated in order to maintain the oppressive system. This is achieved in a number of ways according to Schwalbe *et al.* (2000). Discourse, the things that can be talked about and how they can be talked about, is carefully regulated. Emotional subjectivity is conditioned so that people learn not to feel, or give vent to, feelings of anger or empathy, for example, that might lead them to step out of the oppressor or victim role or question the oppressive system. Lastly, mass events are orchestrated or "scripted" (p. 438) to generate the kinds of feelings that will sustain the oppressive system.

SUMMARY

In this chapter, we have seen how the process of oppression operates and some of its effects on people, individually and collectively. Understanding these dynamics is necessary for us, as leaders, in making sense of much of what we encounter in our dealings with people and groups. In particular, it gives us a way of thinking about what underpins many of the difficulties and struggles in the relationships between people. It allows us to separate what are the effects of oppression from what is true of people naturally or inherently as humans. With this understanding we are able to think more clearly about the sources of difficulties and are less likely to attribute them to simple maliciousness or bloody-mindedness. Understanding these dynamics also allows us to think about the kinds of relationships we develop with other people and about the work we need to do on ourselves in order to make those relationships truly liberating.

Having seen how oppression acts to distort the way people behave, we now need to look in more detail at what happens specifically when oppression becomes internalized. Having a clear insight into the nature of internalized oppression gives us very practical ways of thinking about how to be a resource for the people around us. With a clear model of the dynamics of both oppression and internalized oppression, we can then, in later chapters, look at the process of liberation and its implications for leadership.

REFLECTION

Oppressed identities

1   List the main oppressed groups to which you belong.
2   Which of these do you think has had the most impact on how you are as a person or on your ability to take leadership?
3   How have you personally, or your people, experienced oppression within these groups?
4   In relation to each of your oppressed identities, how have these experiences of oppression left you feeling about yourself, your own people and people from the oppressor group?
5   In relation to each of your oppressed identities, what particular aspects of your humanity have you and your people managed to hang on to in spite of any oppression?
6   What steps do you need to take to heal the hurts and undo the damage associated with your oppressed identities?

Oppressor identities

Oppressor identities can sometimes be difficult to explore because of feelings of guilt, defensiveness, pretence or lack of safety. If you were to be completely honest *with yourself*, however, what would your responses be to the following items?

7   List the main oppressor, dominant or privileged groups to which you belong.
8   Which of your oppressor identities are likely to have the most impact on the relationships you want to build or maintain or the leadership you want to take?
9   In relation to each of your oppressor identities, how have your experiences of power or privilege left you feeling about yourself as a member of this group, your own people and people from particular oppressed groups?
10   In relation to each of your oppressor identities, in what ways has your experience of power or privilege cut you off from close relationships with members of the oppressed group?

11 In relation to each of your oppressor identities, what particular aspects of your humanity have you and your people managed to hang on to in spite of the messages and conditioning you received?
12 What steps do you need to take to heal the hurts and undo the damage associated with your oppressor identities?

8 Internalized oppression

INTRODUCTION

In Chapter 7 we looked at the dynamics of oppression and how the end point of the process results in people internalizing their oppression. More than any other factor, it is internalized oppression that holds external oppression in place. If we did not internalize oppression we would not get confused about our inherent nature as humans and the reality of the world around us. We would see clearly how the oppressive system around us actually operated and what was needed to end the mistreatment. Our natural outrage would lead us to refuse to accept anything that was not completely just and respectful. We would organize, protest and take the necessary steps to eliminate the oppression from our lives. In practice, however, over time, the external difficulties or oppressions that people face do become internalized and leave people confused and disempowered. They come to have a variety of distorting effects on the ways people feel, think and behave. This internalized oppression then gets in the way of people solving the problems facing them externally. If the latter are to be dealt with effectively, it will be necessary to *contradict* or interrupt the internalized oppression in ways that remind people of their goodness, their worth and their power. In this chapter, we shall look at the process of internalized oppression and how it can be contradicted in greater detail and examine its implications for the role of leadership. As we shall see, the ability to apply a clear understanding of this dynamic is a central tool in the repertoire of any effective leader.

LEADERSHIP AND INTERNALIZED OPPRESSION

From a leadership perspective, there are a number of elements involved in this process. The first is simply spotting the particular ways in which the oppression has been internalized by a group. As we spend time with people and listen to them we can notice the things that are special and unique about them. We can notice the particular ways that their inherent humanity expresses itself. We can notice all those aspects of their culture that are positive, pro-human, creative or uplifting. We can also notice, however, elements that are destructive of the people, certain negative patterns or rigidities in the way they think, act or feel. This is where the oppression has been internalized. Sometimes these are revealed directly in things people say to us. They may tell us directly that they are worthless or stupid, for example. At other times, they are revealed indirectly in ways people act, or in the ways they look or sound. They may have difficulty making eye contact with us. They may go quiet and become invisible in certain situations. Their body language and tone of voice may convey an air of despondency or hopelessness. The important point here is that these are not simply individual, idiosyncratic personality character-istics. We see them reflected across the group as a whole. This is not to say that everyone in the group will exhibit exactly the same traits but that, over time, we will see a general pattern or tendency for people within and across the group to feel, think or react in certain predictable ways. For example, when people describe the negative characteristics of particular nationalities, they are often, in fact, referring to precisely these rigid patterns of internalized oppression. When we talk about the levels of aggression in some cultures, or the levels of alcohol or drug abuse, or the sense of inferiority that people demonstrate or the destructive characteristics of their relationships, we are often describing their patterns of internalized oppression.

While the first element is to spot or name the patterns, the second element in this process is holding out contradictions to these patterns. A contradiction can be described as anything that reminds people of, or connects them to, what is true of them inherently, separately from their internalized oppression. It is an alternative picture of reality to that which they have internalized within the oppression. This can include an alternative picture of the reality of what that person or other people are truly like when not acting out their internalized oppression, or the reality of what the world around them is like separately from the oppressive systems that distort relationships and inflict hurt and pain. Making this distinction between true reality, separate from the effects of oppression, and what Jackins (1995a) calls pseudo-reality is extremely important. Oppression operates by substituting a distorted pseudo-reality for an accurate picture of the person, the people and the world. A key part of the process of liberation is, on the one hand, the realiz-ation that what was assumed to be real and unalterable is, in fact, merely a product of oppression and false consciousness and, on the other hand, the decision to live and act on the basis of what we know to be true of the world inherently and in reality.

I have referred on a number of occasions to the notion of inherent human characteristics or inherent humanity. Underlying this model is a set of assumptions about human nature. One of these is the assumption that, *by nature*, human beings are inherently good, intelligent, worthwhile, creative and so on. These qualities are universal and permanent. We all have them by virtue of being human. We are conceived with them and, for the most part, come into the world with our connection to these qualities intact. Our access to these qualities and our sense of connection to them, however, can be disrupted by the experience of hurt and distress. In one sense, oppression threatens us physically; it threatens our connection to life. It also threatens our connection to these inherent qualities. Through mistreatment, we lose a sense of our goodness, our intelligence, our worth, our creativity and many of the other positive human characteristics that we have by virtue of being human. In this sense, people are not inherently evil or bad. They are not inherently stupid. The places where we see people acting in ways that are less than human are generally the results of distress, and of damaging mistreatment and oppression. When we internalize an oppression, we come to confuse the damage we have suffered with our inherent, positive human nature. Liberation involves undoing this confusion and reconnecting with our true inherent nature.

Leadership has a central role to play in spotting and contradicting this internalized oppression. Effective leaders are able to see the places where those around them, individually and collectively, struggle with self-doubt, fear, confusion, self-destruction or other rigid forms of thinking, feeling and acting. They are also able to hold out a contradiction to these rigid patterns. As a simple illustration of this, when Martin Luther King, for example, spoke of having a dream, he offered his listeners a major contradiction to their internalized hopelessness.

The other important element in this process is that leaders themselves model what it means to act outside internalized oppression. This, in itself, is also a huge contradiction. What makes particular leaders attractive, inspiring and effective is that they are able to model a different way of thinking or feeling or acting. They model confidence, vision, courage, hope, love, decisiveness and so forth and, in the process, other people get to see what it looks like to act outside internalized oppression. They hold out a bigger picture and do not seem to get stuck in the ways that trip up those around them. This type of modelling is a key function of leadership as we saw in Chapter 2.

PATTERNS OF INTERNALIZED OPPRESSION

Patterns of internalized oppression show up in a variety of ways. While the details will vary from one oppressed group to another, the broad process is very similar across these groups as has been demonstrated by Adam (1978b), for example. The following sections highlight some of the key forms of internalized oppression along with a discussion of the role that leadership can play in being a resource for people around this.

Low self-esteem

Internalized oppression causes people to feel bad about themselves and other members of their group (Ruth 1988, 1997). It can take various forms. They may lose sight of their own worth or their goodness. They may come to feel deeply ashamed of their identity and have difficulty taking pride in themselves or their people. Sometimes this shame may lead them to deny their identity or to try to pass as members of the oppressor group. They may feel physically ugly and unattractive. They may devalue their thinking and intelligence as we shall see in more detail further on. They may constantly compare themselves or their people unfavourably with the dominant group. They may operate with a deep sense of insignificance and low expectations about how other people will treat them. They may act apologetically, viewing themselves as a bother or burden for others, grateful for whatever time or attention the dominant group chooses to provide. They may have difficulty thinking "big" or having high expectations of what they can achieve. Varas-Diaz and Serrano-Garcia (2003), for example, show how the effects of low self-esteem operate in the context of Puerto Rico as a colonized country.

A variation on this is the way people accept and even reinforce, through language, humour and other behaviour, many of the stereotypes of them created by the dominant group and are uncomfortable with anything that differs too much from these. Women, for example, may buy into stereotypes of being female that link their self-esteem to being physically attractive to men. Irish people may reinforce a stereotype of themselves that makes heavy drinking something to be admired. Even seemingly positive and valuable attributes of a people or culture, such as warm hospitality, may have some of their roots in an exaggerated admiration of the dominant group or a low estimation of their own. The defining characteristics are the relative rigidity of the behaviour or attitude and the implied attitude towards self. Free of internalized oppression, people's behaviour would be flexible and appropriate to the circumstances and their self-concept would be rooted in a connection to their inherent nature as humans.

Low self-esteem can show up in a variety of ways. In some cases, people will tell us directly that they are no good, worthless or unimportant. If we listen carefully, we will hear them put themselves down, demean themselves, play down their talents or achievements. If we do not hear them being self-critical or self-effacing, we will notice them being critical of other members of their group. They will feel ashamed of, or have difficulty taking complete pride in, others of their people who are very visible or successful or who act in ways that are non-traditional or outside their own self-stereotype. In Ireland, this is described as "begrudgery" and people talk about it being a "nation of knockers" where anyone who is successful gets knocked or criticized. Patterns such as this are often confused with some kind of collective, national personality. Yet this begrudging attitude has nothing inherently to do with being Irish. It is, in fact, a feature of many oppressed and post-colonial groups. We see something very similar to it in the description of women as "bitchy". This also has nothing inherently to do with being female and everything to do with being oppressed. This pattern of behaviour in groups is sometimes recognized under the heading of "horizontal violence".

In other cases, these kinds of patterns will show up indirectly in the ways people look or sound. We may spot the lack of belief in themselves in people's postures or tone of voice. We may see it in the difficulty they have in making relaxed eye contact with us. With some groups, we may notice that, on their own, they are full of life, loud and exuberant. When they are part of a wider, more diverse group (particularly when it includes members of dominant or oppressor groups) we may notice that they go quiet, become invisible and melt into the background as the internalized low self-esteem takes hold. We may see it in the throw-away remarks people make about themselves or their people or the things about their culture that they choose to highlight to outsiders. I once visited a small country to conduct a series of leadership seminars. For the first three days, each new person that I was introduced to enquired if I had got used to the potholes in their roads. The first time it happened it was simply a topic of conversation. By the fifth or sixth time, it was clearly part of a pattern and an attempt by people to show me that they themselves were aware of the shortcomings of their nation.

On one occasion, when leading a workshop for a large group of women, I saw another example of how these kinds of feelings can show up indirectly. I was the only male there. The room was quite crowded and, during a break, I had to weave my way through small clusters of women standing round having coffee. As I did so, I heard a voice in the background saying, "God preserve us from women!" A number of the women who heard this laughed. Most either ignored it or attached no significance to it. But I was asking myself why anyone would say such a thing about their own kind. How bad would a person have to be feeling to make a statement like that about their own people? Apparently, one of the women had noticed that the other women were not moving out of my way and clearing a path for me as I made my way across the room. In her embarrassment she then made this remark. From inside this group, no one seemed to think it strange. However, from the outside, it jarred. It told me something about how this group felt about themselves as women.

This last example illustrates another aspect of this dynamic. If most people in a group have internalized the same feelings then these feelings come to look normal. If everyone feels inferior, for example, then feeling inferior does not seem strange. If these are feelings that someone has grown up with and around, then they may not even be noticed. To someone from outside the group, however, who has not internalized exactly the same feelings of inferiority, they are very noticeable. This person may be struck by how bad people feel about themselves even though no one from the group seems to be aware of it. It is in this respect that outsiders can play a key role as allies to an oppressed group. Their ability to spot these patterns places them in a very useful position to offer people a contradiction from the outside.

Being from the outside, however, is no guarantee that we will be a useful resource in this regard. To a large extent, spotting and contradicting the patterns of internalized oppression in other people depends on the extent to which we have spotted and contradicted our own. If we are not challenging our own internalized oppression, it is going to be difficult to notice and contradict someone else's and we may well have the effect of reinforcing the other oppression. We may end up getting confused between the people as they really are inherently and what they have internalized as a result of the difficulties they face in their lives. We may see the survival patterns that have developed in the culture and think that this is what these people are like independently of their oppression. This emphasizes the point that was made in the last chapter about the need for allies to be pursuing their own liberation as part of the process of working with other oppressed groups. It is particularly important for anyone in a leadership role if they are to be able to think clearly about the people with whom they are collaborating.

Contradicting low self-esteem means holding out an alternative perspective that reminds people of their true nature and worth. As leaders, to do this effectively, we need to be engaged in the same process of contradicting our own lack of self-esteem wherever it shows itself. We need to notice where we feel bad about ourselves or our people or where we do not treat ourselves well and we need to *decide* to go against this. At a personal level, in terms of our own identity, this means *deciding* to treat ourselves with great respect. It means looking after our own needs – exercise, good diet, rest, relaxation, fun. It means *deciding* to be pleased with ourselves, *deciding* to give up rehearsing or dramatising negative things about ourselves or our group and *deciding* to focus on what we are doing well rather than on where we fall short. It means modelling true pride in our identity. Jackins (2001) makes the point that one of the effects of oppression is to leave us chronically feeling bad about ourselves and that this requires a decision not to act on or collude with this feeling. It is an effect of oppression rather than a reflection of our true nature.

In terms of leading or being allies to others, we can contradict low self-esteem in many ways. We can listen respectfully to people and communicate empathy. We can find ways to remind people how well they are doing and support them to think well about themselves and their needs. We can believe in them and have high expectations of them. Essentially, it means being pleased with them in all the places where they are less than pleased with themselves and encouraging them to take pride in their identity. Thus, whenever they look at us, we do not seem to be disappointed with them or to have given up on them. This is not something that can be faked. It means we have to get close enough to them to be able to see and be touched by those things that are special about them, which they and others overlook or denigrate.

Some of the ways we can contradict the acceptance of stereotypes involve finding means by which we can remind people of their true nature and qualities, interrupting stereotyping when it occurs, using language that is respectful and affirming and encouraging people to take pride in themselves and their group. The idea of making the effort to get the relationship right like this is sometimes resisted by people in a tone of weariness or frustration associated with the phrase "political correctness gone mad". They get exercised about the demands or apparent restrictions imposed by having to be thoughtful about how they relate to other people, particularly around the use of language. It is as though this were in any way comparable to the effects of the pervasive, insidious and unending communication of disrespect. The fact is that building relationships of support and collaboration with oppressed groups will require work and effort from members of dominant groups. That work, however, will be well rewarded in terms of enriched relationships, enhanced awareness and greater effectiveness.

Many of these contradictions will take place in the context of building close relationships with people. Simply getting close, in itself, is often a major contradiction. As we get near to them we can see more clearly what is precious about them and also where they get stuck. We also allow ourselves to be touched by them and by all that is special about their people. And we get to reflect this back to them directly and indirectly in many different ways. They can see it reflected in the respectful tone of voice we use, in our delight in them, in the importance we attach to their thinking, in our affirmations of what is special about them, in the amount or quality of the time we spend with them, in the importance we attach to, and the committed part we play in, their liberation struggle and so on.

Powerlessness and hopelessness

Over and above low self-esteem people also internalize the belief that they are, individually and collectively, powerless to bring about change and that it is hopeless even to try. When we try to mobilize people or organize them to bring about change, they may tell us that we are wasting our time. They are only a small group with few resources and no one is likely to listen to them. They may remind us of previous attempts to change things and how they failed to make any difference. If we listen carefully we will hear the powerlessness being expressed and, often, closely on its heels will come the hopelessness. "We tried to do something about this a few years ago and nothing came of it. What's the point in trying again? Nothing will ever change around here." Sometimes, people will tell us directly that they are powerless and that it is hopeless to try. In many cases, we will also see these feelings come out indirectly. We will see them in the dejected postures and dispirited tones of voice. We will see them in the lack of energy for taking action and the reluctance to get involved. We will see them in the preoccupation with the obstacles and an inability to think about the ways around the obstacles. Schools and community groups regularly complain about the difficulty in getting people to attend meetings. The same old faces show up each time, usually a small minority at that, and often, in the case of schools for example, the people they would most like to see at the meetings never come. In advance of the meetings, many people may promise to attend, but on the night, a handful of people turn up. Part of the problem here may be due to people's dread of meetings but it is also a reflection of people's hopelessness about being able to bring about change.

For some groups, colonized peoples for example, their history may largely be a history of defeat. There may be many instances of failed attempts at change or liberation to the point where, within the culture, people come to assume their efforts will fail. People stop expecting big things to happen in their lives. Individuals have difficulty seeing how they personally could make any difference. They become cynical about, or dismissive of, attempts to radically change the *status quo*. In a similar way, as with low self-esteem, if most people in the group are feeling hopeless, then hopelessness looks normal. It becomes difficult to see how things could be any different. Hopelessness becomes part of the culture and that culture then operates to suppress hope and to discourage power. Lerner (1991) makes the point that objectively, in many situations, people do face some degree of powerlessness. They may actually have fewer resources or less power than those they oppose. What he points out, however, is that, over and above this layer of objective powerlessness, people themselves add an additional layer of what he calls surplus powerlessness that locks them into being hopeless and taking no action. This surplus powerlessness is not real. It is an emotional reaction to their circumstances rather than an objective assessment of their situation. It is an emotional distress that follows directly from the experience of oppression.

The challenge facing leaders is first to notice how and where this surplus powerlessness and hopelessness takes hold of people, to notice the characteristic ways in which they sink into depression, give up or accept their victim status. The second challenge is to contradict it. Again, there are several different ways this can be done depending on the nature of the circumstances and the relationship. Contradicting these patterns often involves listening closely to people. This is a particular kind of listening where we acknowledge the struggle they face without agreeing that it is hopeless, where we show that we understand *and* that we believe in their ability to change things. I sometimes characterize this by saying that whenever they look at us, we do not ever look as depressed as they feel! Sometimes, knowing that we understand how hard it is and that we still believe in them can give someone the courage and the energy to keep going. We can also help people to organize themselves, we can hold out hope and encouragement in the places where they feel powerless and hopeless, we can help them to reconnect with a vision for themselves, encouraging them to set goals, to make decisions and to take action. We can set it up so they get to experience small wins or early successes. As leaders or allies, our job is not to agree that things are hopeless. Our job is to model hope and power and much of the contradiction is in this modelling.

There is one particular way that this aspect of internalized oppression shows up that is worth highlighting. In this case it is characterized by constant complaining but making no attempt to do anything constructive about the complaints. A typical example of this is a conversation between a group of people that begins with someone stating "I'll tell you what's wrong this organization." This person then goes on to list out their complaints and finishes by saying, "and I'll tell you this, nothing will ever change around here until we get rid of so-and-so". At this point, the next person joins in and says, "I'll tell you another thing that's wrong here" and they finish by saying "and it's not enough to get rid of so-and-so, we have to get rid of all of the people at the top". Sometimes the focus of the criticism is the leader, sometimes it is other people who are visible in some way. This complaining is contagious. People listening get sucked in and before long everyone is voicing their pet gripes and whom they see is to blame. On the surface, this looks like a group of people naming the problems and discussing remedies. If, however, we look at how people feel at the end of such a conversation we can see that it is actually something different. Does this conversation stimulate people's creativity about how to deal with the problems? Rarely. Does it leave people full of energy and mobilized to take some active and constructive steps? Rarely. In reality, this conversation consists of a dramatizing or acting out of people's hopelessness in the guise of a rational discussion of problems facing them. It generally leaves people feeling drained and even more discouraged than before.

Occasionally, the flow of this conversation gets interrupted spontaneously. One of the later speakers breaks the pattern and the mood of the discussion, for example, by saying "I understand what you are all getting at, but I came in here yesterday and so-and-so complimented me on the work I was doing." This person starts to recount instances that give hope and then others join in with their examples. Suddenly, the tone of the conversation changes, it becomes lighter, people's energy begins to increase and the hopelessness has been contradicted. We have to find ways like this to interrupt and contradict the patterns of powerlessness and hopelessness. Dramatizing or rehearsing them at one another can be hugely destructive and rarely leads to useful action. They can also feed into a pattern of negativity and destructive gossip that makes a group much less safe for people to think clearly and rationally or to take proactive steps to bring about change.

Just as we saw earlier, being able to spot these patterns of powerlessness and hopelessness from outside the group and being able to interrupt and contradict them is much easier if we are actively tackling these same patterns within our own oppression. If I am in some way colluding with patterns of hopelessness or powerlessness within my own culture, it will be difficult to notice where this other group is getting stuck. Their hopelessness will resemble my own and my hopelessness will agree with theirs. Or, if I am struggling with feelings of hopelessness in my own life, I may try to motivate and mobilize others by appealing to their despair rather than offering them hope. "If we don't do something, all will be lost." I once listened to a community organizer complain that he had tried everything he could think of to get people involved in community action. He had called meetings, set up committees, organized projects, all with little success. He said he even gave out to them at every meeting but they still would not get involved. Giving out

to people might be an understandable reaction but, in the context of hopelessness, it might not actually be the most useful.

Divisiveness

Internalized oppression causes people to become suspicious of one another,
to fight among themselves, to mistreat one another and to have difficulty
uniting in a common cause. It may be characterized by poor, destructive
relationships, invalidation or "slagging" of one another, distrust, begrudgery
or jealousy. Within the oppressed group, people are more likely to focus on
their differences than on what they have in common. According to Miller
(1978):

> Divisiveness has to do with fighting the people most likely to be your
> allies and failing to tackle the real issue in a situation. Feelings of power-
> lessness lead people to try to organize camps or groups to move against
> other groups close to them.
>
> (p. 40)

She notes that, "Divisiveness counts on organizing 'against' forces and places
people in reactive positions" (p. 40). In this way, it sets up people rather than
the oppressive system as the enemy. So, in a city for example, people in one
housing estate may not want to have anything to do with the people in the
neighbouring housing estate, even though they all face similar problems. One
will look down on the other as inferior to them.

I was once involved in running a diploma course in women's studies. The
first year we ran this programme we had about 30 participants. In the course
of a discussion one day, one of the women indicated that she was working
class. Someone disputed this and said she was middle class. Before long,
others joined in and soon the group split between those who agreed she was
working class and those who maintained she was middle class. Afterwards,
the staff decided we would try to ensure this did not become a divisive issue
on the following year's course. During the course of that particular year,
during a discussion one day, one of the women spoke up and said she was
tired listening to what it was like for single women. We were ignoring the
experiences of married women. The group began to argue about it and before
long they had split between the single women and the married women.
Afterwards, we decided to make sure to address both aspects equally in the
following year so as to avoid any unnecessary conflict. Third time round,
the following year, we were having a discussion one day and during the
discussion one woman got frustrated and asked how come we never looked at
what it was like for older women. The group quickly began to argue about
this and once again split, this time between the older and the younger women.
At this point we realized that something else was going on here. It was not by
accident that, no matter how careful we were, each year the group of women

found some reason to split into factions. Each year we had a different group but the same process took place. This was internalized divisiveness that made it difficult for people to support each other and stay united. Usually splits such as this are along the fault lines of some other oppression, whether it be class, age, sexual orientation, skin colour or any of a long list of oppressions. In situations like these, people sometimes attribute this process to "personality clashes" or rivalry between cliques. However, the pattern is more pervasive than that and, even when the personalities or cliques change, the divisiveness continues. The Irish playwright, Brendan Behan, summed this up when he said that the first item on the agenda was the split!

We see this dynamic at work in many social change movements where there are numerous rival groupings rigidly opposed to one another even though, in the process, their overall strength and resources are minimized. The women's movement, for example, has often been riven with divisions between working-class and middle-class women or between Black women and White women. In some cases, divisiveness may be actively reinforced from the outside. For example, racial divisions have been stirred up in the US as a way of keeping workers from organizing against employers. Historically, anti-Jewish feelings have been fostered among populations whenever it looked as if they were a threat to the ruling class. And Kanter (1993) has shown how divisiveness among women would be encouraged as a condition for allowing some of them to move into non-traditional positions within work organizations.

The fact that divisiveness is a feature of internalized oppression is not that surprising. Given the low self-esteem that people internalize, the difficulty in taking pride or even the shame attached to their identity, this would make it difficult for people to feel good about one another. In some ways, the divisiveness can be seen as the acting out of the low self-esteem against other members of the group. To the extent that groups have internalized the stereotypes held by dominant or oppressor groups, it will lead them to value each other less and to treat each other with less than complete respect. In a similar way, the internalized powerlessness and hopelessness will pull people into venting their frustration at one another rather than taking on the real oppressor.

A variation on divisiveness occurs where individual members of the group isolate themselves or cut themselves off from the larger group. In some situations, it may be isolation rather than outright divisiveness that characterizes members of the group. The internalized oppression leaves them with a lack of any sense of connection to the larger group. I have sometimes worked with groups where there was little conflict between individuals but where everyone in the group operated on their own, in isolation and without any sense of support from others.

Leadership faces similar challenges here as with the other manifestations of internalized oppression. They need to spot the ways in which divisiveness operates within a group, the ways in which people have difficulty trusting or supporting each other, the ways in which they disconnect from each other or any destructive ways they have of dealing with each other. They also have to try to interrupt and contradict this divisiveness. It is not the role of leadership to decide which faction to support or which side to take. Leaders have to be able to see beyond the divisiveness and develop a vision of what unity among the group would look like. Their job is to build unity across these various divisions. I was once asked by an English politician how she could support Irish nationalists to counter the power of the Unionist party of Northern Ireland and its influence on the British government. I replied that if she was committed to being an ally for people in Ireland, then she should try to think beyond the divisiveness and not simply take sides.

Contradicting divisiveness involves building close relationships that cut across the isolation and the divisiveness. The role of the leader is to build bridges across the divisions. There is an analogy here with families. Sometimes adult siblings in a family stay connected to each other through their individual connections to the parents. Without the relationship to the parents, they might have little contact with each other. In a similar way, it sometimes happens that it is the close relationship that each person or faction has with the leader that keeps everyone connected to each other. This, of course, is not ideal but sometimes it is a good starting point in building and maintaining unity. Contradicting divisiveness also involves setting up opportunities for people to be listened to respectfully across the divisions and using constructive problem-solving and conflict-resolution strategies to deal with differences. We shall see more about these in later chapters. As part of this, leaders may also need to find ways to raise people's awareness of how divisiveness separates them. They may need to name what is getting in the way of unity so that people can separate this dynamic from the people involved and not get caught up in blame. Over and above these specific types of contradiction, enhancing pride and self-esteem in the group and going against powerlessness and hopelessness will also have the effect of reducing divisiveness.

Narrowing of the culture

This particular effect of internalized oppression is also a variation on divisiveness. Within an oppressed group, people may accept a narrow and limiting range of criteria for acceptance of others as members of the group (Lipsky, 1979). So, for example, acceptance into the group may require that someone speaks with the right accent, or is of the right religion, or has the right shade of skin colour. Those who do not conform or who do not match these criteria are isolated, rejected, attacked or humiliated. A French-Algerian woman at one of my workshops spoke about how she never felt she belonged anywhere. French people would not accept her as French because, although her parents were French, she was born in Algeria. Algerians would not accept her as Algerian because her parents were French. An Irish Protestant told me how he never felt fully Irish because he was not Roman Catholic, had never played Gaelic games, did not speak the Irish language fluently and knew little about traditional Irish music. The narrow criteria set by groups become a reason not to unite with other members of the group, they keep the group smaller and weaker and they serve as a source of divisiveness. Since these criteria for acceptance are often part of a stereotype of the group, it can happen that no one in the group actually feels that they truly meet all the requirements. No one feels they are "enough".

This process of narrowing the culture is sometimes more pronounced when the oppression is heaviest and when the group feels particularly powerless. It may be noticeable in the early stages of a liberation movement when a group is still struggling for recognition of its oppression and particularly where it is still at the angry, counter-dependent or defiant stage of the liberation process that we shall examine in a later chapter. As the movement matures, gains recognition and becomes more influential, it begins to adopt a much looser set of criteria for acceptance into the group. At this stage, people with any piece of the identity are encouraged to claim that identity fully. They do not have to conform to all the criteria or match exactly some type of stereotype about what a "true" member of this group comprises. Many people who may be of mixed heritage will now be encouraged to claim all parts of their heritage fully rather than thinking of themselves as lesser members of the group or as not belonging at all.

In this sense, the contradiction here is accepting people as fully belonging to the group and encouraging them to claim their identity completely even where their heritage is mixed or where they only match some of the criteria. A key role of leadership is modelling this welcoming and acceptance of all people who share in the identity.

Attacks on leaders

A marked characteristic of internalized oppression is that it pulls people to attack, criticize, undermine, "backbite" or gossip maliciously about, distrust, act suspiciously of, or otherwise fail to support anyone who tries to take initiative or leadership. Often this targets those in formal positions of leadership although it may also affect people who take very visible initiatives. The effect, on the one hand, is to damage the individual's leadership and, on the other hand, to make people in general reluctant to take any initiative for fear of being attacked in the same ways. We have already looked at this particular dynamic in detail in Chapter 5. The important point here is that this is also a manifestation of internalized oppression. It can be seen in the experience of one national women's organization where, over a period of years, each successive chairperson was forced to resign before the end of her term of office. It might be understandable why one person might have to resign because the demands of the job were beyond their capabilities. It would seem unfortunate if this happened to two people in a row. However, when it happens a third time, we have to question what is going on. It is highly unlikely that the organization was that unfortunate that it elected three incompetent chairpersons in a row. More likely we were witnessing this tendency of oppressed groups to attack their own leaders. This is also illustrated in the case of a working-class woman who became a visible leader in her community. She was someone who had left school early, got married young and had children very soon after getting married. Many years later, as the children got older and became more independent, she went on some personal development courses for parents run by the school. These completely changed her life and she began to blossom. Up to then she had not had much confidence in herself and practically all of her energy went into looking after her family. Now she began to have some time for herself and gradually got involved in various community activities. As her confidence grew, she played a more active role, joining committees, organizing community events and becoming visible as a leader. However, the more visible she became the more she was criticized for becoming "big-headed" and "stuck up". People criticized her lack of education and questioned what she would know about leading anything. She found that she had to walk a tightrope, trying not to lose her friends and continuing to lead without being so visible that she drew attacks on herself. She constantly felt under pressure to give up leading and to become invisible. Leaders of many oppressed groups face similar dilemmas.

In our roles as leaders, we need to be aware of this dynamic. We need to be able to see where the attacks are part of the internalized oppression rather than a true reflection of our leadership. As with divisiveness generally, we may need to name the process so that people can see what they do around leadership.

Given the nature of this dynamic, however, it is important that leaders are not left to handle this on their own. As we saw in Chapter 6, the process of attacking leaders happens independently of their competence. Any difficulties associated with how they are functioning in the role need to be thought about and dealt with separately from the process of attacking them. We need to be able to think about people in visible or leadership roles and figure out ways to protect them or to assist them to deal with attacks. This may mean interrupting the attacks for them and pointing out to people that what they are doing is destructive and unacceptable. We need to make the supporting of leaders a key liberation issue. Looking on it as an aspect of internalized oppression adds another dimension to the relevant discussions in Chapters 5 and 6.

Contradicting this piece of internalized oppression involves supporting and encouraging people's initiatives, interrupting attacks when they occur, giving up public criticism as a way of trying to change or correct people and finding *helpful* ways to correct them when they make mistakes or get things wrong.

Mistrusting their own thinking

Most oppressions contain an element that denigrates the thinking and intelligence of the oppressed group. Even if this is not a central part of the oppression, the difficulty that people have in getting anyone to listen or to accept that their oppression is real communicates that their thinking is not valued or trusted. Over time, people internalize this and come to distrust their own thinking or the thinking of people who share the same identity. They may assume that members of other groups are more intelligent or clearer and look to them for answers, for wisdom, for guidance or expertise. They may come to equate intelligence with formal education and assume that people with more education are automatically more intelligent or more aware. Or they may equate confidence and arrogance with intelligence and not speak up in the face of these. Doubting their own thinking and intelligence, they may then look to others for leadership.

This mistrust of their own thinking is another way in which people internalize low self-esteem. It is treated separately here because of its particular importance in holding the oppression in place and because contradicting it is an important step in the process of liberation. At times this mistrust of thinking may be revealed directly – people may tell us they are not very smart. At other times, it shows up indirectly in the reluctance of people to share their thinking or in their tendency to stay quiet during discussions. They may allow others who are more confident to dominate meetings or monopolize the thinking. They may welcome someone from a dominant group who offers to take leadership and allow themselves to take a backseat position. It is very easy for these people from dominant or oppressor groups to be seduced by this and to end up unawarely usurping leadership and reinforcing the internalized oppression (albeit with the best of intentions). This is a point to which we shall return in a later chapter dealing with oppressor dynamics.

It is important that leaders are alert to this dynamic and that they pay attention to whether or not the thinking of the oppressed group is being heard. Contradicting this dynamic involves encouraging people to share their thinking, listening very respectfully to them, encouraging them to trust what they are thinking, and encouraging them to act and take initiative. It can also mean agreeing to follow the leadership of the oppressed group rather than insisting on doing things our way. It sometimes helps also to structure situations in such a way that the thinking of the oppressed group is given greater prominence or that none of the other groups present share their thinking until the members of the oppressed group have first spoken. This gives due recognition to the fact that when it comes to their oppression, they are the experts and that, in many situations, their thinking is actually more accurate, more grounded or more sensible than that of people who display a lot more confidence.

Urge to feel good

Where the oppression is heavier there is often a particularly destructive form of internalized oppression. Where people feel powerless to change things and hopeless about even trying, there can be a pull to focus on feeling good in the short term rather than on organizing for fundamental change. Rather than trying to eliminate the oppression, people look for ways to deaden the pain or to distract them from the hurt. Addictions of one kind or another play a key role here. Alcohol or drugs, for example, will be used to numb the feelings and give some short-term relief. Alcohol, in particular, has been a significant feature of the oppression of many groups (Bulhan, 1985). It has played a very damaging role in the history of Native Americans, of Irish people, of Irish Travellers, of indigenous Australians and of many other peoples. Given the role that addictions have played, it is ironic (though perhaps not surprising due to their addictive nature) that many social change movements have never adopted clear stances on the role of drugs or alcohol in their liberation policies or strategies. Alcohol and drugs, of course, are only some of the ways people might try to seek relief from oppression. There are many other kinds of addictions, whether it be to food, tobacco, caffeine, sex, materialism, shopping, television, sport or whatever, that also can be found to give immediate gratification.

Many of the contradictions we have already discussed will play their part here also. As people recover their self-esteem, their power, their hope, and their connection to one another their dependence on short-term "fixes" to make them feel good becomes lessened. Leadership has an important role to play in modelling what we might call rational behaviour in this area, in being prepared to challenge their own addictions, in encouraging groups to identify the role that addictions play in their oppression and in assisting them to develop rational policies in relation to these addictions. In some cases, the leader's own addictions mirror difficulties in the group and the failure of the leader to tackle his or her own addictions puts a limit on the development of the group as a whole.

Survival behaviour

In order to cope with oppression, and especially to try to avoid some of its worst features, members of oppressed groups develop various behavioural strategies that help them to manage the relationship with members of the oppressor group and to survive with as little hurt as possible. These strategies evolved over time for understandable historical reasons rooted in the oppression and, because they seem to have survival value, they are perpetuated. Gradually, they become part of the culture of that group and long after the need for them has passed they remain as rigid ways of behaving that no longer serve any useful purpose and, in fact, help to keep the internalized oppression in place. Circumstances have now changed. There is no longer the same threat to the group. The oppression has lost some of its harsher or more dangerous elements. In spite of this, these survival behaviours, for which there is no longer any rational justification, live on in the culture. Examples of these might include acting stupid or acting sweet around members of the oppressor group, hiding their true feelings from the oppressor group, not being too visible or outspoken, acting in a sly or cunning way, keeping the oppressor group happy, reassuring them or acting in ways that confirm the stereotype of them held by the oppressor group.

According to Adam (1978b), people develop what he calls defensive behaviour as a reaction to, and protection against, domination. He states that:

> Over time, defensive tactics evolve into accepted habits. Each generation provides a model for its successor; its wisdom enhances the survival of the next. These behaviour patterns moulded by the workings of oppression may accumulate about succeeding generations like a deadweight, easing the work of oppressors and serving the more efficient maintenance of the received social order.
>
> (p. 2)

Because these behaviours have become part of the culture, members of the group may confuse them with what is part of their inherent nature. In some cases, they may even defend them as something that makes their group unique. Giving up particular survival behaviours might feel like going to the other extreme. The alternative to being chronically sweet or reassuring might seem like being all the time angry or confrontational. It can be difficult for the group to give up these habitual ways of behaving and replace them with flexible and appropriate alternatives that may sometimes involve showing their anger or sometimes confronting people. What once might have had survival value now has the effect of locking the oppressed group into its unequal place in the relationship. People are not their real selves and do not expect to have a peer relationship with people from the oppressor group. They can never reclaim their full power in the relationship while these survival behaviours persist.

As with the other examples of internalized oppression, leadership within the oppressed group has an important role to play in modelling a different way of relating to members of the oppressor group. Leaders can also help by encouraging people to act powerfully and assertively. They can support and encourage people to be honest about their true feelings, to express their real needs and to put forward their own thinking. They can model acting with courage and integrity. An important step in this process is assisting members of the group to recognize and name the particular survival behaviours that now hold them back.

Participation in other oppressions

As part of the dynamic of oppression, members of oppressed groups are pulled to seek relief from the oppression by playing an oppressor role in relation to some other group or groups. Essentially, an oppressive system offers people two choices. As we saw in the last chapter, they can either "agree" to be victims and accept their inferior status or they can find some other group that they can oppress and be superior to. Once the oppression has been internalized, it pulls people to tolerate, collude with or actively engage in the oppression of other groups. And so, for example, men who find themselves oppressed in the workplace may, in turn, act oppressively towards women and both groups may be oppressive towards young people. White Irish people, with a long history of being colonized, will often act in racist ways towards people of colour. Some national liberation movements were able to forge broad alliances across oppressed groups during the struggle for independence. However, once this was achieved, the new ruling group introduced policies and practices that colluded with or actively supported the continued oppression of some of the groups that had fought for independence with them. According to Memmi (1968),

> Not the least of the misfortunes caused by oppression is that the oppressed come to hate each other; the rivalry between Jews and Arabs is one of the most regrettable illogicalities in the history of oppression; at best, the proletariat of the different European countries showed little sympathy for the struggling colonies; and domestic servants are rarely on the side of the proletariat.
>
> (p. 11)

In theory, it would seem that any oppressed group, because of its own experience, should be more aware and less likely to be oppressive towards other groups. In practice, however, it often works differently as members of oppressed groups find other groups to pick on. Sometimes, there is a type of rivalry or competitiveness across oppressed groups over which of them is the most oppressed as though some kinds of mistreatment were more acceptable than others. As we saw earlier, all of this also feeds into divisiveness within oppressed groups and makes it difficult for them to unite and support each other. The effect of this dynamic, of course, is to reinforce all oppressions and to leave the oppressive system intact. By diverting people's energy into oppressing one another, there is little effort made to transform the actual system that creates and supports this dynamic.

Contradictions here are similar to those for overcoming divisiveness that we looked at above. In addition, helping people to reclaim pride in their own identity, to organize to take charge of their own liberation, and to build supportive alliances with people from other groups channels energy into transforming the system rather than scapegoating other groups. Leaders play a key role in modelling non-oppressive attitudes and relationships and in being committed to the liberation of all oppressed groups. It also makes a difference for oppressed groups to put forward active policies that enshrine their commitment to, and support for, the liberation of all other oppressed groups as part of their own process of liberation. This helps in giving clear guidelines and a way for people to think about these other relationships.

SUMMARY

Internalized oppression is at the heart of the damage caused by oppression. While the details vary from one oppression to another, the broad process remains the same and involves many of the elements looked at in this chapter. Contradicting this internalized oppression is a key function of leadership. It is part of thinking clearly about people and the situation facing them. It means being able to see the distinction between what people have internalized because of their oppression and what is actually true of them inherently as humans. If we cannot make this distinction, as leaders we risk being part of the problem rather than a useful resource for people. To be able to play an effective leadership role in this context means that we ourselves have to be engaged in the process of identifying and contradicting our own internalized oppression. The failure to see this task as central to good leadership and to do it on a consistent and ongoing basis has seriously undermined the effectiveness of many leaders and allies.

Having looked in some detail, in this chapter, at the dynamics of internalized oppression, it is useful now to go on, in Chapter 9, to expand our understanding by looking at what other writers have had to say about this process. Further on, we shall take a detailed look at what happens at the oppressor end of this dynamic.

REFLECTION

Pick one of your significant oppressed identities as a focus for the following questions.

1   In relation to this oppression, what are you most proud of about yourself and your people? What do you admire, like, love or respect about yourself and your people as members of this group?
2   What are you not proud of, ashamed of, embarrassed about, or what do you dislike about yourself or other members of your group?
3   What messages did you get, growing up, about people with this identity?
4   How have these messages affected your relationships with people who share this identity?
5   If you think about the culture of your group, which aspects are a reflection of your inherent humanity (your goodness, warmth, creativity, humour, intelligence, strength, caring, and so on)?
6   If you think about the culture of your group, which aspects are a reflection of internalized oppression (buying into stereotypes, survival strategies, low self-esteem, divisiveness, addictions and so on)?
7   If you acted with complete pride in yourself and your people, at all times, what would you do differently?

9   Theories of internalized oppression

INTRODUCTION

In the last chapter, we looked at a range of ways that internalized oppression manifests itself and at the implications of these for leadership. The concept of internalized oppression as described here owes its origins to the work of Jackins (1981) who was one of the first people to use this particular term. The idea of internalized oppression was, however, implicit in the works of other writers such as Memmi (1963, 1966, 1968, 1957/1990) and Fanon (1961/1967, 1952/1970), as we shall see. In recent years, it has gained much more widespread acceptance, among social change activists and among academics writing in the areas of critical, community and liberation psychology, as an important component of the process of oppression. Even though the concept is not an entirely new one, however, its significance has not always been clearly recognized. Most academics interested in the process of social change, including most mainstream psychologists, have tended to overlook the role of internalized oppression in maintaining oppression. There are some notable exceptions, however, and what is particularly interesting are the many common elements across these various descriptions of the effects of oppression. In this chapter, we shall examine a range of theories of internalized oppression, highlighting the various elements that constitute internalized forms of oppression and the overall effects of this dynamic.

THEORIES

In talking about the issue of class, Reich (1946/1972) noted that something was operating to occlude the exploitation of workers from themselves. Over the long term, the control of media and other channels of cultural transmission by the ruling class was not enough to explain why workers continued to accept their oppressed situation passively. What we needed to explain, he believed, was not

the fact that the man who is hungry steals or the fact that the man who is exploited strikes, but why the majority of those who are hungry *don't* steal and why the majority of those who are exploited *don't* strike.

(p. 19)

Reich's attempts to explain the irrational behaviour of workers emphasized the effects of early conditioning in the family, particularly around sexuality, in preparing people to accept and commit themselves to authoritarian and reactionary organizations and political parties. His work is part of a relatively small but very significant body of literature in psychology that has focused on the psychological process of oppression. Much of this describes how the oppressed come to accept or put up with oppression, without actively resisting it, and even come to believe in its inevitability and naturalness.

One of the earlier writers to draw attention to this process was Allport (1954/1979) who described the dynamics of prejudice in a work first published in 1954. In particular, he showed how prejudice becomes internalized and leads to a variety of responses from the oppressed person. He notes that prejudices of one kind or another cannot be consistently hammered into someone's head without it doing something to that person's character. Various "ego defences" will develop among members of groups that are subjected to ridicule, disparagement and discrimination. The ego defences that he describes are echoed and developed further in many later theories of what I am referring to as internalized oppression.

Among these ego defences he includes *obsessive concerns and anxiety* where there is a constant vigilance about being attacked or, in some cases, an over-sensitivity to remarks and behaviour of the dominant group. Memmi (1963) touches on this when he states "What was, what still is, Jewish history but a continual alert, punctuated by ghastly catastrophes?" (p. 19). People who are subject to prejudice become very alert to the possibility of being targeted and, occasionally, may even see threats where none actually exist. This relates to a point that was made in Chapter 7 about the subtle nature of oppression. Oppressed persons are highly tuned or sensitized to oppressive behaviour. In some cases, behaviour may be experienced as oppressive without any intention to mistreat on the part of the other person. This is not to imply that the oppression is only imagined and the oppressor group has nothing it needs to do in this situation. It does mean that oppressor groups need to become highly sensitive to the messages they communicate and to the possible meanings that may be imputed to their actions. It means taking the responsibility to inform themselves and learn about the situations that are experienced as oppressive or that create a lack of safety for oppressed groups. It means shouldering some of the responsibility for creating safety in the relationship.

In certain situations, Allport (1954/1979) reports that people may try to cope with the prejudice by *denying their membership* of the group. They may try to pass as members of the dominant group by changing their appearance, their name or some other characteristic. This, of course, is not always an option, for example, where there are obvious physical differences between the groups. Even then, however, the person may avoid contact, or association, with members of their own group or may adopt forms of dress or behaviour that are modelled on those of the dominant group. As we shall see in the context of the liberation process, the reclaiming of identity (or membership of their group) is an important stage in moving beyond oppression.

Withdrawal and passivity is a further type of defence where members of the minority group hide their true feelings behind a mask of acceptance of their situation. They will appear content with the ways they are treated and show no outward hostility or resentment. Weinrach (2002) talks about the profound discomfort that some Jews might feel with the publication of his article on anti-Semitism in the counselling profession. This, of course, is confusing for members of the majority group who take this withdrawal or passivity as an indication that nothing needs to change. Historically, for some groups, this was a necessary survival strategy. To be too visible, out-spoken or assertive would have carried the risk of physical violence or even death. Bulhan (1985) sees the oppressed person adopting an obsequious, submissive or demeaning compliance in response to the violence and aggres-sion of the oppressor group. Groups had to learn how to hide their true feelings behind a mask of acceptance, appeasement or contentment with their lot. The socialization for this would have been carried out within the family in many cases.

A somewhat related mechanism, which Allport (1954/1979) highlights, occurs where, in order to survive and ensure their survival, minority groups may develop traits of *slyness and cunning*. People learn indirect ways to resist and counter the oppression that, because they are hidden, avoid the likeli-hood of retaliation. It is not uncommon to hear members of oppressed groups described as cunning or two-faced. Members of the majority group will say that they never know what the oppressed group really thinks or that what they say to your face is not necessarily what they actually believe. This is probably related to the pattern of "hustling" that Schwalbe *et al.* (2000) describe and that we looked at in Chapter 7. Patterns of behaviour such as this (and the withdrawal and passivity patterns above) can become part of the culture of a group and, even when the prejudice or oppression is no longer active, the behaviour continues. This then comes to be seen as an inherent characteristic of these people rather than a response to oppression and becomes a further reason to distrust them or deny them equality.

An alternative strategy in the face of prejudice or oppression is that people may resort to *clowning*, acting as the happy-go-lucky fool. Individuals may caricature their own group, exaggerating their accent or other aspects of the stereotype that is held about their group. Among other things, this ensures the members of the dominant group will not feel threatened by, and therefore will not threaten, the minority group. This type of behaviour can receive encouragement and reinforcement from the majority group and, again, can come to be seen as an inherent feature of the culture. Kanter (1993) describes how members of minority groups in a non-traditional work setting (for example, women or Black people) may be required to pass certain informal "loyalty tests" in order to reassure the majority group that they are not a threat to the status quo. These tests might include making jokes about feminists or other social change proponents or agreeing to make remarks prejudicial towards their own group. People such as this are often used by the dominant group as an example to contrast with those who are pushing for equality. The latter are seen as angry and strident and told that they should try to be like the more agreeable members of their group. Spender (1980) talks about the dilemma for women who find that when they speak nicely and look for change they are ignored and when they assert themselves or show their anger are told that if they were nicer about it, they would get a more receptive response.

With all of these latter strategies, one of the long-term effects is that members of the minority group lose a sense of themselves and come to believe that the stereotype is an accurate description of their true selves. They lose any sense of righteous indignation about their treatment by the dominant group and come to view their situation in the culture as acceptable or inevitable and not due to any systematic process of unequal treatment. In a similar way, Allport (1954/1979) describes how, in the absence of other explanations for their mistreatment, minority group members may blame themselves or their own people. They develop a *self-hate* (either towards themselves personally or towards other members of the minority group) and come to agree with some of the prejudices of the dominant group in a process of *identification* with that group. This response to prejudice, however (as we saw before), is sometimes closer to a sense of shame or humiliation rather than self-hate with its connotation of self-directed anger. Sometimes it is a difficulty in taking pride or in being pleased to be a member of that group. As a Jew, Memmi (1963) says,

> I do not believe I have ever rejoiced in being a Jew. When I think of myself as a Jew, I am immediately conscious of a vague spiritual malaise, warm, persistent, always the same, that comes over me. The first thing that strikes me when I think of myself as a Jew is that I do not like to consider myself in that light.

(p. 15)

This latter defence may also lead to *aggression against their own group* where various divisions emerge within the minority group that pit members of that group against each other. Although Allport (1954/1979) does not specifically say this, his examples show that these divisions may arise along the lines of other types of oppression, such as class divisions between Black people. Bulhan (1985) refers to this as a pattern of horizontal violence within the group. He see this reflected in the high levels of crime and homicide among oppressed groups. Similarly, Fanon (1961/1967) and Freire (1972) describe how the aggression of the oppressor is directed by the oppressed person against their own people. As we saw in more detail in the last chapter, aggression within the group may even, on occasions, be provoked deliberately and encouraged by the dominant group. Often internal aggression and divisiveness are major stumbling blocks to organizing successfully for social transformation. More recently, the concept of horizontal violence has been applied to oppressed or embattled occupations such as nursing (Hastie, n.d.; Taylor, 2001)

A variation of this aggression is for minority groups to direct *prejudice against out-groups* where they inflict on others the kinds of mistreatment they themselves have experienced. This, again, illustrates how oppressive systems encourage people to seek relief from their oppression by finding other groups to oppress rather than uniting with these groups to eliminate all forms of oppression. The choice is to accept their victim status or become an oppressor of others. The other option of organizing together to transform the oppressive system does not easily emerge under the weight of the oppression and the ways in which it gets internalized.

While stressing the negative effects of prejudice, Allport (1954/1979) also notes that ongoing and systematic prejudice can, in addition, lead to a *strengthening of in-group ties*, where members of the minority group are drawn together in solidarity in ways that support and console each. Working-class people or people who are raised poor often make reference to the strong sense of community that existed where people helped each other out, particularly in a crisis situation. It seems that, for some groups, the self-hate in relation to the social identity that people have, which Allport describes, can coexist with this deep sense of connection at an interpersonal or community level. (In a similar vein, Adam (1978a) and Pettigrew (1978) discuss the disjunction between personal and racial self-esteem.) This sense of connection may be viewed as very "clannish" and exclusive from the outside and lead to a view of people as prejudiced in favour of their own kind. Part of this may simply be the sense of safety that people feel within their own group. When together, they do not have to be all the time vigilant or on guard. Other writers, such as Kanter (1993), have drawn attention to the way in which members of the majority group feel threatened by displays of closeness or support among minority groups. Where members of the minority group are in a token situation, Kanter finds that the pressure from the majority may lead them actually to avoid one another as opposed to giving expression to these in-group ties. Their anxiety to protect the dominant group from discomfort and to avoid being targeted with any retribution may mean that they give up the opportunity to have a safe haven and support for themselves.

Enhanced striving is the response of some groups to prejudice, where people make extra, strenuous efforts to become successful in spite of the discrimination. Success in this often requires them to be even better than members of the dominant group. While Allport (1954/1979) seems to view this in broadly positive terms, other writers would see this as tending to reinforce the prejudicial system. Unlike fighting back, it does not question the legitimacy of the discrimination or attempt to change the oppressive system. As we shall see in Chapter 11, oppressive class systems operate by encouraging working-class and marginalized people to escape their oppression by "climbing the ladder" into the middle class, for example. This response also reinforces the notion that success is largely an issue of individual effort and, thus, those who do not get ahead have only themselves to blame.

In contrast to this, victims of prejudice may also resort to *symbolic status striving* where they settle for status symbols as a substitute for equality. This may show up in conspicuous displays of wealth or fashion or the adoption of speech, accent or language patterns of the dominant group. This also, of course, colludes with the discrimination and leaves the system intact. And, by giving up traditional styles of speech, fashion or lifestyle, it reinforces a negative stereotype of the minority group. This also overlaps with, and is reinforced by, some of the other patterns described above, such as denying membership of the group. In some cases, "progress" and "progressiveness" comes to be associated with giving up the identity or the cultural patterns associated with it. One of the sad aspects of some oppressions is the way in which positive, enriching and pro-human characteristics of the oppressed group's culture are disowned or mocked as old-fashioned, unsophisticated or having no place in the modern world.

The last response that Allport (1954/1979) highlights is the mental health impact of prejudice in terms of hypertension, stress and other manifestations of neuroticism that may arise in extreme circumstances. It is no accident that the clients of the mental health system are more likely to come from within oppressed groups and that, as has been shown by Braginsky and Braginsky (1974) and by Liu *et al.* (2004), the system is more likely to assess members of oppressed groups as mentally ill compared to members of the dominant group.

Not all defences are necessarily negative, however. Allport (1954/1979) points out that people who have been victims of discrimination are usually either very high in prejudice towards others or else very low in prejudice. In the case of the latter, their experiences lead them to have great *sympathy* for other oppressed groups. For example, many Jewish people have been to the fore in fighting for the rights of other minority groups. In addition to sympathy, some members of minority groups will adopt a militant strategy of *fighting back* where they join political or other organizations to try to improve their situation. A question arises as to whether or not it is useful to describe these last two reactions as defences in a strict sense. Whereas the other strategies that Allport outlines have an element of rigidity and irrationality about them, the latter two may, on many occasions, be quite rational and flexible responses to the prejudice. The same question could be raised in relation to some aspects of the strengthening of in-group ties. While this may entail an element of rigidity at times, it could also represent a rational response to adversity and an expression of people's basic humanity.

Memmi (1966, 1968, 1957/1990) and Fanon (1961/1967, 1952/1970) give very clear accounts of the effects of colonization and racism that have many parallels with other oppressions. Memmi (1968) notes the combination of love for the oppressor and hatred of themselves that the oppressed take on. The indoctrinating effects of oppression teach people to look up to and respect the oppressor and to use them as the norm for comparison purposes. By such standards, they themselves are unworthy and inferior. He also notes that the oppressed (colonized people, women, Jews, the poor) resemble one another to a great degree. They develop similar gestures, similar expressions of pain and so on. The burden of their oppression leaves "the same bruises on their soul" (1968, p. 16) and, in similar ways, distorts the way they behave. So, although Memmi talks mainly about colonized people, his remarks are quite applicable to a wide range of other oppressed groups. The worst effect of oppression that he sees is not so much the injustice, the beating, the insults and so on, as the "spiritual ruin" (1968, p. 20) wherein the oppressed consent to their own abasement. At this point oppressed people accept and believe what they are told about themselves and actually become what is expected of them. As Memmi (1963) puts it

> The longer the oppression lasts, the more it profoundly affects him. It ends by becoming so familiar to him that he believes it is part of his own constitution, that he accepts it and could not imagine his recovery from it. This acceptance is the crowning point of oppression. If oppression lasts for even a short time, the majority of the oppressed end by being equally oppressed inwardly.
>
> (pp. 321–2)

He describes them as accessories after the fact of their own oppression. One effect of this is that even after decolonization these effects remain and affect how the person acts and thinks (O'Dowd, 1990; Ruth, 1988, 2000). In other words, political freedom from the colonizer is not the full story as regards liberation from colonization. There is a process of psychological liberation that is also necessary before people are truly free. This again highlights the earlier point that most of the damage done by oppression is done by its internalized forms.

Parallelling Memmi's work is that of Fanon (1952/1970) who shows how colonization and racism generate an inferiority complex among the colonized that leads to their trying to emulate and identify with White people and to look down on and detach themselves from other Black people. In this situation, people cope with subjugation by putting their energy into becoming like the colonizer rather than resisting social structures and asserting their own separate identity. For Fanon, the only way to make sense of this behaviour is to see it in the context of colonialism and the fact that, as a result of economic and other forms of mistreatment, people "internalize" their inferiority. Describing the experience of being Black and repeatedly subjected to abuse and rejection, he says, "I slip into corners, I remain silent, I strive for anonymity, for invisibility" (p. 82). He also notes, as we saw above, how colonial oppression leads to the colonized directing their anger and violence at each other rather than at the oppressor. What both Memmi and Fanon are getting at is that there is a system of oppression (primarily colonialism but with obvious parallels in other forms of oppression) that has not only material effects but also psychological ones and that these psychological effects need to be clearly understood if we are to make proper sense of "dependent", inferior and accepting forms of behaviour.

Similar themes are explored by Freire (1972). Emphasizing the need to "conscientize" people, he notes that one of the main obstacles to liberation is that oppression "absorbs those within it and thereby acts to submerge men's consciousness" (p. 28). A false perception of reality is created by the oppressive system. This false perception is reflected in such characteristics as "horizontal violence" against their own people, fatalism about the possibility of change, and self-depreciation, and effectively obscures the reality of their oppression from the oppressed.

Kenny (1985) and Moane (1994, 1999) have explored the nature of the post-colonial personality with particular reference to the Irish. Kenny describes the strategies adopted by a colonized people to cope with their experience. *Constriction* is a major coping strategy. Here, faced with continuing colonization, deprivation, famine and poverty, a type of national constriction takes place whereby people limit their range of interests, take a near-sighted view of the world, deal with only one issue at a time and do not deal with those they feel are impossible or repugnant. He outlines seven levels of constriction that can be grouped under two broad processes. The first four of these levels of constriction fall under the heading of going underground sociologically (i.e. withdrawing from the environment). The final three fall under the heading of going underground psychologically (i.e. withdrawing into the self).

The first level of constriction is the *creation of secret, micro-worlds* (p. 71), largely hidden from the dominant reality. This can take the form of secret groups or societies organized against the dominant group or other authority. This same process leads to a tendency for these groups to splinter into ever smaller groups over time. *Superficial compliance* (p. 73) is a second form of constriction, where the oppressor is reassured that the status quo is intact. Within this process, there is a lot of pressure on people to conform and appear unified. Appearances become very important. As a result of this process, the oppressed person's overt verbal and non-verbal reactions no longer indicate the reality of what they are thinking or feeling. A third form of constriction is *indirect communication* (p. 73) where people, in order to protect themselves, learn to be evasive and manipulative. From the point of view of the oppressor group, this can look like deviousness, unreliability, deceitfulness and so on. Within the oppressed group, it can lead to difficulties in confronting other people directly and, instead, gossiping or talking about them behind their backs. It can also lead to difficulties in communicating positive things to other people, such as how much we care about them or other types of compliments. Related to this last level is *avoidance of self-revelation* (p. 74) where people do not reveal the depths of their anger or frustration or any other inner feelings publicly, and natural spontaneity is controlled. This also leads to a suppression of any positive feelings of self-regard or ambition. Anyone who acts too pleased with themselves or who wants more out of life is regarded with displeasure and suspected of rising "above their station". These are very similar to Allport's description of the defences of withdrawal, passivity, slyness and cunning. A fifth level of con-striction is the *elaboration of the inner world* (p. 74). Here there is a turning towards fantasy, magical thinking, superstition, creativity, poetry, music and so on. The more people focus on the inner world the less responsibility they feel for what happens in the external world. This can lead to a selfishness, thoughtlessness and an irresponsibility towards other people. It can show up in the belief that if we can get away with something, then it is okay. The sixth level of constriction is *helplessness/passivity* (p. 75) where people simply give up and become dependent. The final level is *elaboration of the negative self* (p. 75). At this level, people learn to hate themselves and this can be expressed in suicide or other forms of self-destructive behaviour (self-mutilation, alcoholism or other addictions). The end result of these processes of constric-tion is the creation of people who are compliant, conforming, evasive, ashamed, withdrawn, inward-looking, destructive, self-critical, dependent, passive, guilty, helpless and self-hating.

The linking of the psychological with the social/political system is taken up strongly by Adam (1978a, 1978b). For Adam (1978b), behaviour must be located in a social and a political context. Dominated people develop a range of coping behaviours that allow them to adjust to, accommodate to, sub-ordinate themselves to, and survive in an oppressive environment. Many of the behaviours he describes are similar to those highlighted by the writers already discussed. The effect of these coping behaviours is often to reinforce and "reproduce" the oppressive system. Over time these behaviours become habitual and are passed on, through socialization, from generation to gener-ation. In the end the oppression comes to be totally accepted and any alterna-tive is unimaginable. Like Memmi and Fanon earlier, Adam sees the same mechanism operating across different forms of oppression. The fact that diverse groups respond to their inferiorized status in much the same ways is evidence, for Adam, that "naturalistic, biological, pathological, psychiatric, and moral theories" (1978b, p. 3) are inadequate to explain the behaviours. The effect of such theories is that behaviour that results directly from oppres-sion is overlooked and treated as an inherent characteristic of those groups, as part of human nature.

For Adam (1978b), domination is a form of structured inequality. One of its functions is to serve as a distraction for social discontent and aggression by diverting unrest against the established order into attacks on "minority" groups. The domination is rationalized and reproduced by educational institutions, churches, the mass media, the publishing industry and other similar institutions.

"Inferiorization" (1978b, p. 1), as he calls it, is accompanied by a stereotype of people that says that they are incapable of "higher" emotions such as love, are uncivilized, unrefined, ill-mannered, unclean, deceitful, excessively sexual, conspiring against the system, overly flamboyant, loud, pushy or aggressive, weak, incompetent and lacking in intelligence. The main effects of inferiorization are worth looking at in some detail.

One of the effects of inferiorization on the dominated and one of the ways the oppression is maintained is *atomization*. Essentially, this means that the inferiorized are kept psychologically isolated from one another. The awareness of the oppression and methods of dealing with it are not shared as a result. Because of this, the oppressed are kept unaware and unable to organize. Atomization is accomplished by excluding members of oppressed groups from the major communication systems (schools, publishing, media and so on). Thus, the stories of the oppressed are never heard and the oppressive system remains invisible.

A second effect of inferiorization is *guilt-based responses* where the oppressed blame themselves for their suffering. Thus instead of taking action against the oppressive system, people feel guilty and put problems down to their own inadequacy. The effect is to maintain the system of domination.

A third effect of domination is *mimesis* where inferiorized people come to adopt dominant values and forms of behaviour. This is very similar to the process of identification described by Allport (1954/1979), Memmi (1963, 1966, 1968) and Fanon (1970) and is particularly the case in situations of extreme oppression, such as, for example, Nazi concentration camps (Bettleheim, 1986a, 1986b). The oppressed look up to and model themselves on the oppressor. This behaviour may be reinforced within the oppressive system by granting extra privileges to some members of the oppressed group who identify most strongly with and assist the oppressor in upholding the system and in maintaining the status quo. An important aspect of this identification with the oppressor is that legal emancipation alone is not enough to eliminate it. It has taken generations to form and is part of the psychological inheritance of the group. Memmi and Fanon saw this clearly in the case of post-colonialism.

A fourth effect of domination is the *escape from identity*. Given the stereotype associated with belonging to an inferiorized group, the individual has a choice: either accept their label and the stereotyping that goes with it or else reject the label and any identification with the group. On the one hand is guilt and self-hatred and on the other is denial and "bad faith". The first choice locates the problem as a personal one and the second isolates the individual from other people in the same situation. In each case the oppression is maintained. These are some of the options explored by Memmi (1966) in discussing the responses of Jewish people to their oppression.

Reinforcing this escape from identity may be *psychological withdrawal* which emphasizes becoming "invisible". Essentially, this involves the hiding of emotion and the presentation of an apathetic attitude towards the oppression. Psychological withdrawal is often accompanied by conservatism and efforts "to prove one's normality". Status displays such as belonging to the "right" clubs or identifying with the leisure classes become attempts to compensate for their inferior status. Again, Allport (1954/1979) and others have also described this particular pattern.

Finally, we have *in-group hostility*. In a situation of inequality, the oppressed can "console" themselves by mistreating other inferiorized people. In this way, the oppressed become victims not only of the dominators but also of other oppressed people. Adam notes that the tendency of Black people to devalue other Black people has been repeatedly confirmed in research. A similar process has been observed with Jews, with women and with gay people.

Addressing similar issues, Moore (1978) makes the point that terror alone is not sufficient to explain why people become helpless in the face of injustice. A process of "self-repression" is engendered which leads people to stifle the demand for justice. This process has a number of aspects. The first, echoing much of the writing in this area, is the inhibiting of self-esteem and its deflection into pride in doing work that sustains the unjust system, for example. The second is material deprivation which forces people to learn how to please those in charge of the environment and leads to an acceptance of social standards held by the dominant group. Thirdly, there are explanations of reality that stifle the impulse to do anything to change the situation by making suffering appear to be inevitable. These have the further effect of turning any aggression and frustration away from the system and against the self.

On top of this process of self-repression there are a number of other processes which serve to further inhibit collective action to identify and resist the causes of oppression. The first of these processes is the tendency for members of oppressed groups to turn on any individual protester. The second is the isolation of individuals from social support by destroying social ties and habits. The third process is "co-option" where the oppressed are forced to accept the system and work within its constraints in order to survive. The final process is "fragmentation" where as, a result of the oppression, groups are left divided into competing factions based on class, ethnic, religious or other divisions. There are obvious parallels here with Adam's work.

Sherover-Marcuse (1986) examines Marx's work and shows how at various points he indicates an awareness of the significance of internalized oppression. The confusion in Marx's thinking, however, between a "dialectical perspective" (p. 4), on the one hand, and a "dogmatic perspective" (p. 6) on the other, is, for Sherover-Marcuse, the source of many of the difficulties that have faced Marxism. The dogmatic perspective leads to a focus on overcoming the external forms of oppression and the assumption that this is sufficient to guarantee liberation. This implies that, if the external forms of oppression are removed, people will easily abandon the internalized oppression. According to Sherover-Marcuse, this notion underestimates the extent to which the past experience of domination influences the present and retains a hold on people's consciousness. The dialectical perspective, on the other hand, argues that merely overthrowing the external manifestations of domination will not be sufficient unless accompanied by an overthrowing of the internalized assumptions and feelings that hold the domination in place. The latter will require deliberate and systematic efforts to transform the consciousness of the oppressed group. The failure to realize this has meant that many revolutions have ultimately failed even though they had taken control of the external apparatus of oppression. The dramatic changes within Eastern Europe during and since the 1980s are a strong indication of this failure. Once the monolithic power structure of the Soviet system was removed, the underlying deep divisions and tensions came to the surface with catastrophic consequences in many areas.

Miller (1986) has described in some detail how the process of domination operates and the effects it has on both dominant and subordinate groups. Her account of this process contains elements of the external oppression and the means by which it gets internalized. It highlights the ways in which noticeable patterns of behaviour within groups can be understood in the context of their experience of oppression and it points to the importance of understanding in detail the dynamics of oppression and internalized oppression. According to Miller, once a group has been defined as unequal, the dominant group attaches negative labels to it, such as being less intelligent, for example. The dominant group also defines what are acceptable roles for the subordinate group. In general, the less valued roles in the society will be given to the subordinate group. Typically these involve providing services that the dominant group does not want to provide for itself, such as cleaning up the dominant group's waste products. The functions that the dominant group values will be kept closed to members of the subordinate group. This inequality will be legitimized often by maintaining that the subordinate group is inherently defective or incapable of carrying out the more valued jobs. In addition, members of the subordinate group are encouraged to develop personal characteristics that the dominant group is comfortable with or finds pleasing, for example, submissiveness, passivity, docility, dependency, lack of initiative, indecisiveness and so on. If subordinates act in these ways, they are judged to be well-adjusted. Fromm (1942/1960) touches on a similar point when he states that the "normal" person in this context is well adjusted only at the expense of having given up their true self, along with their individuality and spontaneity, in order to become the person they believe they are expected to be. People who do not conform to the stereotype risk being judged as abnormal. It is in this type of situation that the mental health system is brought into play to buttress the oppression (Chesler, 1972). The autobiography of the Hollywood actress, Frances Farmer (1983), is a harrowing description of what happens when someone refused to play the role ascribed to her by society. As the book graphically demonstrates, she was committed to an asylum for 11 years and subjected to inhuman treatment, largely because she would not conform to people's expectations of a woman and a film star.

According to Miller (1986), dominant groups also impose varying degrees of sanctions to make it difficult for their own members to act more humanely or more rationally towards the subordinate group. At the height of protests and agitation for greater equality for women, I remember being told by a young father that, when he tried to take his baby for a walk in a pram, he was approached by other men in his local community and told, "we don't do that here". Dominant groups, through their influence over philosophy, morality, social theory and science, are also able to legitimize the inequality and obscure the true nature of the relationship between the two groups. In addition, dominant groups generally do not like to be reminded of the existence of inequality. The inequality will be rationalized in various ways such as that it is in people's own best interests or that the subordinates themselves are content with the situation. Importantly, Miller points out that dominants usually cannot see that the inequality actually deprives them as well, particularly on a psychological level.

For subordinate groups, the focus is often on survival. For this reason, direct, honest reaction to their mistreatment is often avoided. They resort to indirect, hidden ways of reacting, similar to what we saw above in Kenny's (1985) work. On the surface they act in ways that please or accommodate the dominant group, but underneath there is often hidden defiance. One effect of this, however, is that the dominant group tends not to have a clear and accurate picture of what they are doing to the subordinate group. In fact, it will tend to be the case that subordinates know much more about dominants than vice versa. For Miller (1986), this is, in fact, the basis of "female intuition". It is a necessary survival skill for any oppressed group to be able to read the many small, verbal and non-verbal signals coming from the dominant group. Similarly, subordinates often know more about the dominant group than they do about themselves. If the dominant group is the source of power and if it influences the fate of the subordinate group, then that is what people need to pay attention to and understand. This tendency is reinforced by the lack of opportunities for subordinates to experience themselves acting powerfully, confidently and creatively. They are thus unable to develop an accurate evaluation of their own potential. Added to this, as we have seen with other writers, Miller points out that subordinates absorb a large part of the negative stereotypes created by the dominant group. On the other hand, subordinates also have experiences and perceptions of their situation that accurately convey the truth about themselves and the inequality. These experiences and perceptions inevitably come into conflict with the mythology created by the dominant group. When oppressed groups begin to organize against the oppression and to resist the internalized oppression, these alternative experiences and perceptions become an important base for contradicting the stereotypes and redefining their identity. Historically, for example, Miller states that it is the case that subordinates' groups tried to resist their mistreatment.

However, most records of revolt against inequality are not preserved by the dominant culture. This makes it difficult for subordinates' groups to find support in their study of history. It is also the reason why the writing or rewriting of the history of such groups becomes an important part of the liberation process for many groups. Finally, Miller notes that there are also tendencies for members of subordinate groups to imitate the dominants. They may try to act as oppressively towards other members of their own group as do the dominants. Or, they may try to become accepted into the dominant group themselves. Usually this acceptance is not total and requires them giving up their commitment to and support of their own group. As we can see with this account, Miller is echoing, and elaborating on, the processes described by many other writers.

Many of the characteristics of internalized oppression noted here have been highlighted by other writers also. Lewis (1961, 1971) used the phrase "culture of poverty" to describe a large number of traits that he saw as characteristic of people raised in poverty. He noted that people in the culture of poverty had a strong sense of marginality, of powerlessness and dependency along with feelings of personal unworthiness and inferiority. This particular theory was criticized for a variety of reasons, among them that Lewis overgeneralized and ignored more positive aspects of the people he wrote about and that it could be seen as a way of blaming the poor for their poverty. It does, however, reflect much of what would now be called the internalized oppression of people raised poor. Brown (1994) gives a very clear account of the effects of class oppression on people who are raised poor. These include being told that they are worthless, inferior and stupid. When these get internalized, the raised poor person ends up blaming themselves for their own poverty. Similarly, Knupfer (1954) writing about the effects of low status (in terms of income, prestige and power), describes how the economic and educational limitations that accompany low status lead to a lack of interest and a lack of self-confidence in important areas of the world around people. She likens this to a form of "psychological underprivilege" (p. 263) that includes, among others, habits of submission. While both Lewis and Knupfer might be accused of a narrow, psychologistic approach that played down the relevance of wider oppression, the central point here is their recognition of the existence of psychological effects of economic deprivation. In common with the other writers we have looked at, they recognize, in one form or another, the process by which an oppression can become internalized. This was also recognized by Pettigrew (1971) when he wrote about the burdens of being Black in the United States. Associated with the discrimination against Black people was an "impairment of the individual's acceptance and understanding of himself" (p. 159). He also noted that the "confusion of self-identity and lowering of self-esteem" (p. 160) were two of the most damaging effects of their oppression.

INTERNALIZED DOMINATION

So far, the focus here has been on the ways in which oppression is internalized by the oppressed group. However, according to Mullaly (2002), this process of internalized oppression is also paralleled by a process of internalized domination within the oppressor group. We have seen how oppression is installed and maintained by disconnecting oppressed people from a sense of their true inherent nature as humans and replacing this with a false consciousness that distorts their image of themselves and their awareness of their own oppression. For this process to work, it is also necessary to disconnect the members of oppressor groups from their inherent humanness and replace this with a false consciousness of their own superiority or intelligence and a distorted view of reality. The oppressed group is offered various "rewards" in terms of power, status, privileges and wealth in return for "agreeing" to play an oppressor role. They do not do this naturally. As we saw in the last chapter, people are not born inferior. Neither are they born oppressive. Racism and sexism, for example, are not inherent characteristics of White people or men. No member of an oppressor group would play an oppressive role unless they had first been interfered with and "trained" to be an oppressor. This is done largely through a process of systematic mistreatment that dehumanizes them, numbs them to the emotional effects of this mistreatment, and rewards them for abusing or exploiting others. Some of the systematic mistreatment takes the form of oppressing members of the oppressor group themselves. Thus, as we saw earlier, people who have been oppressed in one area of their lives may seek relief from the oppression by becoming oppressors of other groups. An oppressive system, for example, may manipulate a White woman, who is a victim of sexism, to feel superior to, and act oppressively towards, Black people. An important challenge, therefore, for oppressor groups is to examine, become aware of and interrupt the ways they have internalized dominance as reflected in their thoughts, feelings and behaviour.

What is not so clearly appreciated, however, is that apart from oppressing members of the oppressor group under other labels, oppressive systems also impose more direct forms of hurt and conditioning to do specifically with the oppressor identity. Part of men's sexist behaviour, for example, can be explained on the one hand by their experience of class oppression or racism or adultism. It is also due, however, to the systematic conditioning they receive about men and their identity and the mistreatment associated with this (Irwin, 1992; Jackins *et al.*, 1999). For some oppressor groups such as men or middle-class people, there is a way in which their experiences as members of those groups are themselves part of an oppression. They incur damage, particularly on a human level, by virtue of belonging to these groups. Spanierman and Heppner (2004) suggest that racism, for example, involves various costs to White people that are affective (feelings of fear, guilt, etc.), cognitive (distorted perception of reality, lack of knowledge of others, confusion regarding racial inequality and so on), or behavioural (having relationships only with other Whites, self-censorship and so on). In particular, they emphasize the affective or emotional costs. They do not suggest that these costs are by any means equivalent to the costs incurred by the oppressed group but that, for the oppressor group, they do represent negative effects of playing that role. In the context of gender and class, we can talk about men's oppression or middle-class oppression, recognizing that members of these groups are both agents of the oppression of women and agents of working-class oppression, respectively, and also oppressed as men and as middle class. (It is important to stress, however, that this does not mean that they are oppressed by either women or working-class people.) Men, for example, as a result of their oppression as men, may be pulled into destructive competition, violence (against other men, against women or against young people), emotional isolation, emotional numbness, overwork, dangerous risk-taking and a range of other damaging effects. In Chapter 10, we shall see in some detail how middle-class oppression affects members of that group. Because of these processes, we can usefully enquire about men's internalized oppression or middle-class internalized oppression and understanding these is a hugely important part of the liberation process.

Because so little work has been done in the area of oppressor dynamics it is not clear how pervasive the processes I have just described actually are. While it is useful to talk about men's oppression or middle-class oppression, for example, can this be generalized to other oppressor groups? Without detracting from the reality of women's oppression and men's role in that, it has been helpful in understanding that dynamic to think in terms of men's oppression and internalized oppression and how these reinforce sexism and women's oppression. As I hope to show in the next chapter, we can get a clearer picture of class oppression by understanding the operation of middle-class oppression and internalized oppression. There are many other oppressor groups, however, where much more work has to be done (particularly at an emotional level) to see clearly the usefulness of applying these concepts in those cases. The exact relationship between internalized oppression and internalized domination is not therefore clear cut. Does internalized domination simply mean all the thoughts, feelings and behaviours that oppressor groups internalize about their own and the oppressed group's identities – the oppressor group's equivalent of internalized oppression? Or does it refer only to the prejudices, feelings of superiority and other oppressive thoughts, feelings and behaviours that oppressor groups internalize (as opposed to guilt, self-hatred, terror, isolation or other such reactions)? For the moment, my own view is that this more limited notion of internalized domination is a more useful one.

Insofar as it applies to any oppressor group, undoing internalized domination requires tackling the various ways in which we are oppressed *and* tackling the specific feelings, attitudes and behaviour that we have internalized as members of an oppressor group. One of the problems with internalized domination, however, is that there is not the same sense of urgency about unravelling it as there is about internalized oppression. The possession of comfort, privilege and power leaves the oppressor group much more confused about reality than the oppressed group and, initially at least, much less motivated to change. More aware members of oppressor groups are often content to focus on, learn about and support the oppressed group while overlooking the steps they need to take to change themselves and their own people. Becoming aware of the depth of the oppression their group has perpetrated and throwing their lot in with the oppressed group are often naively assumed to be sufficient to overcome their own internalized domination. As we saw in Chapter 7, when members of oppressor groups become interested in oppression, most of their energy goes into learning about the oppressed group rather than into learning about themselves and how they come to play the roles they do. It is a fact that, while most of the work in relation to internalized domination has probably been done around men, very little has been done around oppressor groups in general. There is considerable work to be done in understanding the nature and effects of internalized domination on White people, upper- or owning-class people, heterosexuals, middle-class people, US people, non-disabled people, English people, Gentiles, Protestants and many other dominant groups. While we have been evolving more sophisticated strategies for undoing internalized oppression and achieving the liberation of oppressed groups, we have very few strategies for undoing internalized domination. Similarly, there is very little work done on the process of liberation for members of oppressor groups. Partly, this can be explained by the fact that many of those who write about this area tend to concentrate on their oppressed rather than their oppressor identities. This may well be due to feelings of guilt, confusion and fear that make it difficult for people to focus on being oppressors.

Leadership clearly has a role to play in tackling internalized oppression. We have looked in some detail at how it can do this in the previous chapter. It also, however, has an important role to play in tackling internalized domination. Leaders need to be alert to the ways in which this process can affect their own attitudes, feelings and behaviour and the ways in which it can interfere with building relationships of respect and equality. They also need to model a willingness and commitment to interrupting and contradicting internalized domination both in themselves and others. By being open to learning about their own patterns of domination and showing a willingness to try to change these, they can create the safety and example that enables other members of oppressor groups to do likewise. They can also play an important part in developing structures and processes within groups and organizations that assist people with oppressor identities in dealing with these issues in an organized, collective and systematic manner.

SUMMARY

It is clear that a well-developed body of literature about internalized oppression has existed for some time. There is a high degree of similarity and consistency in the processes described in this literature. In spite of this, it has not figured prominently in courses on psychology or in the training of psychologists. In addition, the significance of this literature and its relevance to our understanding of the processes of leadership and social change have generally been missed. These ideas rarely form any part of leadership theory or leadership training or education. Given the pervasiveness of the processes described in this and the preceding chapters, effective leaders must be sensitive to these dynamics and have a clear picture of their role in assisting people to overcome the effects of both internalized oppression and domination. We shall return to a discussion of oppressor dynamics once again in Chapter 11 when we look at the process of liberation. Before that, however, in Chapter 10, we shall explore the nature of oppressor conditioning in more detail using middle-class people to illustrate the kind of dynamic that operates here.

REFLECTION

Oppressed identities

1   In relation to your various oppressed identities, which of the elements of internalized oppression described in this chapter can you identify in yourself or your people? In what particular ways do they show up?
2   In relation to other oppressed groups, which elements of internalized oppression (from this or the previous chapter) have you noticed?
3   In relation to each of your oppressed identities, tell the story of growing up with, or taking on, this identity. Focus in particular on any feelings associated with your experiences.

Oppressor identities

4   In relation to each of your oppressor identities, what messages or stereotypes did you get about the relevant oppressed group?
5   In relation to each of your oppressor identities, tell the story of your earliest memories in connection with the relevant oppressed group. Focus in particular on any feelings associated with what you remember.
6   In relation to each of your oppressor identities, what negative feelings, attitudes, or prejudices have you internalized as a result of being a member of that dominant, privileged or oppressor group?
7   In relation to each of your oppressor identities, try to name some of the more subtle or covert ways your negative feelings, attitudes or

prejudices manifest themselves in relation to the oppressed group. (See Chapter 7.)

8   When you think about your own or other oppressor identities, what are the main elements of internalized domination that stand out or are reflected in the relationship with oppressed groups?

10 A psychology of the middle class

INTRODUCTION

In Chapter 9, we saw how there has been a neglect of the study of dominant or oppressor groups. The dynamic surrounding the training of people to play roles as agents of oppression has not been closely examined in much of the literature. One area where this is particularly marked is in relation to class oppression. In fact, class is significant because of the neglect of this issue as a whole – both the experience of the oppressed and of the oppressors. While issues such as racism and sexism have received increasingly more attention, class remains as a noticeably neglected area of study in psychology. Langston (2000) maintains there is a reluctance to recognize class differences and that this denial functions to reinforce the control and domination of the ruling class. Commenting on the neglect of class by psychology, Heppner and Scott (2004) remark that although oppressions such as racism and sexism are no longer acceptable in society, classism is still socially acceptable in many situations. Lott (2002) comments that the "near invisibility of the poor in psychology as well as psychologists' lack of attention to social class in general continues even when there is a direct focus on multiculturalism and diversity" (p. 101). For Lott, the reason for this is that psychologists are preoccupied with people who are like themselves, i.e. middle class. They focus on what they know. She makes the point that although those who are middle class can experience the effects of racism or sexism, ageism or heterosexism, or the oppression associated with disability, they do not experience the oppression associated with being poor. And, while a sizable minority within the discipline of psychology may come from a raised-poor or working-class background, it is clearly not a salient feature of their current lives. Thus middle-class people respond to issues of poverty mainly with ignorance because they are largely cut off from, and do not know, people who are poor or they are cut off from, or unaware of, their own early experiences with class. As we shall see below, however, the reasons are actually more complex than this. Lee and Dean (2004) discuss the myth that the US, for example, is a largely middle-class society with a majority of people subjectively identifying as middle class. Given the ignorance around, and stereotyping of, people who are poor and working class, this is not so surprising. In a society that looks down on people who are poor or working class, people will prefer to identify as middle class. We saw in Chapter 9 how this escaping from the identity, or denial of the identity, is one of the characteristics of internalized oppression. Liu *et al.* (2004), Liu and Rasheed Ali (2005) and Borgen (2005) also believe that class has been neglected, holding that it is one of the most elusive and least understood constructs in psychology.

The problem is not confined to psychology, however. In an interview with Shah (1998) and in his own writings, Albert (2000) makes the point that while the New Left has made huge ideological gains in relation to issues such as gender, sexuality, age and race, it has had very little impact structurally or ideologically in relation to class. Like Lott, he attributes this in part to the fact that many of those on the political left are more closely identified with what he calls the coordinator class (for example, managers, lawyers, doctors, academics, engineers) who have a high degree of control over decision making, who do mainly intellectual work, who largely control their own conditions of work and who also define or control the conditions that other more typical workers endure (Albert 2003). These people have only a weak understanding of the dynamics of class oppression and often embody many of the assumptions and prejudices that underpin this oppression. They are, therefore, not in a position to offer any leadership in tackling this issue. A similar perspective is reflected by Hahnel (2005) in his work on economic justice and democracy where he asserts that most people on the left "were blind to the emergence and importance of a new professional managerial, or coordinator class" (p. 65).

While the study of class oppression in general has been neglected, we probably do know much more about the effects on those raised poor or marginalized than we do about middle- or ruling-class people. Much of this comes from the disciplines of politics, sociology and counselling rather than from psychology. Much of it comes also from non-academic, activist sources. One of the challenges we face is to expand the psychological approaches in this area, particularly in terms of liberation psychology. So, for example, we need to develop a much clearer picture of how class oppression and internalized class oppression affect those raised poor and working class. We also need to examine more closely the liberation process as it relates to these groups. Beyond these, however, we need to know much more about the oppressor groups, middle-class and ruling- or owning-class. Given the largely middle-class orientation of the subject, this is an opportunity to turn the spotlight on those who occupy positions of power as being part of the problem rather than focusing solely on the oppressed and treating them as the problem. In this chapter, I want to outline a psychology of middle-class people as an important step in this process. I also want to highlight the need for this kind of work with oppressor groups in general – White people, men, heterosexuals, non-disabled, Gentiles, and so on. Rather than seeing our role crudely as trying to change the oppressed or, more benignly, as assisting the oppressed to achieve liberation, a key part of our role is also learning how to help our own privileged groups to change, to give up power and control, to eliminate their prejudices and to become allies for the oppressed.

From a leadership perspective, just as we need to understand the dynamics of oppression and internalized oppression in order to be able to think clearly about members of oppressed groups, we also need to understand these dynamics in order to be able to think clearly about members of dominant or oppressor groups. We especially need to understand this so that we can keep a clear perspective on the role of leaders in mixed-identity contexts and on how leaders with an oppressor identity can be a liberating resource for people with oppressed identities. As we saw in Chapter 7, leaders' unawareness around their oppressor identities is quite likely to play itself out in ways that are experienced as patronizing, disempowering or disrespectful and thus limit their effectiveness as agents of change and liberation. Rather than looking at the middle class as a whole, a useful way into this subject is to look at the experience of those middle-class people who see themselves as progressive and committed to values of social justice and equality, the kind of people that Albert (2000) sees as playing a leading role on the political left. The contradiction between the values of this group and broader middle-class values makes it easier to see the internalized oppression of middle-class people generally.

In deciding to include a chapter on class in this book, I was struck by the feelings this brought up compared to how I felt about the other issues I have spoken about so far. In ways that were not apparent in relation to other chapters, I noticed that I approached this chapter much more cautiously. I was more concerned about whether or not the reader would be comfortable with what it contained. While I had little difficulty in raising issues to do with racism, colonialism or sexism in previous chapters, when it came to class I wondered whether people would be upset or put off by this discussion. My dilemma around this, it seems to me, is a reflection of a much broader dynamic. People who are comfortable with the concept of oppression as it relates to various groups such as women, people of colour, people with disabilities, Jews, gay, lesbian or bisexuals, older people and so on, are not necessarily at all comfortable around the notion of class oppression. This is partly why the issue has been neglected in psychology generally and more specifically within liberation psychology. It is important that we acknowledge any discomfort around this topic while staying with the struggle to understand it. These feelings are telling us something about ourselves but they are also telling us something about how class systems operate.

MIDDLE-CLASS LEADERS

Many social change organizations and movements are led and actively supported by people who have been raised middle class or who currently live a predominantly middle-class lifestyle. Cotgrove and Duff (2003), for example, found that environmentalists are drawn predominantly from the middle class and, in particular, that section of the middle class that occupies roles in the service sector (for example, doctors, social workers, teachers and artists). In fact, this middle-class leadership has also been a feature of many change movements historically and in different parts of the world. Middle-class leaders, such as Mahatma Gandhi, Martin Luther King, Nelson Mandela, Cory Aquino, Mary Robinson, Aung San Suu Kyi, have played, and continue to play, key roles in the liberation struggles of other oppressed groups. Their middle-class position gave them the education and the opportunity to learn about, understand and offer leadership in the struggles against racism, colonialism, women's oppression and many others. Their access to education and information, for example, has enabled middle-class people such as these to develop critical perspectives on the workings of current economic and political systems that enable them to participate effectively in, and lead, social change organizations. This same class position, however, does not often, or necessarily, leave them very clear about how class oppression intersects with the other oppressions. As we shall see further on, there is a conditioning of middle-class people that makes it difficult for them to think and act beyond the confines of their role in the class system. Being middle class imposes limits and restrictions on the clarity, consciousness and behaviour of people that act as barriers to their effectiveness as leaders and change agents.

Because of our education, because of the confidence in our own thinking but mostly because of an unaware assumption that we know better, there is a real tendency for middle-class activists to usurp the leadership of marginalized groups. Freire (1972), as we saw in Chapter 7, drew attention to the predicament inherent in this when he talked about how difficult it is for people to switch from being exploiters to being on the side of the exploited. As middle-class people we carry a high degree of unawareness into our relationships with working-class or raised-poor people. We trust our thinking and are used to giving it to other people. We easily assume we think more clearly than others. According to Freire,

> Our converts . . . truly desire to transform the unjust order; but because of their background they believe that they must be the executors of the transformation. They talk about the people but they do not trust them; and trusting the people is the indispensable precondition for revolutionary change.
>
> (p. 36)

Under these circumstances, it is very easy for us to take on leadership, to step into a leadership vacuum and to expect other people to follow our lead. In doing this, we may actually make it more difficult for other people to take leadership of their own liberation. A key challenge for middle-class activists is to trust working-class leadership, to support working-class leaders and to be prepared to step aside to allow working-class leadership to emerge. To be effective as a middle-class leader or change agent, to build respectful, peer relationships with the people we are committed to, means understanding the "baggage" we carry into this relationship because of our own class background. It means understanding how this class background can distort our leadership and disempower others. And it means learning new ways to build relationships that are empowering and liberating both for ourselves and those we are allies of.

THE MIDDLE CLASS

According to Liu *et al.* (2004), "social class may be defined as an individual's position within an economic hierarchy that is determined by his or her income, educational level, and occupation". This definition suggests that a person's class is an amalgam of different elements. Nickerson (1991) and Ruth (2005) note that there are different ways of defining class. At a very general level, the working class, for example, is anyone who works for a living as opposed to living off unearned or inherited income. This would include the self-employed and small business owners who do not have sufficient wealth or control over the means of production that would enable them to live off the work of others – they have to work just as hard, if not harder, than those around them. It would also include the middle class. For practical reasons connected with people's lived experiences and connected with how we can do developmental work on class identity, it is often useful to make further distinctions within this broad grouping of workers. From this point of view, the working class is that group of workers engaged in the direct production of goods and services. These are generally valued and paid an hourly wage for what they do and are not, in general, valued or paid for their thinking, even though a great deal of thinking may be involved in their work. A separate category of people again are those who are poor or raised poor. Many of these were forced out of the working class due to unemployment or injury and may at times experience the working class as one of their oppressors, looking down on them or attacking them. A third category of people within this broad group of workers is the middle class. From this perspective, we can define the middle class as that group of workers who themselves do not work in the direct production of goods and (non-professional) services but who work in support of this in their roles as organizers, teachers, managers, coordinators, social workers, consultants and the like. They may also provide specialized and highly paid professional services in occupations that restrict entry or are otherwise difficult to enter. They organize, monitor, control, regulate, facilitate, manage, evaluate, train or educate other workers. They are often regarded as "professionals" and afforded higher pay and regarded with more status and respect. In general, these definitions of the different groups look at class economically in terms of roles or occupations and rewards.

For Nickerson (1991), however, there is also a cultural definition of class. As a result of class oppression, the various classes develop different cultures due to different life experiences and the isolation that exists between them. He maintains that people often become more identified with these than with their actual, objective position in the class structure. These cultures include particular values and lifestyles as well as particular hurts and mistreatment associated with the different class experiences. In this case, it is the combination of culture and hurts that defines class. According to this definition, the working class are those who identify with working-class culture – the values and lifestyles of the people who generally are wage earners and not university educated – along with particular hurts and experiences of mistreatment and their associated painful emotions. In terms of culture, the middle class are those who have internalized certain values such as "getting ahead", economic competitiveness, keeping up with appearances, behaving "properly", fitting in and so on, and who live a certain lifestyle based on access to good education, accumulation, consumerism, financial security and levels of physical and material comfort not shared by other sections of society. In one sense, their lives may be characterized by the absence of the degree of day-to-day struggle for survival that preoccupies those less well off. At the same time, there may also be greater levels of social isolation and a less well-developed sense of community. (We shall look at these characteristics in more detail below). Finally, the other group that we have not yet mentioned are whom we can call the owning class (ruling class, upper class), who are those people who own and control the means of production and who make their living from the labour of others through their ownership of companies or their stocks or from inherited wealth, as well as having the corresponding values, lifestyle and education. The members of all of these groups have particular experiences in common that they identify with. They also have experienced particular hurts and can identify particular painful emotions that these hurts have left them with. Each of the class groups tends to have its own combination of experiences, hurts and painful emotion that are relatively unique and that help to make up the cultural definition of that particular group.

Nickerson's approach is very important in highlighting both the objective and the subjective aspects of people's class identity, but particularly the latter. He sees the definitions as organizing tools, or places to begin, in doing the work of looking at our personal experiences in regard to class. In a similar way, my concern in relation to defining the middle class is less with developing an objective definition and more with defining it in ways that enable people to clarify their own subjective class identity. An important challenge is for people with a middle-class heritage or identity to acknowledge and claim that identity so that they can do the developmental work necessary to free themselves of any "baggage" attached to that identity and to enable them to develop liberatory or emancipatory relationships with raised-poor and working-class people. As we can see in the case of other oppressions, this developmental work needs to be done at both the individual and the collective levels (Moane 1999) and we shall look at this aspect in more detail in Chapter 11. Implicit in this approach is the assumption that many people will actually be of mixed-class identity and may, in fact, need to do developmental work around the middle-class and the other class aspects of this mixed-class heritage. Some people, for example, could have a working-class occupation but middle-class values, education and lifestyle. Others could have a middle-class occupation and lifestyle but with working-class values and experiences. People may have been raised poor or working class and be currently middle class or vice versa. Some people may have little wealth but may also have internalized strong owning-class values through their education or family background. It is also the case that there may be differences from place to place. People who identify as middle class in one country, for example, may be seen as poor or working class by the standards of another country. One of the important questions, among many, for people to look at in all of this, for example, is how their experience of class has left them in any way hurt, damaged or struggling with painful emotion. By working on our subjective experience of class we can undo the effects of internalized oppression and become more effective as leaders and change agents. The nature of the kind of developmental work required by this will be explored in Chapter 11. At this point, I want to focus more specifically on the middle class as one of the more neglected aspects of this issue.

MIDDLE-CLASS CONDITIONING

What then does it mean to be middle class? In what ways does being middle class shape the ways we think, feel and behave? How does it affect our self-image, our relationships and our leadership? These are some of the questions about our identity that face us in trying to make sense of what it means to be middle class. It is clear to me that being raised middle class or currently living a middle-class lifestyle imposes a conditioning on us that we need to be aware of. Psychology has had very little to tell us about this. However, in workshops with middle-class people over many years and in different countries, I have had a chance to build up a picture of what happens to middle-class people as part of our conditioning. Having a clear picture of this process is vital for any middle-class person involved in leadership and social change work. Understanding the broader dynamic will be useful for anyone working in any mixed-identity situation.

Let me paint a picture of middle-class life. My intention is to capture some of the essence of being middle class although the actual details will vary a lot from person to person and group to group. These variations will depend on such things as whether the person is solidly or completely middle-class or else of mixed-class heritage. There will be differences between the experiences of

White middle class and middle-class people of colour. Each oppressed constituency within the middle class will have its own particular story to tell of
what it means to be middle class. So the picture I paint is an incomplete one
and may overly represent the experiences of a raised-middle-class, White,
Gentile male. To be complete, it certainly needs to be fleshed out with all the
nuances and variations of experience that the intersecting oppressions bring
to it.

Allowing for these shortcomings, I will try to describe some common elements of middle-class experience. As middle-class people we have often been
separated physically, socially, linguistically and culturally from working-class,
raised- or currently poor and other marginalized people. We live in different
areas, go to different schools, talk differently and socialize in different locations. We may have few close friends who are poor or working class. This
segregation, which would not be tolerated around some other oppressions, is
considered acceptable to most middle-class people. In the case of middle-
class people of colour, the racism they experienced may have demanded that
they distance themselves from poor or working-class people of colour, which
often meant the majority of their people, as a condition of being accepted by
White middle-class people. In addition, many of us who were raised middle
class were taught to see ourselves as superior in some ways, for example,
intellectually, culturally or morally. We may see ourselves as smarter, more
worthwhile, more sophisticated and as having better taste than working-class
or raised-poor people. Just as with other forms of oppression, our relationships with them may be characterized by high levels of unawareness. As Lott
(2002) points out, such groups commonly experience daily, face-to-face class-
ist discrimination by middle-class people, what Sue (2003) refers to as micro-
assaults. These may include subtle or covert forms of discrimination such as
being insulted, ignored, talked down to or disregarded by others in shops,
classrooms and public offices, including those they must go to for public
assistance. Ehrenreich (1989), one of the few people to focus specifically on
the middle class, highlights the deep level of unawareness around class as
compared with issues such as racism or sexism.

> While ideas about gender, and even race, have moved, however haltingly,
> in the direction of greater tolerance and inclusivity, ideas about class
> remain mired in prejudice and mythology. "Enlightened" people, who
> might flinch at a racial slur, have no trouble listing the character defects
> of an ill-defined "underclass," defects which routinely include ignorance,
> promiscuity, and sloth. There is, if anything, even less inhibition about
> caricaturing the white or "ethnic" working class: Its tastes are "tacky"; its
> habits unhealthful; and its views are hopelessly bigoted and parochial.
>
> (p. 7)

As middle-class, we may have been taught to see our interests as different
from those of working-class people. According to this, they do not appreciate

the important things in life as we do, or apply the same high standards, or adhere to the same strong values that we do. We were told that the current economic system is fair and rational and that anyone who is prepared to work hard and be ambitious can achieve an equal share of society's rewards and resources. Sometimes, we were told that people less privileged than us were stupid or lazy or dirty or dangerous. Some of us then see them as the causes of their own misfortunes. For the middle class, these groups are often either invisible, like janitors and maids or other service workers, and not worthy of recognition, or they are hypervisible and subject to ridicule, disdain, or fear (Lott, 2002). Some of us may see them as bad influences on, or threats to, our own children. If so, we would prefer not to live near them or have our children play with theirs. Many middle-class children, for example, have had the experience of being prevented from playing, or making friends, with working-class children because of their parents' discomfort or prejudices. The result of these kinds of messages and this kind of conditioning is that many middle-class people are prejudiced towards, or uncomfortable around, working-class or raised-poor people. Even when we are not convinced that the current economic system is actually fair and truly reflects people's real efforts and talents, we are still uncomfortable around them because of feelings of guilt or fear.

With the best will in the world, it is difficult for any middle-class person to escape these kinds of messages and this conditioning. Even middle-class activists who, at the very least, intellectually challenge and disagree with many of the messages they have got about other people, may still carry the emotional effects of this fairly systematic conditioning. The messages we got about ourselves and people of other classes were continually reinforced through the education system, through the mass media, through the physical segregation of communities, through the political system, through the legal system, through work and many other aspects of day-to-day life. It is not enough to believe that these messages were wrong or that the current system is actually oppressive and in need of change. It is not enough to know about the damage that has been done to people who have been systematically marginalized and disadvantaged in our economic system. We need to know how we ourselves have been emotionally damaged by this and how the effects of this damage can interfere with our ability to be effective allies for those we work with. We need to understand what we have internalized as part of our own middle-class oppression.

MIDDLE-CLASS OPPRESSION

We can see from the above how middle-class people can play an oppressor role in relation to people who are poor or working class. How then can we talk about the middle class as being oppressed? Sonn and Fisher (2003) describe the coloured community in South Africa during apartheid as being wedged in between the dominant and the dominated, being oppressed but also getting certain social, educational and economic advantages. This is not unlike the position of the middle class. To begin with, middle-class people are oppressed as workers and, in this, we share some of the same oppression as working-class people. For example, we receive back a small portion of the value we produce by our work. Even though some of us receive more than the broad mass of working-class people, it is still much less than is produced. (It is also the case that some of us are paid less than working-class people.) Our jobs exist to the extent that they are necessary to keep things running smoothly and when it is possible to do without them, they are eliminated. In times of recession, we may be just as vulnerable as other working-class people. In the relentless efforts of work organizations to become more efficient by streamlining their systems, middle-management jobs are sometimes the first to go. Long-term financial stability for middle-class people has largely disappeared and our higher salaries cannot cushion us for long once we become unemployed. There are also some specific forms of oppression of middle-class workers made possible by their separation from the rest of the working class. Middle-class workers are expected to identify with their work, to put their personalities at its service and to give up any clear boundary to the working day and working week in order to meet the goals of the organization. We are mostly not paid overtime and many of us work long hours, endangering our health and making well-balanced lives difficult. According to Fraser (2001), "Overwork is epidemic, for men and women whose job demands keep increasing, not because of career advances but because of a corporate environment that has depended upon *squeezing* . . . more and more work out of fewer people with fewer resources" (p. 8). This point is echoed by Bunting (2004) who notes the increasing workloads, the longer hours being worked and the higher stress levels affecting white-collar workers. In the face of increasing intensification of work, the traditional protection of trade union membership is not an option for many middle-class people and collective action is actively discouraged and resisted by employers. Instead, as Bunting points out, "We look for personal, private solutions to our problems, rather than identifying with others and achieving reforms" (p. xxv). Simply as workers, then, middle-class people experience a particular type of oppression.

As part of this middle-class oppression and as part of the larger oppression of working-class people, it is important that middle-class people do not identify, or show solidarity, with working-class people in general. In order to maintain any oppressive system, it is important, as we saw in previous chapters, that the oppressed group is kept divided within itself. This is achieved in part by installing the different oppressions that keep people from being able to unite with one another against their common oppression. As Zinn (1990) puts it,

> How skillful to tax the middle class to pay for the relief of the poor, building resentment on top of humiliation! How adroit to bus poor black

youngsters into poor white neighborhoods, in a violent exchange of impoverished schools, while the schools of the rich remain untouched and the wealth of the nation, doled out carefully where children need milk, is drained for billion-dollar aircraft carriers. How ingenious to meet the demands of blacks and women for equality by giving them small benefits, and setting them in competition with everyone else for jobs made scarce by an irrational, wasteful system. How wise to turn the fear and anger of the majority toward a class of criminals bred – by economic necessity – faster than they can be put away, deflecting attention from the huge thefts of national resources carried out within the law by men in executive offices.

(p. 573)

Part of how class oppression, in particular, operates is to separate middle-class people from the rest of the working class. This separation is accomplished through a combination of four particular processes: bribery; threats; misinformation; and denial of reality. As a result of these processes, which we shall look at below, middle-class people are conditioned to play an oppressor role towards working-class people and to accept the limitations imposed by their own oppression.

Bribery

At a very basic level, middle-class people (in common with other oppressor groups) are bribed to play an oppressor role. We are offered various inducements to help manage, maintain, support, coordinate, legitimize and reinforce the oppressive structures. In our various roles as managers, coordinators, administrators, supervisors, social workers, doctors, lawyers, consultants, teachers and other professionals, those of us in the middle class are induced to help maintain the system in return for promises of somewhat higher wealth and income, somewhat higher status, somewhat greater security, somewhat greater material comfort, and some more opportunities to "climb the career ladder" and get ahead. Zinn (1990) describes us as the guards of the system who are given small rewards to keep things going. The values underpinning this are constantly reinforced through the media, through education and the various other mechanisms of socialization in the culture. In this way, people are encouraged to seek relief from their oppression not by changing the system but by climbing out of the working class into the middle class or climbing out of the middle class into the owning class. This process persuades us to become preoccupied with such things as comfort, security and material well-being as the major determinants of a fulfilling life. We are encouraged to feel good about ourselves to the extent that we have achieved these to one degree or another. And, in the process, the society institutionalizes greed as a positive value. Rather than having a society that is organized around meeting rational, human needs, we have a society preoccupied with greed and profit at all costs. From a psychological point of view, our sense of our own inherent, unconditional worth and goodness is taken from us and replaced with a conditioned sense of worth and goodness based on the non-human values that are useful within an oppressive system. None of the rewards we are offered, however, can ever substitute for the disconnection from our humanity caused by this process. Just as Spanierman and Heppner (2004) pinpointed the numerous psychosocial costs to White people of racism, it is also the case that while individual middle-class people may benefit in terms of power, privilege and status, the costs at the level of our humanity are huge. We shall see this more clearly when we look below at what gets internalized by middle-class people.

Threats

The bribes that are offered to middle-class people are reinforced by various threats about what will happen if we do not cooperate. This process starts when we are young. Often the love that those of us who grew up middle-class received was made conditional on "being good", on "behaving ourselves" or acting "properly", which meant, in practice, being quiet, doing well and conforming to the expectations of the adults around us. For many young people this also meant suppressing their natural spontaneity, not being too loud or not drawing too much attention to themselves. A common threat to children was the withdrawal of approval if they misbehaved. Sometimes, this threat was reinforced with physical abuse. As we got older, we were reminded about how much our future depended on fitting in and doing well. What started out as threats that "Mum/Dad will stop loving you if you do not behave properly" eventually becomes "Your boss will disapprove if you do not behave properly." And so, enormous amounts of energy go into keeping other people happy, not upsetting people, not "rocking the boat" and conforming to what is expected of us. The stereotype of middle-class people as boring, timid and conventional is actually rooted in a very heavy oppression.

The school system plays a large part in reinforcing this conditioning. In spite of the efforts of individual teachers, our education is very often simply a preparation for the middle-class roles we will play as adults. Streaming and setting in schools mimic, and prepare us for, a class hierarchy in the wider world. We are pressurized to do well at school and warned about what will happen if we do not study hard and get good results in examinations. As students, we are reminded of the need to work hard in order to get "a good job". Success in life is held up as doing well career-wise. Much of the education system consists of systematically worrying *at* young people about their future success by teachers and parents, and worrying *at* parents, about the consequences of their children not doing well in school. Our whole future is made to hang on whether or not we get top marks. There are often strong pressures on educationalists to see their role in a narrow way as preparing young people for work. Lip-service is then paid to the notion of educating people for life and only a narrow range of life options is held up to young people as worth aspiring to. It is clear that for many of us, there was a time when we felt we had to give up on our cherished dreams for our lives and for the world in order to fit in with the demands and expectations of the adult world around us. In working with young adults, I have often been moved by their stories of the dreams they were forced to give up on in the interests of being "practical" or because there "was no money in that dream". As people talk about this, it becomes clear that, at some level, this has left them heart-broken. In extreme cases, failure to behave properly and conform to the demands of the system can trigger mental health oppression where the difficult or non-conformist person is described as crazy or mentally ill.

Misinformation

Bribery and threats are powerful means of ensuring conformity. Over and above these, however, we also receive ongoing misinformation about the world around us. The members of each class are given false information about the others and discouraged from forming close, supportive relation-ships across groups. For those of us who were raised middle class, the process of separating us from the rest of the working class starts early on. As we saw earlier we get many negative messages about working-class and raised-poor people not to mention the physical segregation and being prevented from making friends with them. Most of us got very little accurate information about what was happening in the world around us. As young people, we witnessed inequality and oppression but never got explanations for these that made any clear sense. I was raised in a largely middle-class home but in a largely working-class area. From the time I started school, I was aware of the inequality around me. We had a bigger house. We had more money. I had more toys and better clothes. I noticed that I was treated with more respect by adults than were my working-class friends. I could see and feel the differences but none of it made any sense to me. Either it was never talked about or the few explanations that I would have heard put the differences down to per-sonal shortcomings on the one hand or personal initiative on the other. No one ever explained inequality in terms of injustice or systemic problems. The education system ignored the existence of inequality and focused on a world that bore little relation to what I was experiencing day to day. All through primary school, my best friend was working class. On the day we started secondary school, we were separated into two different streams without any warning. From then on, we were never as close. No one ever discussed that or explained why we were separated. There was no place to deal with the feelings around it. It was presented as an inevitable part of growing up rather than something we might question.

In this situation, the adults around us often modelled very oppressive atti-tudes and behaviour towards working-class people that added to the lack of clarity about what was going on. We were warned about the dangers of associating with people from particular areas. We heard the prejudices and the stereotypes that were never challenged or questioned. Even where we were not told directly that we were superior, we could see that the middle-class adults around us treated working-class people differently and did not have them as close friends.

Despite the general encouragement that exists for middle-class young people to explore and think about the world and appreciate different cultures, the subject of class is never addressed. We are left confused about reality. Although many of us have been brought up to ask questions, we do not learn to question our own place in the world. The competitive society is held up as an ideal. Our education prepares us to use the existing system but not to challenge or improve it in human ways.

Denial of reality

Very closely linked to the misinformation is the denial of reality. When we were small, some of us noticed that the world around us did not make sense. It appeared strange and irrational. We wondered why some people were treated differently from others. (It seems to be the case that witnessing mistreatment is always confusing for a young person.) Often we were told it was because *they* were "no good", "lazy", "stupid", "dirty", "violent" and so on. Particularly to a young person, explanations like this do not make any sense but this was coming from people we respected or whom we knew loved us. Sometimes, we were given no information at all. One way or the other, the people around us seemed to act as though everything were perfectly rational and that there was no cause for concern. No one appeared outraged or bothered by the inequality. No one even acknowledged it. As middle-class children, we got the message, repeatedly, that "everything is fine". There is nothing wrong with the current economic system. For both adults and children, there is a widespread denial of the reality of class oppression and the current economic system is held out to be rational, benign, necessary and without any viable alternative (Korten, 1995). The combination of misinformation and the denial of reality are very powerful ways of preparing people to occupy oppressor roles in society. When these are reinforced with bribes and threats we make it extremely difficult for a person to go against the weight of the oppression and act in ways that are non-conformist, challenging, questioning or liberating.

INTERNALIZED MIDDLE-CLASS OPPRESSION

Given the oppression of middle-class people and the various mechanisms that operate to reinforce the conditioning, there are a number of elements that seem to be central to middle-class internalized oppression. These are not the only things that are true of middle-class people (such as the positive ways in which we have retained our humanity in spite of any conditioning) but they are some of the ways that the internalized oppression most damages us. If we scratch beneath any surface appearances of confidence or superiority, and if we make it safe for people to show their real selves, we shall see a range of places where middle-class people struggle. One of these relates to *conditional self-esteem*. As we saw earlier, as middle-class people we are raised to base our self-esteem on successful achievement in school or career or on the accumulation of wealth, comfort and financial security. For some of us, our self-esteem is based on appearances, on looking and sounding right, on keeping the people around us happy, on behaving properly and not "rocking the boat". In other words, our self-esteem is conditional and external. It can be difficult for us to have any sense of our own inherent worth or goodness. Many of us end up leading narrow, isolated lives preoccupied with greed, accumulation, materialism and appearances, addicted to comfort and security. As long as we are successful on these terms we can maintain an air of confidence and self-satisfaction but it is at the expense of being isolated from the reality of the lives of the people around us, cut off from close relationships with them and often with an inability to connect with, or show, our own deepest struggles or even our humanity. (This is not to say that comfort and security, for example, are not desirable goals for all people but rather that a preoccupation with, and addiction to, them leave us with a quality of life that is actually degraded in human terms.) The disconnection from an inherent, unconditional sense of self-worth and the preoccupation with superficialities can sometimes make it very hard for other people to connect with a real person underneath this veneer of polite isolation.

As we become aware of inequality in society, what can get internalized is *guilt* about the privileges we have shared in or about the apparent selfishness, unawareness and lack of concern among middle-class people generally for other marginalized groups. We may feel that, as middle-class people, there is something we have to do to justify our existence. We have to prove ourselves worthy. Sometimes, going with the guilt is also *fear*, fear of being attacked as middle class. Because middle-class people are often the visible agents of class oppression, it feels like we will be blamed by working-class people. These feelings can unconsciously permeate our approach to activism or social change. They can pull us into a *timidity* about taking strong action and a reluctance to upset people. This can make it hard for us to stay with a struggle when it gets tough, preferring instead to stay silent or to give in at that point. When we get into a close relationship with a working-class person, this timidity makes it difficult for that working-class person to know they can trust us, to know that we won't disappear on them when difficulties arise in the relationship. The fear and guilt can pull middle-class people into *being invisible* as middle class, not wanting their class background to be the centre of attention. Middle-class people in one mixed-class group I worked with told me how they had learned to keep their heads down and not stand out. This leads some people into a rejection of their own middle-class identity, along with a dismissive rejection of other middle-class people and attempts not to look or sound middle class themselves. Some people may adopt a lifestyle devoid of conspicuous consumption or comfort or "opt out" of mainstream culture, cutting themselves off from and disliking other middle-class people. Sometimes, they may try to pass as being working class themselves. In their attempts to reject the middle class and to identify with marginalized groups they may even end up romanticizing poverty and "the poor". Deep down, some middle-class people may wish they had experienced more oppression in their own lives so that they could feel better about themselves and less guilty. In a theoretical sense it is actually true that the middle class is a part of the larger working class, but this particular pull to identify as working class is coming more out of fear and guilt and often contains a large dose of pretence about it. This *pretence* is another feature of internalized middle-class oppression. It is one of the things that oppressed groups hate most about oppressor groups. They would find it easier sometimes to deal with outright hostility than the pretence that they are liked or that the other person has no prejudices or no difficulties around them. Although shared with other oppressor groups, pretence is a particularly middle-class characteristic. The combination of guilt, fear and wanting approval, along with the conditioning to suppress spontaneity and behave properly, leads many middle-class people into not showing ourselves, not being real. This can leave us quite isolated. In the middle of this isolation, we do not expect anyone to be there for us or deeply committed to us. It feels as if we have to earn people's support and not that people would be unconditionally pleased to offer it.

As middle-class people, we may bring these feelings and this conditioning into our activism, our leadership and our relationships. The guilt, in particular, that concerned middle-class people feel (just as in the case of men's guilt about women's oppression) is not a particularly helpful motivation for involvement in social change. Along with the pretence, it can leave us operating rigidly from within our own internalized oppression and set limits on how flexibly and creatively we can think about change. With the guilt tugging at us, we may develop a rigid sense of urgency about the work and a need to do it out of a sense of duty. We may feel as if we have to do something to justify our right to exist and to prove our worth. We may find ourselves trying to live up to other people's expectations and trying to keep them pleased with us. We try to figure out what is expected of us now and how we must look and sound in this new, activist situation in order to keep people happy with us. Sometimes, as activists, we simply change one set of expectations and appearances (dictated by an oppressive class system) for an alternative set (dictated by a rejection of class oppression and solidarity with marginalized people). However, we are still just as rigidly caught up in trying to get it right as we were before.

Going with the guilt, the fear and the pretence for many middle-class people is also *confusion*. We have been conditioned to be confused about the reality of economic exploitation and oppression. Many of us are well able to theorize and intellectually grasp complex issues to do with racism or sexism or any number of other oppressions. When it comes to class, however, something strange happens. We have difficulty grasping what happens here, particularly the part we play in it. Unlike these other oppressions, when it comes to class there is some way that many middle-class people simply don't get it. This is another reason why class has been neglected as an issue within psychology and within the political left. In just the same way that men have a difficulty grasping the subtleties of sexism, and White people have difficulty truly understanding the dynamics of racism, so also do middle-class people struggle to really understand how class oppression operates. This is not surprising. It is not a failing on the part of middle-class people for which we should feel even more guilty. Nor is it some wilful denial or deliberate unwillingness to accept responsibility for our role in class oppression. We were set up by the oppression to be confused. As we saw earlier, we were raised with a large amount of misinformation about the world around us and about people from other class backgrounds. The combination of this misinformation and the denial of the reality around us has left many middle-class people very confused. Even if we manage to understand the theory of class we are unable to relate it to our own personal lives and relationships. This is not simply an intellectual confusion nor is it a lack of intelligence on our part. People who otherwise think of themselves as intelligent and clear thinking may find themselves having a hard time making sense of class as an issue. No matter how much they read about it or hear about it, they still find it heavy going. This is an emotional confusion that we picked up as an integral part of the conditioning to be middle class. Listening to theory and reading about it, on their own, will not be enough to overcome this confusion. The feelings that hold it in place will have to be discharged in order to free up our thinking. If we do not do this, we will end up substituting someone else's thinking for our own. Instead of thinking for ourselves, we will parrot someone else's jargon and ideas without really understanding them and, in the process, end up alienating many of the people we try to communicate with. We will have difficulty getting across our thoughts about class to others because we will simply be repeating a formula we have memorized. Our inability to translate what we know into simple, unprovocative yet challenging language will betray the fact that we have not been able to connect our theories with our own lived experience. We will communicate other people's theories, other people's experiences and other people's feelings rather than speaking from the heart about what we ourselves have learned and know intimately about the world around us.

One result of confusion is that we try to lead social change without any clear model of economic or class oppression. Borgen (2005) and Sloan (2005), for example, both highlight the need for psychologists to go beyond their individualistic focus to address the oppressive nature of the capitalist economic system and globalization. As middle-class people, we can identify the problems created by the oppression but not the reasons why they arose or why they persist. This can lead to an approach to social change that is focused on dealing with symptoms rather than causes. We may work to alleviate poverty, for example, rather than confront the root causes of it, preferring minor reforms and charity rather than fundamental change. A mixture of pretence and confusion along with the trappings of either guilt or superiority will tend to come across as "do-gooding" and it is not surprising if, under these circumstances, the recipients of our charity are not appreciative and keep us at arm's length. It is the case that, in some (though not all) situations, the existence of voluntary, charitable organizations seems to absolve society of the obligation to remedy and eliminate oppression rather than simply alleviate its effects. In this, we become part of the problem rather than the solution.

MIDDLE-CLASS ALLIES

I have touched on just some aspects of how the conditioning of middle-class people is internalized and how it may show up in the behaviour of middle-class activists. It is important to underline that this is the effect of the oppression and is not a description of what middle-class people are like inherently. Recognizing that we carry such baggage into this work means that we have to look at how we can counteract it to become effective allies for the people we work with. Some immediate implications present themselves.

First, it is not enough to learn about the effects of oppression on those who are marginalized. We also need to understand the effects on us. As well as raising our awareness about the effects of inequality in society, we also have to raise our awareness about the ways in which our own conditioning as middle-class people gets in the way of our being effective allies. Aguilar (1995), drawing on the work of Cross (1988), summarizes a model of "cultural competency" to describe the stages through which the relationship between an oppressed group and a dominant, or an oppressor, group can progress. He emphasizes that, in order to become culturally competent, oppressor groups have to recognize that, as allies, they are not just part of the solution but also part of the problem and that a key aspect of this role is working to remove the effects of their own conditioning.

To do this, we need to own our middle-class identity. It is important that we do not pretend to be anything other than what we are, that we be visible as middle class. More than that, however, we need to take true pride in ourselves as middle-class people, not a pride based on narrow, conditioned values but a pride based on our deep caring as middle-class people for other people, our commitment as middle-class people to making this a better society, our courage as middle-class people to take a stand, our creativity, our spontaneity, and many other human characteristics not often associated with being middle class. In doing this, we also have to recognize that this work is about our own liberation also. It is not just something we do out of guilt for the sake of other people.

Undoing the effects of our own conditioning critically involves reaching out to, and leading, other middle-class people. We will be selling working-class people short if we build close relationships with them on top of our isolation from other middle-class people. This same isolation poses a real danger of leading us into the usurping of working-class leadership, which I referred to above, because we cannot stand being around the distorted values of middle-class people. It can feel more comfortable and more rewarding to work with and lead working-class people than to try to organize and lead our own middle class. In the same way that male allies of women have to face the challenge of working to change other men, so also do middle-class activists face the challenge to change other middle-class people. To be effective as allies we need both to support working-class people and go after other middle-class people.

A key part of being an ally is learning to listen deeply. For those of us who occupy positions of leadership or power, there is a strong pull to assume that our thinking is clearer or more important.

> How, after all, do working-class people . . . encounter the professional middle class? Not, in most cases, as friends or co-workers but in the role of teachers, social workers, or physicians. All of these are "helping professions," full of generous-spirited people, but they are also roles that confer authority and the power to make judgments about others. . . . For working-class people, relations with the middle class are usually a one-way dialogue. From above come commands, diagnoses, instructions, judgments, definitions – even, through the media, suggestions as to how to think, feel, spend money, and relax. Ideas seldom flow "upward" to the middle class, because there are simply no structures to channel the upward flow of thought from class to class.
>
> (Ehrenreich, 1989, p. 139)

A fairly common dynamic is for dominant groups to have difficulty giving up control or power. We want to be satisfied that people will use this power in ways we approve of before we hand it over. Or, we may refuse to engage in dialogue about change because we do not know the outcome before we begin. We have to resist the temptation to impose our thinking on others, listen well to their concerns and issues, recognize that they may well do things differently from us, trust their thinking and their ability to learn from their mistakes and decide to support their leadership. Our class position makes it highly unlikely that, as a group, we will be clear enough in our thinking to figure things out. In theory, it is possible that an individual middle-class person could achieve this clarity. However, in practice, it is unlikely that we will be able to do this on our own. Working-class leadership will be vital. This means, as middle-class people, getting behind working-class leaders, following them and learning from them.

As an example of the challenge and the complexity of this process, let me describe some of my own personal experience around being an ally and the baggage attached to it. Over many years, in my work and in my close relationships, I have been thinking about what it means to be an ally for an oppressed group. Much of my understanding about this is based on my experiences as an Irish person when I have been in Britain or the US. I have had a lot of experience of people in those countries offering, and trying, to be an ally for me. Some of them have turned out to be excellent allies. Unfortunately, the efforts of others have sometimes had the effect of pushing me back into my internalized Irish oppression rather than giving me a hand with it. People try different things. Sometimes, they simply announce that they are going to be my ally and expect me to be delighted with them. Sometimes they ask me to explain the history of Irish oppression or bring them up to date on what is happening in Ireland. Sometimes, they eagerly ask for my latest thinking and wait to be educated, excited and inspired. In themselves, none of these things is necessarily a problem, except that, on many of these occasions, I simply want people to reach out and make friends with me and not treat me as a category or an identity or a representative of an oppressed group.

I have learned how subtle are the ways in which the internalized oppression around being Irish gets triggered. When I first went to the US, for example, I found people extremely warm and welcoming. What was surprising and confusing was that, sometimes, I also felt awful. I struggled with feelings of humiliation and insignificance on these occasions. When I thought back over particular contacts I had with individuals, I could not pinpoint any situations where people had been in any way oppressive. It took a long time for me to realize that it was not the case that people had behaved oppressively in many of these situations, at least in any obvious or direct way. It was simply that whenever I looked at them, as a group they always looked supremely confident and in good shape. People did not easily show their vulnerability or the places where they struggled. No one acted as if they felt insecure, uncertain, embarrassed, scared or ashamed. For someone who struggled much of the time with feelings like these, to be around people who did not seem to show any struggle that I could see was very unsettling. It seemed that I rarely got to see the full person. And it was not only that they did not show their struggles. A lot of the time, I also could not see their true humanity and instead was shown a superficial, formula friendliness that lacked real depth. It was like being with someone who was being careful to behave correctly but was not able to do this spontaneously or from the heart.

I realized that I could tell someone was truly my ally when they got close to me, made friends with me and showed themselves to me – both their humanity and their struggles. I did not need them to be experts on Irish oppression. I did not need them even to know a lot about Irish culture or history. I did not need them never to make mistakes. I just needed them to show that they cared and that I was not the only one struggling in the relationship. It helped a lot when they stopped trying so hard to be my ally and instead became my friend. It helped when I could tell I was more than just a cause to be supported but a real person they wanted to be close to.

As I got clearer about this, I also began to think about what that might mean for me as a middle-class, White, Gentile man in particular and as a member of any other oppressor group. When I started leading leadership and liberation workshops, one of my fears was that I had not done enough work on my own sexism, racism, classism, anti-Jewish prejudices and all the other oppressive material that I carried. It seemed to me that I simply did not know enough about all the oppressions I would have to deal with. However, I did not have the luxury of waiting until I had done all this work and felt ready. In the end, based on my Irish experience, I decided just to go after people and make friends with them. That decision made a big difference to me and it got me a long way. I was able to build close connections with people of many other identities to the point where they could tell that I understood some of their struggles and was committed to being there as an ally. However, eventually I hit up against some further difficulties that I have since begun to understand much more clearly.

A turning point for me came during one particular tense conversation with a close working-class, female friend. It had started out pleasantly and in a relaxed manner but got to a point where I began to feel criticized and blamed unfairly for things that had happened. I remember telling myself to keep listening and I tried to make appropriate sounds and nods to show I was paying attention. But, in reality, I was gone. As I "listened", my mind drifted away. I found myself looking out the window at the bright blue sky outside, wishing I could just disappear. As I "listened", I was having another conversation in my head where I argued with everything I was hearing and where I felt sorry for myself for having to listen to the "unfair" things that were coming my way.

For whatever reason, at that point, I suddenly became aware of what I was doing. I had disappeared emotionally but was pretending to be present. I also realized that my friend was assuming I was actually listening when, in fact, she had no way of knowing what was really going on for me because I was not saying anything about it or showing it. So, this time, I did something different. I turned to her and said, "Look, I'm having a really hard time listening. I just feel like disappearing. I feel like walking away." As soon as I said this, she stopped what she was saying and said, "Well, would you like me to listen to you for a while?" Although I did not feel particularly safe, I could tell this was important so I told her about how awful I was feeling in the situation. I was very honest about how I felt without in any way blaming her or linking how I was feeling to what she had been doing or saying. As I talked, I could see her relax and take charge of the situation. Once I opened up and she could tell what was going on for me, we were able to focus on the real difficulty and sort it out between us. Previously, where I would have hidden my discomfort, this would have taken a long time to get over and would have left a residue of tension. I realized that on the occasions when things got tense between us, I tended not to show what was happening in my head. Instead, I would either pretend to be paying attention or else get defensive and argue back. In these situations, my friend did not feel that she was truly being listened to and, because she did not know what I was thinking, she often felt angry and powerless. Once she could tell what was going on for me, however, she could then think about what was happening and take an initiative to move things on. The more I could remember to keep saying what my thoughts and emotions were underneath it all, the more we were able to get over difficulties very quickly. My friend's reaction was that "at long last you are listening to me". Instead of feeling powerless, she felt empowered and I could see that something important had happened.

At the same time, privately, I did not think I was actually listening any better or any differently. It was always the case in the past that I could have repeated accurately whatever she had been saying to me so I assumed I must be listening well. I thought that what really made the difference was that I was being more honest about where I was struggling and getting upset. However, the more I thought about this, the more I realized that there was something arrogant about me discounting her thinking about what was making the difference. So I stopped and asked myself how well I had actually been listening. I could repeat the words she said but had I actually understood what she was trying to communicate? It became clear that, as a middle-class man, there were some things she was trying to tell me that I was not taking in. I realized that my belief that I was really listening and that I truly understood everything she was saying was actually a big obstacle in our relationship. In actual fact, I needed to go back and admit that, in a very real way, I actually did not have a very clear sense of what it was like for her as a working-class woman. The truth was, I just did not get what she was trying to tell me and I needed to stop acting as if I did. There were a lot of things I did understand about oppression. There were probably a lot of things I understood more clearly than other middle-class men did. But, the reality was also that, as a member of a privileged, dominant, oppressor group, there is a core piece about what it is like to be oppressed in these various ways that I just do not get and it will make a big difference for me and the people around me if I can humbly admit to myself that I am lost at that point.

This is such a hard thing for me as a middle-class man to do. When it gets tough in a relationship with someone who has an oppressed identity, it is almost automatic for me to disappear, to try to figure out in my head what I need to do to keep them happy and stop them criticizing me. When it gets tough I try to hide what is going on for me and I don't know how to show the struggle I am having. Mostly, I do not notice when I do that, at least in the moment when I do it. Sometimes I can tell I have done it afterwards when there is some distance from the situation. The really hard thing is to spot myself going into automatic while it is happening. For an oppressed person, to be in a relationship with someone who disappears like this can be scary, infuriating, confusing and disempowering.

Since then, I have tried to learn to spot when I am about to disappear, or when I am about to cover up my awkwardness or uncertainty or embarrassment, or when I am about to hide how hard I am finding things. I have tried to learn to spot this when it is happening and show this struggle to the other person so we can both tell that at least part of the problem is me and not just them. I find it really useful for me as a middle-class man to work on the assumption that I just do not get it, that, in some fundamental ways, I do not have a clue what it is really like for working-class people and women in their relationship with me. This is not about being hard on myself or slipping into feeling guilty. It is simply a matter-of-fact assumption that, underneath it all, there is something really important that I do not understand about what people are trying to tell me.

The implications of this seem very big. At last, I can stop pretending that I know. I can stop acting as if I know better. I can stop assuming that my answers and my thinking are more rational. At long last, I can keep my mouth shut and really listen. Doing this means not just that I get to have a deeper and more honest relationship with people but also that I am less isolated and less exhausted from trying to be better and know all the answers. And, I do not have to be so hard on myself for not being perfect. By admitting I do not know anything, I might just learn something!

SUMMARY

Classism and class oppression are some of the most neglected aspects of oppression in general. In this context, being middle class is one of those identities that many people gloss over. If we have this identity, we take it for granted and miss the fact that it carries with it quite a lot of emotional baggage. We carry this unawareness into our relationships with working-class people and end up assuming that any difficulties in the relationship are theirs. This is quite similar to many other oppressor identities. If we are to be effective leaders, however, and effective allies for other oppressed groups, we need to become aware of how our oppressor identities have damaged us and interfere with our ability to think clearly and understand the world around us.

Being an effective ally for working-class people involves a delicate blend of relaxed pride in, and acceptance of, our identity as middle class along with a humble recognition that our conditioning imposes emotional and behavioural blocks that can interfere with truly developing other people's leadership. Crucially, it involves an ongoing commitment to examining, identifying and cleaning up the baggage attached to our identity as middle-class people. This is the same challenge that faces all dominant groups. In our work for liberation, can we own our dominant identities and commit to doing the work to clean up the baggage attached to those identities? And, at the point where it gets tough for us, can we stay with the struggle and show it rather than giving up on the relationship and disappearing?

REFLECTION

Class identity

1   What are you most proud of about yourself and your class identity (e.g. as a working-class, raised-poor, middle-class or owning-class person)?
2   What are you most proud of about the other people who share your class identity?
3   What are you not proud of, ashamed of, or what do you dislike about yourself or other members of your own class?
4   What messages did you get, growing up, about your own class and people of other classes?
5   How have these messages affected your relationships with people of your own class?
6   How have these messages affected your relationship with people of each of the other classes?
7   If you have a middle-class identity, which of the characteristics described in this chapter seem familiar?

Being an ally

8   How have you been an effective or supportive ally for particular oppressed groups?
9   How have you acted with courage and integrity in your relationship with an oppressed group?
10   Where is it difficult for you to make friends with, be with, listen to, follow the leadership of, hand over power to or trust the thinking of the people you are trying to be an ally for? Where do you struggle in the relationship?
11   In what ways do you hold back, not show yourself or not be completely honest about yourself in your relationship with the people you are trying to be an ally for?
12   In what ways do you need to change or develop in order to build more effective, supportive, respectful and empowering relationships with members of particular oppressed groups?

11 Identity and the process of liberation

INTRODUCTION

In previous chapters, I talked about the work that needs to be done to overcome the effects of internalized oppression and domination. One way of thinking about this work is in terms of identity. In the context of oppression and liberation, it is useful to think of people as having a range of different social or cultural identities. We have, in fact, multiple identities rather than one single identity (Mullaly, 2002; Zappone, 2003). These identities have played a role in shaping the way we think, feel and act. Generally, we can classify these identities under various labels or categories, for example, female or male, working class or middle class, Jewish or Gentile. Thus, we can have a gender identity, an ethnic identity, an identity based on skin colour, an age identity, a class identity, a national identity, a tribal identity, a religious identity, an occupational identity, a role identity and so on. Some of these will be more significant for us than others. Nkomo and Cox (1996), for example, distinguish between identities based on social categories, such as gender, ethnicity or class, which are relatively enduring and identities based on organizational function or tenure which may be taken on or shed on entering or leaving a job or an organization. The implication is that the broader social categories are likely to be more salient for people. However, I do not think this can be taken for granted. A person with military combat experience, for example, may find that this identity retains significance long after the person has left the military. As we saw previously, we can also distinguish between oppressed identities and oppressor identities (Tatum, 2000) and some of these will be of particular importance in the ways they affected us.

One way or the other, some of these identities are more significant for us than others – they have played a stronger role in shaping the way we now are. Perhaps they have left us with painful memories from the past that still influence our reactions to situations. Or, perhaps, our experiences within these identities were important in shaping the values and priorities that we attach to our current lives. The significant or key identities will vary from person to person, and possibly also from time to time during our lives. As we experience new situations or develop greater awareness we may claim new identities that seemed to have little or no significance for us previously. We may also drop old identities that no longer represent useful or accurate descriptions of our experience, or who we are, or that no longer exert an emotional influence on how we react or behave. So, each of us can ask what our key identities are at this point in our lives. Often, out of all the identities we have, there will be a small number that stand out for us as central to who we are.

SOURCES OF HURT OR OPPRESSION

For many of us, the key identities represent areas of our lives where we have experienced some degree of hurt or oppression. In particular, as part of these identities we have internalized a variety of painful emotions and rigid, inflexible ways of thinking, feeling and acting that can interfere with our ability to act powerfully and to build effective relationships with others. This, as we have already seen, is our internalized oppression. We bring prejudices, guilt, doubts, misinformation, unresolved conflicts and unhealed hurts that make it difficult for us to think clearly about ourselves or the people around us. These identities may also represent areas of our lives where we have experienced times of great satisfaction or joy and where we are left with powerful or defining memories that we treasure as significant parts of our life story. Often the key identities are a mixture of both positive and negative experiences – we have experienced both great hurt and warm, nurturing or uplifting moments as part of the same identity. Whatever the experiences, these identities have left their mark and continue to affect the way we think, feel and act. Coming to terms with these core identities and our experiences within them, particularly where they have interfered with our intelligence, our self-esteem, our power and our flexibility, will be a key part of the liberation process. According to Mullaly (2002), building and strengthening identity are an essential part of overcoming oppression. This process of liberation entails looking at what has happened to us as part of having a particular identity, identifying what we internalized, healing the hurts associated with it and, in the process, redefining the identity and reclaiming power.

All of this applies equally to us in our leadership roles. If we are to lead effectively and if we are to have flexible, human connections with other people we need to understand the dynamics of identity. We need to know what the key identities are that we bring into our leadership. We also need to heal the hurts associated with these identities and undo the effects of any mistreatment or oppression. To understand truly other people's experiences of oppression and their struggle for liberation, we need to understand our own oppression and our own struggle for liberation. We need to understand how our own identities have shaped us and influence our relationships if we are to have a clear picture of how leadership can be effective. Thus, working on our identity is a central part of the work we have to do as leaders.

CLAIMING THE IDENTITY

As part of the liberation process, doing this work on identity involves a number of steps. The starting point is owning or *claiming our identity*. We have to acknowledge who and what we are. Relatively speaking, this has generally been easier to do in relation to our oppressed identities although it can still be difficult on occasions. Some people, for example, as part of their internalized oppression, have not seen themselves as part of an oppressed group or have been reluctant to claim a particular identity because of the shame attached to it. For the members of some groups, survival meant trying to pass as a member of the dominant group. Perhaps they feared being victimized as a result of visibly claiming the identity. However, claiming the identity, noticing that we have a shared experience with other people, seeing ourselves as part of an oppressed group, are often key first steps towards liberation. It is difficult to clean up the damage until we actually acknowledge the identity. Similarly, people who belong to dominant or oppressor groups have generally tended not to own those identities. In many Western countries, for example, White people often do not think of themselves as White. In working with men, I have sometimes asked them to talk about what they liked about themselves as men. A not uncommon response is for them to say they don't think of themselves as men. They could say what they liked about themselves as "people" but not as "men". This is somewhat similar to a distinction that Mullaly (2002) makes between personal and social identity. Personal identity is how the person sees themselves and social identity is how society sees them. In this case, however, it is probably more useful to focus more narrowly on the difference between how the oppressors see themselves and how the oppressed see them. A White person may not think of themselves as white but no person of colour is ever likely to overlook this aspect of their identity. According to Tatum (2000), people tend to notice their oppressed identities while ignoring their oppressor identities. She maintains that they take their oppressor identities for granted because the society as a whole takes them for granted. So, people overlook the fact that they are White, male, heterosexual, Gentile, and so on. This failure to own their identity has made it difficult for oppressor groups to face the prejudices and blocks that get in the way of relating to members of the corresponding oppressed groups.

I stated earlier that our key identities are often those that stand out for us as either very negative experiences of hurt or oppression or else very positive experiences of satisfaction or joy, or more generally as a mixture of both. The oppressor identities, however, tend not to stand out for us, at least initially. So, if they don't stand out for us, how can they be central? One way they become central occurs when we think about our relationships. If I am in a relationship, or want to develop a relationship with someone who has a different identity to mine, then my corresponding identity becomes important in that context. If I, as a man, for example, want to develop a relationship with a woman that is non-oppressive, then I will have to start dealing with my identity as a man. It may not have struck me before as a particularly central part of who I am but, in the context of this relationship, it now takes on great significance. If I, as a White person, want to develop a relationship with a person of colour that is non-oppressive, then I will have to address the fact that I am White and all that that entails. I may not have seen being White as having had a big influence on me before now, but, in the context of this relationship, it is huge.

In practice, most of us are a complex mixture of oppressed and oppressor identities and all of them have to be owned as part of our liberation. We are not just part of an oppressed group or an oppressor group. In workshops, I often ask participants to make a list of all the oppressed and all the oppressor groups they can think of. When I ask them to look at these lists and say what stands out about them, they almost always comment that, between them, the lists encompass everyone, that they are all represented on both lists. In other words, everyone is a member of at least one oppressed and one oppressor group. In fact, we are members of a number of oppressed and oppressor groups. If I think of my own significant identities, the ones that played a powerful role in shaping and defining who I am and how I now respond to the world, these include being male, White, Irish, middle class, a parent and Roman Catholic – some of these are primarily oppressed and some are primarily oppressor identities. These are not my only identities but they are the ones I know have left me with most of my emotional "baggage".

Many identities have stereotypes associated with them – particular ways that people believe they must be, particular qualities or characteristics they must have – in order to be able to claim that identity. Some people have difficulty claiming an identity because they do not conform to the stereotype. In Chapter 8 we saw examples of this in the cases of an Irish Protestant and a French-Algerian. In the same way, people of mixed heritage sometimes have difficulty claiming all aspects of their identity because it is a mixture and they are not "pure" in the identity. There are elements of this difficulty with most identities in fact. Because of stereotypes, many men do not feel like real men or many women do not feel like real women. People may feel that the colour of their skin is not quite right to justify claiming a particular identity. People may feel they have the wrong accent, the wrong religion, the wrong name, the wrong birthplace and so on. These difficulties are generally a reflection of the way oppressive systems keep people separate and divided. The stereotypes are part of the oppression. For people who do not seem to fit the stereotype, an important step in liberation is to proudly claim their full identity. Thus, all men are real men. All women are real women, and so on. People with mixed heritage can claim each part of their heritage fully. Claiming the identity in these ways is important in contradicting any stereotypes about the identity but it is also important in enabling us to heal the hurts associated with the identity. Claiming the identity will bring to the surface all the feelings we carry about that identity so that they can be dealt with and healed.

For some people, the claiming of such "labels" or "categories" might appear to reinforce the divisions between people rather than heal them. They would prefer to move past or ignore all labels and focus on our common humanity. However, while we carry the damaging effects of conditioning or mistreatment or oppression attached to a particular identity we cannot be free of that identity. Whether we claim a particular identity or not, we are a function of it if we have been hurt or oppressed or conditioned as a member of that group. We are not free to ignore the identity until we have freed ourselves from any remaining painful emotion and rigid behaviour attached to it. Our leadership and our relationships will be restricted and undermined to the extent that we still carry the residue of the hurts associated with that identity.

HEALING THE HURTS

So, having claimed the identity, we now have to *heal the hurts* associated with it. We have to tell the story of what happened, or happens, to us within that identity. We have to talk about what was good about having this identity – the positive experiences and the places where we were encouraged to notice and hang on to our inherent humanness. We also have to feel and discharge the painful emotions that have accumulated around the identity. We have to talk about how we got hurt, or continue to get hurt, as a member of this particular grouping and where we had to give up our connection to our inherent human qualities of being good, worthwhile, courageous, loveable, loving, intelligent and so on. Telling the story of our identity is part of the process of healing the hurts associated with it. It enables us to release, and be healed of, the painful feelings we have accumulated. We may have to tell these stories many times as part of the process of healing. We may have to discharge feelings of grief, fear, humiliation or embarrassment or outrage each time we do this but each time this lessens the hold that the painful emotion has on us. As we discharge the feelings, our perspective on what happened changes and we begin to see our experiences in a new light. Rather than just feeling bad we are now able to think rationally about what took place.

Telling the story to one other person who will listen respectfully is very important. Telling the story in a group of people who share this identity is also very important. As groups of people talk about their shared identity and the feelings associated with it, and as they listen to other people's stories, they begin to notice certain themes or patterns in what different people say. They notice characteristic ways in which people with this particular identity got hurt, or continue to get hurt, certain characteristic ways they ended up feeling, certain characteristic ways they tended to behave as a result, and so on. As they do this, they also come to see that they themselves are not to blame. They begin to identify a system of oppression rather than a personal failing as the real problem. They are able to see those parts of the identity that reflect the ways they got oppressed, mistreated or hurt and disconnected from their basic humanness. They are able to see the ways they learned to act, feel and think that are largely a result of being oppressed rather than being an inherent part of them as humans. In other words, they are able to see those parts of the identity that are distressed or irrational and a reflection of the oppression of their particular group. Gradually they also come to identify those parts of the identity that represent the places where they escaped hurt or were able to stay connected to their human qualities in spite of any oppression. In other words, they are able to see what is rational or natural or inherent about the identity. They are able to see what is unique and special about people with this identity. Martín-Baró (1994) talks about the "recovery of historical memory" which he sees as

> recovering not only the sense of one's own identity and the pride of belonging to a people but also a reliance on a tradition and a culture, and above all, with rescuing those aspects of identity which served yesterday, and will serve today, for liberation.
>
> (p. 30)

During this process, people's feelings about the identity change. Instead of feeling ashamed, for example, they begin to feel pride. Instead of hiding their identity, they begin to proclaim it. Instead of feeling cut off from people who share the same identity, they begin to feel connected and close to them.

REDEFINING THE IDENTITY

As the healing process takes place, we begin to see the identity in a new light. Now, the process of liberation from oppression leads to *redefining the identity* in human, rational terms. We no longer view the identity in purely negative terms where we equate the damage done by the oppression with all that is true of the identity. In previous chapters we saw how oppression causes people to confuse their internalized oppression with their inherent nature. Through the healing process, we are now able to reject this. With a clear picture of what is rational about, and inherent to, the identity and also what is distressed, irrational and simply a function of the oppression, it is possible to redefine the identity in terms of what is inherently true of our people. This process of redefining our identity has three elements. The first is *taking complete pride* in those parts of the identity that are rational, human and flexible and the second is *reclaiming*, with pride, those human aspects that we got disconnected from within the identity. A third element is *disowning*, as central to the identity, those aspects that are simply the effects of our oppression. Women, for example, can redefine what it means to be female in terms of being powerful, intelligent, strong, courageous, as well as loving and nurturing and all the other qualities that any human being is capable of. At the same time, they can disown all the negative stereotypes of women as weak, stupid, "bitchy" and so on, as having nothing inherently to do with being female but as simply the effects of oppression. At an individual level, redefining the identity means contradicting the negative messages I got about myself from the oppressive system and taking pride in the particular human qualities that I had difficulty associating with myself. At a collective level, redefining the identity means contradicting all the negative messages about our people that got directed at us and that we internalized as part of our oppression and taking pride in our complete humanness. Working from a position of pride is a key part of this process. Any shame or lack of pride has to be contradicted in order to move beyond the internalized oppression. This pride has to be without limits and without conditions and based on a recognition and acceptance of our inherent human qualities. In a similar way, it cannot just be a pride in having endured or resisted oppression (although, as we shall see below, these can represent a step beyond shame). In other words, it is not based only on external characteristics of the identity such as, our achievements or the endurance of oppression. It is a recognition that our goodness and worth are unconditional. It could be argued that, by emphasizing complete pride and a disowning of all the negative messages from the oppression, this could lead people to a distorted and unrealistic picture of themselves. In practice, however, the combination of healing old hurts and reclaiming pride tends to balance out the weight of the oppression and leave people in a place where they are able to think rationally and realistically about themselves individually, their group collectively and about the oppressive system around them.

This process of redefinition also applies to oppressor identities. Within these identities, people may have been encouraged to take pride in their superiority over others in one form or another. They may have been raised to see themselves as more intelligent or more worthwhile, for example. Redefining this identity entails giving up a conditioned pride based on assumed or implied superiority, a pride based on comparisons with other groups, or a pride based on privilege or power over others and replacing it with a pride based on inherent human qualities. As a man, for example, I have to take pride in myself as a man not because of some imagined superiority over women or because of my successful achievements at work but because, among many other qualities, I am a good, worthwhile, caring, courageous, intelligent, nurturing and creative individual. Such things as violence, drunkenness, being cut off from feelings, isolation and so on are part of men's internalized oppression and are not an inherent part of what it means to be male. Here again, it could be argued that taking such a positive view of the identity would allow men to avoid taking responsibility for their sexism, for example. As we shall see below, however, having a relaxed pride in our identity and healing the hurts associated with it give us the space to see more clearly where our behaviour is damaging to others and make it easier for us to actually change that behaviour.

For oppressor identities, particularly as members of the group become more aware of the oppressive nature of their relationship with other groups, guilt can become a major stumbling block. It becomes difficult to take pride in the face of the knowledge of how their group has exploited and oppressed the dominated group. Some members of oppressor groups have tried to work for change from within this guilt. It is the guilt that motivates and propels them. Unfortunately, guilt is often not an especially helpful source of motivation. In some cases, it motivates people to reverse roles but not necessarily build a new, equal relationship. Sometimes, as we saw in the case of middle-class people, it leads them to disown their identity and cut themselves off from their own people but not necessarily take steps to bring about change within their own group. In many cases, guilt simply stops people in their tracks. It causes them to become overly cautious, to hold back or in some cases, feeling so bad about themselves, to sink into shame and powerlessness. In practice, the only really useful motivation for change is a relaxed pride in what is true of people inherently rather than how they are as a function of the oppression. Pride gives people energy and hope. If the pride is a relaxed one that is based on inherent human qualities rather than on a defensive, reactive comparison with the oppressed group, the effects will be to loosen the hold of any oppressive conditioning. Rather than reinforcing whatever arrogant and oppressive behaviour marked its relationship with the oppressed, this pride leaves the oppressor in a much better place to be an effective ally.

Within any oppression, identities get defined in such ways as to keep people isolated, feeling bad about themselves or their people, feeling inadequate or feeling that they do not belong. Redefining the identity involves a rejection of the oppressive and narrow stereotypes of the identity. In Chapter 8, we saw how one aspect of internalized oppression was the narrowing of the culture of a group in such a way as to exclude people from membership. Through the processes of listening, telling the stories and healing the hurts, oppressive stereotypes are identified, along with ways in which those stereotypes exclude people from membership of the group, and these are replaced with new inclusive definitions that encouraged all people who share the identity to claim it fully and with pride.

Redefining the identity then means disclaiming any rigid, stereotyped and irrational aspects as having no necessary connection to the identity. The latter come to be seen as a consequence of the conditioning or oppression rather than as an inherent part of the identity. This has been described as a process of "cleaning up" the identity. Thus, from this perspective, aggression or violence are no longer seen as inherently male qualities but simply the result of men's oppression. Timidity or softness are no longer seen as inherently female qualities but simply the result of women's oppression. As part of this process, each group gets to reclaim for itself those human qualities and characteristics that were denied to it. In some cases, however, the conditioning allowed a group to keep its connection to particular human qualities but did so in a way that left the expression of those qualities very rigid and stereotyped. So, a natural human quality of being able to nurture, for example, was denied to men but rigidly exaggerated for women. A woman who was not nurturing was thus not a real woman. Within this oppression, liberation might be seen to involve going to the opposite end of the scale and rejecting or denying the quality altogether. Thus, one rigidity becomes replaced with another. Redefining the identity does not mean rejecting human qualities that were stereotypically associated with the identity. Rather, it means not rigidly requiring any particular quality as a condition of claiming the identity. People can *choose* to be nurturing but are not *required* by the identity to be that way. Instead of being part of a rigid stereotype, the quality now becomes an aspect of a person's humanity to be expressed flexibly as appropriate in any given situation.

RECLAIMING POWER

Typically, the process of claiming and redefining our identities leads to a *reclaiming of our power*. As we work on the identity and how it has left us thinking, feeling and behaving, we begin to recognize the places where we have given up our power. We notice where we hold back in situations, where we have given up trying to change things, where we have settled for a less than rational or less than ideal relationship. We begin to name the places where we need to take charge and act more powerfully, to plan how we will change this, and actually take decisive steps that reconnect us with our inherent power. This, in turn, will involve building close, supportive relationships with people from whom we have previously been separated or isolated. These will include both people who have a different identity from us and people who share our identity. As we saw above, guilt will sometimes pull members of an oppressor group into disowning their own people and going after close relationships with members of the oppressed group instead. We also have seen how shame can lead people to disown their oppressed identity and cut themselves off from their own people. As this process evolves, we begin to reclaim these relationships with our own people and build different kinds of relationships with other oppressed people or with oppressors. This may involve forging new links between, and building powerful alliances across, the different identities. It may involve acting powerfully in places where we have previously felt victimized and powerless within the identity. This reclaiming of power typically means making changes at an individual level but it also leads in many cases to people organizing collectively to bring about change. As people get a clear perspective on their identity and on how the oppression operates, they begin to reclaim power in, and improve the quality of, their personal lives. Quite often, they also look for ways to mobilize or organize other people to work with them for change in the wider culture or society. This may involve acting to change the situation facing the group in the world, to end any mistreatment or oppression and to bring about the liberation of all members of the group.

CHOOSING IDENTITY

Having claimed the identity, having healed the hurts associated with it, having redefined the identity in human terms, having reclaimed pride, and having reclaimed power, we are now *free to choose* whether to continue to use that identity to describe ourselves. The identity is no longer a function of our oppression and no longer contains any charged emotions. Thus we may choose to hang on to the label or to discard it as no longer meaningful or central to who we are. It is not now an imposed identity but one that we can freely choose or not as the case may be. We are now free to think of ourselves as persons and not just as categories. (Other people, of course, may continue to label us in this way but that is a different issue.)

MANAGING DIVERSITY

Central to the process of working on identity is a recognition that the world is an incredibly rich and diverse place. People are not all the same. There is little real homogeneity. We are trying to lead other people and build unity among them in a context of great diversity (Brown and Mazza, 2005). They come with different identities, different experiences, different needs, different feelings, different customs, different expectations, different conditioning, different ways of thinking and behaving.

Traditionally, in organizations and institutions, the issue of diversity was handled by encouraging people to play down their differences. The way to maintain unity was to focus on what people had in common and not to allow their differences to become centre stage. At one level, this seemed to make sense. However, it had the effect of asking people to ignore or suppress huge chunks of their heritage, their culture, their feelings and their humanity. Essentially, this meant that I could be part of this body as long as I did not demand a place for my uniqueness. So, in the West, for example, we had an organizational culture that was largely male, White, middle class, and so on. While we talked about women, the poor, the marginalized, these groups did not have any significant visibility within the structures and culture of our significant institutions and organizations. In fact, one of the problems for some of these groups was the tendency for oppressor groups to pay lip service to, and in some cases to romanticize, their oppressions, while failing to take steps actively to eliminate them. A person could be part of this culture so long as they did not claim a space (visibility, power sharing, equality, parity of esteem, recognition and so on) for their own unique identity.

The model of leadership being offered here suggests an alternative approach to diversity. It is becoming very clear that the way to build unity is actually to cherish and nurture diversity. Far from playing down differences, we have to find ways to make them visible. We have to create the conditions wherein we can celebrate the richness of each social group while facilitating them to become visible, take leadership and leave behind any traces of the oppression they have internalized. At a practical level this means giving these groups a voice. It means creating opportunities for these groups to speak out, be listened to and get support. It means encouraging and supporting them to take leadership.

Setting things up so that people get listened to with respect involves a number of elements. One of these is the creation of support structures (groups, workshops, conferences, for example) where people get to meet period-odically with others who share the same "identity", who belong to the same "constituency" or category, for example the same age group, the same gender, the same ethnic background, the same occupation and so on. In a para-doxical way, the starting point for building unity is to *meet separately*. We have first of all to meet with our own people to share experiences, be listened to and find support without any "outsiders" present. Watts-Jones (2002), for example, talks about the idea of within-group "sanctuary" in providing a safe place for people of African descent to come together to deal with internalized racism. In the safety that this provides, we get to talk about ourselves and our experiences without having to worry about other people's reactions or with-out having to justify, defend or legitimize what we say. We meet in these groups, not to complain or give out about others, but to talk about ourselves and how we feel, think together, break the isolation and get a sense of sup-port. From these groups comes clarity about the dynamics of the relationship with other groups, an identification of key issues facing our own group, important needs not being met, significant ways that others can support us, and constructive steps we can take to reclaim power and bring about change.

As the level of support and safety grows, we then create opportunities for different groups to come together to listen to each other and learn what it is like to belong to a different group to our own. We get to hear what it is like for other oppressed and oppressor people and how we can offer support and we do this in a context where no one gets attacked or blamed. Because there is space for everyone to be listened to, the pull to be defensive is minimized. It becomes possible to focus on building alliances and support across the divisions rather than having them attack each other.

Within this process, the high quality of thinking, the clarity about what is happening in the relationships and the basic down-to-earth wisdom of diverse groups quickly become apparent. It also becomes clear that there is a huge store of untapped intelligence and sound thinking among groups that are often marginalized. In particular, when it comes to understanding the dynamics operating between an oppressed and an oppressor group, the real experts are generally within the oppressed group.

Just as there is a need for oppressed groups to have the opportunity to meet separately like this, so also it is useful for oppressor groups to meet around their identity. As with the oppressed groups, this is not a defensive coming together to conspire against or give out about the other group. Rather, it is a safe place for people to look at their own identity, share with one another their struggles, be honest about where it gets difficult for them in the relationship with the oppressed group, talk about the messages and prejudices they picked up about the oppressed group, get a clear picture of their own conditioning, think about how to be effective allies for the oppressed and reclaim pride in what is inherently true of their own people. The most common example of this would be men's support or liberation groups. Where there is a clear understanding of how oppression operates, and with a safe, non-defensive process, such groups can play a hugely supportive role in helping men to become clearer and more effective allies for women. (This process can be tricky, however, and such groups can go astray in the absence of a clear understanding of the dynamics of oppressor–oppressed groups.) While we are fairly familiar with the notion of men's groups, we are still a long way from applying this model to other types of oppressor groups. For example, this process can be used very effectively to assist White people to work on their racism by providing a safe forum where people can be open and honest about their prejudices without feeling they might offend anyone, where they can get a picture of how they themselves have been damaged by the dehumanizing effects of racism, where they can look at and discharge whatever painful emotion gets in the way of their being effective allies for people of colour and where they can avoid the pitfall of operating out of guilt.

The outcome of this process is to make diversity visible and creative and to produce the conditions for groups that are normally on the margins to play a key role in leadership. Imagine a situation where the various subgroups or identities that constitute an organization or institution came together to listen respectfully to one another, to celebrate each other and to encourage each other to take initiatives that would empower them. This is one way to breathe life into an organization. By giving visibility and a voice to the full range of diversity, the lives of all the members are enriched and enhanced, issues and challenges are named in a non-attacking way that keeps the organization moving forward, potential leaders across all the groups are identified and supported and, individually, people receive ongoing encouragement to take the next steps in their growth and development.

THE LIBERATION PROCESS

A focus on identity and on diversity leads naturally to a focus on the liberation process. To be truly effective in leadership requires us to have a vision of liberation, a picture of what is possible when people's talents and abilities are freed up and the relationships cease to be oppressive. As leaders, we need to understand the dynamic that comes into play as relationships change and people become empowered. Let us first take a look at how relationships develop in the context of liberation.

Cultural Competence

The model of Cultural Competence (Cross, 1988; Aguilar, 1995) describes the stages through which oppressor or dominant groups progress in their relationship with oppressed people. In its original version, Cross used it as a way of thinking about the relationship between caring agencies and their minority population clients. He describes Cultural Competence as "a set of congruent behaviors, attitudes and policies that come together in a system, agency or professional and enable that system, agency or professional to work effectively in cross-cultural situations" (p. 1). At Stage 1, *Cultural Destructiveness*, attitudes, policies and practices are destructive to the oppressed culture and the people within it. The relationship consists of attempts by the dominant or oppressor culture to eliminate or destroy the oppressed group or its culture. At this stage, members of the oppressed group are seen as inherently inferior or a threat to the oppressor group. The solution is to disenfranchise them, control, them, exploit them or destroy them. At its extreme, this involves ethnic cleansing, genocide or cultural genocide. At Stage 2, *Cultural Incapacity*, the system and its agencies are not deliberately destructive but they lack the capacity to help oppressed clients or communities. There is a lot of ignorance, stereotyping and fear of the oppressed who are tolerated so long as they agree to accept their inferior status. Those who do not know their place may suffer particular discrimination. There is bias and discrimination against, and low expectations of, the oppressed group and numerous messages, both subtle and overt, that they are not valued or welcome. It is assumed that they are only fit for menial, second-class roles. Segregation and other oppressive policies may be supported as desirable. At Stage 3, *Cultural Blindness*, there is a denial of any differences between the cultures and a pretence at equality. The system and its agencies operate on the belief that they are unbiassed, that everyone is the same, that colour or culture makes no difference to how people are treated, and that the helping approaches traditionally used by the dominant culture can be universally applied to all groups without the need to take account of the differences. Because of this, the services and institutions of the society are so ethnocentric as to be useless and unusable to all but the most assimilated members of the oppressed group. There is a tendency to ignore the strengths of the minority culture, to blame the victims and to judge people by how closely they resemble members of the dominant group. At this stage, it has become difficult to deny the existence of oppression in the past but there is a pretence that things have changed and that everyone is now treated the same. At the same time, institutionalized oppression restricts access to training, jobs and services and makes it difficult for people from oppressed groups to move into non-traditional areas. With

Stage 4, *Cultural Pre-competence*, there are the beginnings of true awareness within the oppressor group and an acknowledgement of weaknesses in the ways they operate. There is a commitment to equality and a desire to get it right in at least some ways. Some initiatives may be taken such as hiring minority workers or providing awareness training for members of the dominant group. However, there may also be a simplistic belief that undertaking one initiative or experiment is enough to meet their obligations towards the oppressed group. Attempts to deal with inequality may also result in tokenism where a small number of members of the oppressed group are hired by agencies (usually individuals who are more assimilated in the dominant culture). Their token status and their training and socialization often means they may not be much more competent than members of the dominant group. Over and above these aspects that Cross describes, it can be said that while, at this stage, there is some awareness of the nature of the oppression as an ongoing issue, there is still an unease within the relationship. Although there is an openness to seeing how the members of the oppressed group have been mistreated, there is also a large degree of unawareness of how the oppressor group's conditioning and internalized domination have been a source of hurt and damage to its own members, particularly in human terms, and of how the situation feeds into the oppression of the other group. At Stage 5, *Basic Cultural Competence*, there is an acceptance of, and respect for, differences, an openness among the oppressor group to looking at their own shortcomings, and ongoing attempts to become more effective as allies. There is also a lot more listening to the oppressed group and being guided by them. There is a much greater level of awareness, a clarity within the oppressor group about their own prejudices and blocks and about the ways in which oppression has become institutionalized and a commitment to dealing with these issues as part of their own process of liberation. There is also a commitment to the liberation of the oppressed group and the building of close bonds of friendship and support. Finally, at Stage 6, *Cultural Proficiency* (or what Cross calls Advanced Cultural Competence), oppressed cultures are held in high regard and there is an ability to move easily between the two cultures. Old feelings of prejudice or arrogance have been discharged and new attitudes and feelings of equality and acceptance have been internalized. There is an ongoing commitment among the oppressor group to learning about the other culture and about how to become more competent. During Stages 5 and 6, there is the development of a new self-image among members of the oppressor group where their identity is no longer based on feelings of superiority or dominance over the oppressed group. For Aguilar, the role of allies is to build relationships of competency and proficiency with the other culture. This means accepting that, as allies, they are part of the problem and not just of the solution. It means learning how to give up control and arrogance without, at the same time, giving up thinking. If we substitute the word leaders for that of allies, this model gives us a further perspective on the type of relationship we are trying to build with the people around us, especially as leaders. In particular, it shows us how achieving liberation is an integral part of this relationship and how it has to be part of thinking well and fully about people.

Stages of liberation from oppression

The Cultural Competence model looks at the stages that an oppressor group moves through in its relationship with the oppressed. The movement is towards liberation for both groups. We can look at this process in more detail by examining the stages that each group goes through as part of its own journey of liberation (Ruth, 1988). To begin with, let us take a look at the stages for oppressed groups and individuals (Figure 11.1). This has been adapted and considerably expanded from a change model for developing women in organizations (Paul, 1985). We can add to this model some of the contributions of Bulhan (1985), Harro (2000b), Watts, Griffith and Abdul-Adil (1999) and Watts, Williams and Jagers (2003).

Oppressed

At the beginning of this process, we can think of the group as passive, dependent or oppressed. Using the language of Transactional Analysis (Harris, 1973), we can describe how members of the group see themselves and their people negatively or as "not-OK" (I–) and, at the same time, admire, aspire to, or seek to emulate the behaviour, values or qualities of the dominant or oppressor group and its people (U+). Bulhan (1985) refers to this stage as "capitulation" (p. 193) and sees it as characterized by the identification of the oppressed with the oppressor and the assimilation of the oppressed group

Liberated
Interdependent
I+ U+

↑

Independent
Relaxed pride
I+ U?

↑

Angry
Counter-dependent
Defiant pride
Violent
I? U–

↑

Oppressed
Dependent
Accepting
I– U+

Figure 11.1 Stages of Oppressed Group Liberation.

into the dominant culture. For Watts *et al.* (2003) there is a belief that the world is just, a lack of awareness of social inequity or else a belief that the inequity accurately reflects the abilities and motivations of the groups oppressed and their oppressor groups. Watts *et al.* (1999) describe this as the "acritical stage". At this stage people in the group are largely operating from within a self-image and stereotype of themselves that is largely generated and reinforced by the dominant, oppressor group. How long a group remains at this stage varies depending on historical circumstances. While individual members of the group may question its status and its relationship with the oppressor group, it may be a long time before a large number of people begin to change. The process of liberation starts to move very often when a group first becomes aware that what it took for granted as the way things had to be, or thought of as natural, is in fact a reflection of a system-based process of prejudice and discrimination. Sometimes, it is the result of greater access to education and awareness of the struggles of other groups, as in the civil rights movement in Northern Ireland in the 1960s. Sometimes, this is brought to a head by a specific triggering event such as the refusal of an African-American woman, Rosa Parkes, to give up her seat to a White person on a bus in Montgomery, Alabama. Harro (2000) describes the beginnings of the change as the stage of "waking up" (p. 465) and it is followed by a stage of "getting ready" (p. 465). He sees the latter as a process of dismantling the stereotypes, the misinformation, the attitudes of inferiority and other aspects of the old world-view and replacing it with a new perspective using introspection, education and consciousness raising. As we look at the liberation process, we can apply it both to the development of individuals and to the development of their group. Movement through these stages is uneven with people in the group operating at different levels of development. However, when a critical mass of individuals begins to move, we can think of the group overall as moving to the next stage. Watts *et al.* (1999) describe a second stage that can be included under this oppressed heading. They call it the "adaptive stage" where people are aware of the inequality in the system but feel there is nothing they can do about it. Instead they resort to antisocial means of getting what they want and are content with whatever they can grab for themselves without confronting the oppression. This was something we saw also in Allport's (1954/1979) description of the effects of prejudice in Chapter 9. A third stage for Watts *et al.* (1999) is the "precritical stage" where complacency gives way to wanting to understand more about the oppression and how it can be tackled. In terms of the present model, this would represent a transition from the oppressed to the angry stage.

Angry

Whatever the reason for people starting to change, a common reaction is for the oppressed group, or a significant section of it, to become angry and rebellious. Where, to begin with, their attitude to themselves was negative and to the dominant group, in some respects, positive they now begin to question this (1? U–). They no longer automatically accept their own inferiority or the legitimacy of their mistreatment and become much more challenging of the power, superiority and status of the oppressor group. They start to take pride in their endurance of oppression, their resilience in the face of it or their ongoing resistance to it. Or, they may take pride in their moral superiority over the oppressor. Mostly, however, at this stage, this pride has a defiant rather than a relaxed tone to it. While this might have the appearance of throwing off the shackles of oppression it is clear that people are still acting from within the constraints of internalized oppression. The pride is still fragile. Bulhan (1985) refers to this stage as "revitalization" (p. 193) where there is a reactive repudiation of the oppressor culture and a tendency to romanticize the oppressed culture. The oppressed have begun to identify some of the ways in which they are systematically mistreated by the dominant group but they have still not become aware of how this has been internalized and affects their own behaviour, their feelings and their thinking. Many of the patterns of internalized oppression that we looked at in previous chapters are still operating. Their strategies for liberation at this stage therefore are heavily influenced by a victim-type approach to the problem. Although defiant, they still feel quite powerless and hopeless much of the time. A great deal of the violence and hostility we see acted out at oppressor groups is coming from within this victim role and reflects ongoing feelings of self-doubt, anger and powerlessness. Had someone stepped out from the internalized oppression and left their victim role behind, their attitude to themselves and the strategies they adopt would probably look very different. On a more positive aspect, Harro (2000) describes one of the steps that people take at this stage as "reaching out" (p. 466) where people speak out about the oppression instead of staying silent and experiment with expressing their ideas. In doing this, they learn more about how to communicate and reach people to bring about change.

Violence

At this stage, violence may be one of the outcomes of the anger. An important implication here, however, is that hostility or violence (or more correctly, counter-violence), as a means of dealing with oppression, needs to be understood as part of a process of development and not simplistically as the immoral behaviour of fanatics, psychopaths, terrorists or sadists. Taylor (1988) makes the point that applying the term "mentally ill" to a terrorist is not particularly useful although it can be comfortable because it allows people to accommodate to the violence without actually paying attention to the reasons for it. Heskin (1980), writing about Northern Ireland, agrees that the behaviour of terrorists cannot be attributed to their being psychopaths. This does not mean romanticizing violence or ignoring the fact that, in this process, liberation movements tend to get pulled into racketeering, hostage taking, bank robbing, the killing of innocent victims, drug dealing and other highly destructive types of action. Adopting this approach means that we look at the dynamic of those who react with violence or hostility in the context of their oppression and internalized oppression rather than in the context of evil, immaturity or madness. The reaction of many men, for example, to women's anger about their mistreatment is to criticize women for not expressing themselves in a more "reasonable" way. In the meantime, the content of what women are saying is ignored. The revulsion felt by many Irish people against the acts of violence committed in the name of Irish liberation over the past decades is understandable but the "anti-nationalism" which it sometimes led to was almost as irrational as the violence it condemned. Apart from a genuine revulsion against atrocities, underlying much of the condemnation of violence by Irish people was also a feeling of shame in being Irish and a difficulty in thinking clearly about other Irish people which, as we saw in an earlier chapter, are symptoms of internalized oppression themselves. The effect of this kind of difficulty is that instead of trying to understand why the violence is being perpetrated, trying to find other means or channels for people to communicate and represent their anger and outrage and trying to create structures and processes that will empower people, we put our energy into isolating and attacking those who use violence. As a way of eliminating violence it is naive and unworkable. We can see this same dynamic taking place in the Middle East and in the response to what are seen as extreme Islamic fundamentalists (Fekete, 2004). The effects are often to increase the levels of anger and violence rather than decrease them.

One of the responses of a dominant or oppressor group to attacks by the oppressed group is to react defensively in a variety of ways. Often there is a sense of hurt and betrayal at the anger of the oppressed. There can be bewilderment as members of the oppressor group try to understand why anyone would want to attack them. This can sometimes lead to another type of defiant pride that opposes the defiant pride of the oppressed where, for example, national symbols like the flag are emphasized. People are encouraged to take pride in their nation but in ways that portray the oppressed group as evil, uncivilized, misguided, irrational and dangerous. It becomes a pride against, or in the face of, the threat from the oppressed group rather than a relaxed pride in the real human qualities that characterize the people of the oppressor group. The focus goes on resisting the threat or defeating the enemy rather than understanding the anger and frustration of the oppressed and looking for useful, constructive ways to address deeply felt concerns and thus render violence unnecessary or unsustainable.

Given that violence is often a reaction to powerlessness and other aspects of internalized oppression, then one of the least helpful responses is likely to be the suppression of dissent or the restriction of these people's access to non-violent options as in the refusal to deal or have dialogue with public representatives from political parties that represent violent factions. In this situation, even more moderate positions can be viewed as extreme, adding to the sense of powerlessness of the oppressed. Simply espousing the cause of the oppressed can come to be equated with support for violence and ruled out of court as a valid position for any reasonable person to take. One of the difficulties in the Irish situation, for example, prior to the Good Friday or Belfast peace agreement, was the vacuum created by the lack of real dialogue between those with differing views on the political future of the island of Ireland and the consequent elimination of alternative options to violence. For a long period, in the Republic of Ireland, Section 31 of the Broadcasting Act served to reinforce the lack of dialogue and the pull to resort to violent methods by banning interviews on radio and television with political representatives of the IRA – the very people who were eventually central to negotiating the peace accord. The lifting of this ban was one of the key steps in facilitating dialogue and the start of peace talks. The failure to understand this dynamic, which hindered the finding of a resolution to a long-standing division, is currently in evidence in the approaches to similar types of conflict in other parts of the world.

In the case of Ireland, when the legitimate feelings of anger and grief about past and recent events in Irish history were recognized, when such feelings were seen as an understandable reaction of any oppressed group to its mistreatment (even though they led to some destructive and unhelpful actions), it was possible to begin to make progress. It was possible then to talk about ways to bring about constructive change. As long as such feelings and their expression are equated with backwardness, bigotry and evil, the possibility of moving through and past them is prevented by the unwillingness of others to listen and empathize. This applies to all sides of a conflict. The people who have been targeted with such violence also need to be heard and have their fears, their anger and their concerns addressed. Where there is a failure to locate violence in the context of oppression and struggles for liberation, it is entirely predictable that violence and intransigence will occur and continue. What then happens is that two extremes of behaviour develop within the oppressed group. The first is the resorting to violence in the absence of any sympathetic response to demands and, over time, the attempt to find increasingly more dramatic and destructive expressions of this violence. In many cases, the violence actually gets directed at other members of the oppressed group themselves. The second is a reaction to the violence where members of the oppressed group try to show their abhorrence of it by rejecting "extremism" and "terrorism" (terms often taken from the dominant group) and by acting in ways that demonstrate their "flexibility" and "reasonableness". In effect this latter means accepting at least some of the blame for the problem, giving up what were originally seen as legitimate demands, acting in various ways to reassure the dominant group of their moderation and participating with the dominant group in suppressing other viewpoints. There were times, for Irish people, when these extremes meant either asking for change in an appeasing way or else trying to force change violently, rather than confidently assuming our rights and assertively organizing and acting to realize them. Within the oppressed group, the two sides come to view each other as either psychopaths, sadists and terrorists or as traitors and collaborators and the deadlock continues. What we have here is a vivid illustration of the dynamics of internalized oppression where a group becomes so divided within itself that it cannot operate effectively to bring about useful change. The problem, at base, is not violence or extremism, it is internalized oppression. The key issue is the divisiveness within a group, the isolation of people from one another and their lack of respect for one another regardless of political viewpoint. As long as we see one faction or another within the oppressed group as the problem we will continue to fail to solve it.

Some groups can get stuck at this angry and sometimes violent stage. Repressive or oppressive measures by the oppressor group, undischarged painful emotion, a lack of any clear understanding of the ongoing dynamic, a lack of access to non-violent alternatives and a lack of transforming leadership can lead to a cycle of destructive conflict with little useful movement. As we saw above, in groups that adopt violence as their primary strategy there is a strong tendency for this to become infused with criminal and racketeering elements. In many other cases, however, the angry, violent stage gradually evolves into a less destructive approach to change. Particularly as the group gets access to greater resources and to mainstream channels of influence and begins to develop alternative non-violent strategies, the violence begins to wane or is confined to small extremist groups (Brown, 1979). The movement, as a whole, goes forward. This is often facilitated by leaders within the movement who model a new attitude towards themselves and the oppressor that is free of painful emotion. Powerful examples of this are people like Martin Luther King or Nelson Mandela.

It is important to remember also, of course, that many individuals and groups do not resort to violence at this stage. Instead, their anger is directed into campaigning and organizing against the oppression using non-violent means. For some others, anger may not represent a very significant stage in their development and may be bypassed to a great degree. Watts *et al.* (1999), describe this as a "critical" stage where there is a growing desire to learn more about the oppression and the beginnings of social change efforts. According to Watts *et al.* (2003), feelings such as discontent, indignation, urgency and empathy motivate people to try to understand what is going on and to take action. Among the factors that seem to make a difference in these are the kind of leadership that is offered, the levels of underlying frustration and powerlessness, the degree of repression in the system, the degree of organization and access to alternative channels of influence, the opportunity to discharge the anger and heal the hurts, the size of the group and the amount of support in the population at large.

Independent

Over time, some people work through the anger and leave it behind. Particularly, if all viewpoints are accorded respect and allowed expression, the oppressed group can begin to move on to a further stage of development, represented by the term Independent. Here, people have begun to reclaim real pride in themselves as members of their group (I+), as opposed to the defiant pride from before. They feel good about being women, or men, or Irish or working class and so on. Their pride is not based on a comparison with the oppressor group as in earlier stages. Nor is it a reactive type of pride based solely on the endurance of, or resistance to, oppression. It takes the form of liking myself and my people because of our intelligence, creativity, courage, goodness and so on, and not because we are better, bigger, stronger or more honourable than members of the oppressor group. Their relationship to the oppressor group is one of independence. Bulhan (1985) refers to this stage as "radicalization" (p. 193) and sees it as characterized by a commitment to radical change. At this stage there is the emergence of a new culture among the oppressed. People feel good about themselves and are no longer dependent on the dominant group for their self-respect. They no longer need to prove themselves to, or compare themselves with, the dominant group. The attitude of the dominant group to them is not a significant factor shaping their behaviour. They do not need the approval or admiration of members of the dominant group. For women, for example, this is often a stage of great creativity and power as they make changes in their lives to make things more supportive and rewarding for themselves personally and to redefine what they want out of life for themselves without dictation by the needs of the men around them. This can often be a difficult experience for the oppressor group since they are unlikely to have much experience of dealing with oppressed people who act with confidence and high expectations for themselves. The relationship, in the past, was based on a particular stereotype of the oppressed that the latter no longer accept or try to live up to. Once one party stops acting and thinking of itself as inferior, of course, the other party then has to learn a whole new way to relate to it and, if the relationship is to develop, has to redefine its own identity. Harro (2000b) sees a number of steps that would coincide with this stage. One of these is "building community" (p. 466) which involves having dialogue with people who share the oppressed identity in order to build support and having dialogue with people outside the identity in order to increase understanding and build coalitions. The kinds of support groups and networks that we looked at earlier, where people come together to listen to one another and break through the isolation, would be characteristic of this stage. At this stage also, according to Harro, we begin to see that the oppressors are themselves also victims of the larger oppressive system and some of them can be reached to form coalitions for transforming the system. The building of community leads then to "coalescing" (p. 467) and to "creating change" (p. 467). With a new sense of awareness, confidence and power, people now take action and organize coalitions to bring about change. Actually transforming the system means creating a new culture with new assumptions, structures, rules and roles based on a liberatory philosophy. For Watts *et al.* (1999), in the "liberating stage", oppression and liberation are now a key issue in people's lives and such things as community action, solidarity and liberation behaviour come strongly into play.

The major difficulty with this third stage of liberation is that many people are still unsure of, and uncomfortable with, the dominant group as a group. They are clear now about their own worth but are still ambiguous about the dominant group (U?). Individual members of the dominant group seem to be supportive and to act, or least try to act, in general, in non-oppressive ways. As a whole, though, they still find most members of the dominant group, and its institutions and practices, to be entrenched in the same old attitudes and behaviour. They still have to deal with repeated instances of prejudice, abuse or mistreatment. It is as though, at this stage, to use the earlier model, while individual members of the dominant group have reached a stage of cultural competency or even proficiency, the dominant group, as a whole, is still at an earlier stage of cultural blindness or pre-competency. At the same time, as Harro (2000b) indicates, they no longer see members of the dominant group as the enemy. The real enemy is the oppressive system and they are open to support from, and alliances with, progressive members of the oppressor group.

This last point brings us back to an important element in the analysis of oppression that we looked at in the last chapter. This is the point that for oppression to exist members of the dominant group first of all have to be "trained" or conditioned to play the oppressor role. It has been pointed out that much of what happens to children (the physical abuse, the humiliation, the criticism and so on) is a preparation for the mistreatment of others as adults. In other words, the oppression of children is the training ground for all oppressions. In this sense, therefore, identifying the agents of the oppression as the enemy and attacking them is not the way to achieve liberation. It is the system that enforces the oppressive roles that is the problem, not the people who are conditioned by it to act as the agents of the oppression. Attacking the former oppressors often does nothing to change the system that created the problem in the first place. There is a sense therefore in which all oppressions are closely interlinked. For example, one of the things holding women's oppression in place is the conditioning and oppression of men. One of the things holding men's oppression in place (and by extension, women's) is the oppression of gay men which reminds all men (gay and straight) not to step out of their traditional role. These, in turn, are reinforced by oppression in the workplace, by the oppression of children, by racism and by many other kinds of oppression. Because of this interlinking, the complete liberation of any one group will depend on the liberation of all other groups.

Liberated

The final stage of the liberation process is achieved when people become completely free of any trace of internalized oppression and when the oppressive institutions have been replaced. This, however, requires that the oppressor group has also been transformed and all traces of its oppressive behaviour and attitudes have been eliminated. This means that the final stage of the liberation process will not be reached until all groups are in the process of liberation. We have no actual examples of this stage in any liberation struggle. We can see oppressed groups, such as the women's movement, that have made enormous strides and where there are many members of these groups operating at the Independent stage. Logically, however, the whole process cannot be completed until the oppressive system and the oppressor group have also been transformed. For Harro (2000) the liberation process is characterized by, among others, the "practice of love", the "development of competence" in making things happen, the "belief that we can succeed", the knowledge that "we are not alone", "commitment to the effort of critical transformation" and "passion and compassion" (p. 469).

Movement through these stages does not proceed evenly. In any group, it may only be a small minority that operate at the Independent level while most of the members are still at the Angry stage. Or, while most people are still at the Oppressed stage, there may be a very small but outspoken, or sometimes violent, group leading a movement for change. The challenge we face, particularly as leaders, is how to help raise awareness of what is happening while assisting groups to find rational, non-destructive but powerful policies and strategies for change. The more we can understand about the stage of development that people are at and the consequent change strategies that they adopt, the more effective we will be in holding out a bigger picture of what is possible and supporting and assisting them to take the next steps in their development.

Arising from this analysis is the point that the key issue in tackling oppression is not just the mobilizing of people against their oppression but also identifying and interrupting the operation of internalized oppression. It is internalized oppression that is the glue keeping oppression in place and it is internalized oppression that tends to lead people into espousing or supporting policies that are irrational or destructive. Challenging and dismantling structures and institutions of oppression have to go hand in hand with the elimination of the effects of internalized oppression.

OPPRESSOR LIBERATION

It is also possible to describe the parallel process of oppressor group liberation. We know much less about this process than we do about the liberation of oppressed groups. There is an understandable motivation for members of an oppressed group to try to make sense of what has happened and to change their situation. Because of their privileges and confusion about the reality of other people's lives, there is not the same motivation or urgency for members of oppressor groups to question or to change. Very little work has been done within these groups on the dynamics of an oppressor identity. Having said that, we can throw some light on the reactions of the oppressor group to pressures to change from the oppressed group. Some of the elements of this have already been referred to but the main stages of liberation for such a group are depicted in Figure 11.2.

To begin with, members of the oppressor group may be completely unaware of the oppression. Some may have bought into the myths of their superiority and their relationship may be characterized by arrogance towards the oppressed (I+ U–). Things begin to change when the resistance of the oppressed group becomes more overt and challenging. Many members of the oppressor group may initially experience anger or hurt at the accusations of the oppressed group and may resort to denial, blaming the victims and adopting a defiant pride in traditional attitudes and self-stereotypes. They may also

Figure 11.2 Stages of Oppressor Group Liberation.

participate in a backlash against members of the oppressed group. The leaders or other visible members of the oppressed liberation movement may be targeted for attack, isolation or retaliation. Organized repressive violence (by the state, for example) or individual or random acts of violence may also be observed at this stage in some liberation struggles. The oppressors still see themselves as blameless and not responsible for the oppression while reacting very negatively towards what they see as the inappropriate anger and hostility, ungratefulness and unfairness of their oppressed critics (I+ U–). While some members of the oppressor group get stuck at this stage, others eventually move on. For some of the latter, the realization that repressive measures and refusing to have dialogue are simply not working become the spur to look for new ways forward. For others, the tide of change, new legislation outlawing discrimination, increased awareness, greater information about the oppression and progressive leadership within the oppressor group pulls them beyond this stage. Some members of the oppressor group may actually skip this stage, not getting caught up in such defensive reactions, recognizing the injustices that their group has perpetrated, questioning their assumed superiority or their privileges, and instead getting caught up in guilt (I–). As we have already seen, this guilt may lead to some level of pretence at awareness and to a type of support from within the guilt, which sets limits on their effectiveness and their ability to think clearly about the relationship. Although, at this stage, they can see how the system has been oppressive, they are still caught up in their own internalized patterns of prejudice and domination. While being clear about the oppressive system they are unable to see clearly how their own conditioning affects their personal relationships with the oppressed and their leadership (U?). Over time, as people work on their identity and seek to redefine it, as they discharge the feelings of guilt and build closer, more effective relationships with the oppressed group, the guilt can be replaced with a relaxed pride in their own inherent human qualities of goodness, caring, courage and so on. There is also an undefensive acceptance of the role they have played in oppressing the other group. Often the challenges and support from the oppressed group and more progressive leadership from within the oppressor group are part of shifting people out of the guilty stage on to this next stage. At this point, while they recognize that the oppressive system is still largely intact, they no longer see their own people as inherently bad and are able to build warm, close supportive relationships with members of the oppressed group (I? U+). Eventually, as alliances are built and the group as a whole is transformed, there is the possibility of a movement to the final stage of liberation where oppressive structures can be finally eliminated and a new interdependent, non-oppressive relationship developed (I+ U+). As with the oppressed group, movement through these stages tends to be very uneven. In fact, it is often only a small minority within the oppressor group that transform themselves into true, effective allies for the oppressed. Few oppressor groups have been able to articulate a redefinition of their identity and an effective change process for their own group. We still have a lot to learn about how to reach out to, work with, and transform members of oppressor groups.

One of the effects of the struggle for liberation, as we saw above, is that once the oppressed group begins to redefine its relationship to the dominant or oppressor group, the latter is also forced to examine itself. Commonly, the self-image of oppressor groups includes an element of comparison or relationship with oppressed groups. It may involve a pride in their superiority over the oppressed or in their history of conquest. In one sense, their self-image depends on the oppressed group agreeing to be inferior. If the oppressed group changes and no longer acts in a subservient way, then the oppressor group may have to find some other grounds on which to base its own self-image. For example, much of the self-image of the English has been based on a largely imperialist and colonial history. Once this relationship is rejected by the former colonies, English people must find some other basis for their national pride. To redefine Irish identity, for example, so that it is no longer a function of being colonized by the English raises a challenge for English people to redefine their identity and their relationship with Irish people. So, for an English person, if they do not take pride in having oppressed and colonized a large proportion of the world's peoples, what is there to take pride in? If they are not to sink into guilt about their colonial history and involvement in the slave trade and, at the same time, build respectful, peer relationships with the people they have formerly oppressed, how will they define what it means to be English? The same challenge is there for people in the US and in other dominant or oppressor groups. How do you take pride as a member of a dominant or an oppressor group? Real change is unlikely to happen until this is addressed. As we saw in the last chapter, much of this involves redefining the identity in human terms, noticing those aspects of their humanity that they have been able to hang on to within the oppressor group, and reclaiming those other aspects that they have been disconnected from.

SUMMARY

Oppression and liberation form the context within which leadership operates. To really think clearly about people we have to understand these dynamics intimately. We have to understand how they affect other people individually and collectively. We also have to understand how they affect us personally and affect our own groups. We have to be able to identify the challenges facing us in the struggle for liberation, understand the blockages when they occur and be able to offer both the contradictions and the vision that will enable individuals and groups to mobilize, organize and take action to overcome the internalized oppression and eliminate the external oppression. Having a clear perspective on the notion of identity is hugely important in this, as is being able to think well about both the oppressed and the oppressor dimensions. As people struggle to come to terms with their identity and take the steps to transform their situation, the ability of the leader to model a self-confident delight in their own identity and to be proudly pleased with the identities of other people will play a significant role in contradicting any patterns of internalized oppression.

REFLECTION

Identity

Pick one of your important identities.

1   Think about the history of your people and describe how the description of their identity as a people has evolved over time. Which aspects of the identity represent inherent human characteristics and which are a reflection of oppression or internalized oppression?
2   Which aspects of their inherent humanity do your people lose sight of, have difficulty claiming or become disconnected from?
3   Which aspects of their inherent humanity do your people rigidly assert, proclaim or take a defensive or defiant pride in?

Liberation

4   Which change movements have been most effective in counteracting internalized oppression?
5   Give examples of ways in which internalized oppression has been successfully contradicted by particular change movements.
6   Give examples of ways in which change movements have operated from within their internalized oppression.
7   Which change movements, organizations or groups have been most effective in recognizing, valuing and managing diversity?

Part III
Strategies and skills

12 Change and influence strategies

INTRODUCTION

So far, we have looked at the role of leadership as a resource for liberation. At its core, leadership is forward looking and transformative. Working from a vision of how things could be, leaders try to influence their collaborators in ways that encourage and assist them to think clearly about the issues facing them, overcome the effects of oppression and internalized oppression and act with confidence and power to transform the world around them. In doing this, effective leadership is an influence rather than an authoritarian role. Leaders bring people with them rather than impose change or command obedience. In practice, however, this process is not straightforward. At times it gets complicated, it gets messy and it involves dealing with conflict. Often we have to handle all kinds of painful emotion as the prospect of change triggers people's fears or distrust. In this chapter, we want to examine different perspectives on this influence role and workable strategies for dealing with change.

INFLUENCE STRATEGIES

The traditional, hierarchical approach to leadership would have relied simply on commanding people to change. In the context of true leadership, in the context of liberation and in the context of uncertainty and the need for what Heifetz (1994) and Heifetz and Linsky (2002a) call adaptive change, this is not a workable, long-term strategy. Adaptive change is non-routine change that requires questioning taken-for-granted assumptions, methods or policies and learning new, creative ways to deal with emerging situations. By its nature, it cannot be imposed. Apart from its appropriateness, in many situations, those who wish to exercise leadership may not even have the power or the right to command. Sometimes, for example, we want to change things from below where we have little or no formal power. More importantly, in a context where we wish to build empowering, cooperative relationships, to command may actually be counter-productive. So, how can someone become a person of influence in the absence of the power or authority to command? A number of key elements have emerged as central to becoming a person of influence. Some of these are basic motivational tools that have been suggested by management and organizational behaviour theory and some are strategies that have emerged from experience in the context of social change. Many are the natural implications of the model of leadership and of the human person at the heart of this book.

RESPONSES TO CHANGE

A useful starting point is to look at the different ways groups respond to proposals for significant change. We can think of three broad reactions to change from within a group or, more specifically, we can think of three sub-groups within the larger group that are differentiated by their responses to change. While this model risks oversimplifying the process, it is helpful in focusing our thinking on how best to bring people with us. In Subgroup 1, which we can call *enthusiastic/committed*, people are enthusiastic and com-mitted supporters of the proposed change right from the start. They trust us implicitly, they share our vision or they believe firmly in the merits of what is being suggested. It is clear that, from day one, they are right behind us, cheering us on and supporting us in whatever way they can. For some of them, this positive attitude is characteristic of their usual demeanour and approach to solving problems generally and is not simply a response to this particular change. They can generally be counted on to take a positive and enthusiastic approach to initiatives. As leaders, in any change situation it is great to have some people like this with us. They give us encouragement and keep our spirits up. They remind us that what we are doing is worthwhile. We know we will never be attacked or abandoned by these people. Having said that, however, it may well be the case that people such as these are in a small minority. If we are lucky, we will have a couple of people like this behind us. Sometimes there are no such people backing us.

In Subgroup 2, which we can call *uncommitted/neutral*, there is a very much larger group of people who are a lot less enthusiastic about change. Some of them are simply not convinced that the change is worthwhile. They are uncertain about where it will lead and what effects it might have for them. They worry about the possible dangers or negative effects that it might have. Others do not see the change as important. They have other priorities and concerns and perhaps do not see the need for what is proposed. They do not see the same urgency or the same significance in the situation facing them. Others still may have reservations about the motivation behind the proposed change. They may have some doubts or suspicions about what is behind it. And, there may be others who are open to change but simply have not made up their minds yet. People in this larger middle group, while they are not enthusiastic or committed, are not rigidly opposed to change. They have fears, doubts, concerns, other agendas and other priorities that keep them from supporting the change wholeheartedly.

Finally, in Subgroup 3, which we can call *angry/opposed*, there are people who are angry, hostile and deeply antagonistic towards the proposed change. Sometimes they feel this way about any change. They may be deeply distrustful of those behind the initiative and see hidden conspiracies in what is being proposed. Sometimes, the proposed change is seen as part of a pattern of changes that they have felt angry about for a long time. Sometimes, they are a group that has felt badly treated and hard done by going back over a long period and this new change is just another example, for them, of how people are mistreated. Quite often, at its core, this is also a relatively small group. Their opposition is unyielding and inflexible. And their entrenched opposition may be characteristic of their usual demeanour and general response to solving problems. In other words, they are often seen as negative and have a reputation for being difficult people to deal with.

It is possible that we can all think of people who might fit into this last category. Many groups and organizations have some people like this. Having said that, it has been my experience that this group is often smaller than people realize. Some of the people who would be labelled this way are actually people with real and genuine concerns who feel strongly about the proposed change but who are not stubbornly inflexible. More properly, they should be seen as part of the second category. Sometimes, because of poor leadership, they are people who have joined the third group out of sympathy because they saw them being mistreated. At its core, Subgroup 3 may actually consist of only one or two people who have managed to pull a larger group around them by appealing to their upsets, fears or hopelessness. In using these categories to describe this process, this is not meant to imply that all change is good or that opposition to change is always wrong. The proposed change may be a good idea or not. My interest is in how leaders can *influence* a group to support them around change and what is significant here is the way people respond to it, one way or the other. The third category of people are characterized by their inflexibility and often by the level of painful emotion they act out. They are quite similar to the people who act out accumulated hurt in attacking leaders, whom we looked at in Chapter 6. In some cases, there may actually be merit in their opposition but, because of the way it is communicated, it becomes difficult for this to be seen. As leaders trying to bring about change, this latter group can sometimes preoccupy us and take up much of our energy and attention. They can cause us a lot of stress. They may appear difficult, demanding, unyielding, stubborn and threatening. This is the group that we lose sleep over and dread having to deal with. We worry about what to do about them and how we are going to handle them or how we can convert or win them over.

Looking at these three subgroups, the question is – where do we as leaders put our energy in trying to bring about change? The people in the third subgroup tend to soak up our energy but will that lead to change? As a rule,

230 Strategies and skills

significant change rarely comes from the direction of this latter group. Their lack of flexibility and their preoccupation with their upsets make it difficult for them to shift position or to come up with creative, constructive ways of moving ahead. To be effective, we have to put our energy and attention into the first two groups. We have to focus on winning over the people with the potential to change rather than the people who are most resistant to it. In particular, this means focusing on the large middle group who are not yet sold on change but who are also not rigidly opposed to it.

If we have had some bad experiences with the third group, these may have left us so drained that we do not have the energy to face them or any others again. The temptation may be to pull back and keep our distance from everyone. This is one of the strategies that people who get attacked or criticized a lot have for surviving. In response to constant resistance and attacks, some leaders simply give up, stay in their offices and put their energy into administration rather than leadership. While this might be an understandable reaction it will not be helpful. Particularly, when we are having a hard time with this third group, we have to keep going after those in the second group. If we isolate ourselves from them they will get confused about us. The criticisms and attacks from the third group will have a much greater effect. If, however, we manage to stay close to people, these attacks are less likely to stick. People can think about us and see that the attacks are out of line, are inappropriate or simply untrue. They know from their own relationship with us that the things others are saying are simply not accurate. By staying close, they get to think more clearly about us and we get to notice that we actually have some support.

Mostly, winning over these groups involves building solid, one-to-one relationships with people, listening respectfully to them, responding positively to their fears or difficulties, offering encouragement, modelling hope and holding out a vision of what could be achieved. If we can organize a critical mass of people who are in favour of what is proposed and willing to support it, this can outweigh any negative or destructive reactions from a minority of people who are opposed to the change. We can use an analogy here drawing on Peters (1995). He asks how we can handle our enemies. (Thinking of people opposed to change as the enemy is not actually a useful analogy generally but it serves to make a point here.) The answer, according to Peters, is, "Forget your enemies. Work around them. Work instead on developing friends, turning people who agree with you (a little bit or a lot) into passionate advocates and adherents. That is, surround your enemies with friends" (p. 51). Our energy has to go into building our relationship with friends and building a group of committed supporters rather than worrying about or attacking our enemies. Without doing anything directly about such people, we can significantly reduce the negative effects of this third category of people by the efforts we make with everyone else.

WINNING ALLIES

Implicit in what is being said here is a recognition of the importance of allies. Many change agents, organizational and social, are ultimately unsuccessful because they either fail to build alliances or else alienate those with the most potential to be allies. In most change situations, there are many potential allies who, while they are not necessarily for us, are also not against us. They are open to understanding and helping in whatever ways they can if we do not drive them away and can figure out how to reach them. We have to make it easy for them to support us, however, rather than attacking them because they do not. One way to do this is to offer them our support or our help, not as part of some bargaining process but simply as an unconditional offer. If we do not attach conditions to our support and require people to reciprocate, we can build a relationship with people that is trusting and respectful and where they are more likely to listen to us with an open mind.

Listening is also a key skill in doing this. At one of my workshops, a participant stated rather bluntly that she was a fascist. For a brief moment I wondered how I could persuade her to change her viewpoint. Instead, I asked her what attracted her to fascism. When she announced it was because fascism, in her view, was about trying to make the world a better place, I knew we would have no difficulty communicating and finding a way to be allies for each other. So long as we did not get hung up on labels we could go a long way together. By listening closely to people, treating their ideas, their viewpoints, their feelings and their concerns with respect and not arguing with them, we can make it more likely that they will be open to being influenced by us.

It helps also in winning allies if we can avoid the use of emotive language or jargon and instead offer thoughtful, reasoned viewpoints on issues that concern them. It helps if we do not "push people's buttons" by using language that alienates, scares or slights them. It helps to notice what they are able to hear without getting defensive and not to polarize people needlessly. A fairly common mistake that we make is to attack what we disagree with rather than offering people some positive alternatives. Similarly, instead of trying to organize people *against* something negative, it helps a lot if we can organize them *for* something positive. Rather than wasting time attacking other people's positions, it can be a lot more useful to hold out a vision of what is possible that looks interesting and attractive. We are more likely to win people over by holding out a positive vision of the future, making constructive suggestions or proposals and offering practical ways forward.

Apart from thinking about how we might win allies, as leaders, we can also ask ourselves who our potential allies are. Often these are not necessarily the obvious, high-profile actors. They may be the low-key, behind-the-scenes personnel. They may be part of the silent majority. Individually, they may or may not have much power but together they may make a difference. For many effective leaders, the winning of allies, one to one, is an everyday part of what

they do. At every opportunity, they reach out and make thoughtful connections with people who have the potential to support them.

By the same token, if we focus on attacking those in Subgroup 3 above and
resisting their efforts, we risk increasing their opposition, particularly if we
are seen to handle them unfairly or in a heavy-handed way. Some of our
potential allies who are in Subgroup 2 will join them out of sympathy and will
themselves now become more opposed to change. As we saw in Chapter 1, by
thinking about leadership in terms of relationships, we can adopt a very
strategic approach to change. We can think about the people it makes sense to
go after and get close to. We can identify those people with the potential to
change and to influence other members of the group. We can work out in
whom we need to invest energy. For example, we can think about the people
around us and ask which of them we have close, solid relationships with,
which of them we have neglected, not spent enough time with or never built a
close relationship with, which of them could do with some support from us,
which of them we are isolated from and which of them are unlikely to let us
get close. We can think about our relationships like this and strategize about
where best to put our energy and how best to do it.

Pierce (1984) describes how Eugene Debs, a socialist candidate, received
almost a million votes in the 1920 presidential election in the US. He did this
while he was still in prison for opposing US involvement in the First World
War. The reason he got so many votes was that he had spent years travelling
around building relationships with working people all over the country.
According to Pierce, most people voted for Debs not necessarily because they
agreed with his politics but because they felt a relationship with him. As
leaders, we need to understand the importance of relationships, particularly
in the context of leading people through change. It is through our relationships that we become influential. For Jackins (1990) this is also a key aspect
of organizing people. He emphasizes that this is essentially a one-to-one
process. Such approaches as calling meetings, distributing leaflets and printed
information, making speeches and so on are all supplementary to this basic
process of building close relationships and are never a substitute for it. The
enduring results he found always came from the personal friendships he made
with individual people. He says we have to like people and show them that we
like them and he underlines the importance of this friendship in winning
support. Other methods may help but this one is fundamental.

BUILDING RELATIONSHIPS

If building relationships is central to leadership in general and to the winning
of allies in particular, it is important to look in more detail at how this can
be done. It is clear from what we have seen that it is difficult to influence
people at a distance or in isolation from them. The closer we are, the more
influence we have. It is also clear that within a group or organization, the

more supportive and united people are, the easier it is to find solutions to problems. This is not to say that such support and unity will not also create their own problems as Janis (1982) pointed out when he described the process of groupthink. In this case, groupthink is a process whereby a group becomes so comfortable and cohesive that its members fail to challenge each other or the questionable assumptions or policies they are taking for granted. The solution to groupthink, however, is not to avoid support or unity but to ensure that it is safe for everyone to contribute all their thinking without fear of ridicule or attack. So, how do we build close, solid, supportive relationships?

Close contact

At the core of building relationships is keeping close contact with people. Much of what we looked at in Chapter 1 was about this. It may not necessarily mean a high quantity of contact but what does matter is that it is high-quality contact. There are four aspects of this high-quality contact. The first of these is that we listen to people.

Listen

As we saw in Chapter 1, part of our role as leaders is to listen deeply so that we have a sense of what is happening for the people around us, particularly where they struggle. To be influential, people have to know that we understand their issues, their concerns and their struggles. They have to know we want to hear what it's like for them. We have to take an interest in their lives. We have to show that we want to hear their thinking and we have to allow their thinking to influence us if we are to have any influence over them. We have already seen how much of this listening takes place informally or while we are engaged in some common task. The outcome we are aiming for is that people will come away from interactions with us feeling connected to us, feeling empowered, feeling uplifted, feeling accepted and being able to tell that there is a supportive resource there for them. We will not always manage to achieve that but the quality of the relationship over time leads to these kinds of effects.

At one point in my career, I was a trade union shop steward. As part of this role, I used to find opportunities to spend time casually and informally listening to people. I might meet someone in the corridor on the way to my office and spend a few minutes chatting about their day or how they spent their weekend. Or, over coffee, I might listen to someone talk about their family. Whenever I could, I would pay attention to people and hear how things were going for them. There would be lots of relatively short interactions with different people during the day where we would have some relaxed contact like this. Quite often, following one of these interactions, that same person would come to my office and ask if they could speak to me about a difficulty they were having at work. It was clear that the earlier contact we had was enough to remind them that there was a resource there that they could use. This ability apparently to "waste time" with people or to "hang out" with individuals is an important leadership skill. Many managers and administrators have become so busy in their work that they no longer prioritize this kind of contact with the people around them. Their neglect can prove costly.

Encourage

The second aspect of high-quality contact is encouragement. As we listen to people we notice the places where they need encouragement in their lives or in their work. In many work situations that I deal with, for example, people are desperate for encouragement. They may be feeling isolated, overwhelmed or stressed. They may feel that the difficulties they face are unending or that nothing is being done to overcome them. In the face of these feelings and difficulties no one seems to offer any encouragement and people's enthusiasm and morale take a battering. Teachers, for example, are a group that sometimes gets a lot of criticism from parents and the public generally. They face huge problems in the classroom at times, often problems they do not feel they have been trained to handle. Their job can be one of the most isolating of all occupations, particularly if, on top of having to be responsible for a large number of young people on their own in the classroom, there are tensions and poor relationships in the staffroom. Society has huge expectations of what teachers should be able to achieve and often what gets communicated to teachers are disappointments, doubts and criticisms about how well they meet these expectations. It is difficult to stay motivated and enthusiastic under these conditions. A key role for a school principal or any leader in situations like this is holding out encouragement for their staff: offering people hope; reminding people about the important role they play and the difference they make; believing in them and showing them we think they can do it. This encouragement may be communicated in things we say. Often it is communicated non-verbally, in the tone of voice we use or our facial expression or our relaxed manner in the face of their worry.

Praise

Closely related to encouragement is the third aspect of high-quality contact, namely, praise. It makes a difference to people if we show them we are pleased with their efforts. We make a habit of telling them how well they are doing. We point out particular things we have noticed that it would be good for them to hear. And, rather than general statements such as "you did great", we give them specifics. We tell them what exactly they did that was great. However, some people are quite immune to praise. They have learned not to trust it, for example. Perhaps it has been used manipulatively or insincerely in the past and they no longer believe it. Sometimes, praise has been used as a lead-in to criticism and people have come to be wary of it. "First let me tell you what you have done well . . .". The person may not hear the praise because they are waiting for the sting in the tail, the criticism that seems inevitably to follow. Or, it may be that people get praised a lot for some obvious things that everyone notices and this praise no longer has any effect. They know these positive things about themselves and do not need a lot of reminders from the outside. If praise is to be effective, it has to be thoughtful. If we have been listening well to people, we will pick up a sense of where it is they most need to hear praise. What is the thing about them or their work that everyone else overlooks? Where is the place that they are most unsure of themselves? Where do they struggle? What risks have they taken or what new ideas have they tried out recently where it would be useful to get some positive feedback? What steps are they taking that are difficult for them? For each person, we can think about what would be the most useful kind of praise for them to hear. We are trying to build relationships with people where they take it for granted that if they have done well, we will notice this and show it. We do this consistently, we do it formally and we do it informally, we do it publicly and we do it privately. This was summed up very neatly by Blanchard and Johnson (1982) when they talked about the importance of catching people doing things right. We have to switch our attention from spotting what people are doing wrong, notice what they are doing right and communicate this. Leaders can make a huge difference by adopting this approach and using it consistently.

Appreciate

The final aspect of high-quality contact is appreciation. One of the most common complaints in any workplace is about lack of appreciation or being taken for granted. We constantly forget to thank people for what they do. We forget to show that we have noticed the efforts they made and that we appreciate this. This is often particularly the case with people lower down in the hierarchy of organizations who have little or no authority but without whose work things could not function. People need to be thanked. They need to be thanked often and not just for the out-of-ordinary things they do. Where someone can tell that their efforts are appreciated they are more com-mitted and, when necessary, will go out of their way to help in crisis situations or when unexpected problems arise.

These four elements – listening, encouragement, praise and appreciation – are at the heart of high-quality contact. As leaders, we can think about each of our relationships and evaluate the extent to which they are characterized by these elements. We can think about where we ourselves are weakest in this regard and which elements are least characteristic of any given relationship. This does not mean that in every interaction we have with people we will slavishly ensure we have done each of these. It simply means that when people think about their relationship with us, these are the kinds of things that stand out for them. It means that these are characteristic of the relationship as a whole.

Follow-up

Over and above high-quality contact, there are others steps we can also take to build close relationships. One of these has to do with follow-up. If we consistently listen and are open to hearing about people's lives and work, if we consistently seem to catch people doing things right, if we are encouraging and appreciative of their efforts, people will use us as a resource. They will come to us with problems, ideas or suggestions. They will look for our support or our help. The important thing for leaders here is that we follow this up. One group of employees that I worked with once complained that, whenever they raised an issue with the general manager, he invariably said, "leave it with me". And that would be the last they would hear of their issue. It was a huge source of frustration that he never came back to them about what they raised. Even if we are simply telling them we have not been able to figure out any way to solve their problem, people still need us to follow up. They will appreciate that we tried even if we did not succeed. We need to keep people informed about what we are doing with the matters they have raised even if we have no progress to report. In many cases, however, there will be things we can do to help or support them and the follow-up steps we take will strengthen and solidify the relationship we have built.

Do favours for people

Good relationships also require flexibility. There are times when people need us to go easy on them or do favours for them. Sometimes it makes sense not to apply rules too rigidly. On different occasions, I have heard people talk about how much they appreciated being given some leeway when they were under pressure or facing difficulties in their lives. One man, whose wife and child were both ill at the same time, talked about the difference it made to have his boss tell him to forget about work and just look after his family. He was told that they would cover for him and not to worry about anything except his family. The effect of this was to generate a huge amount of loyalty from this man. He would have done anything for his boss. A manager described how, by being flexible around giving staff time off to do errands or attend appointments, the sickness and absenteeism record of her department was one of the lowest in the organization. Where this flexibility is in response to real and genuine needs it is generally not abused. On the other hand, if it is done for the wrong reasons, such as trying to keep everyone happy or to avoid conflict, for example, then there is a danger of people abusing it. As leaders, we have to think clearly about what makes sense and then respond flexibly as situations demand. We have to notice the places where people need a hand and do favours for them.

Treat people with respect

Some of the things we do as part of building good relationships are very basic. They simply involve treating people with respect. Before discussing what this involves, it is useful to point out that while many people complain about being treated disrespectfully day in and day out, very few people will admit to not treating others with respect. This is an area that requires us to be very honest with ourselves about how we behave. We may not say disrespectful things but perhaps our tone of voice is not always respectful. What we perceive as helpful advice may be perceived by others as criticism or interference. While our intentions may always be good, the effect we have may not be what we desire. So we have to be wary of glibly or lightly assuming we always treat people well. We should be particularly wary if we find ourselves stating publicly that we always believe in treating everyone with respect. For some reason, those who espouse things like this publicly can be the worst offenders. We can check out our behaviour, for example, by asking people what they would like us to do differently in the way we relate to them. If we hear the same kind of things from a number of people this might be an area we need to look at.

Among other things, being respectful means that we do not do things that demean or humiliate others, for example. We do not order people to do things when a polite, respectful request would be quite sufficient. We do not ignore people or treat them as less important than we are. We are aware of how various dynamics around classism, sexism, racism or other types of oppression can lead to people being treated badly or insensitively. We are thoughtful about the ways that people with our particular identity can mistreat people with a different identity and we understand the subtle ways that people can feel hurt and snubbed.

Avoid criticism

When we have a difficulty with someone, ideally we talk to them about it privately. We do not criticize them in public. Glasser (1994) states that, "It is criticism from the manager that is the largest cause of the energy-wasting, adversarial relationships that exist between too many employees and boss-managers" (p. 95). In fact, he believes there is no such thing as constructive criticism. This does not mean that issues cannot be confronted but doing this by way of criticism is generally counter-productive. As we saw in an earlier chapter, instead of criticizing people, he believes we should learn to coach them. Very few people can hear criticism in the way it is intended. Mostly, they either agree with it for the sake of peace or because they have no choice in the matter or else they simply resent it and get defensive. About the only exception to this occurs where the person being criticized can tell for sure that the other person cares deeply about them or respects them. Under those conditions, they may be able to hear what is being said without resenting it or getting too defensive. One of the reasons that people at work react so badly to criticism is that it often comes in the absence of any sense that the other person appreciates or notices what they have done well. People will complain that, "I was on time every single morning for the past six months and the one day I came late they were down on me heavily, like a ton of bricks. Not a word about all the days I was on time." Unless we have been consistently putting work into building a close connection with people in all the ways we have looked at so far, it will be difficult to raise issues with their performance in ways that do not generate resistance. Simply attaching a preamble where we mention some positive qualities will not be sufficient to compensate for the lack of recognition in the weeks and months before this. This process of confronting people and dealing with conflict will be dealt with in more detail in Chapters 13 and 14.

Give information

People appreciate knowing what is going on even when it does not directly concern them. Many organizations hoard information and make it a scarce resource. The effect of this, as Kanter (1993) has shown, is to disempower people. Making a habit of telling people all we know is a powerful way of building relationships with them. They come to trust that if we know something, they will be told. This is particularly important when it comes to change, a situation where often people feel they are not being told the full story. If we have built an open relationship with them where we have consistently and willingly shared information, they will trust us when we tell them we do not have information or do not have the answers to their questions. One organization I worked with had set up a steering group to plan and implement a new computerized management information system. This was to involve a lot of changes in people's jobs and the introduction of information technology to areas where individuals had never used it before. When asked how the trade unions felt about these changes they responded by saying they hoped to have the system in place before anyone noticed it! Semler (2003) believes information should be widely available to employees, including company financial information that would normally be kept secret. The more information people have, the more responsibly they can act. In a similar vein, Peters (1995) suggests that nothing is more important than keeping people informed about everything that is going on.

Put the effort in when times are good

The final prescription for building good relationships has already been adverted to in the discussion about criticism. The time to build relationships is when they are in good shape. We have to avoid a fire-fighting approach where we ignore them until there is a crisis. Usually, at that point, trust has broken down and it is very difficult to rebuild the relationship from there.

Building relationships is thus a central and ongoing role of any leader. According to Kouzes and Posner (2001), exemplary leaders are devoted to building relationships based on mutual respect and caring. If we do this consistently, when difficulties arise there is that strong base of trust and connection to carry the relationship through them and to allow a mutually satisfactory, win–win resolution to be achieved.

We have to ensure that day-to-day business and other urgent demands do not relegate the building and maintaining of close relationships to the back seat, to be addressed when there is time. The reality is that there will always be something that feels more pressing or urgent than spending time with people, checking in with them, listening to them and finding ways to support them. Unless we prioritize this aspect of leadership, it can easily be overshadowed by these other demands. Many of the leadership teams that I work with spend insufficient time listening to, and connecting with, each other separately from their other tasks and responsibilities. When conflicts arise, they are less able to deal with them and to create the safety to allow everyone to speak openly, identify issues or challenge what is happening. The purpose of doing all this is not just so people will feel better. It is so that people can function better, individually and collectively. It is to establish the conditions for people to be creative and to use all of their talent and initiative to the fullest. And it is to enable people to exert maximum influence on one another while being fully respectful of each other's autonomy.

LEADERSHIP AND INFLUENCE

To become a person of influence involves, as we have seen, understanding the dynamics of a group and putting the effort into building solid relationships with people. In addition, leaders who are effective at this tend to have certain characteristics that make it more likely they will be successful. These include being strategic, being intentional and being persistent.

Strategic

Effective leaders strategize their relationships. At first glance, this might seem cold and calculating but, more accurately, it is simply thoughtful. They think about their relationships. They think about those whom they are close to and whom they have no connection with. They think about who needs a hand and how they can be a resource for them. They systematically build relationships that matter. They make a difference through relationships and they put a lot of thought into building these relationships. It is not haphazard. It is not peripheral. They think strategically about each of their relationships. As they do this, they also notice who are the people with the potential to play greater leadership roles and they pay particular attention to, and invest time and energy in, these relationships.

Intentional

According to Hestenes (1999), effective leadership that lasts over time and makes a difference is intentional, not accidental. We can go a certain distance by simply responding to the opportunities that happen to present themselves. We can find ourselves propelled into positions of leadership or influence by accident. At some point, however, we have to stop and ask ourselves what it is we want to achieve and how we are going to do it. To become widely influential we have to decide to make a difference. As we do this, we also become much more strategic about how we will make this difference. This transition from accidental to intentional leadership is a significant and decisive one.

Persistent

Woody Allen commented that 80 per cent of success consists of just showing up and Napoleon said that victory belonged to the most persevering. Effective leaders are persistent. In spite of doubts, fears, setbacks or failures, they keep going. At a workshop I was once asked to what I attributed my effectiveness. Spontaneously, and somewhat over-simplistically, I replied that the trick was to show up, look benign and make friends with people. Most of it, however, consisted of showing up. We show up, we take initiative and try things and, if they do not work, we try something else. But we do not give up. The combination of strategic, intentional and persistent leadership is ultimately what makes for success.

RESISTANCE TO CHANGE

Much has been written about change and how to manage it. I want to highlight one particular aspect of this, namely, resistance to change. As a rule, people will resist change when they cannot see clearly how it will make things better for them. Since this is, in fact, often the case, resistance is both very common and very understandable. This is useful to remember because it can prevent us falling into the trap of assuming that resistance is some kind of wilful, malicious or obstinate attempt to obstruct or sabotage change.

A common mistake that gets made is to expect people to be committed to change without taking effective steps to win that commitment. For many groups and individuals, change is, at least initially, a source of difficult and painful feelings. Among other things, it brings up feelings of fear and anxiety about what it will entail, suspicion of those who are proposing it, confusion about what it involves and sometimes anger at the lack of information or consultation. These feelings can lead people to be reluctant to change and to resist it actively. If it is not handled well, it may lead to obstruction of one kind or another, needless hostility or apathy. In work organizations, it may also lead to absenteeism, poor-quality work, sabotage, industrial disputes, demotivation and low morale. This makes very special demands on the leaders of change to develop processes that will allow change to take place without unnecessarily generating resistance from those who will be affected by it. It means looking at how we can approach change in ways that enable people to remain flexible in their thinking without developing rigid mindsets that box them into a limited set of reactions to the process. Achieving this involves using practical strategies and having a clear perception of the role of leadership.

As we saw above and in Chapter 6, there may be times when the resistance from some people is heavily loaded with painful emotion and is a reaction to old, accumulated hurts. We also saw how this requires careful thought and a different approach to resistance generally. Looking at it from the perspective of the group as a whole, however, such people are generally in a minority and it is useful to design our approach to resistance around that broader, less entrenched majority who are more open to movement. I want to look at how change can be approached in ways that will minimize any unnecessary negative or destructive reactions and that allow people to feel a sense of control and ownership over the change process.

To begin with, let me look at one aspect of the context within which change sometimes takes place. This is where there is a past history of difficulties of one kind or another. In particular, there are often the residues of previous conflicts or difficulties in work relationships that have never been fully resolved. Thus the change is proposed in the context of an ongoing adversarial relationship, is greeted with great suspicion or anger and those proposing the change are attacked for their mistakes and failures in the past. Proposals from one side to bring about change will usually result in the other side bringing up what it considers to be the unfinished business from the past. When this occurs, it tends to have the character of a rigid preoccupation with the past or a rigid mindset from which the person or group is either unwilling or unable to move. Such preoccupations and mindsets will be a difficulty not only for the people being invited to undertake a change process but also for the leaders or change agents. Both groups will have to develop an ability to respond flexibly to circumstances as they develop. I want to look in more detail at how this can be handled.

In this scenario, people will ask why those proposing the change should be trusted now, given the previous history? Particularly in the early stages of the change process, there will be a strong pull for people to look back and to bring up all their feelings about how they have been badly treated in the past. What can happen in this situation is that the change agent gets so distracted by the content of the suspicions or attacks that the relevance of the underlying feelings gets missed. Managers, for example, will complain about the unwillingness of workers to forget the past and move forward. They will feel defensive and unfairly attacked. They wish people would leave all this behind, offer their trust, and get on with doing things differently. They will say they understand the anger people are expressing but that it is not getting them anywhere. At this point, everyone feels stuck and the process can become very painful. Managers feel attacked and the workers feel their grievances are not being heard.

We need to understand that inviting people to move from an adversarial relationship to a cooperative one is going to bring up all the feelings people have about how they have not been cooperated with or treated as partners in the past. This does not mean that something has gone wrong with the process. This is part of the process. The job of the change agent is to stand back and notice the pattern in what is happening, without being sucked into it, and to figure out how to deal with the feelings involved. Essentially, this means creating the safety for people to communicate their feelings without getting pulled into blaming or attacking others. As they feel listened to, people will be willing to let go of the past and look ahead.

DEALING WITH RESISTANCE TO CHANGE

Given the above rigidities and difficulties around change, it is clear that for the leader or change agent to view these as wilful obstruction, or as backwardness, misses the point. This is where the rigidity of the leader's own mindset can be a problem. The job of the leader is to stay thinking, figure out how to deal with these and not simply be upset about them. Feeling resentful of people's unwillingness to change is not a particularly useful perspective. Building on the work of Karp (1988), we can outline a number of elements of a proactive approach that help to avoid pushing people into rigid positions and can make a significant difference to the progress of change.

Surfacing the resistance

The starting point is to bring the resistance to the surface. We have to make it safe for people to voice their difficulties by reassuring them that we do want to hear them and that they will not be penalized for doing so. We have to ask for all of the difficulties and listen carefully without arguing. As we listen, we can ask clarifying questions to make sure we understand the concerns. At this point, the role of the leader or change agent is to create the conditions whereby the issues and concerns can be discussed openly without argument. This often fails to happen because the leader reacts defensively to the first piece of bad news they hear. Instead of waiting until all the difficulties have been voiced, the leader gets pulled into defending their proposals against the first objection raised. In Chapter 14 we shall see a set of guidelines for structuring discussions such as this so as to ensure a useful discussion of all the difficulties.

Respecting the resistance

Having brought the resistance to the surface, we then have to respect or honour it. This means listening well and making no attempts to interrupt, argue, state our own position, sell something or imply that the resistance is invalid, while it is being explained. It means taking people's questions seriously and giving them all the information we can to allow them to make up their minds about what is being proposed. It also means acknowledging the resistance by affirming the person's right to have difficulties or concerns and reinforcing the notion that it is permissible and safe to resist. One of the difficulties for change agents or leaders in this process is that, as people confront us with their difficulties, there can be a pull for us to want to give up on them or feel bad towards them because they are not more cooperative. We can see the value of what we are proposing and we can resent people for obstructing something that we cherish and that we think makes perfect sense. Actively respecting the resistance can help us avoid getting stuck in this way. It gives others the space to choose to follow us and allows everyone to feel empowered by the process. Underpinning our respect is the recognition that resistance is normal and understandable. Underpinning it also is a recognition that through dialogue we can identify gaps in, and practical difficulties with, what is being proposed and find creative ways to address these.

Exploring the resistance

As we listen, we have to try to identify people's real interests and concerns and work with them, through a process of dialogue, to find ways to address these. In doing this, we will not be able to impose our own unilateral definition of the problem or announce our own decision on what will be done. We have to involve people in this process and share our power. This has been described as a challenge for us to give up *controlling* what happens without giving up our *thinking*. We saw some other aspects of this in the context of oppressor–oppressed relationships in previous chapters. As we explore the resistance and identify the issues and difficulties, we begin to take on board other people's thinking and modify the proposed changes in ways that address their genuine concerns. Instead of using an adversarial process, we work collaboratively with people to find the way forward that addresses as many of the needs in the situation as possible. In Chapter 14, we shall look at this process in more detail as we examine the problem-solving process.

Staying close and continuing to listen

An important part of this process, and something that was highlighted earlier, in the discussion on building relationships, is the need for some active and visible follow-through on the issues being raised. Where possible, we can agree on specific steps to be taken following the discussion but, at the very least, we need to be seen to have been listening and to have taken people's concerns seriously. At the very least, we need to keep people informed at every step on the way. It is also important that we do not cut ourselves off once some initial progress has been made. One of the big mistakes with change programmes is that of launching and leaving them. Leaders are very visible at the beginning praising the merits of the changes, outlining what they expect to achieve and promising support along the way. After the initial flurry of activity, enthusiasm and promises, those affected by it and those who are trying to implement it find themselves on their own. At this point, cynicism and disillusionment begin to set in. We have to continue to give people support and backup, to listen and be seen to take people seriously. They need to know that our listening is not simply an expedient in order to win support for this particular process. They need to know that we are committed to trying to get things right from now on. They need to see that they can influence what happens in very real ways.

Successful change requires clear, flexible leadership. It requires an openness to hearing other people's difficulties, the ability to think flexibly about people and their concerns and the ability to stay hopeful and inspire people in the face of their suspicions and hopelessness. Resistance to change is a common feature of this process. Handled well it can actually enhance the quality of the change process and make for a more realistic and appropriate set of decisions about the steps to be taken.

SUMMARY

We have seen repeatedly that leadership is primarily an influence process. The job of the leader is to influence rather than command. One of the most important skills here is the ability to step back and think strategically about people and how they can be reached. Being able to identify those with the potential to change and to invest energy in them is a vital part of this process. Being able to build close relationships with them is central to how we make a difference. By putting influence at the centre of how we work we can see the steps we have to take to build relationships, win allies and deal with resistance as a hugely important part of how we use our time rather than as a distraction or a waste of time. In the following chapters, we shall look at one other important aspect of this, and of leadership generally, which is how we can resolve conflict.

REFLECTION

Strategizing relationships

1 List the key relationships in the context of your leadership. Who are the people around you who have, or could have, an effect on what you can achieve?
2 In relation to the people on this list, who are you closest to and have good-quality relationships with?
3 Who is most supportive and is a source of energy and re-invigoration for you?
4 Who has the potential to be a close confidant, shoulder to lean on or safe listener for you to show your struggles?
5 Who are the potential leaders in this group? Who has the potential to play a more active or effective leadership role? In whom could you usefully invest more energy?
6 Who could do with more affirmation, appreciation or positive feedback from you?
7 To whom are you not close or have a poor or difficult relationship with?
8 Whom have you neglected, drifted away from, or lost touch with over the last period?
9 Who is struggling and could do with more support from you?
10 Whom do you need to check in with or spend more time with?
11 Whom do you need to listen to more?
12 Who has absorbed too much of your time and energy without any positive or constructive effects?
13 Who are the chronically negative or destructive people whom you need to "surround with your friends"?
14 Who are potential allies outside your group whom it would be good to build a closer relationship with?

13 Conflict resolution skills

INTRODUCTION

More than many others, conflict resolution skills are a key tool in a leadership role. As leaders we may often be called on to handle other people's upsets and difficulties with one another or with us. We may find ourselves having to handle difficult one-to-one situations where another person is upset, disruptive, challenging, attacking or generally behaving in ways that are inappropriate. We may also find ourselves in situations where the difficulties we confront are within a group with, perhaps, a number of people having trouble coping with each other. Sometimes the conflict will involve us directly and sometimes we will be in the role of a third party trying to mediate and help people to resolve their differences. To handle these encounters effectively, we need to understand the underlying dynamic as well as having finely tuned skills that we are able to use flexibly. For the moment, let us keep the focus on one-to-one conflict.

INCIDENTS vs. RELATIONSHIPS

To begin with, it is useful to make a distinction between two different types of conflict. One of these is where we have a short-term, limited duration, *conflict incident*. This is a row, a clash or a blow-up of some kind between two people. They may be strangers who have never met or friends, acquaintances or colleagues who do not normally have difficulty with each other. Whatever their relationship, something has happened to cause them to be visibly upset with one another. This conflict incident does not last for ever. It has a beginning and an end. Something, such as a provocative word or an upset tone of voice, triggers it and something, such as an apology, a compromise or someone walking away, brings it to an end. When it is over, the parties go their separate ways or resume their previously relaxed relationship. We can contrast this with a situation where there is an ongoing *conflict relationship*. This relationship may be characterized by distance, tension, caution, over-sensitivity to perceived criticism or threats, suspicion, hostility and lack of trust. The parties involved are not comfortable with one another. They have a hard time being around each other, working with each other or living with each other. In some cases there may not be much drama in this relationship as the parties involved have settled into mutual avoidance of interaction and confrontation. There is a type of emotional stand-off. In other cases, the ongoing climate of tension is punctuated with occasional, or fairly regular, run-ins and outbursts of aggression or argument and other short-term, conflict incidents.

This distinction between conflict incidents and relationships is important because the skills involved in dealing with them are not always the same. What might work in a one-off incident with a stranger may not work repeatedly in an ongoing relationship. What might work over time in a relationship may not be enough to handle a short-term incident successfully. Successfully resolving conflict requires us to be able to use a range of strategies and, in the case of conflict relationships, to recognize that there may be no quick fix or simple technique that will easily eliminate difficulties that perhaps took years to develop. The skills for resolving conflict incidents are very helpful and, if used thoughtfully, will assist us in dealing with conflict relationships, but they need to be supplemented with other skills that are specifically geared towards building good relationships. To approach resolving conflict incidents as though the process were merely a question of applying clever techniques or tricks misses an important point. Even in a short incident with a complete stranger, we are also, for that period, in a relationship with the stranger. If we handle this relationship well, it will make the incident easier to resolve and enhance the effectiveness of the incident-handling skills that we use. In this way, a key part of resolving a conflict incident effectively is getting the underlying relationship right – the better the relationship, the easier it is to resolve the conflict – it is about building a good relationship within which difficulties can be dealt with constructively. Thus, keeping an eye on the relationship can even be helpful where the person we are dealing with is a stranger whom we may, or may not, meet again. For this reason, truly effective conflict management is preventive rather than reactive. What we do before the incident erupts makes a difference to how easily it can be resolved or whether it arises in the first place at all. In other words, handling conflict incidents well will enhance the relationship and getting the relationship right makes it much easier to handle conflict incidents.

I want to emphasize the relationship aspect of conflict resolution and downplay a sole focus on techniques or tricks or gimmicks (though these can help a lot if they are in the context of a relationship). Effective conflict resolution is about techniques *and* relationships (Le Baron, 2002). We need to develop skills in both areas if we are to be effective leaders and be able to use one set of these skills to enhance how we use the other set. Since many of the skills involved in building and maintaining good relationships have already been discussed in Chapter 12, the emphasis in this chapter will be primarily on the skills of handling conflict incidents.

THREE USEFUL APPROACHES

The focus on resolving conflict and solving problems in this and the next chapter draws particularly on three very distinct but useful approaches. The first of these is the theory of Re-evaluation Counselling (Jackins, 1978). One general assumption made by this theory is that no person ever becomes difficult or abusive, or mistreats or oppresses others, unless they themselves have first of all been badly treated. They have to be mistreated, abused or oppressed first before they become abusive or oppressive. As we have seen in previous chapters, in looking at the difficulties in the way we or others behave, we have to be able to separate what is true of people inherently or by nature as humans and what is installed or acquired as a result of the hurts or oppressions they have suffered. In general, using blame is not a helpful way to proceed and fails to allow for the full range of reasons why difficulties might occur. Jackins (1997) captures this in a challenging way when he states that

> Every single human being, at every moment of the past, if the entire situation is taken into account, has always done the very best that he or she could do, and so deserves neither blame nor reproach from anyone, including self.
>
> (p. 84)

The second useful approach is that of Rosenberg (2000) who describes it as compassionate or non-violent communication. According to Rosenberg,

> All criticism, attack, insults, and judgments vanish when we focus attention on hearing the feelings and needs behind a message. The more we practice in this way, the more we realize a simple truth: behind all those messages we've allowed ourselves to be intimidated by are just individuals with unmet needs appealing to us to contribute to their well-being.
>
> (p. 107)

His method of communicating involves four elements: making observations that contain no hint of evaluation; expressing how we are feeling; linking that feeling to our own unmet needs (rather than blaming the other person for them); and identifying what we want or desire in the situation. The third useful approach is that of Fisher, Ury and Patton (1991) and of Ury (1991). They focus particularly on the process of reaching negotiated agreement through the identification of underlying interests as well as a number of very practical steps that can readily be applied to any conflict situation. Their work is particularly useful in the context of trying to find ways of dealing with complex or emotive issues.

REACTIONS TO CONFLICT

Before looking at detailed guidelines for resolving conflict, there are some general observations about how we react to conflict that it is helpful to take note of. Self-awareness is a great asset in learning how to deal with conflict. It is very helpful, in particular, if we are aware of how we tend to react when conflict arises. Ask yourself about the feelings that come up when you first find yourself faced with conflict. Focus especially on the difficult or painful feelings that tend to get in the way of handling the conflict relaxedly or elegantly. For some people, the predominant feeling they struggle with in this situation is fear, for example fear of being attacked. For others, the situation brings up self-doubt – "maybe it's my fault". For others, the main feeling is anger with the other person. Or, there may be feelings of shock, outrage, disappointment, hurt or frustration. For many of us, there will be characteristic, common feelings we struggle with under these circumstances. Quite often, these feelings are the residue of old, unresolved hurts and conflicts from our early life. The same old feelings habitually come up for us in conflict situations (Jackins, 1978; Janov, 1980, 1990; Miller, 1987).

Under the influence of these feelings, we will be pulled to react rigidly in particular ways. Some of us, in the face of conflict, go quiet and withdraw into ourselves. Others lash out and attack the other person. Psychologists talk about the fight–flight response in such situations. We may also struggle with fantasies of physically overpowering or throttling the other person or have imaginary conversations where we tell them exactly what we think of them. The feelings we struggle with at this stage may be accompanied by outward physical or verbal indications. Physically, our bodies may tense up as our muscles tighten. Our outward posture changes, signalling the feelings we are struggling with inside. Quite commonly, our facial expression also changes. We take on a worried, anxious, scared or angry look. With that, our eye contact goes from a relaxed, attentive expression to either a rigid glaring or a rigid avoidance of eye contact. Along with these various physical signals, our tone of voice also changes. Instead of our normal relaxed tone and pace of speaking, our speech may become tighter, more clipped and quicker. We may begin to raise our voice, speak more urgently and interrupt more often. Under these circumstances, the person we are dealing with will tend to take their cue from the underlying verbal and non-verbal messages we are sending out. The result will often be an escalation and polarizing of the conflict.

As the conflict progresses, we project a tighter, more serious, more formal and less relaxed image. An emotional distance creeps in. We lose a relaxed, human connection to the other person and begin to communicate from within a more distant, formal role. This, in turn, provokes an equivalent reaction from the other person. All the while, the conflict becomes more difficult to sort out. Many conflicts escalate and become difficult to resolve because, apart from any issues at stake, the people involved get taken over by their feelings and send out physical, verbal and non-verbal signals that reinforce the distance between them. Separately from any special techniques that we might use, if we could learn to maintain a relaxed body posture, a relaxed facial expression and a relaxed tone of voice, this alone would have a huge effect on preventing conflict breakdown. A relaxed, friendly smile is a lot easier to deal with than an anxious, impatient or angry frown.

The first step in learning to do this is to become aware of what happens to us, particularly in the early moments of a conflict incident. We can notice the feelings that come up for us and how they affect our body, face and voice. We can decide and plan to go against this pattern in future conflicts. We can consciously relax those parts of our body that we notice tensing up. We can consciously tell our facial muscles to relax. We can relax our forehead and eyebrows, allow ourselves to blink, move our gaze and shift from staring to paying relaxed attention. We can slow down our pace of speech, breathe more deeply and speak more relaxedly. To the extent that we can communicate a non-defensive, relaxed attitude to what is happening, the conflict becomes much easier to resolve. Adopting this attitude makes it safe enough for the other person to relax and slow down sufficiently for both of us to find creative responses to the situation.

Getting how we look and sound right can make a huge difference to how conflict plays itself out. Having said that, there are particular additional guidelines we can use to assist further in resolving conflict. Before looking at some of these, it is helpful to have a clear understanding of what else goes on during conflict incidents.

FLEXIBLE vs. INFLEXIBLE BEHAVIOUR

There is an additional distinction that it is helpful to make when thinking about conflict. There is a difference in the way people behave in normal, non-conflict interactions and those where there is divisive conflict. In normal interaction, where there is no tension or difficulty between people, they tend to behave in ways that are flexible and appropriate to the situation. What they say and do is relevant and they are open to other points of view. If one of them can give good reasons for the position they have taken up or for the request they are making, the other person will hear these and do what makes sense. This situation, of course, presents people with little difficulty. They do not face any real conflict here.

In contrast to this, on other occasions, when tension arises or when divisive or emotive issues are involved, people may behave in ways that are rigid, inflexible and inappropriate. They rigidly refuse to listen or to change their point of view. Their behaviour becomes inflexible and, given the context, what they are saying or doing is uncalled for in the situation. They may become aggressive, abusive or uncooperative or otherwise act in ways that are inappropriate. This is where difficult conflict arises.

There is a helpful perspective we can bring to bear on this latter situation. As a rule, whenever we see someone behaving in ways that are rigid, inflexible or inappropriate, almost invariably we are dealing with someone who, at that point, is under stress or hurting in some way or other. As a result, they are in the grip of some kind of negative or painful emotion. In other words, people do not just make up their minds to cause us trouble for no reason. A person does not calmly and logically decide that they will become inflexible and behave inappropriately, no matter how it might appear from the outside. Others may accuse this person of deliberately trying to cause trouble or of enjoying making life difficult for people, but this is rarely the case. Something is going on for this person that is pulling them into being difficult. This perspective has a lot of implications for how we approach the conflict and attempt to resolve it. In particular, it helps us to avoid a simplistic, defensive or blaming approach in favour of a more sophisticated one that is responsive to all the factors operating in these types of situations. Let us look in more detail at what happens when someone is under stress or hurting.

EFFECTS OF STRESS OR HURT

When someone is hurting or under stress, a number of things happen to them. To begin with, a person in this situation is in the grip of some kind of painful emotion. They are struggling with feelings of fear, threat, worry, exhaustion, frustration, isolation, embarrassment and so on. These feelings may have been triggered by some immediate occurrence or they may be old feelings about hurtful situations in the past that have been restimulated by a similarity with what is happening in the present. In actual practice, there is often some degree of restimulation operating in difficult conflict situations and not just a purely present-time reaction to current events. The current situation reminds us of similar situations in the past and the feelings left over from those get attached to what is happening now. Were it not for this restimulation, conflict would be a lot easier to resolve. Whatever the source of the feelings, when painful emotion is pulling at our attention and, if we are unable to discharge that painful emotion or if we bottle it up, it will affect how we function in a number of unhelpful ways.

Inability to think clearly

One of the first effects is that, in the grip of this painful emotion, our ability to think clearly or rationally is interfered with. Essentially, *our thinking shuts down*. In a situation where we are under great stress or feeling hurt our minds may literally go completely blank. People describe situations where they were so scared that their mind froze. Or, people talk about feeling so nervous they could not think what to say. Or, they talk about feeling so angry, "they couldn't put two words together". In some cases, people go blank almost instantly. In others, it is a more gradual process. It is almost as though a dull fog creeps up on us and gradually takes over our brain. Our thinking becomes sluggish and we have difficulty concentrating. We cannot think straight. Our brain is functioning but we are not able to use it well. In addition, we may tense up physically, become very serious or very formal, lose our sense of humour and find it hard to treat things lightly. On a good day, when we were able to stay relaxed, we would have no difficulty handling this situation easily or elegantly but not when we start to shut down.

If we apply this to other people, it is clear that, under these conditions, to try to reason with someone whose thinking has shut down is a waste of time. Similarly, arguing with them will get us nowhere. At this point, the person's reasoning machinery is not functioning. They cannot appreciate our logic or make sense of our arguments. In spite of this, it is remarkable the number of times we witness people engaged in fruitless argument or debate where it is clear that, for the moment at least, the other person is unable to think any more clearly than they are already doing. There comes a point in a conflict situation where we have to recognize that the other person has effectively shut down and cannot hear what we are trying to communicate. Our inability to notice when this is the case may well be due to the fact that, at that point also, our own thinking has begun to shut down. Unless we can spot what is happening, we are not likely to make much progress.

Distortion of judgement

Here also, we can see a second effect of stress or hurting. Once our thinking shuts down, we become unable to evaluate accurately what is happening in the situation. *Our judgement gets distorted.* We read things into the situation that are not appropriate or useful. We may, for example, misjudge the level of danger. We may feel threatened when we are actually perfectly safe. We may hear an insult when someone compliments us. We may feel criticized when someone simply disagrees with us or offers an alternative viewpoint. Of course, pointing out to someone that they are misinterpreting the situation usually does not help. If they are not thinking straight, or are unable to evaluate accurately, they will not be able to take in what we are saying. Not only might someone misjudge what the other person is saying but they might also misjudge what would be helpful or workable in the situation. In the middle of our impatient frustration, for example, we might conclude that the other person just needs a good kick. Once our judgement gets distorted in this way, we are then prone to react in ways that are inappropriate and that may even make things worse.

Rigid, automatic responses

At this stage, because we cannot think clearly and because our judgement cannot be relied on, we are unable to invent flexible, appropriate responses to the situation. We are unable to come up with a response that makes any sense in the situation. The reason for this, as was suggested above, is that our reactions are based, not on the reality of the present situation, but on painful emotions that have more to do with old, hurtful experiences than with the current one. Under these circumstances, we fall back instead on *rigid, automatic, unthinking responses* that we have developed over time in the face of similar stressful or hurting experiences. In other words we fall back on old habits that we have developed that are automatic and do not require thinking. It is as though someone presses a button and a computer program in our head starts up. This program takes over our actions for the duration and guides us automatically through a set of responses. Once this program begins, it can be difficult to interrupt until it reaches the end. One moment we are dealing with a relaxed, flexible human being who is in control of their behaviour. Next moment, the computer program has taken over and we are now dealing with a robotic machine that is impervious to our attempts to influence it. And so, faced with a feeling of threat, the person may hit out automatically, or overreact to imagined insults. The person's reaction is inflexible, based on similar feelings in past situations. Unlike how people function when they are relaxed, under stress their brains may be unable to take account of how the current situation is different from threatening situations in the past. There is enough apparent similarity for them to be treated as identical and handled accordingly. Because the ensuing response is automatic and unthinking, it is also generally inappropriate. It fails to take account of how this current situation differs from the earlier one and can be handled in less extreme ways. The automatic, unthinking nature of this process can be apparent in the common reaction of people to their own rigid behaviour after the stress has subsided. We may hear them say, "I knew I shouldn't have said that, but the words were out before I could stop them." Or they might admit "I knew it wasn't helpful to shout at the person but I couldn't stop myself."

Conflict becomes difficult when one of the parties shuts down and goes into automatic. It becomes almost impossible to resolve if both of them do so. In order to resolve conflict, at least one of the parties must stay thinking. Otherwise we simply get two pre-programmed "robots" hitting off each other and triggering additional unthinking, automatic reactions that escalate the conflict further. It has been said that there is one simple rule for resolving conflict that makes a big difference if people can only remember it. This rule states that, in order to resolve a conflict, we have to take it in turns to be upset! In other words, if the other person is too upset and worked up to listen or think clearly, then we have to suspend our upset long enough to think rationally about how to move things forward and take whatever steps are necessary.

We see here some of the blocks in the way of resolving conflict satisfactorily. It is clear that these can apply equally to ourselves and to the other person. Our own rigid, inflexible and unhelpful reactions may be a big part of the difficulty. We can see this in the ways we lose control over our actions and statements. We can see it in the ways we lose control over our tone of voice and eye contact. We go from making relaxed eye contact to a frowning stare and from a relaxed tone of voice to a tight, clipped or loud dramatizing of our painful emotion. Maintaining control over our own reactions can make a huge difference to how smoothly the conflict is solved.

GUIDELINES FOR RESOLVING CONFLICT

Armed with an understanding of what happens to people in conflict situations, we can now look at some guidelines for resolving conflict incidents successfully. There are three important steps in doing this effectively:

1   Get control of ourselves.
2   Calm the situation.
3   Address the problem.

Each of these steps has to be taken care of and, normally, in that order. Apart from a small number of exceptions, the guidelines we shall look at under these headings work extremely well in most conflict situations. In the case of the exceptions, such as we looked at in Chapters 6 and 12, the following guidelines will complement the suggestions already made for dealing with these.

Step 1: Get control of yourself

We saw earlier how much our own feelings and reactions (physical, verbal and non-verbal) influence the course of a conflict. To begin with, it makes an enormous difference in a conflict situation to *remain calm*. This means not allowing our feelings of fear, hurt, anger, frustration or any other painful emotion to take over our facial expression, our tone of voice, our eye contact or our body posture. We may feel any or all of these sensations but they do not need to overwhelm us and determine how we behave. The challenge is to keep our attention on what will be useful or helpful rather than on how bad we are feeling. As the title of Jeffers's (1987) book puts it, we can feel the fear and do it anyway. US President Thomas Jefferson captured some of the spirit of this when he said that, "nothing gives one person so much advantage over another as to remain always cool and unruffled under all circumstances". Things are likely to work even better if we can not only keep our painful emotion under control but also control how we react to the other person. We do not have to match the other person's tone of threat, aggression or negativity but, instead, can actually respond lightly and positively. Responding lightly does not mean being frivolous but rather adopting a relaxed, open, interested, encouraging and hopeful tone.

With this relaxed, positive attitude, the next step is just to *listen and not interrupt*. Before we do anything, we want to get a picture of what exactly the conflict is about. What is bothering this person? What is at issue here? What is this person trying to communicate? The longer we listen, the clearer we are likely to be about what the difficulty is. Quite apart from this, interrupting people, particularly early on in a conversation, is likely to antagonize them or increase their defensiveness. It is also useful *not to react right away* to anything the person says or does. This means ignoring the names they are calling us or the threats they are making, for example. We try not to say or do anything until we have a clear sense of what it is we are dealing with. The length of time we need to pause for may be quite short. It may only take seconds to get a clear idea about what the situation calls for. Alternatively, it may take much longer. During this time, as well as listening closely to what is being said, we are getting a chance to relax ourselves and get control of any feelings that threaten to overwhelm us or push us into a knee-jerk reaction.

Over and above listening, not interrupting, and not reacting to what is being said, it is also important *not to get pulled into an argument* with the other person. As a rule, if we find ourselves in an argument, we have already lost it. Arguing is usually a sign that at least one of the parties has stopped listening. If the other person starts to argue with us, it may be a sign that we have moved too fast. They cannot tell that we are listening or hearing what they are trying to say to us. We may need to back off and listen some more. A useful principle here is that we can listen people into agreement much more easily than we can argue them. It is practically impossible to argue anyone into agreement. At best, they will appear to agree with us simply for the sake of peace or because they feel intimidated.

An important piece to remember is *not to make any decisions while we are under pressure*, feeling stressed or otherwise in the grip of any negative feelings. A decision made out of fear or frustration, for example, is not likely to be the most useful one under the circumstances since it is based more on our feelings rather than on what the total situation calls for. Our primary goal at this stage is to set the tone for the discussion so that we can move towards a constructive and open-minded approach to solving the difficulty and come up with the most appropriate way forward.

Ury (1991) highlights the importance of what he calls *buying time to think* at this stage. So that we do not react inappropriately as a result of whatever painful feelings are restimulated by the conflict, we can take steps to give ourselves time to settle down and think about what might work in the situation. In general, this requires only a short amount of time, often measured in seconds. Faced with a threatening confrontation, I can turn to the other person and say, "let's go in here to talk". As we move into a more private room, my mind has time to think about what I've heard or seen and what might be a useful response. There is time to get over any initial panic about the situation and calm down. Lots of simple ways to buy time exist. For example, we can say, "I'll just tell the switchboard to hold all my calls so we won't be interrupted." Or, "let me take the phone off the hook before we start." Or, "I'll just get out the file on this before we begin." Such short distractions allow us to postpone our first reactions until we are sufficiently relaxed and have begun thinking clearly about how to proceed. (Occasionally, we may need to delay longer and tell the person that this is not a good time to talk. We can arrange to meet them at a later time when we can pay better attention or give the matter more time). Whatever amount of time we buy, the aim is to get to a point where our response to the situation is based on our best thinking rather than on our worst feelings.

Step 2: Calm the situation

Once we have got a grip on our own feelings, we can then take steps to calm the other person. We can try to take some of the heat, the tension or the hostility out of the situation. One general principle about how to defuse a situation is to do the *opposite* of what it seems that the other person is expecting. In other words, if it seems as if the person is expecting us to argue with them, we just listen; if they seem as if they expect us to disagree, then we find something to agree with; if they seem to expect us to discount their feelings, we acknowledge them; and so on. Robert (1982) talks about using distraction to defuse situations, for example, making a request such as asking what time it is or anything else that refocuses the negative energy. Occasionally, people can be very creative in the ways they do this. Some interesting examples from an educational setting come to mind. On one occasion, a primary teacher told me how she asked a young girl in her class to stand and read from a book. The young person stood, picked up the book and then suddenly threw it at the teacher, barely missing her. The whole class froze at that point, everyone waiting tensely to see what would happen next. The teacher paused momentarily, then reached down, retrieved the book, walked over to the pupil, handed her back the book and said, "you missed. You better have another shot!" Immediately, the tension was broken. The other pupils began to laugh and the young girl took the book and began reading from it. This teacher told me that she never had difficulty with that pupil again and, in fact as she discovered later, she became that pupil's favourite teacher. On another occasion, a school principal told me of a teacher who was constantly turning up late for class. The principal disliked confrontation and said nothing initially, hoping the problem would go away. However, in spite of her patience there was no change. One day, in the absence of the teacher, the principal took her class, and, for the want of something to do, got the children singing. When the teacher eventually arrived, the principal was thoroughly enjoying herself with the children. Without thinking, she spontaneously turned to the teacher and said, "You have done a wonderful job with this class. Their singing is just delightful." Having started in that vein, she did not know how to turn it around and rebuke the teacher for being late so she said nothing more. However, she told me that that was the last time that teacher ever came late! Obviously, this is not a general cure for lateness! It seems though that the unexpected affirmation had the effect of enabling the teacher herself to rethink what she was doing. Of course, it is not necessary to be that creative in order to achieve the same outcome. Given the sense of threat or defensiveness that might be engendered in conflict situations, these are the very times when it can be difficult to be creative.

There are two particular responses that will tend to have the effect of calming a situation and that do not depend on being creative. In any conflict situation, particularly if we cannot think of anything else to say, it will help to move things on if we either *summarize* what has been said by the other person or else *ask questions* about what they have said. Summarizing is a simple but rarely used skill. People often do not expect to be listened to in conflict situations. If we try to summarize the points they are making, this can take them by surprise and shift their attention off their upset and onto what we are saying. At an appropriate point in the conversation, we can say, "let me see if I have understood what you are saying. You believe that . . ." They begin to listen to see if we are accurately reflecting what they have said. In doing this, it is important that we attempt to summarize their point of view accurately. We must not try to tone it down or soften it. Our tone of voice needs to be respectful and without any hint of sarcasm or defensiveness. When we finish the summary, we can ask the person if we have captured what they said accurately. At this point, the person may tell us that we have got it exactly right or they may point out some key element that we overlooked or under-emphasized. If we missed something, we can apologize, correct the summary and, once again, check if we have got it right. All the time, while this is happening, the level of tension in the interaction will be easing. Our attempts to summarize communicate that we are not being defensive and are genuinely trying to hear their concerns.

As well as summarizing, we can also ask the person to elaborate on what they are saying. "Tell me more" is one of the most useful phrases we can use at this time. Instead of jumping in to defend ourselves or contradicting what the other person is saying, we can hold off and simply look for more detail. Asking the person to say more about how they felt or how they were affected or asking for more information about what happened also communicates our willingness to try to resolve the difficulty. As we ask these interested questions and show an openness to what the other person is saying, we help to defuse any tension or hostility in the situation. We do this, not to avoid the conflict, but to create the conditions whereby a mutually satisfying response or solution can be found. It is important, of course, that these are genuine, interested questions rather than being manipulative and designed to catch the other person out or indirectly criticize them.

Essentially, what is happening here, while we summarize or ask questions, is that the other person's attention is being pulled off their own upset and onto us. As we summarize, the person starts to listen to make sure we have got it right. As we ask interested, open questions, they begin to notice that we are not fighting them. Any defences that they had primed to protect themselves in the situation are not called into play and gradually the person begins to loosen up and become less defensive. Our responses are clearly communicating that we are open to what they are trying to communicate, that we are listening and that we are not getting defensive. The other person begins to be able to tell that they do not have to fight us. They have our attention and do not need to be quite so desperate or urgent in their attempts to communicate. (In addition to defusing situations, it should be noted that summarizing and asking questions are also other useful ways to buy time to think.)

There are other useful responses that will help to achieve the same goal. Ury (1991) makes the point that, in conflict situations, people often become preoccupied with the things they disagree over and forget to acknowledge the points of agreement. It becomes easier to resolve conflict if we *stay on the lookout for things we agree with* and communicate these. We can agree with facts about what took place. We can agree that some things should not have happened. Being open to agreeing with points the other person makes helps to establish a climate of give and take.

An important aspect of the communication is to *acknowledge how the other person is feeling*. People often need us to show that we understand not just the facts or their perception of what happened but also how people have been affected and are feeling about what happened. Being willing to accept the other person's upset feelings, without requiring them not to feel upset or to have different feelings, means the other person does not have to fight us to make their case. So, we can let the person know that we understand how upset they are. We can let them know that this is also legitimate – "if that happened to me, I'd also feel very upset about it".

There is one other step we can take that may help to calm the situation. This is one we talked about in Chapter 6 when we looked at how to deal with attacks. Sometimes, we can put a conflict to rest simply by accepting responsibility and *apologizing*. This is not always appropriate but there are times when this is all that is needed. "Look, I'm sorry for what happened. It was a mistake and I want to thank you for telling me about it. I'll try to see that it doesn't happen again."

HELPFUL PERSPECTIVES

In addition to the above guidelines, there are some additional perspectives and approaches that both complement these and can enhance their effectiveness. These help us to think more creatively about how to resolve conflicts. They build on our starting assumption that any rigid, unthinking, inappropriate responses are always a sign that the other person is under stress, hurting in some way or other and in the grip of some painful emotion. We may not know the cause of this stress or hurt, but, whatever the cause, we do know that the person is struggling with some difficult feelings.

Pay attention to and respond to feelings

With this in mind, we can start by trying to get a picture of what the feelings are that the person is struggling with. What painful feelings are triggering or fuelling this behaviour? We have to put our attention on how the person is feeling and not just on their inappropriate behaviour (unless, of course, this behaviour is dangerous or destructive and therefore requires intervention). This means listening to them rather than arguing with them, rebuking them or threatening them. It means asking them how they are feeling. It means noticing their tone of voice, their facial expressions and body language. We can ask ourselves how bad must someone be feeling in order to behave like this. If we pay enough attention, we can begin to get a picture of the hurt or other feelings that the person is struggling with at this point.

We may not know why they are feeling this way but it is helpful to have some sense of what exactly the feeling is. In some cases, the actual reason is some recent upset or hurt and the person is still feeling bad about it. In other cases, the reason is some old hurts and painful emotion from past experiences that have been triggered off again, or restimulated, by events in the present. As we saw above, these events in the present themselves do not need to be hurtful. They merely need to remind the person of the earlier hurts. In themselves, they may be quite neutral or innocent.

We do not need to know the reasons for these feelings in order to handle the situation well. What is helpful is to know *what* they are feeling. As we get some degree of clarity about what the person is feeling and struggling with, it is important to base our response on these feelings rather than on their behaviour. We try to deal with their feelings rather than how they are acting out these feelings. The difficulties people have in doing this are illustrated by the typical ways they react to aggression, for example. Here, the loud tone of voice, the threatening gestures and the abusive language become the focus of attention and the response is often to match or mimic these with an equally loud tone of voice, counter-threatening gestures, and equally abusive comments. The conflict quickly escalates and gets out of hand.

Taking a different approach, faced with someone's aggression, we could try to gauge what the underlying feeling is. It might be frustration. It might be humiliation. Quite commonly it is fear. People become aggressive when they feel scared or threatened, for example. In this case, matching the aggression will have the effect of increasing the feelings of fear or threat and, therefore, of reinforcing the aggressive behaviour. On the other hand, once we spot that the person is scared or feeling threatened, we can then take steps to reduce the threat, to ease their fears and act in ways that calm rather than exacerbate the situation.

In an earlier chapter, we looked at the process of emotional discharge. In certain situations, paying respectful, thoughtful attention to a person while they discharge or release the painful emotion will be sufficient to clear up the conflict. As the person discharges, they recover the ability to think clearly, they re-evaluate the situation facing them and are then able to adopt a more flexible and rational response. The discharge process enables the person to remove any confusion between the current situation and any restimulation from old hurtful situations. Being able to provide the kind of attention that will facilitate the discharge of painful emotion will be a lot easier if we can avoid confusing the person with the problem they are upset about.

Separate the person from the problem

Quite commonly, people blame the other person's personality for the conflict between them. Conflicts in the workplace, for example, are often put down to personality clashes. However, it is easier to focus on and respond to the underlying feelings if we do not confuse the person with the problem. We need to resist the pull to see the person as the problem, as though they were born difficult or troublesome. This is almost inevitably an oversimplification. One example of this occurred in a distribution company where staff were having fist-fights. When asked about the cause of the problem, the Managing Director replied that it was due to a trouble-making trade union shop steward who seemed to take every opportunity to stir things up. This person was seen to be a "born troublemaker" and was surrounded by a small clique of workers who also enjoyed creating trouble. The problem with fights had been simmering for about three years and had finally come to a crisis when the shop steward head-butted one of the foremen. Now, the shop steward had worked in this company for 20 years. When asked why there had been no fights for those 20 years if this shop steward was the cause of the problem, the MD dismissed the question as irrelevant, said he was not interested in such subtleties and that he simply wanted to be rid of the man. Further enquiries with other managers, however, revealed a more complex situation. Prior to these problems emerging, there was a manager who sat down with the shop steward on a weekly basis to discuss problems and iron out any emerging difficulties. This arrangement had worked very well and, as a byproduct, the shop steward was accorded a high status in the organization. Unfortunately, three years earlier, this particular manager was promoted and never replaced in this role. His successor did not continue with these trouble-shooting meetings and, without any warning, this vital safety valve and source of status for the shop steward was removed. It was at that point that the problems began to get out of hand. What looked here like a simple personality problem (a trouble-making shop steward) was actually a structural problem (the absence of any forum to resolve problems). It was convenient to blame the shop steward but not particularly helpful.

In one sense, there are no difficult people; there are simply people with difficulties. Glasser (1994) stresses that in most situations, 98 per cent of the time, it is the system that creates the problem not the people. If we can solve the system problems, the people problems will disappear. Often, the difficult behaviour is a symptom of a deeper problem. It is someone waving a big, red

flag in our faces and trying to get us to pay attention to a problem they are
having or to some painful emotion they are struggling with. If we can address
these underlying problems we can often go a long way towards resolving the
conflict.

A GENERAL STRATEGY FOR RESOLVING CONFLICT

In addition to the specific guidelines we looked at earlier, there is a general
strategy that is enormously helpful in resolving conflict. This general strategy is difficult to describe easily because it can take many different forms in
practice. There is no simple recipe for applying it, no simple set of tricks or
gimmicks that can be used to achieve the outcome. Stated briefly, in conflict
situations, it is sometimes possible to bypass the immediate difficulty by
reaching out and *making a relaxed, genuine, caring, human connection with
the person* underneath the hurt. Basically, we have a choice between paying
attention to the rigid behaviour or paying attention to the person underneath who is hurting. Rather than focusing on their inappropriate behaviour,
we can reach past the hurt and show the person that we see them clearly and
are not losing sight of them, their goodness or their worth. We are also
communicating that we are open to the possibility that this difficulty is not
all one-sided; that it is possible we also may have contributed to the
problem.

Making such a connection involves having relaxed but caring body language, tone of voice, eye contact and facial expression. It involves communicating genuine concern, a real desire to understand and resolve the difficulty
between us, and an openness to hearing their hurt. Sometimes it means not
getting too serious – staying light, staying pleasant and relaxed. We can show
the person that, in spite of what they are saying or doing, we have not given
up on them or got disappointed with them; that we are not blaming them or
confusing them with their hurts. We know there is someone there with a
genuine sense of hurt or concern and we want to do whatever it takes to solve
this problem between us. There are no special "techniques" or gimmicks
for doing this. This has to be a genuine expression of understanding and
caring from one human to another. We are communicating that we are really
listening and hearing their pain.

Where we can manage to make this connection with the person, we may
well notice that the inappropriate behaviour dissolves, any defensiveness disappears, the person relaxes and is able to express directly and discharge the
feelings of hurt that they struggle with. Instead of acting out their hurt
feelings, they will now talk about and discharge them. The transition from a
stage of tense confrontation to one of relaxed communication will sometimes
be punctuated by tears or laughter as the other person suddenly realized we
are there for them. At this point, either the initial problem will have disappeared (it was simply a means of getting us to pay attention) or it becomes

possible to have a calm, relaxed discussion about the problem and how it might be addressed.

To the extent that we can maintain a genuine, human connection with people, conflict is easier to resolve and the specific guidelines that we looked at earlier will work much more effectively. Blocks to maintaining this connection include giving up on people, allowing our disappointment with them to control our responses, distancing or isolating ourselves from them, allowing our hopelessness to take over or attacking or snubbing them. These blocks get in the way of our listening and actually seeing the *person* separately from any difficulty between us. They also lead us to set the other person up as the enemy and to react accordingly.

Showing ourselves

As we reach out and connect on a human level with the other person, we are also stepping out from behind any role that we occupy in the situation. We are now responding, not as a manager, supervisor or in any other formal role, but simply as a person. As we do this, it can also be helpful for us to show the other person some of our own struggle in the situation. We can show them where our own feelings of fear, isolation, frustration and so on are getting in our way of staying connected to them in this conflict situation. We can show them where our own painful emotion is tripping us up. And we do this without in any way implying that this is the other person's fault. I gave an example of this in Chapter 10 when we looked at the issue of being an ally for working-class people.

If we can show the other person the struggle we are having with our own feelings in the situation, without attaching that struggle or those feelings to them by way of blame or criticism, the other person can begin to think about us and think about how they can give us a hand with this struggle. Showing ourselves like this can defuse an otherwise blocked confrontation. This is somewhat similar to Rosenberg's (2000) approach where he suggests that we describe our feelings in a conflict situation but show how they are caused by our own unmet needs rather than the other person's behaviour. We do this rather than blaming the other person for them.

SUMMARY

The focus here has been on resolving conflict incidents between individuals. The guidelines we have looked at are simple but powerful. At their core is the challenge to keep thinking and do what makes sense rather than acting out our upsets. As we have already seen, our feelings are not necessarily a good guide to how we should behave. Used thoughtfully, these guidelines can make a huge difference to how difficulties are resolved in most situations. Combined with the guidelines for handling attacks (Chapter 6) and the guidelines for dealing with angry or antagonistic people (Chapter 12) they represent an essential component of effective leadership skills. So far we have dealt mostly with the first two steps of getting control of ourselves and defusing situations so that a mutually satisfactory outcome can be reached. To complete the process, however, we need to look in more detail at the third step in this process, namely, addressing the actual problem. In the next chapter, we shall also look at the problem-solving process and at guidelines for dealing with conflict in groups.

REFLECTION

1   What are your strengths in handling conflict? What are you most skilled at?
2   Where is it a struggle for you to deal with short-term conflict incidents? What do you hate about them?
3   In what ways do these conflict incidents affect you negatively? How do they affect the ways you think, feel or behave?
4   Where is it a struggle for you to deal with ongoing, conflict relationships?
5   In what ways do these conflict relationships affect the ways you think, feel or behave?
6   If you were to be more effective in handling conflict incidents, what would you do differently?
7   What are some ways that you can buy yourself time to think in these situations?
8   What are some of the ways that you can defuse or take the heat out of these situations?
9   If you were to be more effective in handling conflict relationships, what would you do differently?

14 Problem-solving skills

INTRODUCTION

In Chapter 13, we looked at a range of guidelines for resolving one-to-one conflict. In particular, we saw various ways to calm situations and create the conditions for a mutually satisfactory resolution of the difficulties between us. These are crucial skills for a leader. Leaders also need to be skilled in problem solving. In this chapter, we shall look at this third step in the conflict resolution process and apply it to a number of situations, including one-to-one and group conflicts.

STEP 3: ADDRESS THE PROBLEM

Having taken control of ourselves and taken steps to calm the situation, we are now in a position to address the actual underlying problem. Before looking at the elements involved in this, it is useful to examine how conflict is often presented and what can lie behind it. A useful way to think about this is in terms of a conflict iceberg (Figure 14.1).

In thinking about conflict, it is helpful to make a distinction between the *positions* people take up, the *demands* they make or the *solutions* they propose, on the one hand, and the underlying *concerns, interests, issues, problems, fears or principles* that are motivating them. Many conflicts involve disagreements over positions on an issue. Some people are for what is proposed and some are against. Other conflicts involve competition between different demands. Someone is demanding that a particular course of action be taken while the other person is refusing to comply with this or is making their own demands on the first person. Sometimes, the conflict is between competing solutions to a problem. Different people propose different solutions and none of them are in agreement. At times, the conflict can get quite complicated. In the course of discussion, solutions, for example, may clash with demands, positions and other solutions. At any given point, it may not be at all clear that people are actually talking about the same thing. An important principle here is that, for any emotive or potentially divisive issue, it is almost

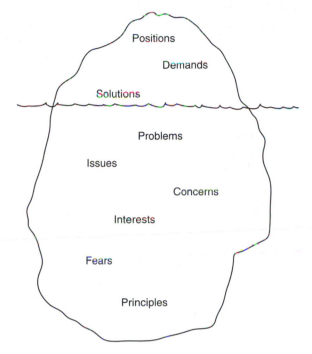

Figure 14.1 The Conflict Iceberg.

impossible to get agreement at the level of positions, demands or solutions, at least as a starting point. Many conflicts get bogged down at this level. People take up positions and refuse to budge from them. They make demands and refuse to compromise. They propose solutions that are incompatible with alternative solutions. These, however, are generally the surface aspects of the conflict. They represent what is above the waterline of the conflict iceberg. Stalemate over proposed solutions to a problem, for example, often masks a lack of agreement over, or clarity about, the actual problem to be solved. We first of all have to get agreement on the problem before discussing solutions or taking up positions. Before we can get agreement, we have to ask what is below the waterline here. In other words, what is the problem that causes people to propose that solution? What is the issue they see that causes them to take up that position? What is the interest they are trying to protect that causes them to make that demand? Unless we can get agreement on the underlying aspects, we are unlikely to agree on the way forward. Yet this is precisely where a lot of conflict gets stuck. Different people are proposing solutions without anyone realizing they are trying to solve different problems and, therefore, their solutions can never be reconciled. Unless we can clarify the underlying issues, interests, fears, principles, problems or concerns we are unlikely to reach agreement on positions, demands or solutions. Fisher, Ury and Patton (1991) stress that it is important that we do not attack other people's positions but rather that we look behind them. They suggest treating these positions as one possible option and that we focus on understanding the interests behind them or the principles that they reflect. They also suggest that we do not defend our own ideas and, instead, invite criticism of them or ask people for advice on how they can be improved.

What this means is that, in order to resolve the conflict, we have to delve beneath the waterline and find out about the underlying issues, concerns and so on. There is no point in disagreeing over positions, demands or solutions until we have clarified what is behind them. This we can do mainly through asking questions. Why do you think this solution will work? What concern leads you to propose this solution? What is your fear about what will happen if we do it another way? Why is this so important to you? Why does it need to be done that way? By asking thoughtful questions and listening non-defensively we can draw out the key issues or concerns that will have to be addressed if we are to find a way forward.

One interesting example of where a failure to identify underlying factors impeded the mutually satisfactory resolution of a conflict involved a group of nurses attached to a hospital ward. Because of space shortages, management in the hospital wanted to take over a linen storage room on this particular ward and convert it into an office. The nurses told me that they fought long and hard to retain this particular room as a storage space. They produced many logical arguments as to why this was necessary but found that management had an answer for each of their difficulties. The sad thing, they told me, was that they were never able to tell management the real reason why they wanted the room in its current form. This they said was because it was the one place they could go to cry when things on the ward got too stressful. Because they did not think this would constitute a valid reason for hanging on to the room, they never mentioned it during their discussions with management. Instead, they invented various practical reasons to support their position. These, however, were easily countered. Because their true interest in the room was never revealed, it was impossible for the people involved to find a solution that would have satisfied everyone. No one thought to ask the nurses why they felt so strongly about keeping this storage space so their interests could not be clearly identified.

Another example of this process occurred in a primary school where a small minority of pupils were members of the Traveller Community. In Ireland, Travellers are a group who face widespread prejudice and enormous difficulties in accessing and using educational facilities. The principal of this school told me that she had a problem in her school she wanted help with. Her statement of this "problem" was quite revealing. She said that some of her staff had come to her privately to demand that all the Travellers in the school should be placed in a separate classroom and not integrated with settled children in the normal classes. She went on to say that she had a very cohesive staff but that this issue could cause a major split as some of the staff were very supportive of, and committed to, the Travellers in the school. Up to now, she had managed to sidestep the issue but the discontent was growing and she could not postpone a discussion of it much longer. She asked me if I would facilitate a staff meeting to help resolve this problem.

The first thing to notice here is that the "problem" described by the principal is not actually a problem at all. It is, in fact, a solution to a problem. The question that needs to be asked is what the problem is that will be solved by putting Traveller children into a separate classroom. The principal is probably correct in her assessment that to put this issue (in the form she described it) on the agenda of a meeting would cause a split among her staff. If she put forward the proposal to segregate Traveller children, members of staff would take up positions for or against it, strong feelings would be stirred up and agreement would be almost impossible to obtain without, at least, some very bruised feelings at the end of the discussion.

A staff meeting was arranged and I proceeded to put two simple questions to the staff. First, I asked them to say, individually, how the present system in relation to Travellers in the school was working well from their own personal point of view. We listed what was going well and noted what people were pleased with. I then asked them to say in what ways the current system was creating difficulties for them. I gave each person a turn to say what their experience had been. One interesting thing about this discussion was that no one got defensive. No one attacked anyone else and people listened respectfully to the various difficulties that were highlighted. The other interesting aspect of this discussion was that no one said anything about placing Travellers in a separate room. After everyone had spoken, I asked the group to look at the list of difficulties, which I had written up on a flip chart as people spoke, and to identify what they now saw as the major difficulties facing them. At this point, the group was unanimous in stating that the problem was simply that there was a small number of children in the school who were extremely disruptive and who all happened to be Travellers. The only disagreement among the group was whether it was four children or five children. Having agreed on the problem, it was now a straightforward process to list possible strategies for solving it. I asked them what they thought were all the possible ways this problem could be addressed. From the list of possibilities, the group quickly agreed on a number of useful steps they thought would make a difference and moved to implement these. I met with the principal subsequently and she reported that these strategies solved the problem and there was no further talk of putting all Travellers in a separate classroom.

What had happened in this case was that individual teachers experienced difficulties with some Traveller children and, without any detailed analysis, jumped to a simplistic solution that focused on the wrong problem. This highlights the importance of identifying clearly and agreeing on the problem before discussing possible solutions. Failure to do this will lead to solutions that are divisive and ineffective and to a recurrence of the problem. Recurring problems that never seem to be solved despite repeated efforts may well be a symptom of failure to identify the problem correctly and the imposition of solutions that merely paper over cracks or fail to get to the roots of the difficulty. If we are to resolve conflict successfully, we need to put our attention on the underlying, below-the-waterline factors.

Once we have pinpointed the real concerns, issues, interests or problems that have caused people to take up particular positions, make particular demands or advocate particular solutions, we can then *reframe*, or restate, the problem in ways that recognize and acknowledge these factors. We can redefine the difficulty in terms of the underlying problem rather than the advocated solution. By focusing on disruptive pupils rather than on Travellers, we make it possible for people to consider a range of alternative solutions rather than the single, divisive one that is first proposed. Scholtes (1998) gives an example of how the definition of the problem, and therefore of the solution, changes the more we ask questions about it. He refers to the problem of a puddle of oil on the floor of a plant. Depending on how we define this problem, we will choose different solutions. If we simply notice the puddle and do not enquire about it, we will just clean up the oil. If we ask why it is there, we might decide it was because of a leak caused by a faulty gasket. In that case, the solution is not just to clean up the puddle but to replace the gasket. If we enquire further, however, we might discover that inferior gaskets are being used, in which case the solution is to buy better gaskets in future. And, on further enquiry, we might discover that the gaskets are inferior because the purchasing agent gets evaluated on how much money is saved on purchases. In that case, the solution might be to change the policy on how purchases are made.

When we succeed in reframing a difficulty in terms of the important underlying factors, the other person will almost invariably agree that this is the issue they want resolved. Once it is clear that we grasp what is really at stake, the person will relax around the particular way it is dealt with. If they have agreed that we now understand the issue clearly, we can say to them, for example, "I don't know if what you are proposing is workable, but maybe if we work together on this we can find another way of solving the problem." As long as they can tell that we understand their difficulty, the other person will be more open to understanding ours. By communicating that we understand and accept their real difficulties and that we are genuinely interested in finding a satisfactory outcome, the other person can be persuaded to let go of an initial, inflexible position and enter into dialogue with us to find some mutually acceptable alternative. In doing this, the process changes from an adversarial, confrontational process to a problem-solving process. Part of the role of a leader, therefore, is to listen long enough and deeply enough to hear the real issues at stake and to build on these as a means of resolving any difficulties. I once mediated in a conflict within a group of fire officers. The sub-officers saw their senior officer as deliberately setting out to undermine them and make them look bad in the eyes of firefighters on the ground. According to them, the senior officer refused to hand over the keys to a storeroom where they could access gloves, boots and other equipment that the firefighters might need as replacements for worn or defective items of their own. Because of this, the firefighters had got into the habit of bypassing the sub-officers and going straight to the senior officer when they needed replacements. This left the sub-officers feeling powerless, undermined and insignificant. During the course of a meeting with this group, the sub-officers complained bitterly about the actions of the senior officer and accused him of bullying them. I then asked the senior officer if he had any principled objection to their having access to the key of the storeroom and he said no. Since he had no principled objection, I asked what was the difficulty from his point of view. He said that he was afraid that stock would go missing if the key was too easily accessible and, since the stock was his responsibility, he would be held accountable for any losses. At that point, having clarified his real difficulty, we were able to move the discussion on to devising a practical method of stock control that would satisfy the senior officer's needs and allow the sub-officers access to the key.

It is possible, of course, that having clarified and reframed the problem, it becomes clear that there is nothing we can do to solve it or that we are not in a position to meet the other person's demands. In this case, however, because we have listened well, treated them with respect and taken their concerns seriously, we can now explain our own position or the difficulties we face in dealing with their problem or demands. We may find ourselves in the position of saying that there is nothing we can do to help. Because of the process we have used, however, it is much more likely that the other person will be able to hear and accept what we are saying without thinking they are being fobbed off or treated unfairly by us. They may not like what we are telling them but they will accept that we have done our best and not hold us personally responsible for their difficulties.

CHECKLIST

Taking what we looked at in the last chapter and what we have seen here so far, we can use a checklist to test how well we are managing any conflict. There are three particular questions we can ask ourselves:

1 Can I see the real person or the human underneath the difficulty?
2 Can I see the real underlying issues or concerns?
3 Can I restate (or reframe) the problem in these terms?

To the extent that I can do each of these, I am much more likely to handle conflict constructively and reach an outcome that meets the needs of all the parties involved.

A PROBLEM-SOLVING MEETING

Brounstein (1993) gives an outline of what he calls an intervention conference where, in this case, a manager or supervisor has to intervene to solve a problem with an employee. It conforms to the broad principles that we have seen in this and the previous chapter. In fact, this model is probably applicable to any problem-solving discussion between two people. Using his approach as a base, we can think of this discussion as a series of stages where one person is raising some difficulties with another and attempting to get their cooperation to resolve them.

Stage 1: Introduction

State the purpose of the meeting and what we want to accomplish. Ideally, this introduction is kept short. In it we say what the concern is that we want to address and that we would like to work out a way of resolving it with the other person. The idea is to present this in a positive, non-threatening manner.

Stage 2: Describe the problem

Here, we describe what the problem, concern or difficulty is and give concrete examples so that the other person is clear about what we are referring to. The more specific we can be, the easier it is for them to understand our difficulty. Again, in doing this, we want to eliminate any tone of evaluation or judgement and stick with factual observations about what has happened. Rosenberg (2000) makes the point that we often imply judgement when we make observations about other people's behaviour but that this makes it much harder for the other person to listen without getting defensive. And so, for example, it helps if we can avoid labelling their behaviour in any way that implies an evaluation. Pointing out that someone has had a number of opportunities to speak while others have not had any is different from telling someone that they are domineering. It is also important that we talk about things the other person can change rather than things that they feel are beyond them. For example, it helps if we focus on people's behaviour rather than their personality. In describing the problem, it can also be useful to say what effects it has been having and why we are concerned about it. Here also we need to describe the effects specifically and factually without labelling or implying any judgement or evaluation. In general, at this stage, we can be more effective in our communication if we speak sincerely, allowing the person to see our genuine concern to resolve the problem.

Stage 3: Listen and clarify

At this point, the other person may want to put their side of the story or, in spite of our best efforts, may be getting defensive. It is now time to listen to their thoughts, feelings and reactions to what we have said. As we do this, bearing in mind the conflict iceberg, we can try to identify the underlying problems, issues, difficulties and concerns from their point of view. We can also explore the reasons behind any of the difficulties we have been identifying. In doing this, it is important to bear in mind the other guidelines we looked at in Chapter 13 such as acknowledging how the other person feels. In particular, it is important not to require the other person to admit blame or accept any judgements about their behaviour. In most cases, this is a dead end and a distraction from solving the problem. People are highly unlikely to listen to blame without getting defensive and we risk derailing the discussion by making this an issue. We do not need them to accept the blame in order to sort out the difficulty. All we actually need from the other person is their acknowledgement of the problem, their agreement that there is a difficulty and their willingness to talk to us about how we can go about resolving it. Two other important guidelines from before are that we do not argue with the person and that, if we find ourselves in an argument, we need to back off and switch to listening to them. Finally, it could happen that the other person complains that some of the difficulty is our own fault. If there is any accuracy in this observation, even though it may be said in an unhelpful way, it can help the outcome of this discussion if we are prepared to acknowledge our own contribution to the difficulty without being defensive about it. Our modelling of openness and willingness to admit responsibility can encourage the other person to do likewise.

Stage 4: Explore the options

As we get a clear picture of all the concerns and issues in the situation and as people remain open and non-defensive, we can gradually begin to look at different options for resolving the difficulties. The whole point of the discussion is to get to this stage. We are looking for a mutually agreeable way forward that addresses all the concerns and interests in the situation. This is similar to Step 3 of the conflict-resolution process described earlier where we invite the other person to explore different ways of sorting out the difficulties. Depending on how the conversation has developed so far, they may come up with some proposals or, in the absence of that, we ourselves may make some suggestions. In a worst-case scenario, where the other person has got very resistant or defensive and refuses to look for ways out of the difficulty, we can draw attention to the implications of our failing to reach any resolution in our discussion. Depending on what the actual difficulty was and the nature of the relationship between the people involved, this might mean that the issue would have to be dealt with in another, more formal forum (for example, a formal investigation or a disciplinary hearing). This can be an incentive for the person to work with us to solve the problem informally. Ideally, at this stage, we will agree a plan of action to deal with the problem. Often, it can be helpful to put this plan in writing so that there is no confusion about what is agreed. The plan should identify what is to be done and who is to do it and should lay out a timetable for this.

Stage 5: Summary and close

Before finishing this meeting, it is very useful to summarize what has been agreed and ensure there is no lingering confusion. It can also be useful to arrange a follow-up meeting to review progress and check if any adjustments to what has been arranged are necessary. Finally, having got this far, it is good to finish on a positive note and thank the person for their help or cooperation.

The success of a meeting like this is largely due to preparation. This outline of the stages is like a map of where we want to get to. In advance of the meeting, we can sit down and plan how we will handle each stage and how we will say the things we want to say. We can anticipate possible reactions and how we will handle these. We can also think about possible resolutions or suggestions that we can bring to the discussion that might be helpful in the latter stages. With a map like this, we can then keep track of the conversation. At any given point, we can tell if the discussion has gone off track and needs to be re-focused. By going in with a clear plan and a picture of where we want to get to, we can keep bringing the discussion back to what is important.

DISCIPLINARY INTERVENTIONS

One particular issue that arises for people in managerial or supervisory roles is that of discipline and how to maintain it. Problems can often arise in work organizations because of a rigid and authoritarian approach to this. Using the principles underpinning these methods of resolving conflict we can describe a more flexible approach to dealing with discipline problems. Templar (2001) outlines a useful way of looking at this process that we can build on here. He refers to three different scenarios. The first occurs where something that is a minor issue is corrected on the spot in a form of instant discipline. The second occurs where the issue is more serious and the person is taken aside for an informal, private discussion. The third occurs where the issue is very serious and requires a formal discipline interview. For Templar, the idea is to use a graduated series of steps to deal with a problem with the emphasis, where possible, on nipping it in the bud before it can escalate into a more serious issue. The mistake that managers make, as he sees it, is to apply more heavy-handed, formal methods early on when a more informal, low-key and less threatening approach would be more useful. We can think of a sequence such as the following:

1 Lightly comment

On the first occurrence of the problem, we can approach people lightly, positively and without implying blame or judgement. Depending on the type of relationship we have with the other person, this can be done in the form of a light-hearted comment. An employee told me once of returning late from lunch and being greeted with an amused comment from his supervisor who said, "that must have been a tough steak you had for lunch". There was no sarcasm or implied criticism in this comment and they both laughed. All that is happening at this point is that we are showing the person we are aware of what has happened without making an issue out of it.

2 Express concern

If the problem is slightly more serious or if this is not the first time it has happened we can communicate some of our concern without treating it as a serious issue or communicating any displeasure, impatience or frustration. We can start by getting the facts straight and giving the person a chance to explain what happened. This can still be done lightly and positively as we enquire interestedly about the problem. When the person arrives late for work, for example, we can ask, "was the traffic bad today?" If appropriate, we can indicate the effects of what happened, still without implying blame or judgement. We can say, for example, "it's just that Joe wanted to go over something with you before the meeting started". However, we are still not making a big issue out of this and may not say any more about it. The aim is to keep the tone positive while communicating our awareness of the difficulty and our concern.

3 Informal chat

Where there are persistent problems of a minor nature, it may become necessary to increase the formality of the approach without making it a very formal discussion. In this case, if the person continues to come late, for example, we might now take them aside for a brief conversation about the problem. When they arrive, we might say to them that we would like to talk to them for a few minutes on our own. We would then go somewhere private and raise the problem with them. We might point out that we were concerned about the lateness problem and that we were worried about it getting out of hand. This is like a version of the problem-solving meeting described above only it is done very informally and relatively briefly. We would check with the other person if there is anything we can do to help solve the problem or if there is anything we should know about it. The aim here is to communicate our concern about the continuing problem and our desire to see it resolved. The emphasis is on problem solving rather than blame or discipline.

4 Formal chat

If the informal conversation does not resolve the issue, the next step is to arrange a formal meeting to discuss the problem more fully. Rather than talking to the person on the spot, we are now going to agree with them a time to meet where we can talk about the difficulty at greater length. This meeting would be very much along the lines of the problem-solving meeting outlined above. The main difference between this and the previous step is in the formality of it and the length of it. If this meeting fails to find a resolution, the person can be alerted to the fact that the next stage is a formal disciplinary meeting.

5 Formal disciplinary meeting

If all these earlier attempts to resolve the problem have failed, then the process can be moved into the formal disciplinary procedure. The mistake that some managers make is to start the process at this point rather than working up to this stage with the other more informal approaches. It is only at this stage that questions of verbal or written warnings come into play. In this whole process, the idea is to try to resolve problems without having to resort to the disciplinary procedure.

Templar (2001) describes this as a three-stage process but I think it is useful to draw out the informal aspects in more detail. Laying it out in this detail can make it seem as if it is a very long, drawn-out process. However, much of this could take place over a period of days in some cases or over months in other cases. Depending on circumstances, the sequence here can be extended or truncated to suit the requirements or the seriousness of the issues.

CONFLICT IN GROUPS

So far, in discussing conflict resolution, most of the focus has been on one-to-one conflict. However, a large amount of conflict takes place in meetings or groups. In fact, many people have come to hate meetings because of destructive conflicts that get in the way of good outcomes and waste an enormous amount of time and energy. One common difficulty that people experience in these situations is that of the domineering individual who takes over a meeting and uses up a disproportionate amount of the time, speaking at length, interrupting people, or making repeated interventions or contributions that prevent others being heard equally. In this situation, people then have to fight to be heard or compete with each other for "airtime". Often, at the end of a meeting, it is not at all clear what the group as a whole thinks. A small number of vociferous people have dominated the discussion and it is difficult to say how truly representative their views are. A second difficulty concerns people being attacked by others at the meeting who dislike what they have had to say. Many a meeting goes downhill when someone expresses a point of view and is immediately responded to by another person stating, "that's rubbish!" At this point, the group begins to become unsafe. Commonly, the individuals involved get sucked into a repetitive back-and-forth argument that takes up a chunk of the time of the meeting. Others get pulled to take sides and join the destructive point-scoring process or else switch off as they wait for this pointless argument to finish so the meeting can move on. In the end, no one shifts their position, the atmosphere is less relaxed and a lot of time has been wasted. Over time, people learn to be guarded, to be defensive and less than open in what they say at meetings. In fact, most of the damage that gets done in meetings happens during open-ended, unstructured discussion when people's feelings take over and the wrong things are said.

Particularly around potentially divisive or emotive issues, it is important to have some way of managing the conflict so that issues or problems can be clarified and workable ways forward invented. In this regard, the same principles and strategies that we have already looked at are equally applicable to group situations. In addition, however, there are some specific guidelines that make a huge difference when applied to the conduct of meetings. The following guidelines are very powerful as a way of structuring out destructive conflict and creating safety for people to address difficult issues.

Give everyone equal time to talk without interruption

To begin with, get people's agreement that everyone will have equal time to talk at the meeting and no one will be allowed to dominate. In general, this is easy to agree on in principle. Even domineering individuals will be reluctant to argue that they should have a right to speak more than anyone else. Translating this aspiration into reality needs a more specific guideline, however. The way to ensure that everyone gets equal time is to have a specific agreement that *no one will speak twice until everyone has spoken at least once*. With this guideline, people no longer have to compete to be heard. There is no longer any need to interrupt anyone. Everyone gets a turn. At the very least, each person will be given the opportunity to speak once before anyone speaks twice. The individual may decide to pass on this opportunity or may decide they have nothing to add to the discussion, but they, at least, are given the chance to contribute. One of the additional helpful aspects of this guideline is that, when someone passes on a turn, we will be able to tell from their tone of voice and body language whether they are passing because they genuinely have nothing to add or because they are feeling unsafe or alienated. Sometimes, because they are given their turn, an individual will start to say they have nothing to add to what has already been said and then, without realizing it, go on to make some additional points! This guideline can be applied very rigidly where each person in turn is asked for their contribution. We can start with one individual and systematically work our way around the group, one after the other. Or, the rule can be applied loosely, with each person speaking when they are ready to contribute and in any order, but still with the agreement that no one comes in a second time until all have had their first contribution. As a rule, the more cohesive, respectful and supportive the group is, the more loosely the guideline can be applied. Where there is much distrust or tension or where people are inclined to interrupt a lot, it could be applied more rigidly. It can happen of course that people forget they have agreed to this and try to be heard a second time before others have spoken. All we need to do in that situation is remind them of the agreement and ask them to hold what they wanted to say until everyone has been heard from. Facilitating a meeting like this is often a lot easier with this kind of guideline. One spin-off effect of this guideline is that, since people no longer have to interrupt or force their way into the discussion, they are now free to relax and listen to what others are saying. Instead of trying to get attention, they are free to give attention and the quality of listening in the group is much greater. With this guideline, we can effectively control the tendency for people to dominate a meeting. We are also in a position to see what the group as a whole thinks and not just the small minority who usually speak up. However, we need another guideline to ensure that when people do contribute they do not get attacked for what they say.

The principle behind this first guideline is to give everyone equal time. In smaller groups this is straightforward. In larger groups and when time is short, it may be necessary to adjust the guideline. So, for example, instead of hearing from each individual, we might pair people off for a couple of minutes to share their thinking with each other and then go round to hear from each pair. Or we might split the larger group into a number of smaller groups where each person would get a turn and then reconvene the large group to get a report from each of the small groups. Whatever the circumstances, we try to keep the process as close as we can to giving everyone an opportunity to be heard without interruption.

Put the focus on listening and understanding

The second important guideline is to get people's agreement that the purpose of the discussion is to listen and understand what people are saying rather than to communicate agreement or disagreement. The point of the discussion is not to debate or discuss what is said but rather to get a clear picture of each person's point of view or contribution. The issue is not whether people agree or not with one another, the issue is whether they clearly understand what the other person is trying to say. One of the main things that interferes with gaining clarity during meetings is the widespread habit of commenting on, or reacting to, what people say after each contribution. Often it is these comments that lead to divisive arguments or to a lack of safety. People become defensive and preoccupied with either protecting themselves or attacking other people's points of view. Once again, it can be relatively easy to get agreement in principle that people should listen to one another. To achieve this in practice, however, we need an additional agreement that *no one will comment on, or react to, what any one person says, at least until everyone has been heard from*. In other words, there will be no discussion at all until everyone has finished making their contribution. Each person will be listened to without interruption and without comment. This guideline means that people do not have to worry about protecting themselves. They do not have to justify, legitimize or defend what they say. The opportunity to attack people has been structured out of the process. If someone has strong feelings about an issue or situation, they will not be argued with about their feelings. The aim is to listen to and understand those feelings. A number of things happen as a result of applying this guideline. The first is that the discussion becomes much safer and there is much greater freedom for people to speak their mind. In addition, however, because there is not the distraction of petty point-scoring or argumentation, it is possible to identify clearly any common themes, threads or patterns in what members of the group are saying. Without the distracting clutter of discussion after each person has spoken, as we listen we can spot the places where people echo one another in what they say and it becomes much easier to identify the consensus that exists or get a clear picture of what the group as a whole thinks. Having heard from each person, we can then have a discussion at the end about what people have heard overall or what they see as the main issues or themes emerging. By keeping the discussion until everyone has finished contributing, we tend to get a much more sophisticated discussion that focuses on the bigger picture rather than nit-picking about the details of what one person may have said. Often, this discussion becomes an overall summary of what was said.

In some discussions, of course, the intention is not just to clarify but actually to make some decisions. By using these first two guidelines to ensure that everyone is listened to, when it comes to decision making, participants are much more relaxed and flexible. This is something we also looked at in Chapter 2. Once people can tell that they are being listened to respectfully and once the process allows the common themes in what people are saying to emerge, it is much easier to come to agreement on what decisions are necessary. Sometimes, by the end of the round of listening to people without comment, it is clear to everyone what the thrust of the discussion is. Those with a minority viewpoint can see that this is the case and are often willing to give the majority viewpoint a try. For this to be workable, however, everyone has to feel that they were listened to.

These two guidelines are at the core of solving problems in groups. They are very powerful but simple ways to manage conflict and, at the same time, facilitate constructive discussion of important issues. They can be applied to all aspects of a meeting or they may be applied only to particular discussions or agenda items. This can depend, as we saw above, on the quality of relationships in the group. There are also some other supplementary guidelines that add to the effectiveness of these core guidelines.

Design the process around simple questions

I have found it useful to structure the agenda for problem-solving meetings around simple questions that allow people to say all that needs to be said about the issue under discussion. Rather than framing the agenda in the form of a descriptive phrase such as "review of progress", for example, it is often more helpful to frame it in the form of questions that focus the discussion without restricting it. In particular, it helps considerably to use these questions to clarify both positive and negative viewpoints. So, in a discussion of any particular policy, for example, members of the group can first be asked to say in what ways the current policy is working satisfactorily or effectively from their own personal point of view. What's good about the policy? How is it working well? What do they like about it? (The same question can be phrased in a number of different ways in order to capture all the possible nuances it might have.) After everyone has spoken from this viewpoint, the group then discusses what they have heard emerging from the various contributions. After the overall reaction has been discussed, the group can then be asked in what ways the current policy is not working satisfactorily or effectively from each person's point of view. How is it creating difficulties for each member of the group? What concerns do people have about the policy? What is hard for them about the current system? Notice that the form of these questions focuses on the particular difficulties or concerns each person has rather than on what is wrong generally or in the abstract. The questions can be asked in a variety of ways with the two themes of highlighting first the positive aspects and then the negative ones.

The first two guidelines create a structure and safety for the discussion. This guideline increases the safety further and keeps the discussion focused. By starting with a positive focus, it makes it easier for people to speak up later on about their difficulties. By including the positive and negative focus, it ensures that all aspects of the issue are covered and that a balanced overall picture emerges. These questions also ensure that the group does not rush on to discussing solutions before it has adequately identified and agreed on the problems.

After everyone has been listened to on these two questions, the discussion then focuses on identifying the key issues emerging, the core problems identified or important concerns highlighted by the group as a whole. The aim is to get a clear picture of these before going on to look at solutions or to make decisions about them. At this stage, a number of possibilities present themselves. For example, it might be useful to try to prioritize the issues, problems or concerns identified. This can be done by using a simple weighted voting system where people are asked to nominate their top three most important issues from all those identified in the discussion at the end. By assigning three points to all the number one choices, two points to all the number two choices and one point to all the number three choices, it is possible to rank order the list of issues, problems or concerns that they have highlighted. The aim is to reduce the full list to an agreed core list of priority items. Once this is done, the group can then be asked to brainstorm all the possible ways to resolve the issues, concerns or problems identified. Alternatively, it may not be that important to prioritize what has emerged and the group may simply take each issue in turn and look at it in more detail.

It is important to emphasize again that for much of the discussion so far complete agreement is either unnecessary or is relatively easy to achieve. If there has been a sufficiently full discussion of the underlying issues, where each person feels heard, it often not too difficult to agree on steps to be taken to solve the problems identified.

Using questions as the focus for discussion has an additional advantage in that it overcomes one of the problems that commonly occur in meetings. This happens where items are put on an agenda without any clear indication of why they are there. For example, a group might find "finance" or "mainten-ance" listed. This, however, tells nothing about the point of itemizing them. What aspects of finance or maintenance are to be discussed? This can be clarified even more if, in addition to structuring the discussion around the questions to be answered, there is also an indication on the agenda of what outcome is hoped for. For example, is the point of the discussion to reach a decision or simply to hear different viewpoints? Or is it simply for people to receive information about the item?

Speak from a personal point of view

It makes it easier to avoid destructive conflict and to ensure people keep listening if there is agreement that each person will only speak from their own point of view. In other words, people are asked not to generalize or talk about what others think. Individuals give their own personal viewpoint, their own personal experience, their own feelings or their own thinking. Other people are much less likely to get defensive if we talk from this personal point of view. It becomes very difficult to disagree with someone as long as they continue to talk only about themselves. Once they start to talk for or about other people, things are likely to become more contentious. As we saw above, the way the questions are actually formed helps this considerably. By putting the questions in the form of how things are from "your own personal point of view", people tend to stay more focused on this and make fewer comments about other people's positions.

Treat each person with respect

Implicit in these guidelines is the understanding that all participants will be treated with respect. This means that there will be no blaming, accusing, name-calling, attacking or other types of destructive behaviour. So, for example, if someone has strong feelings about an issue or situation, it is not necessary for them to blame or attack anyone else in the group in order to communicate those feelings. In line with the previous guideline, where someone forgets and begins to blame or attack, they can be encouraged to talk about themselves rather than switching the focus onto someone else. They can be asked, for example, to talk about the effects on them of what has been happening rather than who is to blame for what has been happening. The guidelines themselves tend to structure out the opportunities for this kind of behaviour but, if it still occurs, a simple reminder of the agreed guidelines will often be enough to put things back on track.

Keep it confidential

Confidentiality is often an important aspect of creating a safe environment in which to discuss potentially divisive issues. It has two dimensions. The first, which we are generally more familiar with, is an agreement that what is said at a meeting stays confidential to that meeting and will not be discussed outside with non-members of the group. So, for example, a group can agree that nothing said at their meetings will be repeated outside attached to any particular member's name or in any way that can identify who said what. This avoids a fairly common difficulty where people refuse to speak openly at meetings because they believe they will hear it repeated back to them (often in distorted or out-of-context ways) by other people who were not members of the group. If someone wants to talk to outsiders about what the group discussed, they agree to do so in ways that protect and respect confidentiality.

There is a second dimension of confidentiality that is less familiar but can add considerably to the safety in a group. This will not always be relevant but it applies particularly where people discuss sensitive, personal or divisive issues. Here, the group members agree not to refer back to what any other member says, outside the meeting or at subsequent meetings, without first of all asking the person for permission to bring up what they said. At that point, the person can say they would prefer not to speak about it any further or they may say they have no difficulty with it being raised. The aim here is to ensure that contributions are not taken out of context or referred to in situations where the person who made the contribution does not feel safe or where they do not consider it appropriate. By obtaining agreement from the person before bringing it up, we respect their right to safety and we ensure that they stay in control of what they said. Obviously, this is not going to be relevant to many discussions but a sensitivity to when it is appropriate can enhance the safety and effectiveness of some groups. Generally, it will be clear when something of a sensitive nature has come up and people can be asked to bear in mind this second aspect of confidentiality.

Because this process is highly structured with a view to minimizing the opportunities for destructive conflict while maximizing the opportunities to contribute and produce a complete picture of what the group thinks, it has the additional effect of making it much easier to time meetings. One of the objections that is sometimes raised about this process is that it is likely to be quite time-consuming if everyone is to get a turn. The other side of that, however, is that because there is little or no open-ended, repetitive discussion, a lot of time is actually saved. Because we know how many people will be taking a turn and how many questions we want them to address, it is possible to time how long it will take with much more accuracy than most meetings. Depending on the circumstances, people may use a very rigid time-keeping schedule where each participant is given a specified time limit on their contribution and it is agreed that, when that time is up, they finish the sentence they are on and stop. Or, they can adopt a more relaxed approach and see that everyone takes roughly the same amount of time, only interrupting them if they go on too long.

EXCEPTIONS

The guidelines described in these chapters work extremely well in a wide range of conflict incidents. There are certain situations where they may not be sufficient, however. We have already come across these exceptions in Chapter 6 when we looked at the destructive ways some people behave around leaders and in Chapter 12 when we looked at how some people react extremely negatively to change. In each of these contexts, we saw how there can be a small minority of people who are so caught up in painful emotion that they have become chronically negative and destructive. Instead of occasionally getting restimulated and acting out destructive feelings of aggression, hostility or distrust, these people are almost continually feeling bad. As we saw before, no amount of listening will drain their attacks. Their effects on groups can be extremely demoralizing and destructive. In those earlier chapters, we saw a range of strategies for dealing with such people so these will not be repeated in detail here.

The guidelines we have looked at in these later chapters will help to prevent situations with such people escalating more quickly than they might otherwise do but they may not be enough to resolve the difficulty. As we saw in the other chapters, we have some limited options with these individuals. Where all else fails and where their influence is destructive, we may have to require such people to stop attacking or to leave. And, we may refuse to listen to them while they are engaging in destructive behaviour. The guidelines for groups above will also often help in structuring out the opportunity for people like this to overwhelm a group. The first two of these guidelines, in particular, make it very difficult for people like this to take over or dominate a group. Finally, as we saw in Chapter 12, we can limit the destructive effects of these individuals by putting our energy into building relationships with, and supporting, those other people with the potential to be flexible.

SUMMARY

In this chapter we have seen how an understanding of the conflict iceberg can enable us to reframe conflict in terms of important underlying concerns and interests. We can apply this approach also in problem solving and disciplinary situations. Similarly, the guidelines for meetings are designed to ensure that everyone's contribution is heard without any one person taking over or dominating the discussion. This can make a huge difference to the quality of thinking that emerges. There are no magical tricks or gimmicks for instantly resolving destructive conflict. Running through all the guidelines we have covered is the challenge for us to stay thinking in the face of painful emotion and to create the safety for other people to communicate in ways that are constructive and undefensive. By being clear about the underlying dynamic we can approach conflict flexibly and thoughtfully and discover ways to identify what is at stake and how it can be addressed to everyone's satisfaction.

CONCLUSION

The model of leadership described in this book brings together a number of important elements. These include a detailed understanding of the content of leadership and the key functions of a leader. They also include a close attention to the context of leadership and the dynamics of oppression and liberation. Finally, they include a range of very practical skills and strategies that enable leaders to play a highly effective role in building relationships of influence and resolving conflicts. Each of these elements adds a vital component to the tool chest or repertoire of a leader. Together, they enable anyone in a leadership role to make a significant difference to the world around them.

REFLECTION

Conflict at meetings

1   What do you like or find useful about meetings?
2   What do you hate about meetings?
3   How would you structure or redesign your meetings in order to increase what is positive or constructive and to decrease what is negative or destructive?
4   How would you apply the guidelines for meetings in this chapter to your own group or organization?

Recurring conflicts

5 List some recurring, intractable, emotive or potentially divisive conflicts in your group or organization.
6 What destructive dynamics have characterized the discussion of these issues?
7 Apply the conflict iceberg to each of these conflicts and list the important underlying factors in each case.
8 Which underlying factors have not been clearly identified within the group or organization? Where are more listening and clarification required?
9 How would you structure a listening exercise around each of these conflicts that would make it safe for people to listen relaxedly to others and to speak openly about their own underlying concerns, interests, problems, fears and so on?

Bibliography

Adair, J. (2002) *Effective Strategic Leadership*. London: Macmillan.

Adam, B. D. (1978a) "Inferiorization and 'self-esteem' ". *Social Psychology*, **41** (1), 47–53.

Adam, B. D. (1978b) *The Survival of Domination: Inferiorization and Everyday Life*. New York: Elsevier North-Holland.

Aguilar, E. (1995) *Re-evaluation Counseling: A "culturally competent" Model for Social Liberation*. Seattle: Rational Island Publishers.

Albert, M. (2000) *Society's Pliers: Class, Race, Sex?!* Retrieved 28 October 2004 from http://www.zmag.org/ZMag/articles/racesexclass.htm.

Albert, M. (2003) *Parecon: Life after Capitalism*. London: Verso.

Alinsky, S. (1989) *Rules for Radicals: A Practical Primer for Realistic Radicals*. New York: Vintage Books.

Allport, G. (1979) *The Nature of Prejudice*. (25th Anniversary ed.). Reading, MA: Addison-Wesley. (Original work published 1954).

Archibald, W. P. (1978) *Social Psychology as Political Economy*. Toronto: McGraw-Hill Ryerson.

Argyris, C. (1985) *Strategy, Change and Defensive Routines*. Boston, MA: Pitman.

Argyris, C. (1986) "Skilled incompetence". *Harvard Business Review*, **64** (5), 74–9.

Argyris, C. (1999) *On Organizational Learning* (2nd ed.). Oxford: Blackwell.

Badaracco, J. (2002) *Leading Quietly: An Unorthodox Guide to Doing the Right Thing*. Boston: Harvard Business School Press.

Baritz, L. (1960) *The Servants of Power*. Westport, CT: Greenwood.

Barker, R. (1997) "How can we train leaders if we do not know what leadership is?" *Human Relations*, **50** (4), 343–62.

Bass, B. (1985) *Leadership and Performance beyond Expectations*. New York: Free Press.

Bass, B. (1990a) *Bass and Stogdill's Handbook of Leadership: Theory, Research, and Managerial Applications* (3rd ed.). New York: Free Press.

Bass, B. (1990b) "From transactional to transformational leadership: Learning to share the vision". *Organizational Dynamics*, **18** (3), Winter, 19–31.

Bass, B. and Avolio, B. (1994) *Improving Organisational Effectiveness through Transformational Leadership*. Thousand Oaks, CA: Sage.

Batstone, E., Boraston, I. and Frenkel, S. (1977) *Shop Stewards in Action: The Organization of Workplace Conflict and Accommodation*. Oxford: Basil Blackwell.

Batstone, E., Boraston, I. and Frenkel, S. (1978) *The Social Organization of Strikes*. Oxford: Basil Blackwell.

Bennis, W. (1989a) *On Becoming a Leader*. Arrow Books.

Bennis, W. (1989b) *Why Leaders can't Lead: The Unconscious Conspiracy Continues*. San Francisco, CA: Jossey-Bass.

Bennis, W. (1997) "The secrets of great groups". *Leader to Leader* [On-line], **3**, Winter, 29–33. Retrieved July 28, 2004 from http://www.pfdf.org/leaderbooks/l2l/winter97/bennis.html.

Bennis, W. (1998) *Managing People is like Herding Cats*. London: Kogan Page.

Bennis, W. (2000) *Old Dogs, New Tricks*. London: Kogan Page.

Bennis, W. and Thomas, R. (2002) *Geeks and Geezers: How Era, Values, and Defining Moments Shape Leaders*. Boston, MA: Harvard Business School Press.

Bettleheim, B. (1986a) *The Informed Heart*. London: Penguin.

Bettleheim, B. (1986b) *Surviving the Holocaust*. London: Fontana Paperbacks.

Beynon, H. (1984) *Working for Ford* (2nd ed.). Harmondsworth: Penguin.

Binney, G., Wilke, G. and Williams, C. (2005) *Living Leadership: A Practical Guide for Ordinary Heroes*. Harlow: Financial Times/Prentice Hall.

Blair, M. (2002) "Effective school leadership: The multi-ethnic context". *British Journal of Sociology of Education*, **23** (2), 179–91.

Blake, R. and Mouton, J. (1964) *The Managerial Grid*. Houston, TX: Gulf Publishing.

Blanchard, K. and Johnson, S. (1982) *The One-minute Manager*. New York: William Morrow.

Blanchard, K., Zigarmi, P. and Zigarmi, D. (2004) *Leadership and the One-minute Manager*. London: HarperCollins.

Block, P. (1993) *Stewardship: Choosing Service over Self-interest*. San Francisco, CA,: Berrett-Koehler.

Borgen, F. (2005) "Advancing social justice in vocational theory, research, and practice". *The Counseling Psychologist*, **33** (2), 197–206.

Boyett, J. H. and Boyett, J. T. (1998) *The Guru Guide: The Best Ideas of the Top Management Thinkers*. New York: John Wiley.

Braginsky, B. and Braginsky, D. (1974) *Mainstream Psychology: A Critique*. New York: Holt, Rinehart & Winston.

Brounstein, M. (1993) *Handling the Difficult Employee: Solving Performance Problems*. Menlo Park, CA: Crisp Publications.

Brown, C. and Mazza, G. (2005) *Leading Diverse Communities: A How-to Guide for Moving from Healing into Action*. San Francisco: Jossey-Bass.

Brown, G. (1994) *We Who Were Raised Poor: Ending the Oppression of Classism*. Seattle: Rational Island.

Brown, L. D. (1979) "Managing conflict among groups", in D. A. Kolb, I. Rubin and J. M. McIntyre (eds). *Organizational Psychology: A Book of Readings* (3rd ed.) (377–89). Englewood Cliffs, NJ: Prentice-Hall.

Brown, P. (ed.) (1973) *Radical Psychology*. London: Tavistock.

Brown, P. (1974) *Toward a Marxist Psychology*. New York: Harper Colophon.

Bryman, A. (1996) "Leadership in organizations", in S. Clegg, C. Hardy and W. Nord (eds) (1999) *Managing Organizations: Current Issues*. (2nd ed.) (26–42). London: Sage.

Bulhan, H. A. (1985) *Frantz Fanon and the Psychology of Oppression*. New York: Plenum Press.

Bunting, M. (2004) *Willing Slaves: How the Overwork Culture is Ruling our Lives*. London: HarperCollins.

Burns, J. M. (1978) *Leadership*. New York: Harper Torchbooks.

Burns, J. M. (2003) *Transforming Leadership: A New Pursuit of Happiness*. London: Atlantic Books.

Businesseurope.com (2004, June 24) *It's Lonely at the Top*. Retrieved July 15, 2004 from http://www.businesseurope.com/cmn/viewdoc.jsp?cat=all&docid=BEP1_-News_0000066598.

Chafe, W. (1977) *Women and Equality: Changing Patterns in American Culture*. New York: Oxford University Press.

Chaplain, R. (2001) "Stress and job satisfaction among primary headteachers". *Educational Management and Administration*, **29**, 197–215.

Chesler, P. (1972) *Women and Madness*. New York: Doubleday.

Collins, J. (1996) "Aligning action and values". *Leader to Leader* [On-line], 1, Summer, 19–24. Retrieved July 28, 2004 from http://www.leadertoleader.org/leaderbooks/l2l/summer96/collins.html.

Conger, J. (1989) *The Charismatic Leader: Behind the Mystique of Exceptional Leadership*. San Francisco, CA: Jossey-Bass.

Conger, J. A. and Kanungo, R. N. (1988) "Behavioral dimensions of charismatic leadership", in J. A. Conger and R. N. Kanungo (eds). *Charismatic Leadership: The Elusive Factor in Organizational Effectiveness*. San Francisco, CA: Jossey-Bass.

Conger, J. A. and Kanungo, R. N. (eds) (1998) *Charismatic Leadership in Organisations*. Thousand Oaks, CA: Sage.

Cooper, C. and Quick, J. (2003) "The stress and loneliness of success". *Counselling Psychology Quarterly*, **16** (1), 1–7.

Cotgrove, S. and Duff, A. (2003) "Middle-class radicalism and environmentalism", in J. Goodwin and J. M. Jasper (eds). *The Social Movements Reader: Cases and Concepts* (72–80). Malden, MA: Blackwell Publishing.

Crass, C. (2003) *But we don't have Leaders: Leadership Development and Anti-authoritarian Organizing*. Retrieved October 9, 2003 from http://www.infoshop.org/rants/crass_leaders.html.

Cross, T. L. (1988) "Services to minority populations: Cultural competence continuum", *Focal Point: The Bulletin of the Research and Training Center*, Portland Minority Project, **3** (1), 1–4.

Cubitt, S. and Burt, C. (2002) "Leadership style, loneliness and occupational stress in New Zealand primary school principals". *New Zealand Journal of Educational Studies*, **37** (2), 159–69.

Darlington, R. (2001) "Union militancy and left-wing leadership on London underground". *Industrial Relations Journal*, **32** (1), 2–21.

Davidson, M. (1995) *The Grand Strategist: The Revolutionary New Management System*. London: Macmillan.

Davis, S. (1996) *Leadership in Conflict: The Lessons of History*. London: Macmillan.

de Board, R. (1978) *The Psychoanalysis of Organizations: A Psychoanalytic Approach to Behaviour in Groups and Organizations*. London: Tavistock.

Dworkin, A. G. (1987) *Teacher Burnout in the Public Schools: Structural Causes and Consequences for Children*. Albany, NY: State University of New York Press.

Dyer, W. (1977) *Team Building: Issues and Alternatives*. Reading, MA: Addison-Wesley.

Ehrenreich, B. (1989) *Fear of Falling: The Inner Life of the Middle Class*. New York: Pantheon Books.

Eykman, H. (1991) "The loneliness of the leader: Reflections on psychotherapeutic leadership". *International Journal of Therapeutic Communities*, **12** (1), 29–34.

Fanon, F. (1967) *The Wretched of the Earth*. Harmondsworth: Penguin. (Original work published 1961).

Fanon, F. (1970) *Black Skin White Masks* (C. L. Markmann, Trans.). London: Paladin. (Original work published 1952).

Farmer, F. (1983) *Will There Really be a Morning? An Autobiography*. London: Fontana.

Farrell, G. (2001) "From tall poppies to squashed weeds: Why don't nurses pull together more?" *Journal of Advanced Nursing*, **35** (1), 26–33.

Feagin, J. and Sikes, M. (1994) *Living with Racism: The Black Middle-class Experience*. Boston: Beacon Press.

Fekete, L. (2004) "Anti-Muslim racism and the European security state". *Race & Class*, **46** (1), 3–29.

Fiedler, F. (1974) "The contingency model – new directions for leadership utilisation". *Journal of Contemporary Business*, **3** (4), 65–80.

Fielden, S. and Davidson, M. (2001) "Stress and the woman manager", in J. Dunham (ed.). *Stress in the Workplace: Past, Present and Future* (109–29). London: Whurr Publishers.

Fisher, R., Ury, W. and Patton, B. (1991) *Getting to Yes: Negotiating an Agreement without Giving in* (2nd ed.). London: Arrow Books.

Fox, D. and Prilleltensky, I. (eds) (1997) *Critical Psychology: An Introduction*. London: Sage.

Fraser, J. A. (2001) *White-collar Sweatshop: The Deterioration of Work and its Rewards in Corporate America*. New York: W. W. Norton.

Freeman, J. (1970) *The Tyranny of Structurelessness*. Retrieved July 28, 2004 from http://flag.blackened.net/revolt/hist_texts/structurelessness.html.

Freire, P. (1972) *Pedagogy of the Oppressed*. Harmondsworth: Penguin.

Friedman, I. (2002) "Burnout in school principals: Role related antecedents". *Social Psychology of Education*, **5** (3), 229–51.

Fromm, E. (1960) *The Fear of Freedom*. London: Routledge & Kegan Paul. (Original work published 1942).

George, J. (2000) "Emotions and leadership: The role of emotional intelligence". *Human Relations*, **53** (8), 1027–55.

Gerstner, C. and Day, D. (1997) "Meta-analytic review of leader–member exchange theory: Correlates and construct issues". *Journal of Applied Psychology*, **82** (6), 827–44.

Glasser, W. (1994) *The Control Theory Manager*. New York: Harper Business.

Gmelch, W. and Burns, J. (1993) "The cost of academic leadership: Department chair stress". *Innovative Higher Education*, **17** (4), 259–70.

Goleman, D. (1996) *Emotional Intelligence: Why it can Matter More than IQ*. London: Bloomsbury.

Goleman, D., Boyatzis, R. and McKee, A. (2002) *The New Leaders: Transforming the Art of Leadership into the Science of Results*. London: Time Warner Paperbacks.

Goodwin, D. K. (1978) "True leadership". *Psychology Today*, **12** (5), 46–58, 110.

Gorz, A. (1982) *Farewell to the Working Class: An Essay on Post-industrial Socialism*. London: Pluto Press.

Greenleaf, R. (1977) *Servant Leadership: A Journey into the Nature of Legitimate Power and Greatness*. New York: Paulist Press.

Gronn, P. (2003) "Leadership: Who needs it?" *School Leadership and Management*, **23** (3), 267–90.

Hahnel, R. (2005) *Economic Justice and Democracy: From Competition to Cooperation*. New York: Routledge.

Halpin, A. (1966) *Theory and Research in Administration*. New York: Macmillan.

Harris, T. (1973) *I'm OK – You're OK*. London: Pan.

Harro, B. (2000a) "The cycle of socialization". in M. Adams, W. Blumenfeld, R. Castaneda, H. Hackman, M. Peters and X. Zuniga (eds). *Readings for Diversity and Social Justice* (15–21). New York: Routledge.

Harro, B. (2000b) "The cycle of liberation", in M. Adams, W. Blumenfeld, R. Castaneda, H. Hackman, M. Peters and X. Zuniga (eds). *Readings for Diversity and Social Justice* (463–9). New York: Routledge.

Harvey, J. (1988) *The Abilene Paradox and Other Meditations on Management*. Lexington, MA: Lexington Books.

Harvey, J. (1999) *How Come Every Time I Get Stabbed in the Back my Fingerprints are on the Knife? And Other Meditations on Management*. San Francisco, CA: Jossey-Bass.

Hastie, C. (n.d.) *Horizontal Violence in the Workplace*. Retrieved July 15, 2004 from http://www.acegraphics.com.au/articles/hastie02.html.

Heather, N. (1976) *Radical Perspectives in Psychology*. London: Methuen.

Heer, K. (2003) *What's That I Smell Burning?* Retrieved July 15, 2004 from http://www.kenheer.com/articles/Whats%20that%20I%20Smell.htm.

Heifetz, R. (1994) *Leadership without Easy Answers*. Cambridge, MA: Belknap Press.

Heifetz, R. and Linsky, M. (2002a) *Leadership on the Line: Staying Alive through the Dangers of Leading*. Boston: Harvard Business School Press.

Heifetz, R. and Linsky, M. (2002b) "A survival guide for leaders". *Harvard Business Review*, 65–74.

Heppner, M. and Scott, A. (2004) "From whence we came: The role of social class in our families of origin". *The Counseling Psychologist*, **32** (4), 596–603.

Hersey, P. and Blanchard, K. (1977) *Management of Organisational Behaviour: Utilising Human Resources*. Englewood Cliffs, NJ: Prentice-Hall.

Heskin, K. (1980) *Northern Ireland: A Psychological Analysis*. Dublin: Gill & Macmillan.

Hestenes, R. (1999) *Leadership and the Christian Woman*. Paper presented to the 1999 meeting of Christians for Biblical Equality. *Arrow leadership articles: Vision and the McWorld* [On-line]. Retrieved July 27, 2004 from www.arrowleadership.org/res/articles/women/christianwomen2.html.

Hope, A. and Timmel, S. (1984) *Training for Transformation: A Handbook for Community Workers* (Book 2). Gweru, Zimbabwe: Mambo Press.

Horton, T. (1992) *The CEO Paradox: The Privilege and Accountability of Leadership*. New York: Amacom.

Howell, J. and Shamir, B. (2005) "The role of followers in the charismatic leadership process: Relationships and their consequences". *Academy of Management Review*, **30** (1), 96–112.

Ingleby, D. (1975) "The psychology of child psychology", in G. Esland, G. Salaman and M. Speakman (eds). *People and Work*. Edinburgh: Holmes McDougall/Milton Keynes: Open University.

Irwin, J. (1992) "The liberation of males", in J. Irwin, H. Jackins and C. Kreiner. *The Liberation of Men*. Seattle: Rational Island.

Jackins, H. (1970) *Fundamentals of Co-counseling Manual*. Seattle: Rational Island.

Jackins, H. (1973) "Leaders and leadership". in *The Human Situation* (223–8). Seattle: Rational Island.

Jackins, H. (1978) *The Human side of Human Beings*. Seattle: Rational Island.

Jackins, H. (1981) "The frontiers of co-counseling", in *The Benign Reality* (77–95) Seattle: Rational Island.

Jackins, H. (1983a) "Insights about oppression", in *The Reclaiming of Power* (63–72). Seattle: Rational Island.

Jackins, H. (1983b) "Why leaders of RC can expect to be attacked and what to do about such attacks", in *The Reclaiming of Power* (247–56). Seattle: Rational Island.

Jackins, H. (1984) "Counseling and leadership theory for wide-world leaders". *Present Time*, **55**, 33–42.

Jackins, H. (1986) "How can we develop more Jewish leaders?" *Ruah Hadashah*, **6**, 11–20.

Jackins, H. (1987) *The Enjoyment of Leadership*. Seattle: Rational Island.

Jackins, H. (1990) *Logical Thinking about a Future Society*. Seattle: Rational Island.

Jackins, H. (1995a) "The 'reality agreement' approach to a session". in *The Kind Friendly Universe* (23–33) Seattle: Rational Island.

Jackins, H. (1995b) "A year of continental and world conferences". in *The Kind Friendly universe* (79–90). Seattle: Rational Island.

Jackins, H. (1997) *The List*. Seattle: Rational Island.

Jackins, H. *et al.* (1999) *The Human Male: A Men's Liberation Draft Policy*. Seattle: Rational Island.

Jackins, T. (2001) "Ending confusion about ourselves". *Present Time*, **122**, 28–9.

Jamison, K. (1984) *The Nibble Theory and the Kernel of Power*. New York: Paulist Press.

Janis, I. (1982) *Groupthink: Psychological Studies of Policy Decisions and Fiascoes* (Revised and enlarged edition of *Victims of Groupthink* (1972)). Boston: Houghton Mifflin.

Janov, A. (1977) *The Feeling Child*. London: Abacus.

Janov, A. (1978) *The Anatomy of Mental Illness: The Scientific Basis of Primal Therapy*. London: Abacus.

Janov, A. (1980) *Prisoners of Pain: Unlocking the Power of the Mind to End Suffering*. London: Abacus.

Janov, A. (1990) *The New Primal Scream: Primal Therapy Twenty Years Later*. London: Abacus.

Janov, A. (2000) *The Biology of Love*. Amherst, NY: Prometheus Books.

Jeffers, S. (1987) *Feel the Fear and Do it Anyway*. London: Century.

Joreen, (1996) *The Tyranny of Structurelessness*. Retrieved July 28, 2004 from http://www.ic.org/pnp/cdir/1995/23joreen.html.

Judge, T.A. and Ferris, G.R. (1993) "Social context of performance evaluation decisions". *Academy of Management Journal*, **36**, 80–105.

Kanter, R. M. (1979a) "Notes on women and power: The organisational side of the equation". *Radcliffe Centennial Conference on Women and Power*. Cambridge: Goodmeasure Inc.

Kanter, R. M. (1979b) "Power failure in management circuits". *Harvard Business Review*, **57** (4), 65–75.

Kanter, R. M. (1993) *Men and Women of the Corporation*. New York: Basic Books.

Karp, H. B. (1988) "A positive approach to resistance", in J. W. Pfeiffer (ed.). *The*

1988 Annual: Developing Human Resources (143–6). San Diego: University Associates.

Kauffman, K. and New, C. (2004) *Co-counselling: The Theory and Practice of Re-evaluation Counselling*. Hove: Brunner-Routledge.

Kenny, V. (1985) "The post-colonial personality". *The Crane Bag*, **9** (1), 70–8.

Kets de Vries, M. (1989) "Leaders who self-destruct: The causes and cures". *Organizational Dynamics*, **17** (4), Spring, 5–17.

Kets de Vries, M. (2001) *The Leadership Mystique: A User's Manual for the Human Enterprise*. London: Financial Times/Prentice Hall.

Kets de Vries, M. and Miller, D. (1984) *The Neurotic Organization: Diagnosing and Changing Counterproductive Styles of Management*. San Francisco, CA: Jossey-Bass.

Kirk, P. and Shutte, A. (2004) "Community leadership development". *Community Development Journal*, **39** (3), 234–51.

Kirkpatrick, S. A. and Locke, E. A. (1991) "Leadership: Do traits matter?" *Academy of Management Executive*, 48–60.

Knupfer, G. (1954) "Portrait of the underdog", in R. Bendix and S. Lipset (eds). *Class, Status and Power: A Reader in Social Stratification* (255–63). London: Routledge & Kegan Paul.

Korten, D. (1995) *When Corporations Rule the World*. London: Earthscan.

Kouzes, J. and Posner, B. (1987) *The Leadership Challenge: How to Get Extraordinary Things Done in Organizations*. San Francisco, CA: Jossey-Bass.

Kouzes, J. and Posner, B. (2001) "Bringing leadership lessons from the past into the future", in B. Bennis, G. Spreitzer and T. Cummings (eds). *The Future of Leadership: Today's Top Leadership Thinkers Speak to Tomorrow's Leaders* (81–90). San Francisco, CA: Jossey-Bass.

Kouzes, J. and Posner, B. (2002) *The Leadership Challenge* (3rd ed.). San Francisco, CA: Jossey-Bass.

Langston, D. (2000) "Tired of playing monopoly?" in M. Adams, W. Blumenfeld, R. Castaneda, H. Hackman, M. Peters and X. Zuniga (eds). *Readings for Diversity and Social Justice* (397–402). New York: Routledge.

Le Baron, M. (2002) *Bridging Troubled Waters: Conflict Resolution from the Heart*. San Francisco, CA: Jossey-Bass.

Leader, D. and Boldt, S. (1994) *Principals and Principalship: A Study of Principals in Voluntary Secondary Schools*. Dublin: Marino Institute of Education.

Lee, R. M. and Dean, B. L. (2004) "Middle-class mythology in an age of immigration and segmented assimilation: Implications for counseling psychology". *Journal of Counseling Psychology*, **51** (1), 19–24.

Lerner, M. (1991) *Surplus Powerlessness: The Psychodynamics of Everyday Life . . . and the Psychology of Individual and Social Transformation*. Atlantic Highlands, NJ: Humanities Press International.

Levinson, H. (1981) "When executives burn out". *Harvard Business Review*, **59** (3), 73–81.

Lewin, K., Lippitt, R. and White, R. (1939) "Patterns of aggressive behaviour in experimentally created 'social climates' ". *Journal of Social Psychology*, **10**, 271–99.

Lewis, O. (1961) *The Children of Sanchez: The Autobiography of a Mexican Family*. New York: Random House.

Lewis, O. (1971) "The culture of poverty", in E. Hollander and R. Hunt (eds). *Current Perspectives in Social Psychology* (3rd ed.) (643–5). New York: Oxford University Press.

Lipsky, S. (1979) "Internalized oppression". *Black Re-Emergence*, **2**, 5–10.

Liu, W. M., Ali, S. R., Soleck, G., Hopps, J., Dunston, K. and Pickett Jr., T. (2004) "Using social class in counseling psychology research". *Journal of Counseling Psychology*, **51** (1), 3–18.

Liu, W. M. and Rasheed Ali, S. (2005) "Addressing social class and classism in vocational theory and practice: Extending the emancipatory communitarian approach". *The Counseling Psychologist*, **33** (2), 189–96.

Lockwood, G. (n.d.) CEO isolation. Retrieved July 15, 2004 from http://www.bizsuccess.com/articles/isolation.htm.

Lott, B. (2002) "Cognitive and behavioral distancing from the poor". *American Psychologist*, **57** (2), 100–10.

McCormack, R. (1996) "Authority and leadership: The moral challenge". *America*, **175** (2), 12–17.

Marchington, M. and Armstrong, R. (1983) "Typologies of shop stewards: A reconsideration". *Industrial Relations Journal*, **14** (3), 34–48.

Martín-Baró, I. (1994) *Writings for a Liberation Psychology* (A. Aron and S. Corne, eds). Cambridge, MA: Harvard University Press.

Maslach, C. (2003) "Job burnout: New directions in research and intervention". *Current Directions in Psychological Science*, **12** (5), 189–92.

Memmi, A. (1963) *Portrait of a Jew* (E. Abbot, Trans.). London: Eyre & Spottiswoode.

Memmi, A. (1966) *The Liberation of the Jew* (J. Hyun, Trans.). New York: Orion Press.

Memmi, A. (1968) *Dominated Man: Notes towards a Portrait*. New York: Orion Press.

Memmi, A. (1990) *The Colonizer and the Colonized* (H. Greenfeld, Trans.). London: Earthscan. (Original work published 1957).

Miller, A. (1987) *For your own Good: Hidden Cruelty in Child-rearing and the Roots of Violence* (H. & H. Hannum, Trans.). London: Virago.

Miller, J. B. (1986) *Toward a New Psychology of Women* (2nd ed.). London: Penguin.

Miller, K. (1978) "Correctness, liberalism and divisiveness". *Present Time*, **31**, 40.

Millman, J. (1978) "Qualities in leaders". *Present Time*, **32**, 44.

Mitchell, R. and Rossmoore, D. (2001) "Why good leaders can't use good advice". *Journal of Leadership Studies* [On-line], **8** (2), Fall, 79–105. Retrieved July 28, 2004 from http://www.csun.edu/~hfmgt001/advice.doc.

Moane, G. (1994) "A psychological analysis of colonialism in an Irish context". *The Irish Journal of Psychology*, **15** (2 & 3), 250–65.

Moane, G. (1999) *Gender and Colonialism: A Psychological Analysis of Oppression and Liberation*. London: Macmillan Press.

Moane, G. (2003) "Bridging the personal and the political: Practices for a liberation psychology". *American Journal of Community Psychology*, **31** (1/2), 91–101.

Moore, B. (1978) *Injustice: The Social Bases of Obedience and Revolt*. White Plains, NY: M. E. Sharpe.

Mouly, V. S. and Sankaran, J. (2000) *The Tall Poppy Syndrome in New Zealand: An Exploratory Investigation*. Retrieved July 27, 2004 from http://www.business.auckland.ac.nz/personal_webpages/mer/people/bfsmouly/tall%20poppy%20syndrome.doc.

Mullaly, B. (2002) *Challenging Oppression: A Critical Social Work Approach*. Ontario: Oxford University Press.

Murray, S. and Keenan, D. (1992) "The role of women as leaders in rehabilitation:

Changing to meet the times". *Journal of Applied Rehabilitation Counseling. Special women with disabilities: Issues of empowerment, influence, and caring*, **23** (4), 34–8.

Napier, R. and Sanaghan, P. (1998) "It's lonely at the top: A look at the symptoms of and treatment for isolation syndrome". *NACUBO Business Officer* [On-line]. Retrieved January 28, 2004 from http://www.nacubo.org/website/members/bomag/9807/napier.html.

Nickerson, D. (1991) "Being sensible about class divisions". *Present Time*, **82**, 53–8.

Nkomo, S. and Cox, T. (1996) "Diverse identities in organizations", in S. Clegg, C. Hardy and W. Nord (eds). *Managing Organizations: Current Issues* (2nd ed.) (88–106). London: Sage.

Nord, W. R. (1974) "The failure of current applied behavioral science – a Marxian perspective". *The Journal of Applied Behavioral Science*, **10** (4), 557–76.

Nord, W. R. (1977) "Job satisfaction reconsidered". *American Psychologist*, **32**, December, 1026–35.

Nord, W. R. and Durand, D. E. (1978) "What's wrong with the human resources approach to management?" *Organizational Dynamics*, Winter, 13–25.

Nygren, D. and Ukeritis, M. (1993) "The religious life future project: Executive summary". *Review for Religious*, **52** (1), 6–55.

Oates, S. (1982) *Let the Trumpet Sound: The Life of Martin Luther King, Jr.* New York: Mentor.

O'Day, R. (1974) "Intimidation rituals: Reactions to reform". *Journal of Applied Behavioral Science*, **10** (3), 373–86.

O'Dowd, L. (1990) "New introduction", in A. Memmi. *The colonizer and the Colonized* (H. Greenfeld, Trans.) (29–66). London: Earthscan.

Paul, N. (1985) "Increasing organisational effectiveness: A training model for developing women". *Management Education and Development*, **16** (2), 211–22.

Peters, T. (1995) *The Pursuit of Wow!: Every Person's Guide to Topsy-turvy Times*. London: Macmillan.

Pettigrew, T. (1971) "Negro American personality: The role and its burdens", in E. Hollander and R. Hunt (eds). *Current Perspectives in Social Psychology* (3rd ed.) (159–65). New York: Oxford University Press.

Pettigrew, T. (1978) "Placing Adam's argument in a broader perspective: Comment on the Adam paper". *Social Psychology*, **41** (1), 58–61.

Pierce, G. A. (1984) *Activism that Makes Sense*. Chicago: ACTA Publications.

Radical Therapist/Rough Times Collective (eds) (1974) *The Radical Therapist*. Harmondsworth: Penguin.

Read, A. (2000) "Is it any wonder we're experiencing a shortage of school leaders?". *School Community Journal*, **10** (2), 57–81.

Reich, W. (1972) *The Mass Psychology of Fascism* (V. Carfagno, Trans.). London: Souvenir Press. (Original work published 1946).

Robbins, S. (1998) *Organizational Behavior: Concepts, Controversies, Applications* (8th ed.). Upper Saddle River, NJ: Prentice-Hall.

Robert, M. (1982) *Managing Conflict from the Inside Out*. Austin, TX: Learning Concepts.

Roby, P. (1998) *Creating a Just World: Leadership for the Twenty-first Century*. Seattle: Rational Island.

Rosenberg, M. (2000) *Nonviolent Communication: A Language of Compassion*. Encinitas, CA: PuddleDancer Press.

Rost, J. (1993a) *Leadership for the Twenty-first Century*. Westport, CT: Praeger.

Rost, J. (1993b) Leadership development in the new millennium. *Journal of Leadership Studies*, **1** (1), 92–110.

Rost, J. (1997) "Moving from individual to relationship: A postindustrial paradigm of leadership". *Journal of Leadership Studies*, **4** (4), 3–16.

Rost, J. and Barker, R. (2000) "Leadership education in colleges: Toward a 21st century paradigm". *Journal of Leadership Studies*, **7** (1), 3–11.

Roy, D. (1980) "Fear stuff, sweet stuff and evil stuff: Management's defenses against unionization in the south" in T. Nichols (ed.). *Capital and Labour: A Marxist Primer* (395–415). Glasgow: Fontana Paperbacks.

Ruth, S. (1988) "Understanding oppression and liberation". *Studies*, **77** (308), 434–44.

Ruth, S. (1989) "Leadership, men and equality". *Equal Opportunities International*, **8** (1), 25–8.

Ruth, S. (1997) "Self-esteem and the Traveller child". *Glocklai* (Dublin: Journal of the Association of Teachers of Travelling People), **2** (6), 6–10.

Ruth, S. (2000) *The Dynamics of Identity: Putting the Peace Process in Context*. Paper delivered at the Visions of Peace Conference. Glencree, Ireland.

Ruth, S. (2005) "Middle-class activists and social change". *Studies*, **94** (372), 51–60.

Sadler, P. (2003) *Leadership* (2nd ed.). London: Kogan Page.

Sarros, J. (1988) "Administrator burnout: Findings and future directions". *The Journal of Educational Administration*, **24**, 272–81.

Scholtes, P. (1998) *The Leader's Handbook: Making Things Happen, Getting Things Done*. New York: McGraw Hill.

Schutz, W. (1966) *The Interpersonal Underworld*. Palo Alto, CA: Science & Behavior Books. (Originally published under the title of *FIRO: A Three-dimensional Theory of Interpersonal Behavior*, 1960).

Schwalbe, M., Godwin, S., Holden, D., Schrock, D., Thompson, S. and Wolkomir, M. (2000) Generic processes in the reproduction of inequality: An interactionist analysis. *Social Forces*, **79** (2), 419–52.

Sedgwick, P. (1974) "Ideology in modern psychology". in N. Armistead (ed.), *Reconstructing Social Psychology* (29–37). Harmondsworth: Penguin Education.

Semler, R. (2003) *The Seven-day Weekend: Finding the Work/life Balance*. London: Century.

Sen, R. (2003) *Stir it up: Lessons in Community Organizing and Advocacy*. San Francisco: Jossey-Bass.

Shah, S. (1998) *Sonia Shah of South End Press Interviews Michael Albert*. Retrieved 28 October 2004 from http://www.zmag.org/ParEcon/shahalbint.htm.

Sherman, D. (2002) "Leader role inversion as a corollary to leader-member exchange". *Group & Organization Management*, **27** (2), 245–71.

Sherover-Marcuse, E. (1986) *Emancipation and Consciousness: Dogmatic and Dialectical Perspectives in the Early Marx*. Oxford: Basil Blackwell.

Sloan, T. (2005) "Global work-related suffering as a priority for vocational psychology". *The Counseling Psychologist*, **33** (2), 207–14.

Sonn, C. and Fisher, A. (2003) "Identity and oppression: Differential responses to an in-between Status". *American Journal of Community Psychology*, **31** (1/2), 117–28.

Spanierman, L. and Heppner, M. (2004) "Psychosocial costs of racism to Whites scale (PCRW): Construction and initial validation". *Journal of Counseling Psychology*, **51** (2), 249–62.

Spears, L. (2002) "Tracing the past, present, and future of servant leadership", in L.

Spears and M. Lawrence (eds). *Focus on Leadership: Servant leadership for the Twenty-first Century* (1–16). New York: Wiley.

Spender, D. (1980) *Man Made Language*. London: Routledge & Kegan Paul.

Sue, D. W. (2003) *Overcoming our Racism: The Journey to Liberation*. San Francisco, CA: Jossey-Bass.

Tatum, B. (2000) "The complexity of identity: 'Who am I?' ", in M. Adams, W. Blumenfeld, R. Castaneda, H. Hackman, M. Peters and X. Zuniga (eds). *Readings for Diversity and Social Justice* (9–14). New York: Routledge.

Taylor, B. (2001) "Identifying and transforming dysfunctional nurse–nurse relationships through reflective practice and action research". *International Journal of Nursing Practice*, **7** (6), 406–13.

Taylor, M. (1988) *The Terrorist*. London: Brassey's Defence Publishers.

Templar, R. (2001) *Fast Thinking: Discipline*. Harlow: Pearson Education.

Tichy, N. (2002) *The Leadership Engine: How Winning Companies Build Leaders at Every Level*. New York: Harper Business Essentials.

Turban, D. B. and Jones, A. P. (1988) "Supervisor–subordinates similarity: Types, effects and mechanisms". *Journal of Applied Psychology* **73**, 228–34.

Ury, W. (1991) *Getting Past No: Negotiating with Difficult People*. London: Business Books.

Varas-Diaz, N. and Serrano-Garcia, I. (2003) "The challenge of a positive self-image in a colonial context: A psychology of liberation for the Puerto Rican experience". *American Journal of Community Psychology*, **31** (1/2), 103–15.

Watts, R., Griffith, D. and Abdul-Adil, J. (1999) "Sociopolitical development as an antidote for oppression – theory and action". *American Journal of Community Psychology*, **27** (2), 255–96.

Watts, R., Williams, N. and Jagers, R. (2003) "Sociopolitical development". *American Journal of Community Psychology*, **31** (1/2), 185–94.

Watts-Jones, D. (2002) "Healing internalized racism: The role of within-group sanctuary among people of African descent". *Family Process*, **41** (4), 591–601.

Weinrach, S. (2002) "The counseling profession's relationship to Jews and the issues that concern them: More than a case of selective awareness". *Journal of Counseling and Development*, **80**, 300–14.

Weinstein, D. (1979) *Bureaucratic Opposition: Challenging Abuses at the Workplace*. New York: Pergamon Press.

Welch, I., Meideros, D. and Tate, G. (1982) *Beyond Burnout*. Englewood Cliffs, NJ: Prentice-Hall.

Westerling, M. (n.d.) "Breaking the isolation: Keeping leadership vibrant". in National Gay and Lesbian Task Force. *Fight The Right Action Kit*. Retrieved July 15, 2004 from http://www.qrd.org/qrd/www/FTR/tblcntnt.html.

Wexler, P. (1983) *Critical Social Psychology*. Boston, MA: Routledge & Kegan Paul.

Wheatley, M. (1997) "Goodbye, command and control". *Leader to Leader* [On-line], **5**, Summer, 21–28. Retrieved July 28, 2004 from http://www.pfdf.org/leaderbooks/l2l/summer97/wheatley.html.

Wheatley, M. (2003) "When change is out of control", in M. Effron, R. Gandossy and M. Goldsmith (eds). *Human Resources for the 21st Century* (187–94). Hoboken, NJ: Wiley.

Wheatley, M. (2005) *Finding our Way: Leadership for an Uncertain Time*. San Francisco, CA: Berrett-Koehler.

Whittington, J. L., Goodwin, V. L. and Murray, B. (2004) "Transformational leadership, goal difficulty, and job design: Independent and interactive effects on employee outcomes". *Leadership Quarterly*, **15** (5), October, 593–606.

Williams, L. (2002) "Fannie Lou Hamer, servant of the people", in L. Spears and M. Lawrence (eds). *Focus on Leadership: Servant Leadership for the Twenty-first Century* (65–87). New York: Wiley.

Wimber, J. (1992) "Why I respond to criticism". *Vineyard Position Paper*, 1. Retrieved July 15, 2004 from http://www.vineyardusa.org/publications/position_papers/criticism.pdf.

Wyckoff, H. (1976) "Between men and women", in H. Wyckoff (ed.). *Love, Therapy and Politics: Issues in Radical Therapy – the First Year* (107–26). New York: Grove Press.

Yalom, B. (1998) "It's lonely at the top". *Inc.com* [On-line]. Retrieved July 15, 2004 from http://pf.inc.com/magazine/19980401/903.html.

Young, I. M. (1990) *Justice and the Politics of Difference.* Princeton, NJ: Princeton University Press.

Zappone, K. (ed.) (2003) *Re-thinking Identity: The Challenge of Diversity.* Dublin: Joint Equality and Human Rights Forum.

Zinn, H. (1990) *A People's History of the United States.* New York: Harper Perennial.

Author index

Abdul-Adil, J., 129, 212, 213, 217, 219
Ali, S.R., 117, 160, 175, 178
Adair, J., 50, 62, 63
Adam, B., 138, 152, 159, 163, 165, 276
Aguilar, E., 191, 210, 211
Albert, M., 175–76, 294
Alinsky, S., 52
Allport, G., 91, 155, 157–60, 163–65, 213
Archibald, W.P., 52
Argyris, C., 11, 35
Armstrong, R., 66, 67
Avolio, B., 51, 61, 104

Badaracco, J., 41
Baritz, L., 52
Barker, R., 3, 48, 51, 52, 63, 65, 97
Bass, B., 50–51, 61, 104
Batstone, E., 66, 67
Bennis, W., 6, 13, 23, 41, 51, 54–57, 80, 95, 98, 164
Bettleheim, B., 164
Beynon, H., 8
Binney, G., 62
Blair, M., 25
Blake, R., 50
Blanchard, K., 50, 235
Block, P., 8, 51
Boldt, S., 79, 95
Boraston, I., 66–67
Borgen, F., 175, 190
Boyatzis, R., 94
Boyett, J.H., 62
Boyett, J.T., 62
Braginsky, B., 160
Braginsky, D., 160
Brounstein, P., 270
Brown, C., 106, 207
Brown, G., 168
Brown, L.D., 217
Brown, P., 52
Bryman, A., 50
Bulhan, H.A., 151, 157–58, 212, 214, 218

Bunting, M., 183
Burns, J., 95
Burns, J.M., 36, 42, 51–52, 58, 60–64, 98
Burt, C., 95
Businesseurope.com, 94

Chafe, W., 129, 213
Chaplain, R., 95
Chesler, P., 166
Collins, J., 23
Conger, J.A., 51, 58
Cooper, C., 95
Cotgrove, S., 177
Cox, T., 198
Crass, C., 39
Cross, T., 191, 210–11
Cubitt, S., 95

Darlington, R., 66
Davidson, M., 63, 95
Davis, S., 55
Day, D., 97
Dean, B.L., 174
de Board, R., 90
Duff, A., 177
Dunston, K., 117, 160, 175, 178
Durand, D.E., 52
Dworkin, A.G., 94
Dyer, W., 12

Ehrenreich, B., 181
Eykman, H., 95

Fanon, F., 155, 158, 160–164
Farmer, F., 278
Farrell, G., 93
Feagin, J., 121
Fekete, L., 215
Ferris, G.R., 97
Fiedler, F., 50
Fielden, S., 95
Fisher, A., 182
Fisher, R., 248, 265
Fox, D., 52
Fraser, J.A., 183

Freeman, J., 39
Freire, P., 117, 127, 158, 162, 177, 297
Frenkel, S. 66–67
Friedman, I., 95, 161
Fromm, E., 166

George, J., 54
Gerstner, C., 97
Glasser, W., 76, 238, 260
Godwin, S., 118, 129, 132–133, 157
Goleman, D., 54
Goleman, D., 94
Goodwin, D., 36
Goodwin, V.L., 97
Gmelch, W., 95
Gorz, A., 128
Greenleaf, R., 13, 29, 51, 56–57, 96
Griffith, D., 129, 212–213, 217, 219
Gronn, P., 93

Hahnel, R., 175
Halpin, A., 50
Harris, T., 212
Harro, B., 129, 212–214, 218–220
Harvey, J., 11, 12, 92
Hastie, C., 93, 159
Heather, N., 52
Heer, K., 92, 93
Heifetz, R., 23, 34, 86, 89–91, 227
Heppner, M., 169, 185
Heppner, N., 174
Hersey, P., 50
Heskin, K., 214
Hestenes, R., 92, 240
Holden, D., 118, 129, 132–133, 157
Hope, A., 52
Hopps, J., 117, 160, 175, 178
Horton, T., 93
Howell, J., 97

Ingleby, D., 52
Irwin, J., 169

Jackins, H. 8, 15, 26, 27, 30, 49, 52, 54, 59, 65–66, 91, 99, 107, 121, 137, 155, 232, 248, 249
Jackins, H., *et al*, 169
Jackins, T., 141
Jagers, R. 131, 212, 213, 217
Jamison, K., 75, 91
Janis, I., 35, 233
Janov, A., 26, 52, 249
Jeffers, S., 254
Joreen, 39
Judge, T.A., 97

Kanter, R.M., 29–30, 49, 146, 157, 159, 238
Kanunjo, R.N., 51, 58
Karp, H.B., 242
Kauffman, K., 26
Keenan, D., 95
Kenny, V., 162, 167
Kets de Vries, M., 51, 90, 152
Kirk, P., 52
Kirkpatrick, S.A., 59
Knupfer, G., 168
Korten, D., 51, 187
Kouzes, J., 15, 23, 51, 62, 98, 238

Langston, D., 174
Leader, D., 79, 95
LeBaron, M., 247
Lee, R.M., 174
Lerner, M., 143
Levinson, H., 95
Lewin, K., 50
Lewis, O., 168
Linsky, M., 23, 86, 89–91, 227
Lippitt, R., 50
Lipsky, S., 91, 93, 147
Liu, W.M., 117, 160, 175, 178
Liu and Rasheed Ali, 117, 175
Locke, E.A., 59
Lockwood, G., 94
Lott, B., 174, 175, 181, 182

McCormack, R., 37
McKee, A., 94
Marchington, M., 66, 67
Martín-Baró, I., 203
Maslach, C., 96
Mazza, G., 106, 207
Meidens, D., 95
Memmi, A., 91, 128, 153, 155, 156, 158, 160–164, 274
Miller, A., 249
Miller, D., 90, 152
Miller, J.B., 52, 166–168, 279, 280
Miller, K., 145

Millman, J., 59
Mitchell, R., 11
Moane, G., 52, 118, 123, 129, 131, 162, 180
Moore, B., 165
Mouly, V.S., 92
Mouton, J., 50
Mullaly, B., 116, 118, 121, 129, 169, 198–200
Murray, B., 97
Murray, S., 95

Napier, R., 94
New, C., 26
Nickerson, D., 178–179
Nkomo, S., 198
Nord, W., 52
Nord, W.R., 52
Nygren, D., 43

Oates, S., 25
O'Day, R., 109–110
O'Dowd, L., 161

Patton, B., 248, 265
Paul, N., 212
Peters, T., 230, 238
Pettigrew, T., 159, 168
Pickett, Jr., T., 117, 160, 175, 178
Pierce, G.A., 31, 232
Posner, B., 15, 23, 51, 62, 98, 238
Prilleltensky, I., 52

Quick, J., 95

Radical Therapist/Rough Times Collective, 52
Read, A., 95
Reich, W., 72, 155–56
Robbins, S., 58
Robert, M., 256
Roby, P., 68
Rosenberg, M., 248, 262, 270
Rossmoore, D., 11
Rost, J., 3, 35, 48, 51–52, 63–65, 97–98, 165
Ruth, S., 129, 138, 161, 178, 212

Sadler, P., 91
Sanaghan, P., 94
Sankaran, J., 92
Sarros, J., 95
Scholtes, P., 268
Schrock, D., 118, 129, 132 133, 157
Schutz, W., 72
Schwalbe, Godwin, Holden, Schrock, Thompson, and Wolkomir, 118, 129, 132–33, 157
Scott, A., 174

Sedgwick, P., 52
Semler, R., 238
Sen, R., 52
Serrano-Garcia, I., 139
Shamir, B., 97
Sherman, D., 97
Shah, S., 175
Sherover-Marcuse, E., 165, 166
Shutte, A., 52
Sikes, N., 121
Sloan, T., 190
Soleck, G., 117, 160, 175, 178
Sonn, C., 182
Spanierman, L., 169, 185
Spears, L., 57, 58
Spender, D., 158
Sue, D.W., 121, 181

Tate, G., 95
Tatum, 198, 200
Taylor, B., 159
Taylor, M., 214
Templar, R., 272, 274
Thomas, R., 13, 98
Thomson, S., 118, 129, 132–133
Tichy, N., 6
Timmel, S., 52
Turban and Jones, 97

Ukeritus, M., 43,
Ury, W., 248, 255, 258, 265

Varas-Diaz. N., 139

Watts, R., 129, 131, 212–213, 217, 219
Watts-Jones, D., 208
Weinrach, S., 121, 157
Weinstein, D., 110
Welch, I., 95
Westerling, M., 96
Wexler, P., 52
Wheatley, M., 15, 24, 62
White, R., 50
Whittington, J.L., 97
Wilke, G., 62
Williams, C., 62
Williams, L., 41, 57
Williams, N., 131, 212–213, 217, 219
Wimber, J., 93
Wolkomir, M., 118, 129, 132–133, 157
Wyckoff, H., 52

Yalom, B., 94
Young, I.M., 129

Zappone, K., 198
Zigarmi, D., 50
Zigarmi, P., 50
Zinn, H., 183, 184

Subject index

Abilene Paradox, 11
addictions, 151, 154, 163
adultism, 169
ageism, 174
Allen, Woody, 240
allies: internalized oppression
  and, 121, 140, 141, 143, 154;
  for people in Ireland, 147;
  middle-class, 176, 178, 182,
  191–6, 262; oppressor, 205,
  209, 211, 222; potential,
  245; winning, 108, 231–2,
  244
anti-Jewish: feelings, 146;
  prejudices, 194
anti-Semitism, 121, 157
Aquino, Cory, 177
Arabs, 153
attacks on leaders, 70, 73–84,
  87, 89–111, 148–9, 230; see
  also oppression
Aung San Suu Kyi, 177
authoritarianism, 30, 34–8, 43,
  48; see also powerlessness
authority, 29, 32, 34–37, 48,
  65, 96, 192, 228, 235; see
  also power

backstabbing, 92
Behan, Brendan, 146
bisexuals, 176
Black: leaders, 91; people, 25,
  158, 161, 165, 168, 169, 184;
  women, 146
bossy bosses, 29–30, 35
bribery, 184–5, 186
building relationships, viii, ix,
  15–17, 18, 62, 69, 232–9,
  282; and divisiveness, 147;
  and handling attacks, 105;
  and influence strategies,
  227, 230, 231, 244, 245; and
  overcoming oppression,
  122, 125, 127, 129, 134, 142;
  and reclaiming power, 206;
  and resolving conflict, 247,

281; and staying effective,
  84; with leaders, **82**, 83; with
  oppressed groups, 192, 197,
  222, 223
burnout, 40, 74, 81–2, 94, 95,
  96, 97

CEOs, vii, 3, 56, 63, 94
change:, viii; adaptive, 89–90,
  227; agents, 58, 176, 177,
  178, 180, 231, 241, 242, 243;
  and attacks on leaders, 106;
  and dialogue, 192; and guilt,
  205; and influence
  strategies, 227–45;
  movements, 224; and
  oppressor groups, 222;
  organizing for, 130, 206,
  219; radical, 218; resistance
  to, 89, 240–4; responses to,
  228–30, 281; and violence,
  216, 217, 220
character:, 93, 109; and
  competence, 50–69
children, 26, 37–8, 185, 187,
  219; see also young people
class: background, 178; and
  confusion, 190;
  coordinator, 175;
  definitions of, 178–9;
  differences, 174; divisions,
  158, 165; and divisiveness,
  146; and exploitation of
  workers, 155; identity, 178,
  179, 197, 198; oppression,
  168, 169, 170, 174–9 passim,
  184–90 passim, 196;
  systems, 160, 176, 177, 189;
  unawareness around, 174,
  175, 181, 187
classism, 117, 174, 194, 196,
  237
Clinton, President, 104
collaborative leadership, 42–9,
  98; see also shared
  leadership

collaborators, 17, 35, 64, 65,
  69, 98, 227
colonialism, 72, 132, 161, 162,
  176, 177
communication: and attacks,
  99, 101, 280; and building
  relationships, 15; and
  change, 229; and conflict,
  249, 250, 252, 255, 257, 258,
  261; and confusion, 190;
  of disrespect, 142; and
  encouragement, 234; and
  groups, 6; indirect, 162; and
  intimidation rituals, 109;
  and isolation, 13; and
  leadership, 4, 22, 30, 59,
  141; and liberation, 214,
  215; and listening, 8, 9, 57,
  231, 276; and oppression,
  123, 126, 142, 150, 156, 164,
  195; and praise, 235; and
  problem solving, 268, 270,
  273; and safety, 15, 242,
  282; and vision, 55; see also
  non-violent communication
compassionate
  communication see non-
  violent communication
competence see character
compliance, viii, 50, 64
conflict: avoiding, 236; and
  building relationships, 239;
  and change, 241; dealing
  with, **12**, 227, 238;
  destructive, 12, 217, 275,
  279, 280; divisive, 19, 250,
  283; in groups, 6, 106,
  274–81; iceberg, 264–6, 271,
  282, 283; incidents, 246–7,
  250, 254, 262, 263, 281;
  management, 247, 269, 275,
  277; reactions to, 249–50;
  recurring, 283;
  relationships, 246–7, 263;
  resolution, viii, 20, 246–63,
  271, 282; strategies for

resolving, 147, 244, 253, 254–63, 266, 268; unresolved, 199; and violence, 216

contradictions, 136–54 *passim*, 167, 201, 204, 223, 224

courage, 25, 27, 57, 131, 138, 143, 152, 197, 218

creativity, 54, 63, 71, 138, 154, 191, 218

criticism: avoiding, 237–8, 262; of children, 219; and conflict relationships, 246; continuous, 91; and destructive gossip, 77; and groups, 78; and hopelessness, 144; inviting, 266; and keeping our distance, 230; and mistakes, 31, 76, 99, 100, 149; of person rather than performance, 92, 93; and praise, 235; public, 83, 84; of teachers, 234; and unmet needs, 248; and unrealistic expectations, **79**

cultural competence, 191, 210–12, 219

cultures: and class, 179, 184; and diversity, 207, 210; dominant, 168, 210, 211, 213; of group, 43, 96, 106, 124, 133, 151, 154, 157; and internalized oppression, 137–44 *passim*, 152; and negative self-image, 123, 125; oppressed, 211, 214; and oppression, 129; oppressor, 210, 214; organization, 86, 96, 106; positive aspects of, 136, 139, 218, 219; of poverty, 168

curiosity, 56, 71

Debs, Eugene, 232

decision making, 19, 36, 46–7, 92, 175, 277

dedication, 54, 55

defensive routines, 11

denial of reality, 184, 187, 190

destructive reactions to leaders, 70–88

difficult people, 13, 98, 103, 186, 229, 260

disabled, 115; *see also* oppression

disabilities: people with, 176; *see also* oppression

discharge, 10, 26–7, 54, 58, 76, 81, 83, 85, 122, 190, 202, 209, 217, 222, 259, 260, 261

disciplinary interventions, 272–74

divisiveness, 145–7, 148, 149, 153, 154

dominant groups: and internalized oppression, 139, 140, 146, 150, 156–62 *passim*, 165, 212, 213, 218 ; and internalized domination, 171, 172; and leadership, 126, 127; and listening, 10, 36; and mistreatment, 117, 121; and oppression, 129–34 *passim*, 166, 167; passing as member of, 124, 168, 200; and power, 36; and relationship with the oppressed, 142, 191, 192, 195, 196, 210–16 *passim*, 219, 223; and rights, 116; study of, 174, 176; *see also* oppressor groups

domination, 130, 152, 163, 164, 165, 166, 174; *see also* mechanisms of domination

double-loop learning, 11

early experiences around leadership, 71–3

Eco, Umberto, 39

effects of stress, 251–54

ego defences, 156–60

elders, 115

empowering people, 10, 28, 30, 75, 77, 215, 243

empowerment, 28, 42, 52, 56

excellence, 51; approach, 98; school, 58; theory, 51, 64

Farmer, Frances, 166

fatigue, 81

female intuition, 167

FIRO-B, 72

flexible vs inflexible behaviour, 250–1

foresee the unforeseeable, 57

four I's, 61

Gandhi, Mahatma, 61, 63, 177

gay:, 96; men, 219; people, 115, 165, 176

generic processes *see* oppression

Gentiles, 171, 175, 181, 194, 198, 200

gossip, 76, 77, 83, 110, 148, 152

groupthink, 35, 233

Harper, William, 93

healing, 58, 125; hurts, 199, 201–3, 204, 205, 207, 217; and listening, 10; process, 10, 27, 58

heterosexism, 174

heterosexuals, 171, 175, 200

horizontal violence, 93, 139, 158, 159, 162

humility, 54, 55, 63

hurts: acting out, 103–7; and class, 179; effects of, 251–4; and healing, 10, 58, 76, 134, 135, 201, 202; old, 26, 241, 249; and oppression, 115; and oppressor group, 211, 221, 237; paying attention to, 259; person underneath, 261; sources of, 199; and young people, 71; *see also* healing

identities: and allies, 193, 194, 237; choosing, 207, 218; claiming, 200–2, 206, 207; giving up, 160, 161, 175; and internalized domination, 170, 171; and leadership, 176; and liberation, 124, 198–224; and men, 169; middle-class, 179, 180, 188, 191, 195, 196, 197; and mistrusting thinking, 150; mixed, 176, 180; mixed-class, 180; and negative self-image, 123, 125, 159; oppressed, 90, 115, 126, 134, 154, 172, 218; oppressor, 36, 126, 134, 135, 172, 173, 221; and pride, 139, 141, 146, 153, 203, 204, 205, 224; reclaiming, 148, 157; redefining, 167, 199, 203–6, 207, 222, 223; *see also* class; power

individual initiatives, 10, 25, 37, 44–5, 47–8, 49, 129; *see also* taking initiatives

industrial paradigm, 51, 63, 98

inferiorization, 164–5

influence strategies, 227–40

inherent goodness, 48, 137, 185, 188

inherent human characteristics, 137–8, 204, 205, 222, 224

integrity: and attacks, 93, 101, 102; and being an ally, 197; and effective leaders, 53, 54, 55, 59, 66; lack of, 55, 56; modelling, 22, 32, 152; and principled stands, 25–6

intelligence, 39, 190, 208, 218; and effective leaders, 53, 63, 65; emotional, 54; inherent, 48, 137; and internalized domination:, 169; and internalized oppression, 138, 139, 149, 150, 154, 199;

and leadership potential, 37
intentional leadership, 240
internalized domination:,
    169–73, 198, 211, 222
internalized oppression:,
    127–9, 134; 136–54, 198–
    205 *passim*, 227; and attacks
    on leaders, 91, 148–9; and
    circles of oppression, 131;
    and class, 175, 176, 180;
    Irish, 193; and leadership,
    136–8, 141, 143, 146–54,
    171; and liberation, 126,
    214, 215, 217, 220, 223, 224;
    and mechanisms of
    domination, 132; patterns
    of 138–53 and
    powerlessness, 30, 91,
    142–5, 146; theories of,
    155–73; *see also* internalized
    domination; liberation;
    middle-class; powerlessness;
    racism
intimidation rituals, 109–10
Irish:, 162, 201, 218; identity,
    223; liberation, 215;
    oppression, 193; people,
    120, 123, 139, 151, 153, 193,
    215, 216; Protestant, 147,
    201; *see also* internalized
    oppression
isolation:, 165; breaking
    through, 12–13, 218; and
    class, 179, 188, 189, 192;
    combatting, 10, 18; and
    conflict, 251, 262; and
    divisiveness, 146, 147; and
    leaders, 27, 36, 70, 73–5,
    78–83 *passim*, 86, 89–96,
    111, 126, 230; and
    liberation, 204, 208, 222;
    and relationships, 232, 234
isolation-attack dynamic,
    73–82, 84, 87, 89; *see also*
    destructive reactions to
    leaders

Jefferson, Thomas, 254
Jewish:, 198; history, 156;
    people, 160, 164
Jews, 115, 121, 153, 157, 158,
    161, 165, 176

King, Martin Luther, 22, 25,
    107, 109, 138, 177, 217

leaders: authoritarian, 30; and
    defining reality, 6, 14;
    developing, 18, 28–32, 46,
    59, 69; effective, viii, 3, 7, 8,
    18, 22, 32, 50, 53, 68, 98,
    138, 172, 196, 231, 239, 247;
    functions of, viii, 3–33, 34,

282; good, 4, 7, 54, 81; and
    healing, 27; potential, 37–9,
    48; and process of decision,
    27, 34, 35, 37, 40, 42, 69, 85,
    141; qualities of effective, 3;
    role of, viii, 3, 4, 14, 19, 20,
    28, 58, 147, 268; as thinker,
    4–16, 37, 21, 40, 41, 44, 47;
    trade union, 3, 8;
    transactional, 51;
    transformational, 61–2;
    transforming, 51; *see also*
    attacks on leaders;
    isolation; middle-class
leaderless groups, 39–40
leader-member exchange
    (LMX), 97
leadership: abusive, 21, 40, 43,
    72; and acting responsibly,
    41; authoritarian, vii, 21,
    22, 29, 42, 43, 46, 72;
    charismatic, 38, 58, 59; and
    decisiveness, 20–1, 27, 32,
    69, 86, 138; and delegation,
    28–30, 34, 35, 37; effective,
    7, 10, 13, 15, 16, 18, 23, 41,
    42, 48, 52, 53, 54, 57, 59, 62,
    70, 87, 90, 127, 154, 227,
    240, 263; good, 4, 17, 20, 40,
    54, 55, 56, 86, 154; and
    influence, 16, 35, 64–6,
    239–40, 244; and inspiring
    people, 22–5; *liberation*,
    16–17, 37, 39, 40, 42, 48, 49,
    53, 57, 58, 62, 69; and
    modelling, 22, 31, 32, 59, 66,
    84, 138, 143, 148, 151, 152,
    153, 230; model, of vii, 4,
    32, 37, 41, 208, 228;
    necessity of, 39–40; and
    organizing, 21–2, 32, 65, 66;
    practices, 62; and principled
    stands, 25–6, 32, 69; and
    proposing ways forward,
    18–20, 32; qualities, viii,
    53–9; role of, 8, 15, 25, 31,
    36, 40, 42, 43, 63, 147, 148;
    staying effective in, 84–7;
    trade union, 50, 66–8;
    transactional, 60, 64;
    transformational, 51, 61, 64;
    transforming, 51, 60–1, 63,
    69, 217; and visibility, 41–2,
    103; widespread, 40–1;
    see also internalized
    oppression; liberation;
    listening; oppression
lesbian, 96, 176
liberation, vii, viii, ix, 52, 118,
    121, 124, 129, 282; and
    allies, 127, 141, 176, 191,
    196; and internalized
    oppression, 138, 143, 161,

162, 165, 171; human, 65;
    and leadership, 59, 115–16,
    125, 126, 134, 149, 153, 177,
    227; movements, 128, 148,
    214, 222; policies, 151;
    process, 128, 129, 131, 134,
    137, 148, 150, 153, 157, 168,
    170, 172, 175, 199, 200, 203,
    209–24; psychology, ix, 155,
    175, 176; stages of, 212–20;
    struggles, 142, 177, 199,
    216, 219, 222, 223; *see also*
    identities; leadership;
    racism
listening: and allies, 194, 195;
    and attacks, 102, 106; and
    building relationships, 235,
    236, 239; closely, 129, 143,
    231; and conflict resolution,
    255, 258, 259, 261, 262, 266,
    283; deeply, 7, 8–17, 18, 59,
    69, 192, 233–34, 268; to
    feelings, 9–11; to leaders,
    83, 85; and leadership, 4, 15,
    18, 41, 52, 53, 84; and
    problem solving, 269,
    270–1, 276, 277, 279; and
    resistance to change, 242,
    243, 244; respectfully, 150,
    230, 267; and servant
    leadership, 57, 58; to
    thinking, 13–15; *see also*
    safety
loneliness, 73, 90, 93, 94, 95

magnanimity, 54, 55
management:, 50, 51, 63, 65,
    68, 266; skills, viii
managers, vii, 3, 50, 65; and
    backstabbing, 92; and
    building relationships, 234,
    236, 237; and class, 178,
    184; and conflict resolution,
    260, 262; and problem
    solving, 270, 272, 274; and
    resistance to change, 241,
    242; women, 95
managing diversity, 207–9,
    224
Mandela, Nelson, 22, 177, 217
Mao Zedong, 14
Marx, 165
mechanisms of domination,
    131–2
meetings: agenda of, 267,
    278–9; and attacks, 78, 103,
    104; and building
    relationships, 15, 232; and
    collaborative leadership, 44,
    45, 47; and conflict, 282;
    and decision making, 19;
    and domination, 150;
    formal, 8, 9, 11; guidelines

for, 274–81; and
hopelessness, 142, 143, 144;
and safety, 11–12; *see also*
problem-solving meeting
men: as allies, 192, 194, 209;
and identity, 200, 201, 204,
206, 218; internalized
oppression of, 170, 204;
oppression of, 117–18, 169,
170, 183, 205, 219; as
oppressors, 10, 90, 115, 139,
153, 171, 175, 190, 215; *see
also* middle-class; women
mental health: impact of
prejudice on, 160;
oppression, 186; system,
130, 131, 160, 166
middle-class: activists, 177,
182, 192; conditioning,
180–2, 187, 190, 191, 192,
196; groups, 175; and
identity, 198, 201, 207;
internalized oppression,
160, 170, 176, 187–91;
leaders, 176–8; men, 10, 95,
195, 196; oppression, 170,
182–7; psychology of,
174–97; values, 176, 179,
180; women, 145, 146; *see
also* allies; identity
misinformation, 184, 186–7,
190, 199, 213
mission statement, 23–5
mistakes, 31, 39, 75–80 *passim*,
102, 104, 106, 193, 231, 240,
241; admitting, 59, 72, 100,
258; correcting, 75, 79,
99–100, 108, 149; learning
from, 56, 62, 192
mistrusting thinking, 149–50
motivation, 43, 46, 56, 60, 97,
189, 205, 220, 228

Napoleon, 240
narrowing of the culture,
147–8, 205
Native Americans, 151
negative messages, 122–3, 204
negative self-image, 123–5
New Leadership approach, 50
nibble theory of leadership,
75, 91
non-violent communication,
248
Northern Ireland, 213, 214

openness, 54, 55
oppression, vii, viii, ix, 6, 57,
58, 73, 127–38 *passim*, 141,
143, 144, 148–76 *passim*,
180–224 *passim*, 227, 237,
248, 282; agents of, 117,
126, 170, 174, 219; and

alcohol, 151; and attacks on
leaders, 91; circles of,
129–31; colonial, 162;
definition of, 116–18; and
disability, 174; and generic
processes, 132–3; and
leadership, 115–35, 141; and
mistreatment, 116–18,
119–22, 127–8; operation
of, 118–25; *see also* identity;
liberation; middle-class;
stereotyping
oppressor groups, 10, 134; and
identity, 200, 201, 205–23
passim; and internalized
domination, 169–72 *passim*;
and internalized
oppression, 139, 140, 146,
151, 152, 156, 157, 162; and
leadership, 126, 127, 150;
and middle class, 174, 184,
189, 191, 192, 194, 195, 196;
and mistreatment, 117, 121,
122; and power, 36; and
pretence, 120; *see also*
dominant groups
oppressor liberation, 220–3
overload, 80, 81, 86, 95, 96
owning class, 179, 184; *see also*
ruling class
owning-class: groups, 175;
people, 171, 197; values, 180

painful emotions: listening to,
9, 10, 11, 54; and isolation,
13; and thinking, 14, 25, 47,
59, 78, 282; and discharge,
26, 27, 58, 76, 77, 83, 85,
202, 209, 260; and decision
making, 46; and leadership,
55, 59, 71, 80, 88; and
attacks, 99, 100, 105–11
passim; and oppression,
119, 121, 125, 126; and
class, 179, 180; and identity,
199, 202, 217; and resistance
to change, 227, 240, 241;
and conflict, 249, 250, 253,
254, 255, 258, 259, 261, 281;
acting out of, 76, 229
painful feelings *see* painful
emotions
Parkes, Rosa, 213
participation in other
oppressions, 152–3
people of colour, 10, 96, 115,
116, 121, 153, 176, 200, 201,
209; middle-class, 181; poor,
181; working-class, 181
political correctness, 142
poor, 51, 56, 115, 161, 168, 174,
175, 189, 207; raised, 116,
159, 168, 174, 174, 177, 178,

179, 180, 181, 182, 186, 197
post-colonialism, 52, 91, 164
post-colonial personality,
162–3
power: and authority, 29, 30,
35, 36; and collaborative
leadership, 46, 47, 48; and
criticism, 76; and discharge,
10; and groups, 6; hoarding,
28, 35; and identity, 199,
204; and influence, 227, 228,
231; and internalized
oppression, 143, 151, 152,
167, 168, 214; and
oppression, 115, 116,
125–34 *passim*, 169, 171,
175, 176, 185, 192, 197; and
potential, 16; reclaiming,
199, 206–7; and
transference, 90; and young
people, 38
powerlessness:, 56; and
attacks, 78, 79, 84; and
authoritarianism, 29, 30, 35;
and burnout, 94; and guilt,
205; and internalized
oppression, 131, 142–5, 147,
168; and violence, 214, 215,
216, 217; *see also*
internalized oppression
power wielders, 36, 51, 60
prejudices: and
authoritarianism, 30; and
internalized oppression
156–60 *passim*, 170, 172,
199; and liberation, 209,
211, 213, 219, 222; and
oppression, 118, 119, 124,
126, 127, 131, 175, 176, 181,
182, 187, 189, 200; and
reactions to leaders, 91
pretence, 120, 189, 190, 210,
221, 222
problem-solving: meeting,
270–2, 273, 274, 278;
process, 243, 263, 264, 268;
skills, 264–83

racism: and allies, 194, 237;
and circles of oppression,
129; and class, 174, 176,
177, 181, 185, 190; forms of,
121, 122; and internalized
oppression, 161, 169; and
liberation, 209, 219, 237;
white, 91
rational responses to
leadership, 82–4
Re-evaluation Counselling,
248
religious: groups, 22, 42, 115,
119; identity, 198; leaders,
3; life, 43; superior, 46

Robinson, Mary, 177
Roosevelt, F.D., 63
rotating leadership, 47
ruling class, 146, 155, 174,
    179; *see also* owning class
ruling-class: groups, 175;
    people, 175

safety: and attacks, 110;
    building, 18; creating, 8, 10,
    11–12, 27, 31, 156, 171, 239,
    242; lack of, 120, 275; and
    listening, 83; and meetings,
    11–12, 208, 276, 278, 280
sanctuary, 23, 86;
    within-group, 208
Saro-Wiwa, Ken, 107
schools, 38, 133, 142, 149, 164,
    181, 184, 185, 186, 188, 266
school principals, 3, 25, 79, 95,
    96, 234, 256, 266, 267
self-esteem:, 125, 147, 151,
    165, 168; low, 138–42, 143,
    146, 150, 154; and identity,
    199; and middle class, 188;
    personal and racial, 159;
sense of the unknowable,
    57
servant leadership, 13, 29, 41,
    56, 69
sexism, 129, 169, 170, 174,
    176, 181, 190, 194, 204, 237
shared leadership, 22, 42–7;
    see also collaborative
    leadership
Silkwood, Karen, 107
social change:, 51, 52, 64, 107,
    128, 172, 188–91 *passim*,
    228; activists, 3, 155;
    groups, 22; movements, 50,
    128, 146, 151;
    organizations, ix, 52, 127,
    176, 177; proponents, 158
stereotyping: acceptance of,
    139, 141, 158; and class,
    174, 185; and identity, 201,
    204, 205, 206; and
    liberation, 213, 218; and
    oppression, 118, 119, 123,
    131, 132, 146, 148, 152, 154,
    157, 164, 166, 167, 172, 210
strands: Academic
    Psychology, 50;

Organization
Development/Management
Theory, 50–2; Social
Change, 52
survival behaviour, 151–2

tall poppy syndrome, 92
taking initiatives: and attacks,
    148; and criticism, 76, 91;
    and diversity, 209; and
    leadership, viii, 18–26, 31,
    35, 39, 41, 48, 52, 66, 87, 88,
    240; and oppression, 125,
    126 150, 195; and safety,
    32; and trade union leaders,
    67; and young people, 38,
    71; *see also* individual
    initiatives
teachers, 42, 93, 95, 96, 177,
    178, 184, 185, 192, 234, 256,
    257
thinking:, 150, 152, 178, 192,
    211, 262, 282; about
    everything, 45–6; about the
    group, 40, 44, 45, 46, 47, 65,
    66; clear, 10, 14, 18, 25, 41,
    47, 58, 59, 106, 190; clearly,
    viii, 4, 5, 14, 29, 53, 54, 58,
    69, 77, 78, 82, 84, 85, 87,
    105, 107, 122, 129, 133, 154,
    199; as an oppressor, 10;
    other people's, 7–15, 197,
    233, 243; *see also* listening;
    mistrusting thinking
threats, 184, 185–6
transference, 90–1
Transactional Analysis, 212
Travellers, 124, 125, 151, 266,
    267, 268
trust, 6, 22, 31, 55, 62, 238,
    239, 241; lack of, 51, 96, 247

unrealistic expectations,
    79–80, 88, 89
urge to feel good, 150–1

values, 22–4, 33, 42, 55, 63,
    107, 129, 179, 182, 192, 198;
    end, 60, 61
violence, 25, 107, 119, 130,
    131, 157, 162, 170, 204, 205,
    214–17, 222
virtue, 56

vision, 7, 22–5, 32–3, 43, 47,
    48, 55–9 *passim*, 62, 63, 64,
    81, 85, 86, 101, 129, 138,
    143, 223, 227, 228, 230, 231

Watson, Lilla, 126
White:, 207; bigots, 121; men,
    10, 95; middle class, 181,
    194; people, 122, 153, 161,
    169, 170, 171, 175, 185, 190,
    200, 201, 209, 213; women,
    146, 169; working class,
    181
women: allies of, 192, 196,
    201, 209; and diversity, 207;
    ethnic, 95; executives, 93;
    and identity, 203, 204, 206;
    and internalized
    oppression, 139, 140, 145,
    161, 165; leaders, 90, 95;
    and liberation, 212, 215,
    218; managers, 95; and
    mistreatment of men, 117;
    and oppression, 115, 123,
    124; oppression of, 118,
    153, 158, 167, 170, 176, 177,
    184, 189, 205, 219;
    relationship with, 10, 200–1;
    see also men; middle-class;
    working-class
women's movement, 39, 146,
    220
workers, 115, 155, 156, 175,
    178, 183, 241, 242, 260
working class, 175, 178, 179,
    180, 181, 183, 184, 186, 189,
    198
working-class: background,
    174; culture, 179;
    leadership, 178, 192;
    oppression, 170; people, 10,
    123, 159, 160, 170, 177,
    180–8 *passim*, 192, 196, 197,
    262; values, 180; women,
    145, 146, 149, 195;
workshops, 3, 53, 54, 125, 126,
    140, 147, 180, 194, 201, 208,
    231, 240

young people, 38, 55, 70, 71,
    72, 115, 153, 170, 185, 186,
    187, 234, 256; *see also*
    children